APOCALYPSES AND
APOSTROPHES

APOCALYPSES AND APOSTROPHES

John Barnes

The right of John Barnes to be identified as the author
of this work has been asserted by him in accordance with
the Copyright, Designs and Patents Act 1988.

First published in Great Britain in 1999 by
Millennium
An imprint of Orion Books Ltd,
Orion House, 5 Upper St Martin's Lane,
London W C2H 9EA

To receive information on the Millennium list, e-mail us at:
smy@orionbooks.co.uk

A CIP catalogue record for this book
is available from the British Library

Printed in Great Britain by
Clays Ltd, St Ives plc

Copyright Acknowledgements

"How to Build a Future" © 1990, 1992, 1998 by John Barnes. First appeared in *Analog*, March 1990.

"Stochasm" © 1986, 1998 by John Barnes. First appeared in *Isaac Asimov's Science Fiction Magazine*, December 1986.

"Under the Covenant Stars" © 1988, 1998 by John Barnes. First appeared in *Isaac Asimov's Science Fiction Magazine*, April 1988.

"Finalities Besides the Grave" © 1985, 1998 by John Barnes. First appeared in *Amazing Stories*, September 1985.

"Restricted to the Necessary" © 1989, 1998 by John Barnes. First appeared in *Amazing Stories*, March 1989.

"Delicate Stuff" © 1988, 1998 by John Barnes. First appeared in *Amazing Stories*, July 1988.

"Information and Unfictionable Science" © 1995, 1996, 1998. Given at the Chicago National Convention of the American Library Association, 1995. Published in *Information and Library Science*, Summer 1996.

"Between Shepherds and Kings" © 1997, 1998 by John Barnes. First appeared in *Free Space* (Tor Books, edited by Brad Linaweaver and Edward E. Kramer), 1997.

"Digressions from Second Person Future" © 1987, 1998 by John Barnes. First appeared in *Isaac Asimov's Science Fiction Magazine*, January 1987.

"My Advice to the Civilized" © 1990, 1998 by John Barnes. First appeared in *Isaac Asimov's Science Fiction Magazine*, April 1990.

All other material copyright 1998 by John Barnes.

This one is for William S. Yellow Robe, Jr.,
who will want to argue about practically everything.
I'm looking forward to it.

CONTENTS

FOREWORD

I'm not a particularly adventurous or interesting person, but I try to write about them. I was born in 1957 in Angola, Indiana; grew up in Detroit and in Bowling Green, Ohio; went to school at Washington University in St. Louis, where I picked up an A.B. in Economics and an A.M. in Political Science and got married for the first time; worked for a while as a systems analyst at Middle South Services in New Orleans; moved to Missoula, Montana, and attended the university there, eventually getting an M.A. in Drama (Direction), an M.F.A. in Creative Writing (Fiction), and divorced. I moved to Pittsburgh, got a Ph.D. from Pitt in Theatre Arts, got married again (this time to Kara Dalkey, who has written a bunch of good books that all of you should run out and buy after you finish this one), and have settled in, reasonably happily, on the faculty at Western State College, in Gunnison, Colorado, a small isolated town in the Rockies where scenery is abundant and people are scarce. I teach a bunch of different communication and theatre courses, cook, ski, or read when I have time, and have settled into a pleasant state of mild academic vegetation.

Sometime back there in St. Louis—to be precise, in the furnace room of 749 Heman Street 2 South—not long after I got married for the first time, I started to write science fiction, plus a little bit of fantasy and men's action adventure. I've had enough success with it so that I've continued to do it through all the moves and changes. My publisher thought there might be demand for a collection of short pieces, some of which appeared more than a decade ago in science fiction magazines, and some of which had never seen publication till now. Speculation about why is discouraged.

Also included here are some essays and notes that I felt like throwing in; science fiction is supposed to make you think, so presumably you'll tolerate other things that possibly may make you think as well.

I've omitted several of my early stories because I no longer like them very much.

An apostrophe is an address to a person or a personification who is not literally present: "Oh God our help in ages past . . ." "O Love, thou art cruel . . ." and so forth. That should at least spare me critical analyses of my punctuation.

Here are the expected announcements: Thanks for buying the book. Come see a show in Gunnison some time—it's only a four-hour drive from Denver, or six hours from Santa Fe, in good weather, and it's a beautiful drive. If you like this one, do feel free to buy more of my books.

And here's the expected aknowledgment: if you write, everything that happens to you makes your work a little different than it might otherwise have been. I have known far more than my share of fine people, and often, without their knowing, they put my feet on a just slightly different path. So—and most of them won't know why—I'd like to thank Jim Holloway, Jeff Radel, Debbie Williams, Dean Turner, Glenn Browne, David Donley, Mrs. K, Mike Watkins, Lisa Newman, Dave Lathrop, Vicki Dunbar, Greg Tiede, Neil Caesar, Steve Leon, Steve Legawiec, Phil Cary, Mike McIntyre, Beth Fell, John Miller, Chris Knapp, Bong Yul Shin, Victor Le Vine, Dick Palmer, Mike White, Gary Salazar, Lance Hill, Eileen San Juan, Ashley Grayson, Eric Baldwin, Carolyn Grayson, Tom Whitmore, Jonn Jorgenson, Russ Gay, Sean Walbeck, Rolly Meinholtz, Neil McMahon, Randy Bolton, Bill Kershner, Chris Ransick, James Crumley, Adria Brandvold, Jerry Oltion, Craig Holdin, Todd Case, Bill Raoul, Earl Ganz, Mike McClintock, Corey Wolverton, Frank Dugan, William S. Yellow Robe, Jr., Joni Rio, Frank Vigil, Liane Treiman, Rick Williams, Dan Hooker, Stephanie Preissman, Sherry Caldwell, Frazer Lively, Ellen Seeling, Mark Kittlaus, Ron Richards, Lynn Bernatowicz, Jeff DeVincent, Buzz Aldrin, David Fielding, Nathan Hurwitz, Anna Rosenstein, Gregg Dion, Melissa Gibson, Kinneret Noy, Dennis Kennedy, Buck Favorini, Ron Vince, Paul Edwards, Jim Gelwicks, and everybody else. Somewhere in this book, there's a word or a sentence or something that wouldn't have been the same without you, and looking back, I think I have been very lucky in the people who entered my life.

WHILE YOU WAIT

TWO CHEERS FOR NED LUDD, ONE FOR CRAZY EDDIE

One of the standard sneers at science fiction is that it's adolescent power fantasy. Like most sneers at things people do for fun, it tends to be simultaneously accurate and beside the point. Accurate, as even a cursory reading of what people are actually buying will tell you; and beside the point because it leaves out anything that might be interesting about the subject.

Such as, why would it be bad for adolescents to fantasize about having power? After all, would any adolescent fantasize about being powerless? (In real life, if we are to believe the sex studies, the people who have strong fantasies about being dominated are people who never experience it in real life—hard-driving leaders, alpha types, tough guys. But how many adolescents—in fact, how many people—experience getting shoved around so rarely that they have to daydream about it?)

Seriously, what *else* are adolescents (of any age) going to fantasize about?

And if you're about to tell me that they shouldn't be fantasizing about anything . . . well, now. The alternative to fantasy, for anything that really interests human beings, is not complete restraint, but actuality.

Before you sneer at adolescent power fantasy, at least ask yourself whether you would prefer them to have power in reality.

Now, what do adolescents want with power? Well, human beings seem to have an innate craving for power of their own, only exceeded by their craving not to be under someone else's power. Borrowing Mao, and starting from the simplest formulation, if one man is holding a gun on another man, the first man has power. There is something he could do to the second man that the second man could not do to him. Similarly, when you were six and were given that ultimate argument ("Because I'm your mother, that's why!") notice that you couldn't have said the same thing to your mother (well, you could, but it wouldn't have meant anything).

Power is asymmetry. It's the thing one party can do to the other, and the other party can't do back.

Which is exactly why we keep it out of the hands of adolescents, and restrict them to fantasizing about it. Would you want to discover that your boss was a fourteen-year-old boy? Do the households in which teenagers dominate the family strike you as unusually pleasant?

The reality of power, blessedly, is that it's rarely as complete as it is made out to be. Generally if the powerful person wants something from the powerless person, it will still be more effective to get the powerless person's consent (even if it's grudging) and best of all to get the powerless person's genuine enthusiasm. This is why so many managers and business leaders spend so much of their time being trained in "leadership," which is a polite way of saying "Getting people to want to help you instead of scaring them into it."

Leadership is not what most adolescents fantasize about; power, raw and lots of it, is. And for our own peace and sanity, we generally keep it out of their hands.

Now, one effect of the craving for power and the fascination with it that runs through the genres of fantasy and science fiction is that any fantasy about having it is usually enmeshed with a fantasy in which some bad person is trying to take it away from the hero. (Think about rightful-king, saboteur-at-the-spaceport, and all the rest of it).

Which brings me to my title.

One of the more popular epithets in current science fiction, especially among the devotees of hard SF, is "Luddite."

A short history lesson: in 1811, in Nottingham, workers in the textile industry, predominantly weavers, were being laid off in immense numbers due to the introduction of weaving machinery. Those who were not laid off experienced a drastic fall in wages (as workers who were desperate to keep their jobs bid the wage down and down). The quality of stockings and other garments made from the machine-woven cloth was abysmal, but first of all it was possible to sell them to the government, then engaged in fighting Napoleon, as part of the old tradition of enabling capitalists to get wealthy by gouging and cheating on military supplies; and secondly, although working people probably spent more on stockings once the machines came in (because machine-made stockings wore out much faster) they spent it in much smaller increments. (If you only buy stockings twice a year, they have to be pretty sturdy, and you end up paying a lot for them; if they're cheap enough to replace every other week, then it's somewhat more tolerable to have them fall apart.)

The workers seized factories, usually briefly and by night, and smashed machinery, claiming to be followers of Ned Ludd, variously known as General Ludd or King Ludd. The major targets for destruction were stocking and lace frames, those being the two commodities from which the most workers had been displaced, and also the two whose quality had collapsed the furthest.

In the spring of 1812, Ned Ludd's followers were a busy lot, as they began to operate more boldly, in the daytime, and in Yorkshire, Lancashire, Derbyshire, and Leicestershire—all textile centers. That summer, at the request of a Mr. Horsfall, who owned a factory, troops fired into a Luddite crowd. Horsfall was later assassinated, probably by the Luddites. A series of laws was passed, and in 1813 many of the Luddites were brought to a mass trial at York; some were hanged, most were transported to Australia, and the movement collapsed and disappeared.

King Ludd reappeared in 1815–1816, bad harvest years when the price of bread went up. Apparently having acquired some skill from the previous outbreak, the Luddites were systematic about setting sentries and guarding factories while the machinery was smashed. Good harvests and better economic times seem to have driven Ned Ludd from the field (although many historians speculate that if there was a single, real Ned Ludd, he may have been among those executed or transported in 1813 or 1816, under another name).

Luddism and Luddite, almost ever since, have been synonymous with machine-wrecking.

The first odd thing to notice about that fact is that the Luddites do not seem to have been angry at machines per se; they were angry at low wages, layoffs, and poor-quality products, but it wasn't the machines that caused those—it was the factory owners using the machines. Some of this perhaps can be explained as the same silly impulse that makes people want to ban guns rather than lock up those who use them; bad inanimate objects rarely invite pity in the way that bad people do.

A more likely explanation for the Luddites' behavior, it seems to me, is this: The machine had given the owner power over the workers, a power he had not had before—to fire most of them and reduce wages for the rest. What the Luddites had discovered is that the power went both ways; true, the owner could destroy their lives and livelihoods with his machines, but the owner had a very large amount of money tied up in those machines, and if the machines ceased to run, the owner went broke. The owner had asserted a power to disrupt and impoverish the community; the Luddites asserted a power to bankrupt the owner. In an era when a strike, boycott, or building occupation would have been swept aside instantly, it was the one way they had to hurt the ones who were hurting them.

This is not, of course, the standard hard science fictional take on the matter. That take might be summarized as "Machines were Progress, especially because they led to better machines in the future; destroying them was therefore holding back Progress; therefore the Luddites were opposing Progress." From there it is only a small step to note that since the owners brought in the machines, defended the machines, and replaced the machines when they were smashed, clearly the owners were on the side of Progress, and ergo they were heroes.

And notice how beautifully it now reads into adolescent power fantasy: just one guy, the owner, is right. He has power. Having power, he makes Progress. Bad people momentarily take his power away, but he regains it and makes more Progress, which leads to our world of today and the better world of tomorrow.

The real-life capitalist has been rewritten into the angry teenager who just plain knows things could be done better.

Now undoubtedly some readers are pointing out that eventually machines led to higher production, the quality got better, the goods got cheaper, and the descendants of those workers live in a world that is considerably more comfortable than those workers could have dreamed of—indeed, more comfortable than the owners could have dreamed of, if you count later mechanized innovations like electricity, indoor plumbing, and central heat.

Which of you would be willing to lose his job, or take an 80 percent pay cut, so that his grandchildren could take vacations on the moon?

In hindsight, it is good to be living at a time when we can see earlier ages in hindsight; but that doesn't mean that if only they could have known that their misery and danger were going to make us comfortable, that they would then willingly have endured it.

Nor could the owner have known. He was out to make a fast pound; he had found a way to pay less in wages while making more from stockings.

Yet, from Robert Heinlein's D. D. Harriman forward, our science fiction is filled with the visionary capitalist whose only real purpose is the magnificent future he is building, which he somehow visualizes in vivid and accurate detail.

Oh, probably the Luddites had to be suppressed; they eventually became more violent against people and less controlled in their behavior, and besides once there was a rapidly expanding economy their primary grievance went away. But without the Luddites, how much more misery might have been inflicted? How far would owners have felt free to go? (They certainly felt free to go a long way as it was.) Are you so sure that naked power unleashed and unchallenged is what you want to be ruled by?

Remember that in any given era, the number of people at the top is small; your odds are much better of finding yourself standing out there in the mud, needing a job and unable to find one, than they are of being inside the factory, growing wealthy and Making the Future Now. And remember too that power and adolescence have another link through fantasy; the adolescent fantasizes what he or she would do with unlimited power, but unlimited power gives people the ability to behave like adolescents. That is, to ignore the input of others, and to say, "What I say goes."

Are you really so sure that, in 1811, not knowing a thing of the history to follow, you'd be able to tell that the Luddites were the bad guys and the owners were the good guys? Is it possible that up close, and in their own time, they're all just guys?

Take another example, one famous in science fiction. In Niven and Pournelle's *The Mote in God's Eye,* the Moties, an intelligent alien race who breed without any control whatsoever, are bedeviled by Crazy Eddie. Crazy Eddie is described as a condition that Moties go into, a kind of permanent insanity, in which, for example, if a city is barely able to deal with its refuse problem and is still growing, a Motie becomes Crazy Eddie, and organizes a garbage workers' strike.

Crazy Eddie brings on the population crashes that prevent complete extinction, by starting religions that lead to religious wars, by launching irrationally large projects that destroy vital resources, and so forth. Once a Motie goes Crazy Eddie, he or she is a danger to every other Motie.

A defense of Crazy Eddie would be much tougher to mount than a defense of Ned Ludd—but not utterly impossible. Niven and Pournelle make it clear that Crazy Eddie is an ecological force, the thing that keeps the Moties from breeding to extinction—by doing insane things that kill a lot of them. Ned Ludd was a message—don't go any further. Crazy Eddie is a force—he hits you to make you stop. It's the difference between having a dog that growls at intruders, and putting a land mine under your front porch—both keep something undesirable away, but one of them treats the undesirable as having some rights and a human nature.

It's hardly surprising that in adolescent power fantasy the villain is the thing that gets in the way of the power and stops or blocks it. Adolescents are forever getting told no, just when the fun is really starting.

But think back to your own adolescence, if you're out of it, and about some of the things you did or wanted to do, and just ask: Is it always so bad to be told no?

GENTLEMAN PERVERT, OFF ON A SPREE

This story never quite found a home before; but then, every time it's been out in front of some editor, it's had a different ending. It's set in the same universe as my novel Mother of Storms, *but nine years before the events of that book. Billy Crystal has said that when virtual reality reaches the point where the average guy can experience sex with the supermodel of his choice, it'll make crack cocaine look like aspirin. I really think he's badly understating the case.*

A brick slams the hood of Ken Greer's Angel Excellent, but the new cars have good dent resistance and from the back seat, where he's almost done fucking Nikki, he shouts "riot help." Nikki barely bothers to open her black-eyeshadowed eyes or make a little noise of curiosity through her bruise-purple lips; she's probably drugged or maybe just tired and burned out.

But if she doesn't hear or listen, the car does, and it sets about getting him out of the crowd of protesting busybodies who are determined to spoil his fun. Even as the car's brain guides it out of the angry, chanting crowd, Ken notices the play of bright lights on the back of the Angel Excellent; they're getting a good video shot of the plate as it drives away. If they keep that in their own files, it might not ever have any effect on his life, but more likely they'll put it out in their netfeed; even if it's in something as archaic as a web site, it'll get into general dissemination soon enough.

Once the protesters make it available, some enterprising datarodent will carry it to Ken's parole officer's incident cache, and Ken will be looking at another three years on his sentence. Furthermore, even though he's never seen it, Ken suspects that his wife, Linda, has an incident cache of her own to track his movements—anyone thinking of a divorce does that these days, just as they have a private investigator AI—and so just about for sure his wife is going to get it, too, eventually.

There is probably one chance in ten that Linda will know before he gets home, one in five by end of day tomorrow. He doesn't like the odds, but he still might get the weekend at the lake with her before Linda discovers that he has broken all the promises that he made to get her to take him back, nine months ago when he was convicted on a soliciting charge.

No, it is certain that Linda will eventually know that the car was down here in the stroll. She'll know within a week at the outside. The added time on his sentence and the fact that they'll either read the Angel Excellent's memory (and discover that Ken picked someone up in that block) or else he'll erase it (and violate his parole in another way) all mean that Ken is going to be doing more time wearing a bracelet, and he's going to be doing it without Linda.

Well, he's already paid for Nikki, and she's about as zing as anything on Jefferson Avenue. The little kitty is lying sprawled on her back on the back seat, short denim shorts around one ankle and halter top lifted off her tiny, slack breasts, her long coat folded neatly on the front passenger seat. His penis is limp inside her. It's hard to really see a facial expression on anyone whose face is done in contrasting reds and blacks, but it would appear that she doesn't really care in the slightest whether he comes, gives up and pulls out, or does anything at all.

He has a very uncomfortable moment wondering if that bright flash was one of those cameras that's supposed to be able to shoot through the opaquing on the car windows, in which case it almost certainly caught his face and body, plus enough of Nikki to let everyone get a clear image—a balding paunchy thirty-two-year-old, still wearing his white shirt and necktie, with his pants pulled down and his pale white soft gut hanging out from under his shirt, on top of an ivory-white anorexic blonde girl who is probably about eighteen but looks more like twelve. She's his idea of zing but she probably isn't most people's, so even if it weren't for the difference in age and his ridiculous body, there would be a lot of people who would wonder *why that gross guy wanted something like that?*

Somehow being photographed in a situation with so little dignity, and with a kitty who really powers him up but who most people would think was a strange taste, seems even worse; there's some netlectors out there that specialize in finding and collecting humiliating pictures of ordinary people, and Ken and Nikki will probably be in all of them a month from now. Plus probably making that horrible netzine, *Foolshots,* that so many of the people at work like.

"Wayya wan' do?" Nikki asks; it's one of about five sentences he's heard her utter tonight. She doesn't seem to feel any need to cover herself or bother to look at him; she just lies still, in the back seat of the Angel Excellent, while the car takes a random tour of this old, run-down part of Jefferson Avenue.

He sighs. Things are not turning out at all the way he wanted them to. Today, Friday, is his first day with the bracelet turned off; he has a three-day weekend pass during which he wears the little tracking and monitoring bracelet on his ankle but it doesn't record or report, and he's no more monitored than any other ordinary citizen. If he were to complete ten of these paroles-from-parole, he could get the bracelet off two years early, and have his record expunged.

Instead, just ten hours into it, Ken has screwed up pretty thoroughly. He'll end up wearing the bracelet for the full term, plus three, and of course word will go back to MitsDoug, which will fire him, and to Linda, who will divorce him. The whole complicated, badly running, undermaintained works of his life will come crashing down within a couple of days at best.

He might as well make it a weekend to remember—a real spree, as he has been promising himself—because it's all he will have to remember for a long, long time.

"Nikki, honey," he says, "I guess it's your lucky day. I'll give you a second payment, as big as the first, to start over. Harden me up in your pretty mouth, and then we'll fuck again." He hands her the bills.

He sits back and she gets on the seat beside him, then puts her head down in his lap. While she sucks, he rests his hand on the thick blonde hair on the back of her head, and watches what she does.

The car, told to keep the windows semiopaque so that no one can see in, and to do a random wander of the city, drifts through good neighborhoods and bad, past factories, wrecking yards, office buildings. Once it wanders through a big shopping district, hung with bright Christmas lights, ringing with Christmas carols played too loud on the overhead speakers. As the Angel Excellent passes between the mobs of shoppers, Ken gets on top of Nikki again, and this time, knowing how long it might be till he can afford to see her again, he does what he wants and goes at it fast and hard.

She's so tiny that the force of his thrusts bumps her head on the door, and he can see that her small breasts are red from where he has pinched and squeezed them, and that powers him up a little extra, so that he comes in a few hard, wet squirts into a blob of warm disease-blocking foam in her vagina. She turns her head a little to the side and sighs as it happens, which is more response than he's had from her so far.

Afterward, as they cruise back through the shopping district, toward the Jefferson Avenue area so that he can drop her off discreetly, he gives her some more cash and tells her she's the best he's ever had and a beautiful girl. She accepts the cash and the compliment alike with a shrug and an embarrassed little smile. The smile is the final touch on the evening for him; one thing he likes about these young kitties is that even the toughest ones can still be touched by some small courtesy or some little taste of lagniappe. One of them—another thin blonde like Nikki—told him once that she thought he had treated her like a princess and that he was a real gentleman. That powered him up so much that he paid her to do him again.

He has the Angel Excellent pull over to a curb on Jackson Street, three blocks from Jefferson, to drop off Nikki. She pulls on her long coat, steps out of the car, and struts off toward Jefferson. He watches her go till she's out of sight.

Chances are she's the last of it for the weekend. Probably he will get home and have a screaming fight with Linda, ending in an immediate divorce. Then on Monday MitsDoug will fire him, and the parole officer—a very unsympathetic and cold artificial intelligence—will inform him of the months added to his sentence. And without income, with a divorce to pay off (he has to expect to be found a hundred percent at fault) and subject to constant monitoring, it will be an eternity before he can be back on the street looking for kitties again.

On the other hand, it is just possible that his original plan will hold on till Monday. He'd been planning this for ages—a sort of one-person do-it-yourself orgy out among the kitties, plus a romantic weekend with Linda—sort of a traffic jam of emotions and sensations. Hell, for three days he's been humming

Gentleman pervert, off on a spree
Out having fun just like he's free
God, I hope they don't catch me

over and over to himself, trying to make sure he doesn't subvoke those words since the bracelets are reputed to be sensitive enough to pick that up.

At least, he thinks, as the Angel Excellent drives him back toward the house, where Linda will be waiting to go to late dinner and a movie—unless she already knows—he's going to be spared the expense of trying to find Christmas presents for her. Linda always complains about whatever he gets her, anyway, and the cost of a pile of Christmas presents that isn't completely disgraceful is more than twice what it costs to do Nikki. This year at least some of his money can be saved toward the day when the bracelet comes off and he can go do what he likes.

When the Angel Excellent pulls into the garage, Linda is standing there waiting for him. He gets out of the car and it's obvious; she knows. The protesters must have put that picture out right away, and probably her private detective AI has a datarodent with a priority sensor, so that it would call that kind of thing to her attention right away.

She's wearing a robe but in full makeup; it must have alerted her while she was getting ready to go out, so she took off the dress but left the makeup on. Probably she hasn't eaten, either, and that always makes her cross. He stands, and while he waits for her to do or say whatever it's going to be, he looks at her. He feels strangely calm, as if nothing mattered to him.

Linda's hair is still red—after all, she's just twenty-nine—but there are some little traces of crow's-feet showing up as cracks in her makeup, and there's something about her skin that is not as fresh as it used to be. Ken notices, too, that since she's not wearing a bra under the robe, she sags some; that's what happens when big tits age. For the ten thousandth time in his life he wonders why he didn't just dump her, back when she was nineteen and he'd already done her as much as he would ever need to.

She's in shower shoes, and she steps onto the dirty garage floor gingerly, looking down at the oil stains and grit, as if not wanting to wash her feet afterwards. Then she looks up at him, directly into his face. He can't seem to look down or away, so he looks back at her, but all he sees is a woman who has begun to age and fatten a little, still sexy enough so that if she weren't familiar he'd want her, glaring at him in a fury.

After a long while, she says, "You son of a bitch." She repeats it twice, each time a little softer, as if the anger is giving way to pure amazement. "You son of a bitch, you son of a bitch."

Then she walks forward and hands him a printed sheet of paper, obviously from the home fax, with that annoying dashed stripe in the right margin that no maintenance man has been able to get rid of for them.

It's the divorce decree; with no kids and fairly simple property to divide, she was able to get one from the twenty-four-hour AI court, for a couple hundred dollars, in just a few minutes. The AI court listened to her testimony, read and examined the whole body of evidence, found him 100 percent at fault, and issued this decree, all in eleven minutes and thirty-four seconds according to the header. Almost all of that time must have been her testimony. He could appeal it but human reviewers rarely overturn an AI's decision nowadays, and besides Linda seems to have told nothing but the truth. She's that way; sometimes she seems not to know how to lie.

"You want to come in and let me yell at you?" she asks. "Or to get a few things? I guess I could let you get a few things. The AI court gave me the house, and you're not sleeping in my house tonight. Tomorrow I'll be out from two in the afternoon till five, exactly, and in that time you can move out. I'm keeping practically everything except your clothes, books, CD's, and wedges—*mustn't forget those,* asshole. You'll find full directions in the decree, and it's been uploaded to your data access. Follow the directions exactly."

"If I don't it's another felony," he points out. "Okay, let me get a change of clothes, my toothbrush, and—can I have my pillow?"

"It's yours. Decree says so. It was fitted for you, anyway."

Ken nods. The world is strangely cool, gray, and textureless, as if he were watching a barely out-of-focus movie of this moment in his life, through a slightly foggy glass. He walks back to the bedroom, gets the pillow and change of clothes, and has a moment of trying to think of a way to stay there just a minute or two longer. Ken was actually sort of looking forward to trying to get it up and do Linda in here tonight, like it was an interesting challenge, or maybe because she had been so nice to him for so long, ever since the counseling this past summer, that he was feeling more affectionate.

Anyway, they could have done it in the dark and he would have thought about Nikki or some other girl while he did it. A lot of times that saves him. *Saved.* He doesn't need saving anymore.

Whatever the Friday evening might have been, it won't happen in here, again, ever. He feels his stomach sink heavily, sighs, and goes into the bathroom.

His toothbrush is not on the rack. He looks around and sees it floating in the toilet.

"That was petty," Linda says behind him. "I wish I were ashamed of it, but I'm really not. After I threw it in I used the toilet. If you don't want your toothbrush anymore, get it out and throw it away yourself."

He picks up the toothbrush and wipes it on his pants; he can clean it somehow when he gets to the hotel, or throw it out there.

"Come in here," she says, from the living room.

Ken knows it's a bad idea but he goes anyway, and there in the living room, right in front of him as he comes through the hallway door, Linda is clutching a tight red dress on a hanger, with high heels tied together by their straps around the top of the hanger. "I had this on. I was going to try to show off for you and get you powered up for me. I was horny and looking forward to it," she says, and tosses the dress—

Onto the Christmas tree.

Ken stares. In the ten years they've been married, they've always gone to Christmas at his mother's house, and never had a tree of their own, but Mama died last April, and . . . he hadn't even thought about it. Linda had put up a whole Christmas tree, decorations and all. "That's right," she says. "I did that for you. I even had champagne chilling for when we got home from dinner and the show."

Then Linda lunges under the tree that is now festooned with the red dress—he wants to yell at her to be careful and not hurt herself—grabs the base, and heaves the whole thing backwards over the couch. Water from the base spills everywhere, and Ken cries out in surprise.

Linda grabs the base—she's not a particularly large woman, and it's a six-foot tree, but she has the force of rage behind her—and swings it against the wall, three times, smashing everything. When she finishes, she brushes the pine tar and splinters from her hands, and gives him the same dead stare she gave him in the garage. "A maid service will clean that up tomorrow," she says, "and the charge will go on your account. One less whore, more or less, that you'll ever be able to afford. My little revenge, I guess."

She stares and stares; Ken doesn't know what to do, and stands there as if paralyzed, shirt, pants, socks, underwear draped over the arm that holds his custom pillow, his toilet-soaked toothbrush in his other hand. Finally Linda gestures toward the door into the garage; Ken walks toward it with his legs still and numb. Distantly, he thinks he ought to say something or do something; all that seems to register is how far it is to the door, and the powerful smell of freshly crushed pine limbs.

"You son of a bitch," she says again, as he goes out into the garage. "You son of a bitch," she adds, one more time, as he throws his possessions into the back seat—he notes that it still smells vaguely of Nikki's cheap scent, disease-guard foam, and sweat, and realizes that he could never have concealed it from Linda anyway.

The only things he could think of to say would be stupid—"I'm sorry," "I love you," "It just happened," "Nothing personal." So he says nothing, gets in the car, and tells it to take him to the nearest Comfort Inn with a vacancy.

He's not sure how he gets through the process of interacting with the desk clerk, but late that night he's in the room, making the arrangements with Ryder. When he finishes arranging his next day, and sets up the program on his laptop to find himself a list of temporary apartments to look at in the morning, he feels like going down to Jefferson Avenue, but it's late, and a freezing rain is falling outside, so he decides not to. It feels awful, somehow, that he decides not to, as if he's lost the point of everything.

He brushes his teeth before he remembers. The toothbrush doesn't taste any different from usual, and so he just rinses it out and figures that he's already gotten whatever he's going to get.

When he goes to bed, he doesn't think he'll be able to sleep, but after just a few breaths, he catches his drifting mind wondering how to explain it to Mama, and, remembering that she's dead, he starts to cry. Sometime after the tears begin to flow, he falls asleep, and sleeps till ten o'clock the next morning.

At three-thirty the next day, Saturday, Ken Greer is standing in what used to be his living room, with his back to the stain from the Christmas tree that the maid service apparently couldn't get off the wall.

Maybe all the trouble was that Linda has red hair and a big soft chest. For Ken, the zingest kitties are pale blondes with no extra fat. *Maybe Linda could always tell she was second best, and it bothered her and made her angry, and everything spiraled downwards from there.*

Probably not. She's divorcing me because she doesn't want to die from AIDS, SPM, or ARTS. And I have treated her like shit.

He's packed all his CD's, clothes, and wedges. *Mustn't forget those,* he can hear Linda saying sarcastically in his mind's ear. His new apartment has dishes, furniture, and such. There's nothing else in his old house to pack.

He looks over the furniture they bought together. The house is a convertient and at one time they were way ahead on that—back when he was putting a tenth of every paycheck into it—so she's got some equity. Probably she'll be able to leverage that into keeping it.

At least they didn't have kids, they had some savings that weren't wiped by the Flash, and they had a few good years.

At least. Yeah. Things are at their least.

Now all he has to do is three or four things and then he can . . .

Do anything he wants, he supposes. What does he want?

Wrong question, very definitely wrong question. He could have thought about what Linda wanted before this happened. He could have thought about what the country wanted and gone off to be a volunteer worker in the Duc, right after the Flash.

Wild stories coming back from there about young kitties at night moving around from tent to tent of male rescue workers, think about the excitement of working all day and then nailing soft young—

Ken's hand is already creeping toward his crotch. He is having fantasies a lot lately, which is pretty bizarre—making it up himself when he probably has two hundred wedges in the crate right now.

I ought to squirt a farewell to Linda onto her pillow.

He doesn't. Since he got up this morning he's been having these weird ugly thoughts; not like he's never had them before, but he hasn't had them every five minutes.

He's going to miss the house. And Linda.

Six Ryder rental crates, and all of them are heavy. There's a dolly that came with the crates, and Ken can move all these without too much trouble. The only reason he is not moving just now is that he is soaking up the feel of the place. It's weird. For the last several years he's constantly longed to get out of it.

The house still smells right, even a little like Christmas because of the pine scent. Besides that, there's a slight lingering odor from those white-sauce dishes Linda makes all the time (because they're easy to warm up and he gets home at late hours). Ken can remember the discussion behind buying every chair and lamp, and where a lot of the little stains on the cushions came from. The TV they haven't used much since they got XV is hanging on the wall behind that curtain, and he remembers how long they saved for it, and that one corner is dented from when they moved in here.

Fair trade. No real home, but freedom. And if he doesn't have a home, it's time to stop standing around getting morbid in the home he used to have.

Task list for self. One, get crates into MitsDoug Angel Excellent. Two, leave house keys on table per agreement. Three, car to new place. Four, crates into new place. Five, unpack and return crates. Six, live through rest of weekend; it's the last spree before the job goes away and he is resentenced. At least he knows it's the last spree, so he can make it count.

Step one takes almost an hour. Ken is out of shape and the crates take a lot of wrestling. Weird how with the Angel Excellent configured for cargo there's so much room in it.

Wedges are small and light. Their crate doesn't weigh much. They go in last, and he doesn't really need the dolly but he's tired so he lets it take that last crate to the car. One quick swing, up and in, then fold down the dolly and toss it into the Angel Excellent.

He takes a last look around the living room, trying to remember it without the gray stain. Linda will be back at five. He needs to be out of here.

The keys hit the table and crash to the floor. Ken turns back, puts them on the table, steps out the door, lets the autolock lock, and gets into his car.

He turns the key, presses his thumbprint to the reader, folds down the keyboard when it unlocks, types his new address and redefines it as "home."

With the crates, there's no room to fold down the seat and take a nap, but he opaques the windows so he can see without being seen. (Maybe there will be a couple kitties walking by or something. There are supposed to be lots of young ones in his new apartment complex.)

But after several blocks there are just a couple of high school girls, wearing the Forties Comment style where all the underwear and shoulder pads and so forth are pinned loosely to the outside of the overalls. Young girls seem to like it but it does nothing for Ken, not like when he was in school, back in the early Oh's, when they thought AIDS was beaten—*I was a kid and good-looking and there were all those X-Po's out-fits around, it seemed like you could smell every vagina on campus*—god, why had he spent his whole senior year, when he could have been nail-ing freshkitties by the dozen, bouncing on Linda?

Because I liked *her,* he admits to himself.

The Angel Excellent passes one petite kitty who's wearing a scalpnet, but since she's walking she has no goggles or muffs—she's experiencing XV but only as a ghost layer over reality. (She moves her butt a lot, which you can see through those tight shorts, her muscular little back is taut through the swimsuit top, he's instantly hard for the deep tan and the way the long hair sways.) As the car overtakes her, at only twenty mph in the heavy traffic, he sees her legs are thick with cottage-cheese fat, and when she turns and glances toward the car he sees crow's feet. *Jesus, Grandma, get off the street. You must be three years older than I am.*

He can see the irony. Hell, Linda has a great body for their age, but a guy can't help it, can he, that those first signs of aging power him down? *Older women need to get real about what they look like. Maybe I do too. Maybe I need to give up the whole sex thing, or admit there's only one way I can get what I want. Well, at least this is going to be a spree to remember, and since I don't have to hide it, I can make it count.*

The Angel Excellent turns left into the big Westview Gardens apart-ment complex and parks itself.

At least he doesn't have to drive himself. If he did and the cops pulled him over and saw the stressor levels in his bloodstream, they'd nail him for driving while emotionally distressed.

Well, he's as home as it gets just now. Get out the dolly, put on two crates, wheel it to the omnivator, up to the apartment that looks like a hotel room with a kitchen.

Two crates off, back down to the Angel Excellent, two more crates— jeez, these are heavy, but then suits are heavy and that's mostly what's in them—back up via the omnivator again. He's never gotten completely used to having these things move sideways as well as up and down. Mama used to give a little half-scream every time the first one in his hometown changed directions.

He misses her a lot. Maybe he'll save a few bucks out from the spree, for flowers for her grave.

Offload the two crates he has, go back and get the last two more crates. They're fairly heavy. After he rolls them into the place he looks around. Two crates by the closet, clothing. One crate by the entertainment center, CD's for audio and video. One in the bedroom, books and souvenirs. One in the kitchen, the mealmaker. Linda let him keep it because she'll be getting a new one. One by the big lounge chair, the one he'd rather open first . . . but if he opens it first he will get nothing more done tonight, and it will cost him more to return the crates tomorrow.

Pick up Allen key. Start opening crates. Get clothes into closet, toss socks and underwear into drawer. Now the entertainment center, and lift and stack and lift and stack and lift . . . it's like exercise.

Same routine gets the books and souvenirs into the bookcases. One hard lift gets the mealmaker onto the counter in the kitchen. Doesn't leave him much counter space but then he doesn't really need any. Mama would have a fit, but Ken knows nothing about how to turn raw stuff into food—that's what the mealmaker does.

One crate left. Since he has to make sure he returns the crates tonight, before he gets involved with this, he doesn't look at his wedges, much, especially not at the color holes on the boxes, and as soon as he's unpacked the wedges and set the scalpnet, goggles, and muffs by the lounger, he gets busy with the Allen wrench and takes the crates apart. Total time to move, probably, about five hours. Not bad at all.

The disassembled crates make an easy single load for the dolly, and it all goes into the car. He closes the rear door with a thud, gets in, and sets the car to go to the Ryder office where he rented them, *on Jefferson Avenue.*

He sets the car seat for a nap but doesn't sleep. It's only about twenty minutes anyway, so he pulls on the scalpnet for the car to catch up on the news, and tunes in to experience some XV. Naturally he goes with Passionet—it'll help him get into the mood—

Right now he's experiencing Rock. Rock is a muscular, handsome younger guy who is noted for his sensitivity and affectionate style, and he's working with the new girl, Synthi Venture, a busty flame-redhead.

Ken laughs to himself for a moment—his very first no-guilt experience after Linda divorced him is another redhead with big tits. Must be fate or something.

There's a law that says that you're not allowed to wear goggles or muffs in the car—*as if anyone ever sits close enough to the steering wheel to grab control, nowadays!*—but with a little practice you can tune out the real world around you. Ken slides into experiencing Rock as naturally as a kid jumps onto a bicycle.

The background info runs into his mind quickly. May 24, 2019, 4:45

Eastern, delayed broadcast of experiences of Rock Guardian and Synthi Venture. The story is called *Assignment in Singapore*. Rock is an intrepid reporter and Synthi is a young cub trying to make a big name for herself.

The story they're covering is about Singapore's role in the market for European teenagers bound for Japanese "rape clubs." It's pretty predictable—Synthi is going to go undercover and get raped a lot. Rock is going to rescue her. Then they're going to do a fancy, super-zing fuck scene for prime time, and the pillow talk will be about the web of connections between businesses, governments, and crime syndicates that underlies the rape clubs—followed by a barrage of flashcuts of Japanese, Singapore, and Euro cops beating the shit out of various creeps.

Ken likes being shocked by the brutality the police use on XV and the terrible crimes Passionet reporters uncover. You're reminded ceaselessly that it's really happening, though the reporters are too valuable to put in real danger—they just don't show you the guards that are trailing Synthi or Rock. Usually some detectives have paved the way, or that's what people say. They leave some whorehouse unbusted so the reporter can go undercover there, and they have it surrounded by Passionet private troops undercover. You wonder why you never see one of the bad guys catching on.

There's a rumor that Ken has heard a lot: somebody at the different XV nets invents the crimes and scandals, puts the crime syndicates in business, gets politicians and cops on the take, and then arranges the bust for the XV story.

He's not sure why the idea excites him so much. He fantasizes actually sitting at a desk and giving the orders: "Yeah, blonde and red-haired Euro kitties, kidnapped from the streets, plugged into d&p jacks in Singapore clinics, rewired to come when they're hurt and scared, fat Japanese businessmen buying them like horses at an auction, beating them and holding them down while they helplessly come and come—set that up, and send one around to me as a free sample."

Synthi has been flirting a lot with Rock, probably for a consummation next Thursday when experiencership peaks. Right now she's giving him a lot of eye-batting and smiling, always turning so those huge tits show to best advantage. Ken feels how Rock's pulse races, feels the burning need for Synthi, knows that she would be different from all the others, finally give Rock the love he's really looked for all his life . . . but business must come first.

"Let me tell you what I found yesterday," Ken says, millions of men say, feeling Rock's mouth move like their own, and Synthi looks atten-tive—she's a good listener. "Six of those big old hotels all belong to Paraglobal, a bank controlled by the Mitsu under-*keiretsu* of MitsDoug. There's big money in this, and that's why the Singapore syndicates have been able to keep going for so long—"

He traces the financial relationships, the system in which Paraglobal top *kaishajin* are getting pick of the kitties and then throwing them into rape clubs for drug-and-plug until they have too little memory to func-tion as witnesses or even to call for help if they run away—

With a ping Synthi's face freezes over. Three-dimensionality goes first, then the feel of Rock's trench coat on his back, of Rock's hard mus-cles and the taste of his warm accent in the mouth, is gone. Ken is back in the car, the scalpnet dead.

MitsDoug has pulled signal for all its employees; they can do that in the Angel Excellent because they hold the loan for it. He shakes off the feeling, looks around at the warehouses the car is now driving past. There are going to be some memos coming down pretty soon about how to handle it when customers ask. No question that the sales force is go-ing to have a tough time for quite a while. First from the scandal itself, and then as indictments happen there will be some suicides, some exiles, some guys who run off to Euro, Siberia, or the UNARs.

The Ryder truck rental storefront looks like it was probably a KFC, then a Pizza Hut, and hasn't had a full remake since. Ken tells the Angel Excellent to back up to an open bay, the dock there comes down level with the rear door of the Angel Excellent, and he pushes the crates and dolly onto the dock. The last he sees of it, the dock is gliding back, car-rying the returned materials. The Angel Excellent datalink winks green, indicating that they know they got it all back and there are no further charges. He's free to go.

Jefferson Avenue is a long street, several miles of indo stuff, big metal and concrete buildings to keep the weather off machines and office workers. In fact Linda's data patterning shop is somewhere on Jefferson Avenue—but a long way from the part that Ken knows well.

There's a stretch of six blocks or so where about half the ads are old-fashioned yellow lighted signboards; asphalt and concrete crumbled, iron rusted, and dry fast-food wrappers strewn in the gutter like greasy autumn leaves. People who work at the few legitimate businesses there tend to lunge from their cars into their workplaces, as if afraid to be seen against their background.

But legitimate businesses are exceptions, down there. Most businesses are virtual parlors, which are full of pretty kitties; whorehouses, which are full of old, psychotic, and diseased kitties; or whorehouses that pretend to be virtual parlors, which are full of very pretty kitties at extremely high prices. Ken can't afford one of those, which is why he wants to go to one so badly.

In a plain old whorehouse you pretty much know what you're going to do. See if there's a half-assed pretty one that doesn't look crazy. See if her HIV clearance is current. If it is, look for the purple blotches of ARTS on her chest and arms, check her for lumps, ask her to flex her mouth a couple times to prove it's not locking into the characteristic grimace. If she flunks that, get out. Even though half the ARTS cases test HIV-negative, at least the rumor has it that the HIV strain that causes ARTS is actually much more infectious.

If not, are her veins inflamed? Eyeballs yellow? Gums spotted? You can get just as dead from SPM.

Once she's passed all those tests, all you have to do is get powered up enough to fuck her.

In a virtual parlor, the pretty girl has a partner she likes. You experience the partner via scalpnet and neural rig—signal comes in via merkin for genital and butt plug for visceral, long gloves on the arms and socks on the feet so the big muscles get stimulated. You get, not just the ghosts of pleasure and pain from the scalpnet, but deep muscle and skin stimulation, your heart beating in time with the guy's, your breathing in rhythm with his, feeling it in your own bowels when his gut muscles clench. When orgasm happens they give you a loop-and-slowdown effect so that it lasts half an hour.

It leaves Ken sore, drained, and almost satisfied, and you can't get any disease by virtual.

So why does he always go to the whorehouse afterwards? Shit, most of the time, it's not even a house, sometimes it's a streetwalker, some kitty who's either underage or too crazy and dangerous for a legal house, out living by her tits, probably had the AIDS shot so it will now be twenty years till she dies from ARTS. It doesn't seem to matter what Ken does, there's no real satisfaction from the virtual world; he can come and come and come, but he still can't go home until he has stuck his nonvirtual dick into the mouth or vagina of a realtime woman.

Maybe Nikki will be out tonight. He really liked her bony chest with just little lumps of tits, flaccid flesh that's always white and cold, and legs so thin he could wrap her thighs in his hands. And it might be interesting to continue the spree with her; since he's been generous, and was fairly polite, chances are she'll take more chances with him. And, as he reminds himself, this spree is going to have to last a long time in memory. Good thing that last night he really *was* a "gentleman pervert," because the wild time he's hoping to have will be a lot easier if he can find people he was nice to in the past. And at least Nikki ought to remember him.

The car takes the turn onto Jefferson. Now it will randomly prowl the area and the side streets near it.

After two circuits of the area, there's no Nikki, just a couple of old fat ones. They need to do some quality control around here.

One of the whorehouses has shut down since he was last here, ten days ago. No big surprise there. They're legal these days but regulated to death, and more importantly, the Community Standards Enforcement Act lets every nut and crazy that doesn't like what happens in those places stand outside, yelling, chanting, threatening the customers. People protesting the various kinds of sex store are not allowed to use actual violence, but unlike protesters outside other businesses, they are allowed to block traffic, make threats, cause noise for its own sake to get on the workers' and the customers' nerves, and in short do pretty much whatever they want that isn't actually assault. It was part of the deal when they legalized the houses; they're legal but they don't have much legal protection. And in this city it's a bit worse; local police don't seem to do much about emergency calls from a house.

In fact all the law enforcement seems to be aimed toward suppressing the trade, even though it's legal. Let one little kitty in a house come down with something and the owner and everyone is in jail, even if she got it from a cop taking a freebie.

Cheerleaders&Majorettes, the virtual parlor Ken likes best, has a lot of cars outside it. He's tempted but he won't have much to spend on action till he gets another job if he blows it all here. Besides, there are still three whorehouses along Jefferson Avenue.

The car has been set to run a random pattern in the area, occasionally looping out a couple of blocks past the usual cruising zone. That way the cops will find it more work to follow, if they decide to go hunting for unlicensed streetwalkers. Besides, there might be a new house or parlor on any side street.

Unfortunately, the other thing that can turn up on any side street is a demonstration or a picket line; now that there aren't as many vice cops, there seem to be ten times as many protesters. Ken checks to make sure the opaquing is on as his car slows down, confronted by about twenty people with signs who are walking slowly up the street toward him. They part around him; but they may just be hoping to get his car close enough to batter it with rocks or their picket signs. That's not exactly legal under the Community Standards Enforcement Act, but the police have acquired a habit of looking the other way.

But they seem to be parting to let him through. It's a church group, not Deepers, so they're annoying, not dangerous. This is a quiet little group. *Frozen-faced bitches and pious eunuchs,* Ken thinks. Their faces are held rigid, as if God never wanted them to smile, and they are singing and carrying candles. Ken doesn't see any reporters, which is a surprise. Usually when you have two or three young pretty ones and a couple of old sincere mommy-looking ones, and they're all candlelit, the local stations get a camera or an XV crew out here to get the sharp contrast between those images of purity and the avatars of filth and corruption, like Ken.

He's clenching his fists, glad that the marchers can't see him. They're all around the car now, candles at about the height of the windows so that there's an odd effect of headless bodies with burning candles in front of bulging tits. The tits are in muting, smothering baggy T-shirts and dresses, but Ken can tell some of them are all right. It's sort of like the tits are the idols to which the candles are burning.

The car makes a hard right when it gets the chance and goes down an alley. Normally it only does that when it reads "surrounded not threatened" from its sensors, so its little AI pea brain must have decided that this was a mob that might turn violent. The car's mistake might cost Ken a lot—there have been plenty of people taking off cars in alleys down here. It's so easy to block them in, so easy to hook the frame into an RF circuit and chew out the brains, causing all the safety doors to unlock. . . .

Ken shudders. *God, if they'd just let people enjoy this the way they were meant to, it wouldn't be hooked up with crime and all. And a better class of kitty might go to work down here.*

He thinks about Linda with a mouthful of some stranger and it makes him laugh, but it gets him more excited. Since Nikki isn't out, and apparently won't be coming out for a while, time to find a place.

It's a long alley, barely paved. The Angel Excellent lurches and bounces furiously, keeping speed up for security as it has been programmed, through and over the fierce potholes, making Ken catch his breath as the car tries to pick its way between them.

Abruptly it yanks itself onto Jackson, three blocks from Jefferson. Normally there's nothing over here—the Jackson Avenue Merchants have been pretty tough at fighting any parlors or houses that set up here, and there's a neighborhood watch that hassles customers—but a big sign flashes at him:

JOY HOUSE. COME IN AND en-JOY!

Above the sign are six screens, one girl on each screen. A slim blonde slides a strap down. Cut to an Asian girl with a big chest, back to you, turning sideways to show the breast in profile, yanking her short shorts up into her crack. Cut to a black girl, eyes big and wet, undoing the belt on her skirt. Cut to another blonde, winking as she drops her hands from her bare breasts. Cut to a fat brunette with big droopy tits, leaning forward in a leotard and shaking them. Cut to a rangy redhead with a lot of teeth and inflated hair, uncrossing her legs as she sits in a short, tight dress. One image per screen, and at each cut all the images move left. All six of those three-second flashes are always up there, marching left, one after another—

Ken has told the car to park before he's even begun to consider that this location must have cost something in bribes, from the look of the sign this place has a high overhead to meet, and there's no guarantee that what you see on the billboard is on sale inside. But it can't hurt just to know what it costs. He can save up or something. He has a little credit left on his Commandline account. He's just been divorced. He needs something.

Better still, the place has underground closed parking. No confrontations with demonstrators—except one woman standing out there with leaflets. Just one is more annoying than scary.

She looks like she's about Linda's age, could be a coworker or friend of Linda's—old, worn-looking, turning fat. Baggy jeans and loose pullover don't hide her pot gut enough. She's just in the edge of the car's headlights as it makes the turn—could she be a Deeper, might the purse hold a Self Defender or a grenade? She looks so normal.

As the Angel Excellent rolls into the drive and the steel doors open, she leans forward and slaps a leaflet on his windshield with a flat-handed thud.

He yells because she startles him, but before he has time to be really frightened or really angry, the car rolls through the steel doors, and they slam shut.

If she had been a Deeper she might have shot his engine. They say they're "gentle in their anger" but that doesn't always include "self-defense" against machinery or white males, both of which are "centric." Whatever that is. MitsDoug once assigned him to experience a long dull wedge about Deepers, or "Values Clarified people" as they call themselves. He got to experience thinking about them as a sociologist, a reporter, a religious historian, and then as a Deeper. All of them used the word "centric" a lot, some defined it repeatedly, and he still has no idea what they mean by it.

But this woman was either not a Deeper, or a mild one. Just one scary thud from the leaflet on the glass. She didn't even look angry as she did it.

The MitsDoug Angel Excellent pulls into a parking slot, facing a blank gray concrete wall. Set in the wall, about ten feet away, is a big door made of some dark, warm wood. There's a large brass handle, and a sign over the door in raised wood letters: WELCOME, FRIEND, PLEASE COME IN.

Ken shivers in the unheated parking area and hurries to the door. He turns the handle and walks onto thick soft carpet. Beside him there's a coatrack, to his left a wood-paneled alcove with several armchairs around a fireplace, and directly in front of him, an antique desk.

The girl sitting behind the antique desk is wearing dressy office clothes—soft silk blouse, pearls, hair neat and nicely done in a practical way, makeup carefully understated. She looks like a young, pretty receptionist—not at all whory. She looks up and smiles; she's the slim blonde on the video board outside. "Hi, welcome to Joy House. My name is Aura."

"Uh, I saw the place was new and I, uh, came in."

"Great. Was there anyone on the board outside you especially liked? Not all of us are working at any one time."

"Uh, well—"

Aura is his type. She's wire thin, just the suggestion of breasts under the silk, a pert little-girl face, and a little pursed mouth. But usually when you're asked to pick out a girl she's standing in front of you in a nightie or a swimsuit, obviously for sale, not sitting like the receptionist at some company where he's making a sales call.

Still, he remembers the video of her sliding that thin stretchy black strap down her arm, the hint of a bared nipple. "Er, um—are you um—"

She beams at him. "Yes, that's me up there. Do you really want me or is it just that I'm here?"

"I—uh, really, you *are* my type. No kidding."

Her smile gets wider. "Well, you'll be my first client."

Client. Not "customer," "john," or just "guy." *So nice.* He reminds himself to say, "Uh, I'm kind of on a budget—"

She gets up from behind the desk and comes around to him, and he gets to see the rest of her. She's wearing a little tight pink skirt, black stockings, and fashionable midcalf-length spike-heeled black boots, worn unlaced and with the tops pushed down into a rumple. It's attractive and tasteful—Linda might have worn an outfit much like it to work at the data patterning center. "The money isn't usually an issue," she says, "but the time is. We insist on a minimum session of three hours the first time and two every time afterward."

"Uh, I—um, I guess I still need to ask about money. I don't know if I can afford even one hour, let alone your minimum." He feels embarrassed and ashamed.

"Certainly," she says. "Why don't you come this way with me; we'll go to one of our private rooms—there's no charge for that—and I'll explain everything, and then if you feel you can afford it, we'll just go from there."

"Sure." No *charge?* Most of these places are obsessive about collecting money up front—a lot of guys come really fast, sometimes just from looking at a girl or talking about the deal, and it's tough to repo an orgasm.

Aura pushes a button on the phone and beckons Ken to follow her down the short hallway behind the desk. He checks the line of her bra strap through the back of her blouse and her panties through the short pink skirt. She really is fully dressed, not like she strips to fuck every hour, and it powers Ken up like nothing else. He's her first "client." (Does that mean she's never done it for money before? God he's hard.)

He was expecting either a bed or a doctor's office table. Instead, when she opens the door and gestures for him to go in, there are a couple of big armchairs and a writing desk in it. She closes the door behind her, sits in one chair, and gestures for him to sit in the other, handing him a piece of blue paper; it reads

JOY HOUSE
The Samuel Ordhaus Clinic
for Sexual Compulsive Disorders
Rate Schedule for Standard Therapy

and below that are some figures. He looks it over once, then once again. "Therapy for Sexual Compulsive Disorders" . . . that's a new dodge. A lot of places claim to offer "massage therapy" or "whole-body healing," but he hasn't seen this exact routine before. He says, "Uh, this list of rates doesn't include a tip, does it?"

Aura shakes her head vehemently, making blonde hair flip around over her face. *God I want to fuck this kitty.* She even smiles when she says, "We aren't allowed to accept tips or gifts of any kind. The fee is complete."

He gulps hard. For the three hours, it won't be any more than what he was planning to spend anyway; if it doesn't satisfy him there will even be enough of tonight's budget left for Nikki or one of the girls at the whorehouse. The two-hour return sessions are even cheaper. And this is on one of his two last nights of freedom for god knows how long. Clearly he was meant to have this spree, and it was meant to be the best he's ever had.

Ken glances up at Aura. Any other place, if the customer seems to be waffling, the kitty starts sliding the skirt up, undoing buttons, talking dirty—but Aura seems to be just waiting for him to decide, not putting on any more pressure than her slim legs and fine features do.

Which is more than enough pressure, given the combination of last chance, just divorced, and an unbelievably good rate. His mouth is as dry as it was the first few times he did this kind of thing. "Sure," he says, "I'll take your standard three-hour session."

She beams at him. "I wish we could get people's insurance to cover it, but right now Dr. Ordhaus's methods are too controversial and the insurance companies won't touch it."

They are really carrying this routine about a clinic a long way.

"Now," she says, "what we're going to do is this—and remember the three hours doesn't have to be, like, exactly three. It can go longer if you really need to."

Have I died and gone to heaven? What they're offering is pretty weird, and she makes it clear that it is all they offer. Still, with a kitty like Aura, he doesn't expect to mind.

Ken will put on a reader scalpnet—one of the rigs that lets him transmit, to a limited extent. It won't send precise thoughts the way a full jack in the head will, but vague impressions and feelings come through okay. Aura will plug a remote into the jack in the back of her head. They will talk about sex, touch and kiss for a long time, and at the end of it she'll give him "a release—no need to figure out how just yet, we can kind of let that flow." She recrosses her legs. *Her thighs are perfect,* he thinks.

The requirement for three hours is partly because it takes time to get used to having sex while plugged into each others' brains, and partly because they're going to take a blood sample of him and get it analyzed so that they know he's free of HIV and virus-modified spirochetes before she gets around to handling his semen.

He's never seen a better deal than this. *How can they afford to stay open? Maybe they can't. Maybe this place will be broke next week. But at least it was here for my last spree. That's certainly good enough for me.*

The room is like a small, tasteful bedroom in a country bed-and-breakfast, or a maiden aunt's guest room. They put their scalpnets on, and she puts her jack in, and she says, "Tell me about the first time you had sex. Was it nice?"

Actually, it was one of his big sister's friends, and it wasn't nice at all. She just pulled Ken's pants down abruptly and yanked his penis around in front of his sister and her friends. They all laughed at him, especially when he came. He was twelve.

He's never told anyone.

Ken starts to tell about being fifteen and out after dark with the neighbor girl, who was thirteen—they were kind of wrestling around and he got his hand down her shorts, she was crying but she was very wet and she pressed against his hand—

Something feels very weird. Aura knows that he is lying and she can feel it. Not only that, she *doesn't mind, but she'd like to know the truth.*

He blurts out the whole miserable, embarrassing story, being jerked around by the dick by a girl, in front of all the other girls. Halfway through he's starting to cry. He's clawing at the scalpnet to get it off—

Aura's arms are around him. She's holding him and soothing him. His hands unclench a little, and he reaches forward, lets them slip around her tiny waist—god, she's so thin and so young—

And she likes him. She really likes him and feels sorry for him, and—

She kisses him. Really kisses him. Like he can't remember when that last happened, that way. He feels his tears stop flowing, runs his hands along her slim back through the soft silk—

Now I want to grab the little whore by the tits and shove her onto the floor and fuck her. The thought hits him as he takes her small and soft breasts in his hands, stroking the firm little lumps of her nipples with his thumbs, through her sheer bra.

She knows what I'm thinking. He feels her fear, the quick scared surge of adrenaline, like stepping over a log and finding a snake. He feels his own thoughts making her uncomfortable, powering her down, feels her trying not to be disgusted and trying not to think about his out-of-shape, flabby body.

I couldn't help it, the thought just happened!

She relaxes, kisses him again, and whispers "I can't experience your thoughts very well. What words do you think about me?"

He sighs. "You're not—"

"Tell me." She kisses him again. He feels through the scalpnet that she does want to know—feels too that his hands were rough and clumsy on her breasts and that he's made them a little sore, that he wasn't caressing them as much as he was crushing them and bending her erect nipples uncomfortably. It's too much, he knows she's hurting, he doesn't want to say—

"Now tell nice Aura. Am I a slut? Am I a whore? Am I a cunt? Am I just a nice blonde kitty to play with?" He feels her detect his responses. She kisses him longer and deeper. He is terrified, confused, more aroused than he's ever been.

"Those are the words, aren't they? I'm a nice girl, I'm a pretty little kitty, and I'm a whore, right, Ken? Do you like to hurt the whore's tits?"

He is hard as a rock. He feels her hating the words in her own mouth and disgusted with the idea, hating her body for receiving such attention, hating Ken for treating her this way and hurting her. He feels another part of her mind staying level, calm—*professional*—

"This really is some kind of therapy," he whispers, shocked.

Friendly irony comes through the link. "Yeah. So far they say no one has believed it till they got to this point." He feels her detached amusement, and also that she's fighting down her fear and disgust at being treated like this, and that another part of her is still terribly sad about what was done to him as a kid. And he reaches to see which feeling is the true one—

He ghosts in completely, sees his own body through her eyes. She sees his bald spot, she sees where his shirt and belt are straining to retain his out-of-shape gut. She knows he's erect.

He tastes his slight bad breath with her tongue, feels what it's like to have her body, to be dressed up in a way that feels pretty and be treated like a pork chop.

She wants so much to like him. She wants so much to help him. And through her eyes he looks so lost and bewildered.

It's not the way he ever sees himself at all. He feels like a complete dork, and more than that he seems pathetic—sad—*comic.*

Do I look that way to all these bitches? Bitch. Bitch in heat. Aura bent over for a gang of men, squealing and crying out for more. Aura the orifice.

He feels her revulsion and can't stop; his penis is so hard and he's so angry at her for being someone he wants to fuck that will never fuck him except for money.

Aura chained at bus stops so men can have something to do while they wait for the bus. Aura lying out on her porch naked reading a magazine and satisfying any man who comes by without ever losing her place in the article. Aura frantically dialing random numbers to find a man in the city she hasn't exhausted yet and at last settling for a large carrot while the dead, passed out, and exhausted men of the city lie in heaps around her apartment building.

He pushes her to the floor, yanks her skirt up; he feels her fear and then pain as his fingers thrust into her dry vagina. For the first time ever he feels that he is hurting his partner, humiliating her, making her want to vomit, feels how disgusted she is at the same time that he jabs a finger *up that dry little cunt and teach the bitch a lesson and let's see if I can just twist her tit right off—*

At the feel of her nipple in his fingers and her terror at the pain he is planning to inflict, something short-circuits through him and he ejaculates so hard that it feels like being punched in the stomach; he feels the wet goo shoot into his underwear. Letting go of her, he lies down on the cool floor, crying, retching, terrified of himself.

It felt so good to hurt her tits. When he stared at her legs she didn't mind that meant she wanted it needed it deserved it she's just to fuck to fuck to fuck to fuck—

He screams so hard he can feel it in his balls. Uncountable snakes in the brain hurting him. Aura feels them too. He feels them hurting her too.

He looks up and sees her face smeared with tears. The ghost of her experience slides back onto him and he feels what Aura feels, hating herself, hating seeing her whoring self with his eyes, hating herself for drawing his eyes for leading him on for being with this nauseating old creep. Aura suddenly whirls away from him, and Ken feels the vertigo of her rolling over so quickly, and her desperate need to run out of the room. He rolls after her and their feet hit the floor at the same time—he starts to scream that he's sorry he's sorry he hates himself too—

She vomits. Linked through the neural connection, he heaves as well, though his stomach was already emptied by the first time. Side by side, crouched like dogs, they sob and heave.

Finally she draws a deep breath, holds her voice carefully even and low (they are still connected, he feels her controlling her voice), and says, "It was worse than I imagined. The other therapists all said it would be. There's a bathroom where we can clean up. Let's leave the neural connect in place while we do, okay?"

"Okay, are we going to talk more?"

She sighs, and tears course down her face. Still linked through the scalpnet, she sees her own tears with his eyes, he feels them on her cheeks. "Cindy and Rainbow both had exactly this happen to them yesterday. Clarice had a guy get hysterical—he ran out five minutes into the session. But I thought, I'm a good therapist, I can do this."

They wash and shower together, cleaning each other's backs, wiping each other's faces, often holding hands. Sometimes tears surge up, usually from Ken. He says, "I had no idea that would happen and now I think I'm afraid to have sex again. Where did all that hate come from?"

Aura sighs. "Let me clean your back. Well, the short answer is it was always there. Fear and hate and all that. What got you so turned on was that you finally found out, absolutely and for certain, that you were having the effect on me that you wanted to have. At least that's the theory and it certainly felt as if it made sense while it was happening. So you got the most complete release of your life, probably, because you got exactly what you've always wanted. The catch was that you had to face up to what you really want, and it's not a very pretty picture, is it?"

"I always thought I was a gentleman, and pretty decent to most of the kitties," Ken says, and begins to cry again, because he can feel her wince right after he says "kitties" instead of "women." "I really thought I was a nice guy. And they all said I was but I suppose that's because I paid them."

She shrugs. "Compared to the way a lot of men treat them, you probably were relatively nice. But you know, a streetwalker isn't going to have much of a sample of male behavior to judge by. If you didn't hit them, try to cheat them, or threaten them, and you paid without too much argument and got off quickly—well, that's what they're looking for. It's not like they'd want you for a boyfriend or anything. They're just glad that you're not a psychotic killer. That's a pretty easy standard to meet."

Ken nods and takes a turn washing Aura's back. "I keep wondering if there was ever a time in my life when I wasn't this way." He feels like crying again; he can't believe this woman knows so much about him, and he can feel both her disgust and the way she's trying to fight down her disgust and be professional.

She shrugs, and he feels the warm cascade of water on her back as she rinses. "This will be no comfort to you at all but you're not untypical. In fact if anything you're a modal case, somebody with the most common set of problems there is. So you aren't a typical man and you might not think you're a very nice one, but for what you are you're absolutely normal, if you see what I mean. A lot of men with SCD's have no real intimate experience with a woman—they've been intimate every way except the way it counts, with all kinds of women except ones who matter to them."

"Well, that's me, all right," Ken agrees, sighing. "What's an SCD?"

"Sexual compulsive disorder. Guys who have sex when they don't mean to, guys who can't seem to behave themselves, like that."

"That's me, too. I thought I was just a pervert. Shall we turn off the water, and can I dry your back?"

"Please." She cuts off the shower and hands him a towel.

Her body is soft, slender, young—vulnerable. Someday there will be crow's-feet, a roll of fat under the navel, and—perhaps after children—her breasts will be too big and saggy and stretched out. She's only this way for a moment, and it's so very sweet, and I want to gobble her up and use her.

"You're sad about something about my body."

He starts to answer, thinks again, starts to answer again—"I don't know what to say, even if I try to answer honestly," he says. "I guess . . ."

She smiles. "You have half an hour left in your session, Ken. Let's get dressed, and while we do, try to tell me about it. And let's stay wired while you do—unless you don't want to."

Ken can feel how much better Aura feels, and why. They are out of the scary, dangerous part, and now it's just straight therapeutic work. She can help him without bleeding inside herself.

Her feelings don't bother him. He's glad the worst is over for her. As they pull on their clothes—she's putting on a clean blue low-backed dress, in which she looks very pretty but doesn't power him up at all— he finally says, "I *hate* how I react to the bodies of women my own age. I think of Linda, my ex, as an old bag. The only way I ever got it up for her was to pretend I was using my dick to punish her for . . . oh, for being fat. Or old. Or something. And it was pretty hard to manage if I liked her, so the sex was always better if we'd been fighting. She said it was fun to make up, but she was the only one that made up. I just got to hate her more."

"Was she so hateful?"

He's crying again. "I don't know. I didn't know her well enough to know."

Aura holds him for a long time—he can feel that this is professional and that she is actually a little impatient with him—dries his eyes, and says, "If you've got a little time, you could talk to Dr. Ordhaus. He's here tonight. Or I could talk to you about it, but he really can explain it better, and anyway, uh—"

He says, "You have more work to do," meaning to sound reasonable about it. But they're still linked neurally, and she feels at once that he's dismissing her, turning her into one more anonymous body that he scored on, and that hurts. The pain it causes flashes back to him before he draws another breath, and he feels his face go slack, sees (through her eyes) his expression get dull and heavy. "Will I ever get better?" he asks.

"Did you ever try to think only of Linda when you were with Linda, and maybe to think loving thoughts?"

"Now and then. It made me impotent and she took that personally. Which I used to think was terrible." He scratches the back of his head. "Now, though, I think it was good for her to take it personally. It might have been a start."

Aura hugs him. "Well, if you come back for more therapy, then *I* will take everything personally."

"I don't think I'd have it any other way," Ken says. Then he feels that

that is a lie, and that she knows it is, and chuckles. "Well, okay, the truth is, if you were just a plain old whore I'd have been thrilled shitless to get you. But I still feel like—well, it wasn't very sexy or anything but at least it kind of touched the place that needed to be touched, and that's more than you can say for rolling in the back seat with a streetwalker."

"Okay. Let's unplug."

They do, and they stand facing each other: a guy in his thirties with Not a Success practically carved on his forehead, and a girl who ought to be her sorority's candidate for homecoming queen. They stand there awkwardly for a long moment, saying nothing, before she returns to the front desk.

Ken finishes dressing. He doesn't really consider talking to Ordhaus. He's delighted not to feel the need to go get Nikki or some whore.

He nods to Aura, who is back at the desk, and goes out through the door into the garage again.

It's not like he needs to be able to see, but he finds he's a little angry when he pulls the leaflet off his windshield. He glances at it and reads "Dr. Samuel Ordhaus is using completely untested theories on human subjects and is exploiting a group of young women who—"

The place has only been open one day and they're already targeting it specifically. Must be the christboys and the godgirls, they have more resources and better data patterning than the Deepers.

He gets in the Angel Excellent, cues it to take him home, and sits back. The big steel door slides open and the car rumbles out into the streets, now getting a good soaking in the icy Christmas rain. There won't be any streetwalkers out tonight anyway.

A figure looms in the darkness, thumb out, wearing a red raincoat, looking miserable.

It might even really be a hitchhiker, he says to himself, telling the car to slow and pull over. It does. The woman comes up to the window; he turns up the outside ears and she says, "Honest to god, my car broke down and I really just need a ride—I can't walk home from here and I don't have emergency road repair insurance."

A knot unties in Ken's stomach. If she'd been a whore he's not sure what he'd have done. He unlocks the door and lets her in; it would seem too stupid to get paranoid considering what he has been letting into his car routinely for all these years.

She slides in, pulls the door closed, and says "Thank you so much." When she pulls back her hood he sees it's the woman who was leafleting

Joy House, the one who scared the shit out of him by slapping her stupid pamphlet on his windshield.

She sees that he recognizes her. "I can get back out if you're angry at me."

"Naw." It's raining like mad, and the whiff of air from her door was like the frozen breath of a morgue. Ken can't quite bring himself to make anyone go back out in it. Besides, this way he won't be tempted by streetwalkers, if there are any out there. "I'll give you a ride. Where to?"

"Marlowe Apartment Complex, over in the corporate apartment area."

It's the one next to Westview, where he just moved in. He keys up the address on the car and they're off.

She sighs. "Thank you. I don't seem to be able to do anything right."

The raincoat was probably bought when she weighed less. It makes her look like a little girl who has outgrown her clothes, but the coarse skin of her face and the width of her hips say she's about Ken's age.

"Are you with some group that's picketing?"

"If I were I wouldn't be stranded. No, I'm doing this on my own."

"How come you picked Joy House?"

"Have you been there? Did you go there tonight?"

"Yeah."

"Well, my name is Suzelle Ordhaus. Dr. Ordhaus is my ex-husband."

"So it's revenge or something?"

The windshield wipers slap twice before she says, "God, I hope not. But I couldn't really say."

Her accent is the mall-chick lisp that he remembers from high school. Most of the girls who had it married some guy who fixes electronics— the great dependable job, even now, three years after the Flash—and have settled into lives of visiting their mothers and having babies. A name like Suzelle should have tipped him.

Ordhaus must have married this one when she was young, hot, dumb, and zing. Probably when she was right off the bus from the Plaza Nowhere Mobile Home Community, dressing and looking cheap but ripe. When the inevitable happened and she started to sag and get fat, he dumped her. Shrinks have the money to do that. Shrinks are lucky bastards.

After another long breath she says, "Did you read the leaflet?"

"No."

"Well, uh . . . it's like this. You know that there's a whole bunch of different problems they call SCD's, sexual compulsive disorders—basically men who can't seem to leave sex alone, especially sex for money, and their lives get messed up because of it, right? I'm sure they told you about that much. Well, Sam thinks he can cure it by getting them to dislike the kind of sex they're having, and teaching them to have healthy, healing, affirmative sex instead. I think all he's doing is running an unusually pleasant whorehouse for telepathic voyeurs. But you have more experience than I do. How was it?"

"Uh, nice, actually. Very different. Um . . . satisfying." *Why did I answer? Maybe just to have somebody to talk to. When I park this thing at my complex, with just one day left to go on this spree, with nothing to look forward to but a long sentence wearing the bracelet, probably doing community service, that little apartment is going to be the emptiest place in the universe.*

"Sam thinks if it's closer to real love, it will start you looking for the real thing. I think the men who go to those places are looking for a substitute for love, and the very best he could hope to achieve is giving them a better substitute; for a lot of them he'll just show them what they don't like about love. What do you think?"

Ken sighs. "I *don't* think, much. I just *do* these things. I mean, it's much nicer than a virtual parlor, and that was probably the first girl I ever really liked. And the scalpnet link was weird and it scared me, but it also powered me up like nothing before ever did. And anyway, she was very patient and kind even though I was making her really uncomfortable, so since I got to know her through the scalpnet, I got to like her more than I have most of the whores before. But I might have liked her even without the link. She's got more class and education than . . . uh—"

Suzelle stirs in her seat as if holding herself down. "She should. They're all seniors or grad students in Sam's clinical psych program." Her fists clench. "Maybe that's my revenge coming out."

"You might as well tell me."

The car turns onto the expressway and begins to climb the ramp.

"Well, Sam is kind of a guru type, you know what I mean? He likes to get under everyone's skin and be the wise man they all feel like they have to talk to. He likes to analyze everybody at first glance and then use his charm and charisma and all that to talk them into doing whatever it is that he thinks they ought to be doing. More messiah than doctor, I guess.

"He talks a lot about how these girls need to get over their inhibitions. As if inhibitions were the big problem a woman has in our society!

Naturally most of them get *that* part of the program pretty fast. You don't go into our line of work if you're a prude or religious or uptight. If you ask me, they need no help. But if you ask Sam, not only do they need his help, but, although Sam's ideas have changed a lot over the years, no matter what else changes, his current thinking always involves students going to bed with him."

"Well, I'm sure it's good for him." *God did I go into the wrong line of work!*

"Exactly. Anyway, I was one of them. Nice little girl from a not-great school and a not-great background, and Dr. Wonderful walked into my life. The trouble was, he walked into a lot of other people's lives." She sighs. It sounds like there's a lot of pain in it. "So maybe it's revenge, and that's all it is. It doesn't feel like it but maybe that's all it is."

They ride on in silence for a while, and Ken says, "But you think what he's doing is bad for people? I mean, going to places like that . . . well, shit, I don't even know that it's been bad for me to go to the *other* places, the ones that don't claim to do any therapy."

"How's your life going?"

"It sucks. Tomorrow is the last day of my first three days of nonreporting bracelet, and I've got so many violations that they'll automatically add three years to my sentence and put it back under close supervision. My wife just divorced me last night and she was absolutely right. I expect to get fired on Monday morning. And I just spent the Saturday night of my last fling, for some stupid reason, throwing up and crying."

"Does that have anything to do with your SCD?"

"Yes. Everything. In fact I don't know what life would be like without it, because I've never been without it, but I can tell you right now, life stinks." *Why am I talking to her about this? Because she'll listen. Because she already knows I go to those places and doesn't care.* He feels a sudden, unclear impulse, and gives in to it before he has time to examine it. "Listen, I live close to you. And tomorrow's Saturday. Want to have coffee or something tomorrow morning, and talk about this in more detail?"

She seems to be grinning at him. "That's about the best offer I've had since I moved out on Dr. Wonderful. Most of my meals with people are in the cafeteria at the data patterning place."

He asks, but Suzelle doesn't work in the same place as Linda, and doesn't know her. It was a possibility; data patterning is so much the "job you can always get" that it was quite possible they'd have worked together at one time or another.

Suzelle says, "I've really only been doing it for two years, though, since the funding ran out for my dissertation. It's pretty stupid of me—if I'd just finish the thing I could get a job as a clinical psychologist and roll in money—but you know how that goes, I guess . . . sometimes life just drifts."

"Yeah."

They agree to meet tomorrow at the coffee shop in a nearby mall, and Ken drops her off. A few minutes later, as he gets into bed, he thinks that at least his life has a few new directions and possibilities in it, even if they aren't anything like what he dreams about.

His eyes open on blank white walls, washed with early morning sunlight. He hasn't been up so early on a weekend in years. But then he hasn't gotten to bed, or even *home*, so early on a Saturday night.

Ken showers and shaves. (This isn't exactly a date and Suzelle is not his type at all, but it's sort of practice.) He gets dressed in ordinary knock-around clothes and walks over to the shopping center coffee shop.

Since Suzelle isn't there yet, he takes a table, drops a five-dollar coin in the slot, and slips on a scalpnet to get a five-minute newsscan from ExtrapoNet. They're an okay service for news, but you sure don't feel it the way you do on Passionet—you just experience being a very knowledgeable listener being told about the news.

He ghosts in to find himself sitting at a table and being briefed by the foreign affairs expert. Clearly it's a slow news day because the lead story is that the UN Recovery Forces hope to be gone by next Christmas. The experience pops to walking down a street in the ruined part of LA, wearing the blue helmet, hoping not to get shot at, wanting to go home to Ghana. It's a stock experience—Ken must have had it twenty times.

UNRF has been hoping to go home ever since they came here, in the weeks after the Flash. Now it's coming up on the third anniversary of the Flash, about a month away, and the smart money is they'll be here at least two more years.

The sticking point in the talks is that large parts of the United States are still getting UN relief, and the UN won't let the feds administer it or assign it to private agencies—they say because the private agencies are controlled by the giant corporations and would be used for corporate purposes, and everyone suspects it's a way of keeping the United States from dominating world affairs again. Certainly since Europe has fallen into nativism and racism, they don't want a "mongrel nation" standing up to them, and hence the French, British, and Russian vetoes of every proposed withdrawal plan are understandable enough. China probably likes the power vacuum in the Pacific as well.

The second story is another predictable one: although the U.S. still controls a bigger armed force than the UN or any other member nation by far, Washington, D.C. is still digging out after the Flash. Briefly, in another bit of stock experience, Ken experiences standing on the blast-swept Mall and looking at the stump of the Washington Monument. In a burst of esthetic sense, Congress has decreed that though the Capitol and the White House will be rebuilt, that shattered hundred-foot column will remain blackened and vitrified as long as it stands, memorializing the Flash itself.

Then there's a quick click through the basic business news. Unemployment is low but underemployment is high; after the Flash there were plenty of jobs but very few high-paying ones. Ken was lucky that so much of MitsDoug was in Hawaii and overseas. If he'd been able to behave himself he'd still be lucky.

It's funny to realize that even here, less than a thousand miles from Washington, you can't see any direct signs that the Flash ever happened. Ken remembers what it was like. He and Linda were sitting on the couch, sharing popcorn and beer, catching the State of the Union address from a live experiencer sitting in the gallery. "Hail to the Chief" was playing and the president came striding in, all ebullient confidence. Then it went blank and they were back on the couch in the living room.

That must have been the last time they tried turning on the TV. The old set's picture took a second to come on, and it was on the Home Shopping Network. They started to click to CNN, and got a man saying his name and announcing that he was in Arlington, Virginia, about a kilometer—

The TV went dead. So did the lights, and all electric power. When Ken and Linda went to the window to look, the street was dark as far as the eye could see. Phones were dead. They couldn't get into the car—it wouldn't read thumbprints or voice.

Finally a man down the street turned out to have a radio that had been inside a metal drawer, and all the neighbors, gathered in the spitting rain, heard the word from him: no local stations on at all. An AM station that said it was broadcasting from Mexico City said there had been a bright light over the United States. They waited, checking every few minutes. Most of their homes had no heat, and city water pressure was dwindling; some smart ones ran home and filled bathtubs and sinks, and made sure the kids didn't flush toilets.

Seven hours later, almost the morning, they were all still standing there. The radio was running on its third set of batteries. Then the man looked up and shouted "We have it."

People stood silently in the drizzle as he played the radio loud enough for the closest to hear; then he and two others repeated the news.

Clevis Macauley, the Secretary of Education, who had been in Hawaii at the time, had taken the oath of office and become president of the United States. Naval reconnaissance aircraft from overseas bases had determined that a nuclear weapon of unknown origin had been detonated, somehow, on or just above the Mall at the beginning of the State of the Union Address. Approximately four minutes later a second nuclear weapon, probably enhanced to increase electromagnetic effects, had been launched on a rocket from somewhere just west of Kansas City, and had detonated in the ionosphere, causing an electromagnetic pulse that had shut down, damaged, or destroyed virtually every electrical appliance in the continental United States, along with most of Canada and the northern third of Mexico.

The president and vice president, all but four representatives and one senator, all but two of the fifty state governors, the whole Supreme Court, the Cabinet, all were dead. Macauley was the forty-seventh president of the United States because years ago the custom had developed of sending one Cabinet secretary out of Washington during the State of the Union Address; no one had ever really thought of sending an important one.

It took two months to get electric power back on across the country. In the first two weeks, almost half a million Americans died of exposure or froze to death. It was April before broadcasting was resumed. Most of the money that had existed on January 20 had disappeared, recorded only electronically. Smaller tragedies littered the landscape; aircraft that had lost all electrics and glided as best they could down into forests, lakes, mountains, or desert miles from any help; pacemakers, artificial hearts, and other medical equipment abruptly shut down; fires that raged out of control in cities with no gravity storage of water; the few people who had been outside in the middle of the country who had looked up and been blinded, then not rescued for hours since most people had more important things to do.

Ken sighs; he doesn't even know anymore why he lets himself experience all this stock footage. The thought crosses his mind that he'll never say "Remember when . . ." to Linda again. It's a small point but it hurts.

The last featured story is that Brittany Lynn Hardshaw, American ambassador to the UN, is planning to run for president next year. Ken experiences sitting in the audience and hearing her say it, having her come forward and shake the hand of ExtrapoNet's experiencer. It's a good feeling and Ken notes with some amusement that even through the fuzz of XV and the careful obscurity of professionalism, anyone can tell that the ExtrapoNet reporter is planning to vote for her. Ken is too; Hardshaw has been fighting hard to keep UN Recovery troops out of our internal affairs, UNIC from controlling American news, and in short to make them go back where they came from.

"Anything interesting?" Suzelle asks, sitting next to him.

"The usual; for the last three years everything's been a footnote to the Flash."

She nods. "Yeah. The Flash is everything—it's part of why my dissertation didn't get done, I suppose even part of my divorce. How about yours?"

He shrugs. "The Flash probably held it off. Linda was a data patterner even before, so when her pay went up, and everyone had to buy replacement stuff from MitsDoug, and most of our old debts vanished, it took a lot of pressure off."

They talk for a while about where they grew up. Ken was right in his first impression of Suzelle; she's from the not-good end of a backward town, one of those bright kids that escapes, and, ten years later, has nothing to talk about with any of her relatives, but can't quite shake the accent, attitudes, or tastes.

She's not bad looking if you don't have to have a young kitty. But Ken does—though admittedly it's his loss. *Plenty of guys would be glad to go out with Suzelle. But you can't help liking what you like, can you? And what if you don't like older women?*

After the food, when the subject turns back to sexual compulsive disorders, Ken finds himself on the defensive. "Well, but okay, what if you just don't like love? Then who's getting hurt? Women do it voluntarily and men get what they like."

Suzelle grins. "'What if you don't like love?' That's a great question. You said last night was more satisfying, despite being so upsetting, right?"

"Oh, yeah."

"Well, was she prettier? Was she more skilled? Was it purely physical?"

She was a little prettier, Ken thinks, and then realizes that that's in retrospect, he's not sure what he originally thought. *Now* he thinks Aura is beautiful. "Okay, so, uh, I like love. Probably almost all other guys do. But then what's so wrong about your ex's place?"

She shrugs. "If he's right, I'm a very silly person and I've thrown away a brilliant career because I could never get over being what he called a 'mobile-home majorette pouf-haired Puritan'—and a 'monogamist,' which, coming from Sam, is a much bigger insult than 'whore.' Do you think there's anything wrong with monogamy?"

"I don't know," Ken admits, "I've never tried it."

He's glad she laughs.

The long breakfast turns into going to lunch—Ken can remember that from college, how some days you blew off classes because you never got out of the cafeteria—and from there they end up wandering around the mall just looking at all the Christmas decorations, and going to one of the new movie theaters where you can rent a few-person viewing room and select a movie to be downloaded over the wire. They see Hierman's new one, another carefully worked-up allegory, a story about a high school track team that pretends to be training for the never-held San Jose Olympics of 2016, that manages to poke the UN pretty thoroughly without getting the censors of UNIC down on it.

Ken has to admit it's a very nice afternoon, and they sort of agree they'll do something next Sunday as well. She hugs him good-bye. It feels better than he'd have expected.

As he goes back into his new apartment, he finds himself wishing she was just ten years younger . . . better yet, fifteen years younger and without any of the emotional scars she's picked up from Ordhaus . . . about like Aura. Who no doubt is getting some emotional scars from Ordhaus even now.

Well, Ken's pretty broke, but since he's getting fired tomorrow and they'll turn his bracelet back on for good and close-supervise him for months, he supposes that he should finish out his spree. On the other hand, after the day with Suzelle, he feels a little bit better, and maybe he doesn't really want to go back to the Ordhaus place, especially since he might very well be tempted to get a streetwalker instead. So maybe for tonight, he'll just settle in and experience some of his dirty wedges; he's got a terrific "outlaw" one, where they used a couple of real young street kids and gave them time to really get zing with each other . . . there's another that was put together by a bunch of inspired amateurs at some California college. At least it will keep him from thinking about Jefferson Avenue. *First Blow Job* or *Dorm Room Orgy,* that's the question.

Ken's phone rings and he unclips it from his belt. "Hello?"

There's no picture. The voice of his phone company says he has a fax coming in. He says he's at home. They click off. A moment later the slot by the kitchen ejects a sheet of paper onto the still-perfectly-vacuumed smooth gray carpet.

He picks it up and reads.

MitsDoug has fired Ken. Apparently somebody in Human Resources is working this weekend. The stated grounds are substandard productivity, and his reversion to criminal behavior.

He *has* been a pretty lousy salesman for several months, and no wonder. If you figure how often he's been down to Jefferson Avenue, he's actually been working about a ten-hour week. Not good for a man on commission.

He'd probably have fired himself.

Still, his stomach really hurts and the air feels thin in his chest. He's not a candidate for a heart attack but right now, while he's still covered by interim insurance, would be a good time to have one—

Sit down. Take stock. I can get a data patterning job. It's dull, just sitting there running your screen through all sorts of graphic representations and pointing to any regular geometries or patterns you see, letting that in turn suggest to the artificial intelligence the various congruencies between the many millions of databases. Kind of like playing computer games for money, or solving jigsaw puzzles. Since the Flash disrupted millions of information processing operations, and since probably only a quarter of the nation's recoverable data has been recovered since the Flash, it's the one job you can always get.

A data patterning job will cover rent, groceries, debt payments, and keeping the Angel Excellent. And the bracelet will keep him off Jefferson Avenue, which will reduce his expenses more than he wants to think about.

He checks his status. He has more credit left after last night—plus the cheap date with Suzelle Ordhaus—than he expected to have. A two-hour session is affordable, and Aura said this is one of the nights she works.

Ken is in the car and has keyed in the address for Joy House in less than a minute.

When the car turns onto Jefferson, Nikki is out, in little white shorts and black satin top; she's a very zing kitty tonight. He's tempted, but he'd rather fuck Aura than Nikki, and besides, he's seen Nikki around often enough in the past to know that she usually works all night. If he's still horny after Aura, he'll draw out his last credit in cash and do Nikki to finish off this spree. The car takes the turn and heads up to Jackson Avenue.

It's not quite dark yet. As he approaches Joy House, he sees a crowd of about a dozen, churchies rather than Deepers—the picket signs are bigger and worn around the neck. Deepers tend to favor small signs on big sticks because they make better improvised weapons.

The Angel Excellent draws nearer and he sees the video screens above the big sign more clearly—Aura, pulling down her strap. He needs this so badly his chest aches.

The protesters chant and point. One of them photographs his license plate. Ken almost laughs. With no wife, no job, and a pending administrative punishment for violating parole, he has no reason to care.

The big steel doors slide up to let the Angel Excellent in. Just as they close behind him, a small rock booms off his rear window. It makes him jump, and the rock skips forward and thumps on the hood before bouncing to the side. As Ken gets out of his car, something clangs against the steel garage door behind him.

His car's finish seems to be undamaged. There are three other cars in the customer garage, and a lot of rocks and brick chips he doesn't remember from before.

He goes inside and finds a tall, thin, bearded man sitting at the desk. The guy looks like Santa Claus from the eyes up, and like Pan or Mephistopheles below that. "According to our security software," he says, "you must be Ken. I'm Sam Ordhaus. Aura is with another client just now but she should be able to see you in forty minutes or so, if you would like to wait. We've got comfortable chairs, some music and reading, that sort of thing. Or if you want we can talk—"

"Uh, I'm *really* short on cash this time," Ken says, "and if talking means counseling, I guess I'd rather just read."

Ordhaus's eyes twinkle. It's going to be difficult not to like this man. "Mostly," Ordhaus says, "I was getting bored. One more bug in the system; nobody wants to wait, or talk. Either they go around the corner for a quickie with a streetwalker, or they take off and come back later. I was just hoping you'd hang out and talk with me. If any counseling happens, tell my professional association it was an accident."

Ken smiles back. After Suzelle's description he hadn't expected to like this guy. "Well, then, sure. I don't really feel like seeing anyone except Aura."

Ordhaus grunts, sounding pleased. "In that case, I really do want to talk with you. You're one of our few signs of hope. I've got coffee and tea; want to sit down over here, where I can talk to you and keep an eye on the door?"

As Ken sits, mug of tea in hand, he thinks how unlikely the combination of Ordhaus with Suzelle seems; how could two people that different have been married for so many years? He ventures, tentatively, "I met your ex-wife."

"Suzelle, you mean? I've got three, but she was the most recent."

"Yeah."

"Nice girl. Too nice for what she was getting into. I suppose she's told you about what she thinks of all this—I think her phrase is usually 'pimp with a Ph.D.'" Ordhaus takes a sip of tea. "Well, you've had the experience and you're back. What do you think?"

Ken shrugs. "I like Aura and I like what we did and how we did it. But I couldn't tell you if it's therapeutic." The words pop out. "I just want to fuck her again."

Ordhaus's face goes slightly sideways and he says, "How did you feel when you just said that?"

"Thought we weren't doing any counseling."

"Counselors lie all the time, and you're not getting billed. Besides, you're also my Most Favored Guinea Pig at the moment. How did it feel to say that about Aura?"

"I guess it was kind of fun." Ken hadn't expected to think about this, and how he says, "That's weird, though. I mean we both puked and cried afterwards. Usually that's not a sign of having fun."

Ordhaus nods. "Usually not. Or else you both have fun so rarely that that's how you react to it."

"Unless we both—she can't possibly be having any fun!"

"Oh, of course, she's having all kinds of fun. She loves being hurt and treated like shit. She's really a slut, isn't she?" Ordhaus says, taking a sip of tea. "Right now she's got some other man up her hole and she'll probably fuck another one after you tonight. Plus the little whore has a boyfriend. She'll go home with sperm dripping down her legs, and suck his cock before she goes to sleep."

Ken sputters, speechless, painfully erect.

"Isn't it interesting how the words work on you?" Ordhaus asks, nodding at Ken's erection as if it were an old acquaintance. "Like old-fashioned crude software with no fuzzy logic. Just push the button and off you go."

Ken squirms. Ordhaus's eyes are still kind but the odd turn of his mouth makes Ken uncomfortable.

"I don't know what you're getting at," Ken says. "If this place is supposed to be about love and all that, that's a really strange way to talk. I know it hurts her feelings when I think those things, even though they really power me up. If you want me to admit that I got off on hurting and humiliating her, well, then, yeah, I guess I have to admit to that, and it probably means there's something wrong with me. But I don't see why you're sitting there encouraging it and anyway I don't see how anyone can fix it, because it's just the way I am, the way I've always been. I don't get what you're after."

Like a shrink in an old movie, Ordhaus makes a tent of his hands and says, "Well, now, *that* is an interesting question. What if everyone you were ever attracted to had immediately consented to have sex with you?"

"I wouldn't have time for much else."

"Wouldn't you get tired?"

"Temporarily."

Ordhaus leans back and laughs. "All right, I understand, speaking from inside your own situation, that's how it feels. But do you see what I'm driving at? Just the idea of availability gets you excited. As soon as I call her a 'slut' or you talk about 'fucking her,' you're off and running, because permission has been granted to think that way. You always knew there was some pain and suffering involved, didn't you?"

"I guess I always did."

"But you didn't say that to yourself, and you didn't have to. You could pretend, and still get what you wanted, right?"

"All right, I see the point. So last night I got what I've always wanted, is that what you're telling me?"

"And you were so disgusted by it you threw up and cried. But you wanted it anyway, and it was what you wanted." Ordhaus smiles at him, and there's something creepy in the smile. Ken thinks *I am not the only person in the room who gets some kind of pleasure out of hurting others.* Ordhaus continues. "You're a salesman, right? What if I said—and you believed—that the receptionist at the first place you call on Monday is a slutty little bitch who spends her lunch hour giving head to her boss? Wouldn't you suddenly be fascinated with her? And wouldn't that be because—"

"Uh, I'm not a salesman anymore. They gave me the Saturday slip today; my things from the office will turn up by street mail next week sometime. And I always avoid thinking stuff like that—"

"Because if you did you'd start to behave inappropriately, right? Don't you see that—" A bell. "Excuse me, we have another client coming in here."

Ordhaus gets up and is at the desk before the door opens. The man who comes in looks like he must be close to sixty, and is massively overweight. "Hello, I'm Dr. Ordhaus, Mr. Samson, and—"

"Yeah. Hey, you people keep records? That's not cool if the cops raid the place, you know."

"We have reason to believe what we're doing is legal under—"

"Yeah, save that. I've got about an hour and I was wondering if that blonde chick I had last time wants to make some quick cash?"

"I'm afraid Aura is with another client, and there will be a client after that—"

The guy's voice drops lower, and he lets a folded bill in his hand show. "C'mon, at least check with her, I always come right away and I just want it sucked a little. We don't have to do any of that other shit and I'll pay the full rate."

Ordhaus sits back, looking puzzled; from the way his feet are curling around the legs of the chair, Ken figures he's getting mad. "Look, Mr. Samson. There's no under-the-table here. You can either wait your turn for a minimum two-hour session, or not. But that's all we sell here."

"See ya." The fat old guy goes. The door bangs shut behind him.

"Sorry," Ordhaus says, coming back.

"Is *that* what's been happening with your repeat customers?" Ken asks.

"Mostly. I admit I'm stumped at the moment. The women report all kinds of things coming out of the encounters. Things you wouldn't necessarily think of. We had one guy who came in here three times in two days, who's about a hundred and twenty pounds overweight, and what he likes about it is that he can *feel* how disgusted the women are. He got worse, not better—the more attention and sympathy they tried to give him, the more he liked hurting their feelings. We had to tell him no more. But most of them are like Samson, that clown that just came in. They enjoy whatever happens but they don't have a fucking clue what it's about. I'm feeling like a fairly shitty therapist, to tell you the truth, and the women are pretty demoralized. Most guys can't see this place as anything but a whorehouse." Ordhaus groans from the heart, then takes a long sip of his tea. "And then here's the other weird one. We get a half dozen or so guys like you. You don't just respond as hoped, you respond better."

"You've only seen the one session—"

"It went a lot better than anything we planned on, though it's still much too tough on Aura."

Ken shifts uneasily in his chair.

"And now you've lost your job," Ordhaus says, musing, looking into space. "You know, historically, most therapies that achieve any notice at all have to work really well for at least some people. And there's a historic phenomenon that goes with that. . . ."

He stares into space a little longer; it occurs to Ken that it's entirely possible that Ordhaus is staring into space in order to make a carefully thought-out idea seem spontaneous.

"Unemployment?"

"What?"

"Just my guess about the phenomenon you're talking about," Ken says.

Ordhaus laughs, and it's just phony enough for Ken to decide he can't trust this guy. Aura is all right, and Ordhaus's therapy *might* be all right, but definitely not Ordhaus. It takes a salesman to smell a salesman.

Then Ordhaus says, "In a way, though, 'unemployment' is what I was thinking about. This operation is going to have to run on its start-up grants for longer than I had hoped, but that's okay, there's some cushion.

"But I'm finding that there's a lot more need for counseling outside of the sessions we provide . . . if for no other reason than to screen the men who aren't introspective enough, or empathetic enough, to learn anything from the procedure. And the women are getting too busy to answer the phone and serve as receptionists.

"What I was thinking about was the way so many other psychotherapies have been launched. Historically, with every new form of talk or communication-based therapy, a high percentage of the first patients end up as 'disciples' or whatever you want to call them. The first cadre of patients end up working full-time for the therapist, sometimes, eventually, as therapists themselves. Happened with Freud, Jung, Adler, Reich, a lot of different therapies. I hadn't planned on it, but . . . how about you? I can show you what there is to it in a couple of hours, and you could start Monday. It wouldn't pay much, but while you were working here your therapy would be free."

Ken sighs and says, "I don't think I can. It sounds like something I'd probably like to do, but—" He lifts his left pant leg to reveal the bracelet. "See? I'm in process of violating the hell out of my parole. They're going to have me locked down and under close supervision for months. I won't be able to play with myself without having cops come to the door."

Now Ordhaus is really grinning. "You haven't realized the beauty of the therapeutic context yet, have you? I'm not a licensed whorehouse, Ken, so being here was probably *not* a strike against your parole. I'm a therapy center. So"—he consults the records on his laptop for a second—"ha. Okay, you do have a violation, of course, that your car was photographed on Jefferson Avenue and there's a suspicion that you were with an underage prostitute. But see, immediately after that you were divorced—aren't the new electronic systems a bitch? I've had clients who've been remarried to the same person five times because they kept divorcing each other over whose turn it was to clean the bathroom—the very next thing you did was go to a therapeutic institution. Twice, in fact, over the weekend. Let me see if I can get your AI to do me an early approval here." His fingers click on the keys for a minute, and then a sheet scrolls out of the wall printer. Ordhaus hands it to him.

Ken is on regular observation, just as he was before. His sentence has not been lengthened. He will get more free weekends six months from now if he has no more violations.

And he has been okayed to work at Joy House and ordered to get "therapy" here at least twice a week for the indefinite future.

Ken looks at the sheet and whistles. "How come every whorehouse on Jefferson Avenue isn't a therapist?"

"Because they don't want anyone to get well," Ordhaus says. "If you want to look at it cynically, they generate my business for me. When a guy gets tired of going around the loop of those places forever, he finds out he's dug himself a moat so deep he can't climb out by himself. What I do is charge him a whole lot of cash for a ladder."

"What's he get out of it?"

"From me? He gets out. From them, nothing. I'm still the better deal."

Ken nods, slowly. "Uh-hmm. Just making sure I really understand what the product for the business is. You already mentioned that I get covered for the major health benefit I need, the therapy here. Is there any other kind of health plan?"

"Just basic. You're on the same one with the women. That does mean you have unusually good coverage for pregnancy and VD, but you're okay otherwise—legal minima and catastrophic."

Ken nods. "Not only can beggars not be choosers, but this seems like a pretty good idea anyway. You have a number in mind for pay?"

Sure enough, Ordhaus has a number right then and there. To at least some extent, this was all planned. On the other hand, Ordhaus may have been planning to do him a favor—or may be doing him a favor even if he wasn't planning on it.

By the time Aura is available, Ken has a job, even if it's only about as lucrative as data patterning, he has a regular way to get sex and to pay his bills without living on the line or going broke, and most of all he has a clear pathway off of parole that might not be too hard to stick to. Not bad—only unemployed for about three hours. It had a big element of luck in it—but what doesn't?

He's actually cheerful as he goes back into the other room with Aura. She's quieter this time, and sort of subdued. When they put on their scalpnets, he feels at once that she's tense and scared.

"Was the last guy rough?"

"They've all been rough. Not physically, but it's very hard to be inside their heads for any length of time. Even you, and Dr. Ordhaus says that you're my success story." She stares at her feet. "Five clients, counting you. And I feel sick and I want to cry and I hurt pretty much everywhere you want to touch me."

A weird split happens in Ken's mind; one part exclaims *She's just a little girl! What did they do to her?!* and another part loves the thought that this little whore has fucked five men in a day and that she's crotch-sore from it.

He feels her mind feeling both his feelings, and says, "Wow. I'm sorry, Aura. Maybe I should just go up the street and get a streetwalker. I can tell you're really hurting but if we do anything, that's what's going to power me up."

Aura shrugs. "Why do you care what I think? I'm just a slut."

He can feel that it hurts her to have said it. He feels an erection starting, a sort of pleasant pressure against the front of his pants, and sees her watching for it. He asks, "Are you saying that for part of my therapy, or are you trying to hurt yourself?"

"Maybe me hurting myself is your therapy. Maybe you need me to do that so you can get better." She's wiping her eyes; whatever the truth may be, about the therapy or her own feelings, he can feel how upset she is, the ghost of a constriction in his throat mirroring the way hers feels. *The last guy grabbed her hair and jammed his cock in her mouth till she choked.* He has a sudden rock-hard erection, and she groans and stares at him.

"I . . ." he says. "I feel stupid saying I can't help it. But I've never tried to control it and I don't know how."

"If you're controlling it, it's still there," Aura says, dispiritedly. "That's not exactly a cure, is it? This whole idea is insane, I think. I think Sam just wanted us to fuck a lot of men and tell him about it. He's never had sex with any of us while wearing the scalpnet, you know. I know a lot more about what you think about while you're having sex than I know what he thinks about. For all I know he's a lot worse than you. God, I felt so brave and tough and like such a pioneer when I said I would do this. Now . . . Christ, Ken, all I really do feel like is a slut."

"Maybe it costs too much for me to get better," he says.

She shrugs again. "If you go to streetwalkers, what do you think is happening to them? Something not too different from this. You think they don't know how you feel or what you're thinking? The only difference is that you don't know that they know, and you can pretend not to know how they feel about it."

He kisses Aura's neck gently, not to arouse but to tell her she's pretty, and special, and that he likes her. He used to do this for Linda after she'd had a bad day, very long ago. The thought makes him so sad that he feels his own eyes getting wet.

She hangs on to him and whispers, "I'm so sorry. I wish you were the first one tonight. I wish they were all like you. I'm in terrible shape to give you any help."

A little bit of laughter rises unbidden in his chest. "It's all right. There will be lots of chances. I work here now." He explains it; she nods and smiles.

"That's Dr. Ordhaus," she says, "always so willing to help. God, I wish I could be like him. He always knows just the right thing to say or think to make you feel better about yourself."

"Dr. O doesn't have to do therapy while he's blowing the patient," Ken says firmly. "You have a much harder job."

"The loyalty is touching, Ken, but . . . oh, hell." She sighs. "I feel better, but I'm not sure how well I can deal with any more of . . . oh, the kind of thing I've been dealing with. You're not nearly as bad as the others—"

He can feel through the connection that she is sort of lying; he *is* as bad as the others, but not all the time. And she feels that there is someone good and decent inside him, and wants to know that person.

Ken feels very strange and disoriented; he likes her judgment of him. It feels fair, yet kind. He likes her, and he thinks she's more beautiful than ever.

And his penis is limp and he couldn't imagine having sex with her. *It would be like having sex with Mama, or my sister, or my wife.*

He realizes what he has thought and feels sick. Aura, still linked to him, asks what's wrong, and he starts to explain; then they're both crying because it's all so frustrating, there is no way for him to become better, nothing she can do to make him get better, all that the scalpnets have done is made them feel how urgently he needs to get better. It's like giving an appetite-inducing drug to the starving. Looking at himself through Aura's eyes, he is identifying with her, hating the things she hates, liking the things she likes—

But wasn't it always that way? Doesn't she hate the parts I always wished would go away? Doesn't she like exactly the parts I felt good about? For that matter, exactly the parts that Linda loved?

He feels dizzy, moves to sit down, and suddenly she's taking care of him, worried about him, and he's crying about something or other again.

They spend all two hours cuddling and talking and trying to make each other feel better. There's no conclusion to the time; it ends because

Aura has to work with another client, and she says this one is "sort of creepy with promise—we can't write him off yet but I wish we could."

Ken has never felt less horny in his life. After dressing, and making sure of his time to come in to work tomorrow, he rolls into his car, and it roars out through the steel garage doors, catching two more rocks thrown by the protesters. The Angel Excellent zips by Nikki, who is looking pretty tired at this hour and has a sort of expression of bleak hope. That expression used to power him up. Now Ken realizes it means only that a chance to make more money is more important to her than her sore body and misery of spirit.

His bed back in Westview seems very large and empty. The best part of today, definitely, was the time spent with Suzelle Ordhaus; maybe if Aura had actually wanted sex it would have been different—but then maybe it would have been worse.

Ken's dreams are full of nightmares and half-memories. He wakes up after one bad dream, lies still in the silent dark, and tries to count the number of women who he's made some use of sexually when they didn't want to. Start with Angie, the girl he wrestled down when he was fifteen . . . she really didn't want to do anything sexual, and he knew that, even if she did want attention from an older boy. Some other younger girls, when he was in high school. High school girls while he was in college, freshmen when he was a junior, Linda herself the first time.

The list gets pretty long. He itches all over; maybe a shower would help him relax and get to sleep?

He starts to wonder if anyone ever actually consented to have sex with him, except for money.

He gets up to get a drink of water; it's still dark, but then he went to bed pretty early, and it doesn't take that long to have a nightmare, does it? The clock says it's four A.M., but he's wide awake. At least he isn't due at work till noon.

He rummages through his wedge collection, looking for anything where he's sure the girl wants to and is enjoying herself; probably he's just muzzy and confused, but he can't remember any that are quite what he's looking for. He has a feeling that he did try some wedges like that at one time or another, in the shop sampling booth, and didn't buy them. He wishes to god he had, now.

There's a very old one, one that came with the first XV rig he owned back before the Flash, called "A Walk in the Forest"—just a walk through a state park in Minnesota that you experience as an old naturalist—and he ends up putting that in, pulling on the goggles, scalpnet, and muffs and settling back into the lounger.

It's surprisingly good for an old wedge, and a free sample too. He feels crisp cool air in his lungs, and a sense of the world being clean and fresh, from the first moment as he and the ranger step onto the path.

Somewhere in the middle of the experience he falls asleep; his dreams are of sunlight through the trees, water gurgling from little springs into creeks, ducks flying on and off the river, the rustle of the wind in the leaves. He wakes up at nine, feeling much better.

He's not due at Joy House for three hours, and the world seems a little better to him, so he figures he might as well get out in it. He ends up taking a longish walk and eating in the first little diner that smells good. When he gets home he catches the news on ExtrapoNet—more Flash recovery, Hardshaw's campaign is picking up steam, UNIC has just banned four books—then showers, shaves, dresses, grabs a sandwich for the car, and lets the Angel Excellent take him over to Joy House.

If he really gets better, he realizes, he will have a lot more time, and he knows very little about how to fill it.

The job at Joy House, in most regards, is like any office job. Answer the phone. Tell them the truth even though they don't believe it. Say no to people who want anything other than Ordhaus's therapy. Keep the filing system and records straight—and all that means is read the ID's off the cars pulling into the garage, then see who he was with last and whether or not he's allowed to come in here. Call the cops if protesters break in.

That last one is getting more important. "We've been open four days," Ordhaus says, "and look at it. A few pickets the first day. The second day it rained, and we got Suzelle and that was all. Yesterday twenty-five people, today seventy or eighty—other places don't get this. There are places three blocks over that have underage girls with active ARTS, and they don't draw this kind of protest. Who'd have guessed we'd become such a focus?"

The outside video cameras show the marchers; it's a mixture of Deepers and Christers. They've managed to form a single circling picket line but they're not interacting otherwise. A Deeper woman, face set in hard lines, goes by with a sign that reads "Men *NEED* Feelings"; the man behind her carries a sign that says "GIVE UP THE CENTER." Then there are a couple of "Jesus Is Lord" preprinted signs, worn as sandwich boards, and another that says "SALVATION IS THE ONLY REAL JOY," hand-painted. A group of fresh-faced, scrubbed-looking young godgirls is giggling and laughing, carrying a banner that reads "look not with lust"; they seem to have a flirtation going with a couple of Deeper boys who are carrying signs that read "The Center Cannot Hold."

"Well, it's a nice day," Ken says, "even if it is Monday. And with Christmas on Thursday, I bet a lot of them have time off. A lot of married men won't be able to sneak out, either. So the ratio between customers and protesters is going to be a little skewed for the next couple of weeks, I imagine."

"But why are they picking on me?" Ordhaus says. "God, listen to me, I sound like a classical paranoid. But they don't do this to anyone else—"

"Well, not all the time," Ken says. "But I've seen protests bigger than this over on Jefferson. They put a couple of businesses—Strutters and Baby Luv's—out of action, just by scaring off customers."

"Why did *those* get targeted?"

Ken shrugs. "Who can say? But . . . well, Strutters was high-end and expensive. Great, great-looking girls, models really. One of those places where they pretend you're going to do it all by virtual, you go into the little room after you pay your money, and then the girl comes in, claims she shouldn't do this but she can't control herself, and then makes a real show out of giving head. Baby Luv's was a plain old whorehouse. It wasn't very expensive, and the crowd was kind of downscale, but they had mostly very young-looking girls and all of them dressed and made up to look even younger." He remembers it vividly. They had an ash blonde named Collette there, who dressed like a perky cheerleader type, looked about fourteen, and would do no more than take off her clothes and lie on the table, not even talking with you. Ken used to get very powered up for that one; now he wonders what she was thinking, or if she was thinking anything, while men used her body?

"You look far away," Ordhaus says, sitting down.

"Just remembering Baby Luv's. Nasty place, really. I guess I'm a little glad they closed it down. The women there were pretty miserable, I think."

Ordhaus sighs. "Yeah. Not that the women here aren't. Who'd have thought they'd . . . well, *mind* so much? You can show them all kinds of TV and XV of men with SCDs, and it doesn't seem to prepare them at all."

Ken shrugs. "Reality's different."

"No shit. I ought to have that made into a sampler for my wall. 'Reality's different.' Anyway, it's been what, an hour since anyone came in?"

"At least."

Ordhaus sighs. "Well, I'm still glad I hired you. I appreciate the company. And with just Cindy and Chantelle working, I guess if we did get a rush you'd be handy."

Ken raises his hands in the no-blame gesture, and shakes his head. "I don't really have anywhere else to be. And I think you're having some kind of effect on me—I just wish I knew for sure what the effect was." His eye is caught by something, and he turns to stare at the outside video monitor. "Holy shit."

There are about twenty of them now linking arms, surrounding a car with its windows opaqued. Ken has hit the button for police assistance before he even begins to see that they are now beating on the car with picket sign handles—it's a late-model car so they're unlikely to break the windows or even dent the body, but the driver must feel like a mouse inside a bass drum.

With a screech and squeal, the car lunges left, fakes right, turns its front and rear wheels to opposing directions so that it changes direction almost ninety degrees, and crashes through. There's a lot of screaming and as the car peels out away from Joy House, Ken sees that two of the young church girls are lying on the pavement, and there's a lot of blood around. He hits the police call again.

"That car must have had the full-fledged antiriot package," Ordhaus observes, looking at the screen over Ken's shoulder. "Had he signaled an ID?"

"Yeah, but we hadn't opened the door yet. And he was a new one. The cops'll want the record, I'm sure. The car didn't decide to do that on its own. He told it to. Let's go out and see what's going on. Are you an MD?"

"Haven't practiced in a long time, but yeah. Right with you."

Outside, they find that the protesters had two paramedics among the Christians (no Deeper would go to medical school since medical knowledge is based on killing animals). The Deepers are doing a fast fade from the scene, probably to avoid being made witnesses. The Christian group seems guardedly polite as Ordhaus examines the girls and determines that one has a broken ankle and the other may have a concussion. Ken is sent inside a couple of times to get compression bandages and then a cool wet washcloth. Chantell and Cindy want to come out and help—

and they're not dressed in a way that would be a problem, but Ken figures it's better that they don't.

When he gets back with the washcloth, a small police staticopter is descending to the pavement, its monofilament rotor making a high-pitched whistle. Ordhaus flags it in, and the two Christian paramedics get the girls aboard; Ken watches as Ordhaus stops and talks for a minute with the two protest leaders still there, a minister wearing a clerical collar and an older woman in a blue parka. They all seem sort of embarrassed.

"At least those girls are taken care of," Ken says, when Ordhaus comes back. "And the cops caught the guy less than a mile away. How can their parents justify getting them involved in crap like this?"

"You've got me. Same parents who raise young girls to think their hymens are their most important organs. Well, this'll make the news for sure. At least we have a little bit of human connection with the leadership out there, and even though they don't approve of us, they say they'll pray for us and our patients. Maybe if you pray for people you don't throw rocks at them."

"I think it was mostly the Deepers throwing the rocks," Ken says.

"When they do the TV program, probably they'll interview Suzelle. . . ."

"Are you worried about that?"

"Not really." Ordhaus sits; he looks drawn and tense. "At least she understands what this is about, and she's really a very fair and honest person even if she's a little limited in the imagination department. What worries me is only that if you look at their written material or if you were listening to their speeches, they seem to be angry at this place exactly because we claim we're helping people get better. The church people don't want us competing with Jesus and the Deepers don't think you're better until you're noncentric. And they both agree that wanting to get laid a lot is a disease or a sin or something, that the problem is with wanting to and not with how you go about it. So naturally they aren't crazy about us here." He groans. "They wouldn't let me run this on the campus or at the med school or at any hospital—too afraid of controversy. So here we are, in this completely exposed position. What I'm afraid of, if they interview Suzelle, is that she'll be *accurate* about what we do here. Because what we do here seems to be what really sets them off."

Later the cops come by to get a statement, but since Ken and Ordhaus don't know anything that isn't already recorded on video or in the database, it goes very quickly. Business picks up that evening, as expected, and Ken agrees to stay till midnight after his eight o'clock appointment with Aura; hard to believe that a few years ago the United States had eight-hour laws, but since the Flash, no matter what you work at, you tend to work a lot.

Aura is feeling better today, and she and Ken spend the two hours touching, holding, and talking. Ken would like to do more, and maybe Aura would too, but every time they start he thinks *slut* or *cunt* or something like that, she feels hurt, he gets turned on, and suddenly they're out of synch. Now that his bracelet is turned back on, he won't have the option of going to a streetwalker, either; they finally settle on having him masturbate while she monitors his thoughts. By thinking about other women and keeping it vague, he finally manages to get off while only nauseating Aura a little bit. It doesn't feel like a victory, and since it's disappointing, they end up spending the last twenty minutes just sitting and staring at the walls, trying not to have feelings that bother each other.

The last two hours are when a lot of people who don't seem to have the concept come in, many of them repeaters, and Ken begins to wonder if the place needs a receptionist or a bouncer. There's a Self Defender—a pistol that radios a 911 call and its location when it's fired—under the desk, but at least he doesn't have to think about using that on any of these guys. On the other hand, he keeps expecting to have to use it on the *next* guy.

When Ken goes home, finally, he cleans the place a bit—Mama would be shocked and Linda would never believe it—and goes to bed.

He's not quite asleep yet when the phone rings. "Hello?" He fumbles keep the video send from coming on.

Suzelle appears on the screen. "Ken, I'm sorry, were you in bed?"

"Yeah, but not asleep yet. What's the matter?"

"Not exactly the matter . . . well, maybe. I, uh, I need someone to talk to about something important and you're about the only person I can think of, but it could wait a day or two, and—"

Ken shrugs before he remembers that she can't see him. "Well, I've only just gone to bed. I don't have to be to work until noon. If you want to talk on the phone, I can pull a robe on or something, or if you'd like I could meet you at that coffee shop again. They're open twenty-four hours."

"I—uh." Suzelle blinks and then says, "I was going to suggest that.

You're sure you don't mind? It won't be long, I have to be up for work tomorrow."

"I don't mind at all. It's your sleep, not mine, that's at stake."

"All right then. Sorry to be such a nuisance. You must be wondering what kind of maniacs you're acquiring as friends."

"Maniacs I like," Ken says, firmly. "See you there in twenty minutes."

"Thanks, Ken, you're a prince."

As he dresses he finds himself laughing and not sure why; then he realizes that when you meet a woman because she's picketing the whorehouse you frequent, you don't really expect her to call you a "prince."

Why do I still think of Joy House as a whorehouse?

And another thing . . . he certainly went out of his way to be charming. Not only Linda, but Ken himself would have been surprised to see him being that way with someone who wasn't either a sales prospect or a woman he was trying to fuck. *Could Joy House affect me that much? In such a short time? Or the shock of the divorce? Or is it just the way I always wanted to be?* Mama always told him he was a little gentleman.

Suzelle's there when he gets there, stirring her coffee just a little nervously. "I already ordered a slice of pie," she says, "and it's the first time I've broken my diet in two weeks. I guess I'm really upset, Ken."

"Unh-hunh." The waiter delivers Suzelle's pie; Ken just orders decaf, and waits till that arrives before speaking. "So, all right, I still don't know what you really *are* worried about."

She winces. "It's stupid and maybe nothing."

"Yeah, but I'm here now. You might as well."

She takes a large bite of pie, chews slowly, and swallows. "Uh, okay. Did you say you have a job? Did you get a new job that fast?"

Ken thinks about lying for just a second. "Actually, uh, your ex hired me to work the desk at Joy House. I got fired on Saturday evening, right after I saw you—"

Suzelle nods vigorously. "And Joy House was the first place you headed to. That's what I'd expect from a guy with an SCD."

"I'm not sure I like being predictable." Ken is surprised at how much edge there is in his voice.

She looks down at the table and shakes her head. "I don't imagine you do, Ken. And I really didn't mean it to sound that way. But it's true. Addictive behavior is predictable—that's what it's all about. There's no way around that—the predictability is what makes it feel good, and it's what causes all the problems, because you can't modify it when you need to. You were probably broke and close to the financial edge—"

"But I went to Joy House. Yeah." Mentally, he stares at the picture of himself doing that, to keep it in mind from now on. "Well, as it turned out, it was a fairly lucky thing. Because what happened was that I got hired for the desk, and the treatments there are free now. And Sam, uh, claims that I'm his biggest success story."

Suzelle nods slowly. "That may reflect more on you than on the treatment method. But I am sincerely glad it's working, if it is." She takes a long sip of her coffee and then drops her voice, so that she is speaking so softly he must lean forward to hear her. "And I think maybe it's a good thing, too, because I was wondering whether I should tell Sam about this—and now I won't have to deal with him directly, which is sometimes very difficult. You will pass this along to him?"

"Whatever it is," Ken says, wondering why he whispers back.

"Yeah. I hope it's nothing." Her face looks a little dry and stretched, as if she's gone without sleep for a while, and he notes that her big mass of hair doesn't seem quite adequately combed; probably she's been running her hands through it so much today that it won't behave. "Here goes, anyway. On Friday night, before I went off to picket, I posted a long message onto the net explaining exactly what Sam was doing, what the theory behind it was, why I didn't think it would work. It was aimed entirely at other professionals, you have to understand that. I had no notion at all of doing anything other than getting some other shrinks to take a look at it and ask him some of the questions I thought he should have asked himself."

Ken nods. "I bet when you checked the access trace on it, you found out it was downloaded by a lot of Deepers and church people."

"Right. How did you guess?"

He tells her about the mob outside this afternoon.

"Shit, it's too late already, then," Suzelle says. She shakes her head, hair swirling around. A distracted part of Ken thinks that's pretty, and wonders whether her body would feel like Linda's under his hands. He fights the thought down, trying to keep himself listening to her. "Ken, there are tons of follow-ups and queries to me. The Deepers are worked up about it because they think all those men need to start feeling orgasms with other parts of their bodies and not caring who they get them from, as far as I can make out. It looks like the usual babble and it will probably blow over in a few days. But the church people are completely crazy about the subject. Not all the churches, but the ones that are really big on the net, the same little denominations that you see out picketing all the time. As far as I can make out, it's one thing for all those other places to promote 'harlotry'—that's their word for it—for purely commercial reasons. That fits into their worldview, I guess you'd say— wicked men doing wicked things. But what Sam is doing slaps them right in the face. The idea that a man might be *healed* or *helped* by such a thing—let alone that sexual pleasure might be the doorway to love— Ken, they're *foaming* about it. There are *busloads* of them coming hundreds of miles next weekend to demonstrate, *busloads*. Sam's hit some *amazing* raw nerve there. And I don't think he's ready to deal with it."

"Probably not," Ken agrees. "And yes, I'll tell him."

"I don't want to see him get hurt because of something I did," Suzelle adds. Her eyes look wet. "I mean, I've been very angry at him and I don't like him anymore, but . . . but I didn't mean—"

Ken nods. "I'm sure he'll understand that. You didn't mean that information to get picked up or used in that way."

"Yeah." She sniffles a little. "Everything I do, I fuck up."

"No. Don't say that."

They end up sending their cars back to their complexes without them, and taking a long walk together. An unseasonably warm wind has blown in, with a little spitting rain now and then, and gusty winds whip at them during the half-mile walk; Christmas decorations and ornaments dance all over the street. Sometimes they talk about things they remember, and mostly they don't talk. It's almost three when they arrive at Suzelle's door, now both damp from the wild wind and warm rain. It occurs to Ken that it's now officially Tuesday and that he has Wednesday and Thursday off for the holiday.

"Ken?"

"Yeah?"

"I'd like to be kissed good night, but only if you want to."

He glances at her. The big pile of hair is now an utterly sodden mess, and her makeup has smeared and run a little. The crevices in her skin are more apparent than ever. Her red raincoat is stretched over her full breasts and bottom, and the voluptuousness appeals to him a little . . . just a few years ago, he thinks sadly, and then realizes that even that fantasy doesn't interest him. Nothing seems to just now.

"Sorry," she says, turning away.

"No," he says, "I'm not feeling . . . uh, well, I don't think I want sex with anyone right now. And I guess that's real stupid because you just asked for a kiss, not for sex. But . . . I like you. We're friends. I'm not . . . I don't want to . . . I'm really confused."

"Obviously." She turns around and gently brings her face up to his. Her lips just brush his, and her arms go around him. He embraces her, feels the warmth and weight against him, kisses her a little more firmly this time.

They kiss once more, very gently, and he says, "I, uh, I like this, but . . ."

"But you're not the kind of boy to go further on a first date," she says.

Ken laughs and hugs her; she hugs back. "Wednesday or Thursday," he says. "Christmas or Christmas Eve, reserve me at least one day. Both, if you want. And we'll try to talk by phone a couple times before then."

"Fine. Is this okay? Are you feeling pressured into it?"

He shrugs. "This is okay. I had been kind of drifting. It gives me something to do, even if it doesn't go anywhere."

"Yeah, me too."

Back in his bed again, he can still feel her dry lips pressed on his, the warmth of her body through her coat. His memory of it seems so strange. She's even heavier than Linda has gotten, and she's older than he likes . . . but he likes her. But . . .

He falls asleep, finally, and his dreams are puzzling and fearful. He can remember none of them at eleven, when he finally gets up and hurries over to Joy House.

Sam Ordhaus doesn't seem terribly worried about what Suzelle told Ken. "At least it explains where they all came from and why they came out in such numbers," Ordhaus notes, "and that's more than I knew before. And tell her from me that I sure as hell don't hold any grudge. People reading over scholars' shoulders is getting to be a big problem—look at the way Congress back-seat drives every research grant. Suzelle has a right to her concern—it's not her fault that some of these people are assholes."

As they're talking, Ken is watching through the monitor. The crowd is only about twenty, but it's all Deepers today. Maybe the Christians are embarrassed or they have too much to do at church or something. All of a sudden Ken wishes that the Christians were there; he'd feel safer with people out there praying for his soul, instead of chanting that he has to die for the earth to live.

That afternoon, the four men who come into Joy House have all had to run a gauntlet of the protesters beating on the car with fists and signs, and rocks have sailed in after the car into the garage each time.

Even after the fourth one, getting on toward dinner time, the police are refusing to come out; they don't want to guard the place, and they tell Ken that since the crime is over before they get there, they can't prosecute. When he points out they have videotape, the cops merely say they'll send someone around to pick it up the day after Christmas.

"What I can't believe," Ken says, "is that anyone is coming in here at all. But we did get those four, and they seemed like they really felt like they had to come here. Probably it means something that every one of the guys that was willing to go through that is somebody who's been here at least twice."

"Yeah. In fact they all called in advance, the two for Aura and the two for Tabatha. So either the therapy is a rip-roaring success or I've just found something more addictive than sex clubs themselves," Ordhaus says. He's pacing the floor, gloomy and frustrated. "You know, if you'd like your session with Aura now, I doubt that there will be too much traffic for me to handle."

If anything, Ken is a little afraid of the session, especially since Aura has already had two clients today, but she seems all right when he gets in there.

The link is stronger this time; the additional practice is making them more completely telepathic. She's wearing a dancer's leotard top and practice skirt, looking very pretty and athletic, and he senses her pleasure at his liking the way she looks.

She's also noticing that he didn't think crude or nasty thoughts about her body, and appreciating that professionally. He feels like she's pinned a gold star onto his soul.

Strange. It used to power him up to notice that a kitty was disgusted, bored, or angry with him. Now he . . . well, he's changing. He came here to change.

He feels his confusion meet her friendliness, and then she smiles and says, "Well, do you want to make love?"

Ken is startled to realize that he's not sure. "Let's touch and kiss for a while and see if the mood develops."

Her hair is soft and clean under his hands, her mouth is open, yielding, her tongue light and gentle on his. She brings his hands down to her breasts

slutty tits

and he feels her warming to him, guiding him in what will please her

little bitch is getting hot for it

reaching for his penis

whores love cock!
ram the little bitch's
dripping slutty hole
till it fucking bleeds!
rip her nipples off and eat
them like fucking pink gumdrops!
MAKE THE DIRTY WHORE SCREAM!

They push away from each other, panicked, frantic with anger, tearing the contacts from their heads to end the telepathy, so that she won't hear what he's thinking, so that he won't know that she hears. When they are no longer ghosting in each other's heads, they sit at opposite ends of the room, gasping for breath, weeping, angry at each other, angry with themselves, angry with God. It is half an hour before he manages to look up from the floor and say, "I'm sorry," and a long breath after that before Aura answers, "Me too. Ken, I don't think this will ever work. That program that runs in your head isn't a defect in your personality, it *is* your personality. At least that's how I experience it. I don't think I could even try again, and I bet you don't want to because I know too much."

"You got that right." He sighs.

Comparatively, it is wonderful to get back to the reception desk.

He watches the video screen as the crowd builds up in the late afternoon's gathering dark. As it gets noisier and more frightening, Aura, Cindy, and Tabatha come up front to join them, and everyone sits watching the screen, trying not to jump at the thuds of things striking the building.

By eight P.M., there have been no customers for two hours. Rocks are bouncing off the video screens, a couple of people out there are waving torches (though there's not much outside that they could ignite), and the police finally agree to come and clear a path as long as everyone inside just goes home for the night.

Ordhaus is shaking his head. "We'll have two days off, and that might help. And I'll pay everybody for a full day on Friday and Saturday, but I'll call you and let you know when to come in—we'll open late and close early. Throwing their rhythm off might help. Besides, after Christmas, maybe the Christian group will come back and help to make things a little calmer and kinder out there.

"I suppose I could just give up but I can't quite bring myself to do that. We're making such good progress with a few of you—don't wince, Ken, really, it is progress. Before you didn't know how you felt. Now you know way too much, but you don't know how to react. You'll learn. No big problem. Really. We've about got you fixed." The twinkle in Ordhaus's eyes seems real, and Ken feels better for it, until he looks at Aura, who is staring at the rug with a grim fixity.

Ken shrugs. "If you say so. At least there are fewer of the assholes that come in here trying to get just plain sex for money. Nobody's going to run through that circus outside unless this is the only place that will do."

"Yeah. Well, so all of you have a good holiday and don't think about this place too much. Ken, take my ex to the movies or something, and tell her all's forgiven. I know that Suzelle doesn't have a mean bone in her body and she wouldn't wish this on me or on anyone. Ladies, we're going to limit you to one client per day for a while, and we'll do extensive debriefings after each one. And if you want to just bag a day, or two, you can do it with pay, as long as you let me interview you extensively."

"Dibs on bagging Friday," Aura says.

"You have it. Now let's get ready to run for it, people. I hired you for your empathy, not for your heroism. Get everything together, everyone goes straight to their cars, all cars head straight home. No exceptions to any of that."

The cops call a couple of minutes later, to let them know that the way is clear. They move silently to their cars, starting them as soon as the doors close. No one waves or says "Merry Christmas," and Ken thinks that this is one of the bleakest times he's ever left work for a holiday.

When the employee garage doors open, Ken's Angel Excellent goes out first. Two rocks ring off it, and he shrinks down into the seat, as if trying to hide. The faces out beyond the opaqued windows are filled with fury; he dreams of them all that night.

He wakes from the dreams of them screaming to a phone ringing at nine in the morning. "Hello?"

"Ken, it's Sam Ordhaus. I hate to do this to anyone this early, but it just happens that Joy House is no more. The fuckers broke in and burned it out, and the insurance won't pay to reopen. If you can believe it, the cops are claiming it was an accidental fire that just happened to happen—maybe due to occupant carelessness of some kind—during a misdemeanor break-in. I know it's Christmas Eve today and I know you need more sleep, but could we all meet at my office on campus at noon? I think we all need to discuss what's to be done now, and see if we can figure out something to meet everyone's needs."

Ken is about to suggest just shutting the whole works down when he realizes that the light terms of his parole partly depend on keeping Joy House, or some such operation, going. "I guess I'll be there," he says, rolls over, and sleeps another two hours.

All six women are at the meeting, as is Ordhaus. The doctor looks around the room for a minute and it looks like he senses something; finally he says, "All right, I admit, I have no idea. Somebody talk."

"I'm getting therapy the day after Christmas, and I'm not coming back to work," Cindy says, looking straight at him. "The whole damned thing turned out to be rape and abuse. I feel like I wasted the last two years of my life having you as my guru and philosopher-king and all that. You made me feel very special and important for being your favorite, and I thought I was the luckiest woman on earth, and I ended up getting treated like that. Not to mention that for the rest of my life I'm going to wonder what any man I get involved with is thinking. You really suck, Sam. You are a pig, you experimented on me in a way that I really can't believe, even now, you could stoop low enough to do. Fuck off and die."

She goes out the door.

"She said it better than I could," Tabatha says, and goes. The rest go until only Aura is left.

Ken's gut is clenching; he's very afraid that it is not just Ordhaus that she will be tearing into. *Whatever she says, I've got it coming,* he reminds himself. *It all seems so stupid; before, I'd never have let anyone like Aura be my friend, and now, she'd never let anyone like me be hers. What was it all for?*

Finally Aura shrugs. "I feel pretty used, too. I just wanted to ask Ken if he feels like I did him any good."

Ken wants to look away, but he looks her straight in the eye, and tells the truth as far as he knows it. "I really don't know at all. You made my old life impossible, you know. I think that's great, and it's a gift I could never repay, but I think it cost you more than anyone should have to do for anyone else. But if it makes you feel better, you should know that I don't think I can be quite the same guy again. I think I'd puke if I tried to do the things I used to do. I might never manage a normal relationship, but at least I can't act like as sick a bastard as I did before. I do wish I could say more, but I can't."

Her eyes soften for just an instant. "If I knew what it was going to do to me, I'd never have done it. Still, I did. And if you really are out of that life, I'm glad for you. It wasn't worth it, but you're welcome to whatever I did for you." She turns to Ordhaus. "You see?" she says. "You see?"

Ordhaus is sitting slumped in the chair, tears running down his face, and does not answer.

"Well, then," Aura says, "I guess Cindy said it best. Fuck off." She turns to go and then turns back, shouting, "Fuck off and die!"

Ordhaus starts to weep, his shoulders and back shaking, and Aura, after giving him one more contemptuous look, says, "Ken, if I were you, I'd stay away from him. But you're probably not that smart."

"My parole," he says apologetically.

"I forgot. Good luck, then." And she leaves, quietly, her footsteps making faint echoes in the hall.

After she's gone, Ordhaus wipes his eyes and says, "That reminds me. I can offer you sort of a deal. With the Joy House project closed, I'm falling back on a couple of grants that have something left in them, and trying to hustle some more soft money. How would you like to be my patient and my research assistant? You'd be absolutely unique."

Ken shrugs. "Well, it beats going for a longer time on the bracelet. Don't I have to enroll, though, to be a research assistant?"

"Oh, yeah. Stay in long enough and you might end up as a shrink, yourself. One of the occupational hazards of grad school. But at least you'd be completely unique among my grad students." Ordhaus sits back and sighs. "Completely unique."

"How?"

"You wouldn't be a woman. And you'd be the first one I didn't try to fuck."

Ken can't help it; he starts to laugh. "Oh, hell, how can I turn the deal down? Maybe we can figure something out together. And if not, we can always just drink a lot, or something."

"Or something. Okay, I'll call you after the holiday."

At Suzelle's that evening, they have a little bit of her spaghetti and a great deal of his red wine, but they only touch each other lightly, and now and then. He tells her the story, filling in details that broadcast news got wrong. They both agree that the Deepers are getting really danger-ous, and that it's lucky no one was hurt.

Then they're silent for a long time before she says, "Ken, did you like sleeping next to Linda?"

"Kind of. Well, maybe a lot. Maybe even more than I liked sex with her."

"It's been a week since you did. Is that too soon for you to share a bed here? We don't have to have sex."

He thinks about it. "Would it help you?"

"It's been a few months for me. And there's hardly anywhere lonelier than a bed, once you've gotten used to not sleeping alone. But I know the whole world's gotten turned upside down for you, and I don't want to push it if you don't want to yet."

"We could just kind of let it happen."

In the next long silence they move over to where they can look out over the city; for a Christmas Eve night it's very warm, and she opens the window a little. "There's four sets of church bells you can hear from here," she explains. "I thought it would be nice at midnight. Let me know if you get cold. We can always close the window."

He's getting to like the silences better. She slumps against him, and he notices that her breast is pressing his arm a little. He looks down and sees the bubble of flesh dented in by the pressure of his arm; her eyes are hidden by her bangs, and he can't see if she's doing it on purpose or not. After a while it occurs to him that *it's just a breast,* and that this is the first time he can remember thinking that thought.

The church bells catch them kissing, and Ken breaks off to say "Merry Christmas."

"Merry Christmas to you too," she says. "Are you staying the night?"

"Maybe New Year's, okay?"

"'Kay." They kiss one more time, and he gets up to go.

He walks home, taking a while to do it. There are lights and colors everywhere; a lot of places leave them on, on Christmas Eve. The streets are full of people driving home from church. But Ken is all by himself, with dark whispering ugly thoughts, and hopes for the future, and a vague feeling that he's made a couple of friends and knows a few things that he didn't know before.

New Year's Eve will start the 2020s. Maybe that's why he's feeling suspended, at the beginning of everything, as if God had just said "Let there be . . ." and was enjoying a little teasing, not saying what there would be yet. Maybe it's all just stress from too much change at once. But tonight he'll sleep, tomorrow he'll deal with the day that turns up, and someday—he's sure of it though he has no evidence—he'll kiss Suzelle, or somebody like her, and there won't be a thought in his head.

A gust of cold rain blows out of nowhere, into his face, and for one instant he concentrates on keeping his hat on and getting his balance back. Two blocks home, then bed.

HOW TO BUILD A FUTURE

This is my most reprinted article, so let's take it for one more trot around the track; mostly it's been reprinted in editions for would-be writers, but I think it may be of interest to people who have liked the Giraut Leone's books. If nothing else, some 1988-vintage computer neep may be good for a nostalgic chuckle. The reading guide at the back is now ten years out of date, but a little improvisation should allow anyone who wants to try this at home to substitute more recent sources.

So without further ado, here's how I came up with the world for both A Million Open Doors *and* Earth Made of Glass, *plus, I hope, three more novels still growing in the files.*

Building worlds mathematically is so basic to hard SF that we rarely think about *why* we do it.

I won't presume to say why anyone else does, but I do it because I have too little imagination.

Does that seem a shocking admission from a science fiction writer?

Think about what most fictional planets are like. The writer who doesn't worldbuild usually creates the familiar in drag: a single, excerpted environment. Jungle planets, ice planets, or desert worlds are usually just like the Amazon, Antarctica, or the Kalahari without the research or detail a story actually set in those places requires.

Not merely limited in variety, they all seem to be the size of Chicago, or at best Georgia. Jerry Pournelle has aptly described this with the phrase "It was raining on Mongo that morning." Though SF writers claim to explore the wonder and vastness of the Universe, many forget that a planet is *big*. The Earth includes places as diverse as the Grand Canyon, the Black Sea, the Pacific atolls, Greenland, and the Mid-Atlantic Ridge. Yet how often are we told some planet is a "steamy jungle world" or a "polar waste?" (So what's the Earth—a "room temperature world with an oxygen-rich, water-saturated atmosphere?" Tell that to the poor tourist dropped off, wearing only his bathing suit, in the Whichaway Nunataks or Qattara Depression.)

Now compare those bastardized Earth environments with the wonderfully diverse created worlds of Poul Anderson, Larry Niven, or Hal Clement. I think it's exactly because those writers do calculations that they reach as far as they do. The calculations spur them to leap over the usual walls of imagination. The imagination must really stretch to take what the numbers say is plausible and see what that looks like standing on the ground. (The vivid picture Clement gives us of what it's like to *be* on Mesklin is what really makes that a classic piece of worldbuilding.)

It Was Raining That Century. . . .

What's true of physical environments is true of social ones. How many versions of the Roman Empire, the high feudal period, or Tokugawa Japan, are there in SF? Just as many SF writers invent familiar environments, they also invent familiar history.

This does have the advantage that everything "goes together"— a first-century polity with a first-century economy and society automatically has some plausibility. (So do crocodile-like reptiles on jungle planets.)

Yet it cheats the reader of the excitement of going somewhere *really* new. How many *Star Trek* fans would argue that the "set-of-the-week club" episodes in the last year of the original series were as good as the earlier ones?

You also get the social equivalent of it raining on Mongo that morning. Just as we forget that there are a lot of very different places on a planet, we forget that a lot of different things happen in a century. When John D. Rockefeller was born, the last Revolutionary War veterans were still alive; when he died Neil Armstrong was seven years old. Thomas Jefferson lived through one-quarter of the nineteenth century, Thomas Edison more than half of it—that same century contained clipper-ship races, the experimental development of radio, the Romantic movement in music and literature, the birth of modern advertising, Greek Revival and Victorian Gothic, the canal era, Freud's early work, Lewis and Clark, Impressionism, the 1848 revolutions in Europe, the opening of Japan, and the first hints of atomic energy.

Yet many science-fiction future histories have less happening between now and 3000 than actually happened between A.D. 900 and 1200. Often, in SF, social change seems to have arrested anywhere from ten to fifty years after the present, technological change a century at most.

THE SAME SPUR FOR ANOTHER WALL

Just as doing the numbers can drive a planet builder into realms of possibility he wouldn't otherwise enter, calculations that grow out of mathematical social science can help the society builder envision the unprecedented.

I have a fairly extensive background for this (a math-heavy B.A. in economics and a math-methods-emphasis M.A. in political science) so my bag of tricks is bigger than will actually fit into any space reasonable for an *Analog* article. What I'm going to do now is take you along as I build a future, with some substantial commentary on why I'm making the choices I am and what other ones you might make. I'll only use a few tools from the kit, but this should at least give you some feel for what can be done.

Let me warn you that this is all just fun. With all respect to other writers (Flynn 1987), I do not believe that the use of math methods in the social sciences will ever lead to social forecasting even on the level of pre-satellite weather forecasts. Sensitive dependence on initial conditions and measurement error are both intrinsically too extreme in social data for that. This stuff can be a good basis for stories, but if you get the feeling that you are forecasting the future, I suggest you lie down until it gets here.

STARTING FROM AN IDEA

I wanted to do a story about the introduction of instantaneous travel (the transporter booth, if you like) into a civilization that had spanned several solar systems for centuries. Expansion and intensification of contacts between cultures has often caused spectacular events, so I was sure I could find plenty of excitement in such a world.

What kind of future would FTL break into?

If you're going to write about a new way to do something, you first need some understanding of how it was done before. I arbitrarily decided to limit my pre-FTL starships, at least the colony-sized ones, to a velocity of one-half lightspeed—fast enough, with suspended animation limited to one century, to put many nearby stars within reach. At .5c, relativistic time dilation only slightly extends the human crew's range of travel. Additionally, limiting accelerations to 1.5g maximum for any time more than a couple of days put the outer reachable limit for manned expeditions at about forty light-years.

If I were doing a story about the exploration/colonization period, I'd need to do much more elaborate detail work, but with a non-scientist hero in a future where these technologies had been familiar for centuries, I could leave the suspended animation as a given, and needed only cursory work on the propulsion technology.

Again arbitrarily, I decided the starships would be photon rockets with a power plant that converted mass to energy with perfect or near-perfect efficiency. Allowing for acceleration and deceleration in a one-way trip, a speed limit of .5c could be set by limiting the ratio of propellant mass to total mass to .75 maximum. Whether that limit is imposed by problems in handling antimatter, or the necessary size of the "field generators" (whatever they might be), or the tensile strength of Larry Niven's "balonium," doesn't matter because ship operation won't figure in the story, so again I left the problem for the physicists to play with.

FROM THE BUDGET FOR BALONIUM TO THE TEA CEREMONY

Assuming that interstellar colonization would be a relatively low priority for future civilization (important for prestige or PR, perhaps, but not truly vital), how long before colony ships would be cheap enough to represent little or no strain on the global budget? That would mark the beginning of a plausible colonization era.

Where physical worldbuilding uses equations, social worldbuilding generally must use models. A model, technically, is a "system state vector" (a set of numbers, like population, growth rate, GNP, economic growth, and per capita income, that characterizes the system at one moment in time [say 1989]) plus a "transformation rule" for calculating a next vector in the same format ("multiply the growth rate by the population and add it to population to get new population," "divide GNP by population to get per capita income," etc.). By applying the transformation rule over and over, you can project a set of values indefinitely into the future.

To do modeling, I usually set up a spreadsheet (a columnar pad, for the rare *Analog* reader not yet computer-initiated). Each row is a system state vector, the values for one time period; each column is a social variable of interest. The cell formulas are the transformation rule. The values of social variables are calculated partly from present-day, and partly from lagged (previous period, next row up) values of other social variables. You simply record the initial state of the world in the first row, set up the cell formulas to calculate the next row, and then generate more rows until you reach the desired year. (If you're using pencil, calculator, and columnar pad, you'll be at it a *long* time—probably the major reason this wasn't done much before the early '80s. And be aware, if you're using a computer, that spreadsheet models tend to be huge—one I discuss below eventually took up about 600 kb of hard disk space.)

Initially I just wanted a quick-and-dirty estimate of the earliest quarter century in which a colony starship might reasonably depart Earth, so I set up my spreadsheet with one row equal to twenty-five years.

I started forward from 1985 with the following assumptions:

1. The fully loaded ship, exclusive of fuel, masses about 330 million kg. (60 percent of the size of the biggest present-day oil tankers). Dividing by 25 percent gives 1.33 billion kg of mass at launch, so 1 billion kg of fuel are required (regardless of destination because the ship travels ballistic most of the time).

2. GWP (gross world product, the annual total value of all production and services worldwide) grows at a conservative 2.5 percent indefinitely. (This and other unattributed specific numbers are either found, or calculated from values found, in the 1989 *World Almanac.* There are better and more esoteric sources of numbers, but you can do just fine with that one simple source.) Working in increments of twenty-five years, that's about 85 percent per iteration.

3. The starship is a government venture. As Earth continues to industrialize, the public/private mix, and the growth of the public sector, will tend to approximate those of the Western democracies of today.

(If you think that's a whopper of an assumption, you're right. Feel free to play around with drastically different values.)

Right now the average size of total government budget among Western democracies is about 37.9 percent of GDP (gross domestic product—GNP without foreign trade, to more accurately reflect the actual size of a national economy) and the public sector claims an additional 7 percent per twenty-five years (Heidenheimer, Heclo, and Adams, page 173). We might simply figure a future date at which the government budget becomes 100 percent of GWP, but I chose to assume that the private sector is actually *losing 10 percent share* per twenty-five years. Thus the private sector dwindles but does not disappear (in fact it continues to grow in absolute terms—just more slowly than government.)

4. The first colonizing starships will be built when one of them represents one half of one percent of five years of global government budgets. Modern nations rarely pursue non-vital projects of more than five years' duration, and one half of one percent of total government budget is about two-thirds the proportion of all federal, state, and local outlays going to NASA, and thus a conservative estimate of what the future civilization might find a sustainable funding level.

5. Fuel is the cost bottleneck. (A century or more of unmanned or small-crew exploration has developed the necessary technology.) This seems especially credible because the fuel converts to five million times present American annual energy production.

6. The price of energy remains constant. Energy price automatically sets a boundary on fuel price because the price of any fuel must lie between the price of the energy it will yield, and the price of the energy it takes to obtain it—below that range, none will be made; above, it will be too valuable to burn. I assumed starship fuel (antimatter or balonium) could be produced from electricity with perfect conversion, so it cost exactly what electricity did—good enough for the one-digit-or-so accuracy needed. For greater precision, I'd have had to specify a fuel-to-energy conversion efficiency and an energy consumption per unit fuel made, and calculated prices based on those.

Given a starship budget and a price of fuel, I just put a column for "starships per year" (annual starship budget divided by the price of one billion kg of fuel) on the modeling spreadsheet, and scanned down the sheet to see where it exceeded .2; that date plus five years would be a good figure for the first launch.

Unfortunately, with energy prices at present levels, launch year came to 3165. From past experience, that's much too far into the future to model at all, not to mention being extremely discouraging.

To get out of that situation, I added more balonium to the technology mix. I came up with the "Von Neumann powersat" of "VNP"—a space-borne electric power plant that puts out fifty trillion watts and reproduces itself every eight years. Whether VNPs are solar, nuclear, antimatter generators, or balonium transformers didn't matter to me any more than it usually matters to a mainstream author whether the electric power in his fictional house comes from hydro or coal. If it were relevant to the story, I'd simply work up some specific physical rationale to fit those economic parameters.

So this gave me a new Assumption 6, to replace the one above:

6. Sometimes in the early 2000s the first VNP is constructed; within a few decades, their rapidly growing population is virtually the whole electric production for the solar system.

VNPs increase about eightfold every quarter century. GWP increases 1.85-fold in the same time. Demand for electricity is roughly a function of the square of national GDP, so presumably that means demand is going up $(1.85)^2 = 3.24$ fold per quarter century at the same time supply is increasing eightfold.

In the very long run—and in twenty-five years you can modify machines, homes, practically anything—you can use an almost infinite amount of electricity if it's cheap enough. Assuming society holds growth in its electric bill at the same proportion of total expenditures, then, every twenty-five years the planet is buying 8 times as much electricity for 3.24 times as much money.

Or, to the one digit of accuracy we needed, the VNP causes price of electricity to halve every twenty-five years.

Under the new assumptions 2285 began the quarter century in which launching was feasible. Humankind's first interstellar colony would be launched in 2290.

Three centuries is still a very long way into the future—think back to 1690—and that's just the beginning of the colonization era. Since the idea I started out to work on pretty much demands that other solar systems have been colonized for some centuries, it takes a while to build and launch hundreds of starships, and it might take as much as eighty-five years travel time to some of the colonies, the date of the story is still further away from the present than any reasonable ability to extrapolate. (My experienced-based rule of thumb is that five hundred years is the absolute maximum.)

I didn't want the world to get utterly unrecognizable (though that might make another good story), but clearly I would need a reason *why it wasn't* unrecognizable. I decided to add an event to the background: at or around the time the colony ships are leaving, for some reason or other, the global human culture decides change in general is bad, and begins the Inward Turn (a period like the Enlightenment or Renaissance). There will be much refinement but little new development after A.D. 2300.

Such things have happened. The familiar case is Tokugawa Japan, but China, Persia, and India have done similar things at times, and the tendency was clearly there in other cultures (e.g., Dark Ages Ireland, fourth century Rome). So it's a reasonable human possibility.

Of course, after several centuries of the tide running the *other* way in our culture, we're out of sympathy with such a cultural turning, and may think of it as "decadent," as "stagnation" and "degeneracy." But it need not be. The Inward Turn simply means people will value and explore one set of possibilities at the expense of another. It will tend to favor skills, arts, and crafts that require extensive refinement and disciplined training: gymnastics, martial arts, formal or classic styles in the arts, religions requiring elaborate meditative practices, taxonomic or "catalog" sciences, ethics and ontology in philosophy. By the same token, it will devalue that which requires novelty and personal passion: team contact sports, romanticism and subjectivism in arts, religions based on fervor and conversion experiences, theoretical sciences, epistemology. That's a choice—not a moral collapse. They'll have fewer Beethovens and Rimbauds, but more formal gardens and tea ceremonies.

And at the time of the story, centuries later, the Inward Turn will be as automatically accepted, unremarked, and beyond debate as the Renaissance is today.

CYCLING FORWARD

What triggers the Inward Turn? We need to have some major event happen three hundred years from now, give or take fifty. What could it be?

If I already had a clear picture of the society of 2285, I might simply make up a shock to impose. Since I don't, I'll develop the society first. Because good social models tend to be unstable, there may be a big enough shock occurring "naturally" near the desired date.

For this projection, I calculated annual values of the social variables, giving a more elaborate fine structure, because the social event I was looking for would lie somewhere in the rich detail of history. I'll discuss only the seven variables that gave me a result I would use for the story, but I actually modeled more than forty variables. (Like photographers, modelers have to shoot a lot more pictures than they keep.)

We'll start with the economy, taking Woodward and Bernstein's advice—as good in the social sciences as it is in investigative journalism—to "follow the money." It also happens to be a good example of cyclic phenomena.

The major cycles in economic growth rate are the Kondratiev (54 years), Kuznets (18.3 years), Hansen 1 (8.3 years), and Hansen 2 (3.5 years). The error bars on those times are so wide that you can arbitrarily flex values plus or minus 10 percent.

There are cycles in the rate of growth, not in the actual size of the economy itself. You can take growth of GWP as varying from 1 percent to about 6 percent annually (postwar values for industrial nations except for peculiar cases like Japan and Germany during postwar reconstruction) with the average at around 3.8 percent; or, taking data going much further back in history, you can assume annual economic growth can fluctuate between −3 percent and + 9 percent, with an average of around 2.7 percent. I chose the smaller range.

The effect of each cycle is about 1.8 times as large as the effect of the next shortest—thus the Hansen 1 is 1.8 times as big, the Kuzents $1.8^2 = 3.24$ times as big, and the Kondratiev $1.8^3 = 5.83$ times as big as the Hansen 2.

I usually just use a sine wave with a period equal to the length of the cycle. First pick a year when the cycle "troughed"—went through a minimum. The year 1795 seems to have been the last four-cycle trough, but all cycles except the Kondratiev seem to "reset" during very deep depressions, so you might arbitrarily pick three years during the 1930s for the Kuznets and Hansen troughs.

The trough will be one quarter cycle before the start of a new cycle, so you add one quarter of the period to that year, and now you have the zero year for that cycle. For the value of each cycle at all future dates, then:

Cycle value = sin ((Current date-zero year)/(Period/2π)).

Total cycle value = sum of all the cycles times their coefficients (those powers of 1.8).

Growth = average growth + k(total cycle value), where k is a normalizing constant, a simple fudge factor to make the results come out within the range of growth you've selected.

The value of GWP in year Y is then simply:

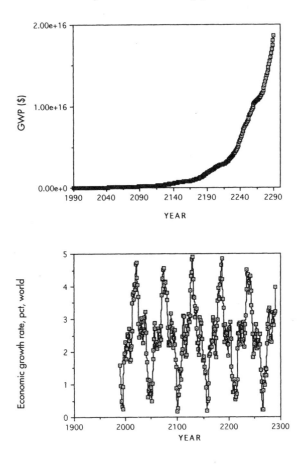

Figure 1: Annual growth and GWP to the beginning of the Inward Turn.

$$GWP_Y = GWP_{Y-1} (1 + \text{growth rate}).$$

As you can see in figure 1, in the next three centuries the growth rate flexes all over the place, but in the long run of history what we see is simply the same explosive growth that has characterized the last century or so. By the time of the Inward Turn, everyone is a lot richer. But what is available for them to buy?

HALF MAGIC

I need not tell an SF audience that technological advance has dramatic effects. There are a lot of different ways to model it; this time I used the "shopping list" approach—gadgets are invented at a steady rate, but they are economically deployed (that is, come into actual widespread use) in bursts. Schumpeter suggested deployment might correlate with the upswing in the Kondratiev wave; it's also a truism that war brings rapid technical development.

To express this, I simply assume significant new inventions go onto a "shopping list" or "technological backlog" of potential technology, and move off the list and into real deployment at a rate that varies between 0 and 100 percent, depending on the Kondratiev cycle value and the values of warfare indicators (see below).

As you can see in figure 2, this gives a fairly credible situation: technology sometimes stagnates as nothing new is deployed for a long time, and at other times skyrockets, especially after a long hiatus. This gave me as much information as I really wanted: eight major surges of technological innovation between now and the beginning of interstellar colonization. (A "major surge" is something on the order of the highly innovative periods 1900–20 or 1940–65.)

To envision the surges, I use a rule of thumb that has no justification other than gut feeling. Each new surge is 90 percent what you might have expected from the last one, plus 10 percent magic (in its Clarke's Law sense). So from the viewpoint of 1920, 90 percent of the gadgets of the (roughly) Manhattan Project through Apollo Project boom would be imaginable (indeed, some, like TV, were abortively available in the previous boom). But 10 percent (lasers, nuclear power, transistors) would be absolutely incomprehensible—magic.

I further arbitrarily assume that the major discoveries for the next surge have all been made as of today.

The graph shows a major surge in the 2000s and 2010s, Surge Zero,

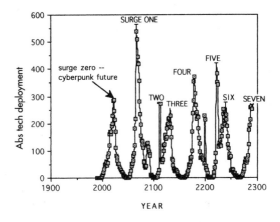

Figure 2: Technology deployment (index of number of major innovations) annually 1990–2290.

which should deploy everything in SF that seems pretty likely right now. *Everything.*

Does that feel like a real explosion in the brain, like Bruce Sterling or William Gibson at their dazzling best? All the same it's only the start.

Surge One must be an immense extension of everything in Surge Zero, *plus a 10 percent addition of things that work according to as-yet-undiscovered principles.* Surge Two must be extensions on everything in Surge One (including the 10 percent of magic) plus 10 percent *new* magic. From our viewpoint it's now 19 percent magic.

And Surge Three . . . well, you see where this gets to. Since the Inward Turn starts at the end of Surge Seven, 52 percent of significant new technology in the culture we're imagining must be stuff we currently would not find comprehensible.

Realistically, the world should be half magic. Who'd have thought calculations, the lifeblood of hard SF, could drive us that far into fantasy?

THREE HUNDRED YEARS OF SEX AND VIOLENCE

Since we've already been through the business of setting up cycles, I'll just mention that there are four prominent cycles in the Index of International Battles, of lengths 142, 57, 22, and 11 years, in battles per year.

(Any separable clash of armed forces between competing sovereignties is a "battle.")

The same cycles apply to "battle days per year." Each day contains as many "battle days" as it does battles—so that, for example, if ten distinct battles go on for ten days duration, that's a hundred battle days.

Like the economic cycles, the longer the cycle the bigger its effect, but it's not quite so pronounced, and one-digit accuracy is about as far as I can comfortably go, so I suggest coefficients of 3, 2, 2, and 1 for those cycles.

Estimates on actual numbers of battle days per year vary wildly; all sorts of international, defense, and peace organizations publish estimates, and no two are even remotely close to each other. (The problems include defining when a battle starts and stops, which incidents are big enough to be battles, and how separated things must be to be separate battles.) Thus there's no good guidance on what the numbers actually should be.

Once again flying by the seat of my pants, I simply estimated a range. In all of human history, I doubt there's been a day of peace—somewhere on the Earth, two military forces were probably fighting each other on every day of history. So an absolute minimum would be four hundred battle days per year (one-digit accuracy, again).

On the maximum side, the most battles probably occurred either during the nineteenth-century European colonial conquests or during World War II. There were eight major European colonial powers, and most of them were fighting one insurrection or another most of the time. Add in the American Indian wars, and assume the larger British and French empires were usually fighting two insurrections at once, and you get eleven battle days/day.

In World War II, counting four Allied fronts against Japan and five against Germany/Italy, plus partisan activities in occupied areas, and counting each front as a battle day every day, we get eleven battle days/day.

Either way it comes to about four thousand battle days per year, which is obligingly one order of magnitude greater.

After about 1900, the percentage of global population killed in war per annum is an exponential function of the number of battle days. (This is just something I've found in playing with UN and various other statistics. It's purely do-it-yourself social science and comes with no institutional pedigrees, so if you don't like it please feel free to cook up your own.)

Again, I set this up as a function that would flex between a minimum and a maximum. According to UN figures, in a very good year only about 1 in 100,000 people worldwide die of something directly war-related.

About the highest figure I can conceive (excluding genuine nuclear wars of annihilation so that there will be a future to write about) is that a twenty-year war might kill half the global population. That's about an order of magnitude worse than World War II, which, if you extend to include the Sino-Japanese, Ethiopian, Spanish, and Russo-Finnish wars leading into it and the many aftershock wars (Greece, Malaya, Korea, China, Ukraine, Palestine, etc.), killed around 5 percent of the global population between 1931 and 1952. So the global fatality rate varies between .00001 percent and 3.4 percent per annum, as an exponential function of battle days.

Wars are allegedly about something or other. We aren't interested in every little brushfire conflict, of course, and neither will our descendants be—when was the last time you heard anyone refer to the War of the Pacific, Queen Anne's War, or Prussian-Danish War in passing, and expect you to follow the reference? But the two really heavy periods of fighting that appear in the three hundred years should have some global significance.

In the theory of international competition, the classification "great power" comes up frequently. I like a modified version of Kennedy's definition: a great power is, first, a nation that can, if it has the will, militarily enforce its wishes on any other nation not classified as a great power, and on credible alliances of non-great powers; and second, a nation that is able to make conquest by any other great power too painful for the aggressor to contemplate.

If you apply those rules the way I do, there are five great powers in the world today: the United States, Japan, the Soviet Union, China, and the European part of the NATO alliance.

Great powers come into being from sustained periods of economic growth. Major wars against other great powers produce very high death tolls and economically ruin great powers, busting them back to secondary status, sometimes permanently and often for decades.

The great powers normally get and consume the bulk of the world's wealth, so an ambitious secondary power needs a generation—twenty-five years—of fast world growth to rise to great-power status. Success for one rising power precludes anyone else's success. There are finitely many resources, power vacuums, and unclaimed turf in the world, and the secondary power that gets all or most of them is the one that becomes a great power—while shutting out everyone else, so I also allowed only one new great power to emerge per decade.

To express the way wars between great powers quickly knock them down the scale, I assumed that if annual global war deaths exceed 1 percent, twice their WWII value, all the great powers must be involved. I expressed this as a simple fraction—every time war deaths went over 1 percent, I busted three-eighths of the great powers (to the nearest integer) to secondary status. Thus a three- or four-year war at those historically unprecedented levels is enough to break all the great powers in the world.

The numbers of great powers, along with war deaths, are shown in figure 3. There are two truly big wars in this future—World War III and IV, let us cleverly call them—and the starship launches come right when a second power manages to lurch up to great powerhood again. Normally that would be time for another war . . . so why not this time?

Let's look at population statistics. (This stage of the creative process approaches sex, like violence, in terms of its quantitative results, rather than its messy particulars.)

How many people are there in 2290, and where do they live?

The results of the model can be seen in figure 4.

Virtually all the growth of population in the long run comes from rural populations. This is caused by something that always startles elitists: people are not stupid. Agriculture is labor-intensive, and as long as an additional person can produce food in excess of its consumption, it pays to have another baby. (Famines are generally caused by a drastic change from the expected future—war, drought, or land confiscation changes the value of children after they're born.) In most parts of the world, the expected value of children doesn't reach zero right out to the limit of human fertility.

By contrast, life in cities is expensive, and work children can do there is less valuable, so having kids really doesn't pay. Thus over the long run (it takes time to alter perceptions, and peasants who move to the city don't suddenly de-acquire children), city dwellers will have children at

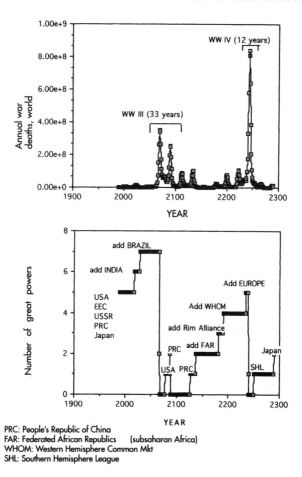

PRC: People's Republic of China
FAR: Federated African Republics   (subsaharan Africa)
WHOM: Western Hemisphere Common Mkt
SHL: Southern Hemisphere League

Figure 3: War and the Great Powers to the Inward Turn.

or below a replacement rate and rural people will have all they can. "All
they can" globally currently corresponds to a global rural population increase of about 2.3 percent per year.

Luckily, practically everyone would rather live in the city. (The American back-to-the-land fetish is an extreme minority taste.) Currently a bit
under half of one percent of global population moves from country to
city per year. If that continues, by 2056, the growth of rural areas has reversed, and as they decline in population the rate of population growth

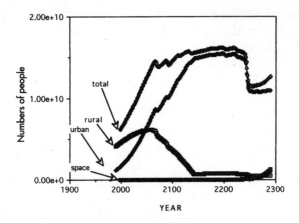

Figure 4: Solar System population, 1990–2290.

slows. In fact, World War IV is so big that global population actually peaks at around fifteen billion in 2237 and declines to just under eleven billion by the beginning of the colonization era. Global population is then more than 95 percent urban (as opposed to 22 percent today).

For a quick extrapolation of spaceborne populations, assume a VNP makes work for 100 people and the percentage of spaceborne population that would be working in the energy industry declines steadily by 10 percent every twenty-five years. That gives a population growth rate of 6 percent (most of it supplied by immigration at first).

By the beginnings of interstellar colonization, there are 1.256 billion people living permanently in space. Go ahead and gasp—but it's a slower rate than the European population increase in Australia 1788 to 1900, and Australia effectively cost more to get to.

BEYOND MEGALO

Megalo- is the prefix for "real big." Hence the SF idea of "megalopolis," the giant city.

I won't report full details here—it's another article in its own right—but in playing around with statistics on the world's very largest cities, I've noticed there are roughly three groups: (1) New York and Tokyo, (2) eight industrial centers with populations of ten to fifteen million, and (3) about twenty Third World population jams.

They seem to group unusually clearly according to what I call a "respiration statistic"—how many dollars worth of goods per year must flow per unit perimeter to keep the city functioning. Tokyo and New York have respiration statistics about an order of magnitude greater than the eight giant industrial centers, which in turn have respiration statistics two orders of magnitude greater than the Third World giant cities. (The one interesting exception is that the respiration statistic for Osaka-Kobe-Kyoto (OKK) is about one-fifth that of New York or Tokyo, so it may be an intermediate case, or one in transition.)

It doesn't take a lot of travel to discover that the fundamental experience of living in these three kinds of places is drastically different, especially that categories 1 and 2 are different from category 3. So I set up a simple system to let categories 1 and 2 grow as population grew. Category 2 I call a "megalopolis"—similar in lifestyle and scale to LA, London, or Moscow today. Category 1, of which New York and Tokyo are the existing representatives, I dubbed a "hyperpolis."

And because in three centuries it didn't seem unreasonable to have at least one more kind come into being. I created the imaginary category of "transpolis" to cover a respiration statistic one order of magnitude greater than that of Category 1. This works out to a city of a hundred million with a population per unit ground area like that of a modern high-rise apartment building. The technology to feed such a thing doesn't exist today, but I see no inherent impossibility.

I simply set up allocations so that some of the world's urbanizing population would flow into megalopoli, some megalopoli would grow into hyperpoli, and a very few hyperpoli would become transpoli. Which cities or areas became which, again, wasn't critical for the time in which I wanted to set my story, so I simply left it as a piece of cultural background to be filled in as necessary.

THE TIME OF THE INWARD TURN

In A.D. 2290, global population is steady at eleven billion, down 27 percent after World War IV, forty-one years ago. Practically everyone lives in town, and about 17 percent of the population lives in giant high-density towns—the equivalent of twentieth century LA or bigger. Half the technology is, by twentieth-century standards, magic. Global per capita income is about 110 times 1985 American per capita income. World War IV reduced transpoli from seven to five, and hyperpoli from twenty-three to seventeen, well within living memory. There are many veterans, former refugees, and survivors around, and the ruins of the destroyed hyperpoli and transpoli are still in existence, raw scars visible even from the cities on the moon, visited by grieving pilgrims as Auschwitz is today. In the last few years, the hegemony of one superpower has been challenged by the rise of another, and the fear of another war is in the air.

And that seems to me enough to explain the Inward Turn. At such a moment a charismatic leader might successfully move for an effective global sovereignty. The Earth becomes a loose federation, committed to develop internally, refining and integrating its culture, bringing technical, social, and political change to a near stop, letting humanity find time to knit together. (Again, that sounds unattractive to us—but we don't have four billion dead in a landscape of ruins, and a recent scare that it might happen again. People whose world was shattered only forty years ago might feel very differently.)

If they take the Inward Turn, why would they launch colonies at all? Perhaps as a bribe—"your way of life must be assimilated here—but you can perpetuate it in the stars." Any group that can raise the money can launch something the size of a big twentieth-century ship on a one-way trip to a preselected colony site on some other habitable planet. (I assume unmanned probes, and perhaps some manned scientific missions, have thoroughly scouted the feasible worlds.)

Arbitrarily, I've set the colony ship size at ninety-six adults, one million preserved human embryos, plus everything needed to fully establish the colony. I also assume that because our descendants get better information faster, and perhaps have a better way of using it, there are no mistakes on the order of Jamestown or Botany Bay. (You could write a terrific story about such a mistake, though—remember these ships are much more strictly one-way.)

PLANETS WHOLESALE

The physics/astronomy/geology side of worldbuilding has been covered extensively and well elsewhere (see Gillett 1989 for a good update and reading list) so I won't deal with it here. When I need a lot of planets in a hurry, I set up a spreadsheet of the basic equations, one row to a planet. I put in randomizing factors that will keep planets within habitable zones and give acceptable mass, surface gravity, etc. In this case I used some real stars (G's, warmer K's, and cooler F's) within forty light-years of Sol, so the stellar information was a given and only the planets had to be generated.

For more colorful place names, I assigned habitable planets preferentially to stars that had individual names over stars with constellation names.

This is very unlikely to turn out to be the actual case.

Nearby stars that have individual names are almost invariably red giants, too old to have living worlds; several of the ones that aren't have white dwarf companions so that any living world there was cooked long ago. But for purposes of fiction and romance (and I hold few purposes higher), I preferred to use those star names. So I cooked up a hypothetical process that would cause practically all such stars to have, not living planets, but extremely easy to terraform planets—so easy, in fact, that robot equipment sent at near lightspeed would be able to have them "ready to move in" by the time the colony ships got there. Since the story itself was to be set only a few hundred years after terraformation, this immediately suggested all sorts of interesting local color that wouldn't have been there otherwise. Just such a dialogue between calculation and art is what worldbuilding is all about.

The planet sheet can be as sophisticated as desire or skill can make it, but in practice you'll always end up doing a great deal of further work on each generated planet, drawing maps and so forth.

This time, rather than use a random number table, or the supplied random number generator, for the six randomizing factors that went into each planet, I used the function $y_{n+1} = ky_n (1 - y_n)$, going down the columns of the spreadsheet, with k in its chaotic range between 3 and 4, to make values cluster irregularly, creating just a few kinds of planets plus a few weird outliers.

I did that for several reasons. It fit my basic feeling that the universe is made up of endless variations on just a few themes. There aren't an infinite number of kinds of stars, the gas giant planets we know are all clearly of the same family, and there are just a few common kinds of ecosystem on land on the Earth . . . so why not just a few common kinds of habitable planet, plus occasional "Australias" and "Galapagoses"?

It also created an interesting potential situation in interstellar trade, because the more alike two places are the less they have to trade and the more they compete with each other. If there are just a few types, then most planets will have several serious trade rivals and a finite number of good markets.

Finally, there's only room for a finite number of symbols in any story or collection of stories, and if you intend that the environment mean something, contrasts will work better aesthetically if they're to a small number of alternatives (Arrakis v. Caladan, for example). You need enough "normal" planets to establish that one in particular is "weird."

This time my generator gave me three basic categories of planet:

- Six "Wet Mars" planets, smaller and cooler than Earth with big oceans and just scatterings of volcanic islands and some Greenland or New Guinea sized pieces of continental rock. Colonies tend to huddle in their tropics.
- Fourteen "Utah" planets, worlds 5- to 15-percent larger than Earth with much more extensive continents and 10- to 35-percent of their areas covered with dense briny seas (mostly long and narrow like the Red, Mediterranean, or Timor seas), intense insolation, and high axial tilts. A lot of their surface area is fantastically hostile—deserts drier than the Atacama, enormous daily and seasonal temperature swings, mountain ranges that dwarf the Himalayas—but seacoasts are habitable well into arctic latitudes.
- Eight "Cold Indonesia" planets—earthlike but cooler, with bigger polar caps, and somewhat less land area broken into many smaller pieces. The tropics and lower temperate zones are pleasant.

In addition to these, the sheet also generated five outliers, mixed or peculiar cases that added variety.

WHEN DO WE GET WHERE?

With the set of destinations worked out, the next question was timing of colony arrivals. Obviously that depended on when they were launched.

The simplest assumption is that since economic growth continues, if we leave the starship budget at a fixed five hundredths of global government budget, starships will be launched at a rate proportional to cumulative economic growth. There were thirty-three habitable planets in twenty-five solar systems, presumably all well-surveyed. Knowing what is available, what does the world government do?

Trying to think like hypothetical bureaucrats under the circumstances, it seems to me that a system whose overriding concerns are peace and stability would want, first of all, to insure that there was as little basis as possible for rivalries between colonies on any one planet, and that there were no "wild" or "open" frontier worlds out there where dissidents or malcontents might build up strength in isolation. There's going to be a lot of looseness for cultural development, but you don't want to create, or leave, a space for an actual enemy to exist in. In fact, if you're trying to keep social change slow, you don't want anywhere out there undergoing uncontrolled growth—you risk creating a potential Commodore Perry in a few centuries, and a culture that thinks like this one thinks in terms of millennia.

So clearly, to avoid having untenanted open real estate anywhere, the first priority is to get *some* colony down in every system, and then on every planet. The first twenty-five colonies go one to a solar system, and the next eight go to empty planets in solar systems that have more than one habitable world.

To insure quality, you make sure nobody has to live in the truly nasty parts of the planet. Every colony is granted a land area with resources and worst-case climate comparable to France, Texas, or the Ukraine. In the whole set of habitable worlds, 1,240 such spaces were available, four-fifths of them on the 14 Utah-type planets. (For comparison, the sheet gives a value of 46 such spaces for Earth.)

For political stability, you want most of the colonies on any one planet to be close together in age—as we'll see, these colonies grow so fast that in a century or two they might well start grabbing land assigned to somebody else. So you want the last colony to land within one hundred years of the first colony's arrival.

Thus after the "elder" colonies are planted on each planet—three planets don't have good spaces for more than one—you "fill up" each planet rapidly with younger colonies. That way the younger colonies will all be close together in age, and can, if necessary, support each other against the large elder colonies.

Obviously the fewer colonies assigned to a planet, the faster it can be filled up, especially in the early years when you're still not launching many ships per year. So each successive colonizing mission goes to whichever planet has the *fewest* open slots.

Knowing ships per year launched, order of colonization, and travel time, working up founding dates of every colony is no harder than coming up with a simple bus schedule. The first colony, on a Utah planet circling Alpha Centauri, is planted in 2299; the last colony arrives at another Utah planet, this one circling Theta Ursa Major, in 2475, having left Earth in 2390. (Coincidentally, exactly one hundred years after the first colony left.)

With those missions, the "colonization era" is over. Colony ships can't reach any more systems from Earth, and none of the colonized systems is as yet ready to launch a secondary colony. Of course, colonies could be set out from Earth to be refueled in distant systems, but remember that this is a century after the Inward Turn began—the interest in reaching out may have dwindled. So the colonies get planted, and grow, and time goes by. . . .

THE NUCLEAR FAMILY:
TEN FROM THE WOMB, THIRTY FROM THE VAT

I gave each ship forty-eight couples of childbearing age and one million frozen embryos. What would that grow into?

This required only a very rough demographic model, because I just wanted to know what the population age profile and size would look like, and from past experience I knew that a "point entry" demographic model would give me the two digits of accuracy needed.

The quick-and-dirty spreadsheet I created is thus extremely crude. A point entry model is one in which all the major demographic life changes are assumed to happen simultaneously for everyone. So in this model:

1. The ship arrives on the nineteenth birthday of all ninety-six adults.
2. Exactly one year later, on their twentieth birthdays, each of the forty-eight couples adds a decanted baby (a former frozen embryo) to the family. In addition, one-third of the mothers give birth on their twentieth birthday.
3. Every birthday thereafter, through the forty-ninth, all adult couples adopt a decanted baby (until the supply runs out) and one-third of them have an additional birth.
4. All children pair off into couples on their nineteenth birthdays and are part of the reproductive pool beginning with their twentieth birthdays.
5. Everyone drops dead on his or her eightieth birthday.

No doubt Lewis Carroll could have a lot of fun with such a society. One can imagine Big Day celebrations every January first, in which the whole family gets together to unbottle a new crowd of babies in the morning, attends a mass wedding at lunch followed by a mass birthing, and then goes out to the cemetery to watch old people drop into their predug graves before going home to the traditional dinner.

Yet although the results this model yields are different from the real world, for the story I want to tell, four hundred years after landing, they aren't different enough to matter. The demographic profiles for two planets (size of cohort by age) are shown in Figure 5.

If you need a more accurate model (e.g., to get accurate effects of baby booms, plagues, or wars in the age profile), you can always improve the precision by cutting down the time represented by one iteration, making deaths or births depend on variable fractions of many age cohorts, and installing more leaks (bachelorhood, early death, individual preference, sterility) into the reproductive pool.

Just one warning—if you do try a more elaborate model, make sure that the total death fractions applied to each cohort add up to 1, as do the total fractions moved out of the reproductive pool. Few things screw up a demographic profile as thoroughly as immortality, negative people, perpetually fertile dead people, or reverse mothers!

By prior assumptions, these would be planets without significant technology gains or wars, so I didn't put these cycles into the process. You could probably do interesting things with diffusing technology via radio from multiple points, and the shopping list model might be very interesting for that, but again, that's another story.

For the economic cycles, I suggest starting the Kondratiev wave with its minimum value on the landing date, the Kuznets cycle whenever you think they'd start putting up buildings, the Hansen 1 cycle at the point where they'd be setting up factories, and the Hansen 2 cycle whenever they'd start making their own goods rather than living on what came in the ship, because the three shorter cycles are traditionally identified with building, physical capital, and inventory investment.

THE STUDENT EXCHANGE ECONOMY

Before the introduction of FTL travel, is there anything to trade between planets?

It is a basic principle of transportation economics that, if there's a faster way to get it for the same price, the slower way won't be there at all.

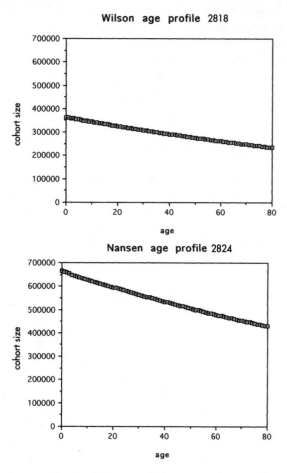

Figure 5: Age profiles for Wilson and Nansen at the time they get instantaneous travel. Wilson was colonized some decades prior to Nansen—notice that the downward slope of the profile is less acute. The downward slope indicates a growing (hence youthening) population.

First of all, since a radio transmission can carry instructions on how to make certain goods and gets there in half the time of a ship carrying the goods, given the speed of construction possible with self-replication, it's very hard to see how any finished goods could be involved in trade. Designs will probably travel by radio, and thus money and information might flow between star systems, but cargoes of finished goods won't.

Given the quantities of energy available at the very low prices that make colonization possible at all (presumably every colonized solar system has VNPs), it's equally hard to see what raw materials could be in short enough supply to be a problem. With 50 percent magic technology, even if somehow you had a whole solar system with none of some vital element, I would guess transmutation would be cheaper than transportation.

Works of art can also go by radio, even paintings, sculptures, and dances if the recordings are precise enough holograms. Scientific papers are no problem either, though biological specimens might have to go by ship. Again, though, with our 50 percent magic technology, it's more likely that a full genetic description would be sent by radio, and the life-form of interest "constructed" on site, and if the technology base also includes really sophisticated computer simulations, rather than doing the traditional random searches for interesting pharmacological materials, biochemical engineers will be constructing specific molecules for specific receptor sites. In that case no one will be interested in exobiotes for potential new drugs or spices—which have traditionally been high-priced for low-shipping-cost goods, and hence great openers of trade routes.

Are we left with nothing but one-way tourism?

Well, almost. Although all kinds of information comes in via radio from thirty-three other worlds, the big problem is that it gets increasingly hard to understand. Other cultures diverge from your own, and it can take up to eighty-five years to get an answer to a question.

Ideally you want someone to talk to about it who won't take decades to reply. So maybe you get the equivalent of interstellar Fulbright scholars, students on life-abroad programs. They might serve as "interpreters" for data from their home system and perhaps from those beyond it (from the standpoint of their adopted system).

They probably do *not* spend all their travel time in suspended animation; instead, they put a lot of time into reading and viewing transmissions from back home and from their destination, so that they'll be fluent in the culture they left (though behind it) and fairly fluent in the one they're joining—thus making good interpreters for some decades afterwards.

On the other hand, the older they are, the less useful life is left in them—so perhaps they spend half their time in the tank. Further, since we've established that suspended animation is risky (remember, after a hundred years, odds are you're dead—which is why the ships can't get much further than their forty-light-year limit), a few of them probably die on the way.

Well, then who will go? You can hardly send condemned criminals (usually not the academic type), dissidents (not representative), or desperate poor people (probably no poor people—living standards are likely to be as high as Earth's in short order).

Probably most of them will be self-selected. In a population of millions, you can surely find one hundred or so acceptable people who will have personal reasons for taking a one-way trip to somewhere else entirely, especially if the "somewhere else" is a place where they'll be in a very high-prestige, high-authority position. They will have five major characteristics—they'll be:

1. young enough to be worth sending.
2. smart enough to be able to enjoy the years of study aboard ship.
3. socialized enough to be endurable company for everyone else on board, and
4. abjectly miserable enough in their home culture to leave it forever, but
5. not actually incapable of happiness (if they were, they'd stay home and kill themselves).

One hundred such people confined in a small space for several years . . . that sounds like a story to me. It's still not the one I'm writing, however.

THE NETWORK IN THE STARS

To do this next step, you need to do enough simple trigonometry to figure out how far apart the stars all are. This gives you a "distance matrix," not unlike the mileage charts found in road atlases. Then, given the known performance of the starships, it's fairly trivial to convert the distance matrix to travel time matrix.

Assuming we don't want people to spend much more than fifteen years out of suspended animation (too much aging, since they must leave as educated adults and arrive with some decades of vigorous health still ahead of them), and that they need to spend about half their time awake to keep track of the cultures they're moving between, the practical travel time is about thirty to thirty-five years. Planets will exchange only within that radius, *unless* there are no closer neighbors with which to exchange. In that case, a planet will exchange with its closest neighbor, paying enormous premiums, plus any other planet that is insignificantly further away than that (say less than 10 percent greater travel time).

The acceptable routes by these rules are shown in the "route map," Map 1. It shows the major trade routes (those that make economic sense) and the secondary trade routes (those within a few percent of making sense, plus the routes to the nearest neighbors for those planets that don't have any choice in the matter).

GETTING DOWN TO CASES

The map immediately drew my attention to the Mufrid and Arcturus systems. Though they exchange easily among themselves, they're quite remote from the hub. That combination of close relationship with each other and being a long way away from the rest of Human Space suggests really deviant subcultures could grow there, more so because there are only two colonies in the Mufrid system and one in the Arcturus—fewer elements in the mix means it will be less homogenized. Cultures there can be both very archaic (i.e., comprehensible to my twentieth-century readers) and truly bizarre to the rest of Human Space. If I chose a protagonist from there, when the transporter booth was invented, I would have a good pair of eyes to go see twenty-ninth-century Human Space through.

I set up a convention to avoid having to do too much thinking about names: habitable planets are named, in order of distance from Earth, after winners of the Nobel Peace Prize, beginning with the oldest. So Alpha Centauri's habitable planets are Dunant and Passy, Arcturus's is Wilson, and Mufrid's is Nansen.

Circling Mufrid, Nansen has good spaces for only two colonies. This world, one of the five "outliers" (fitting none of the three classifications) is cold, wet, and heavy—oceans almost saturated with salt, just to keep it from freezing (and even then I had to add a great deal of calcium chloride in solution as well), gravity 1.2 Earth's, Antarctic conditions on small continents in its temperate zones, continent-sized rafts of polar ice on which CO_2 snow falls every winter. But at the equator, there are a few islands with year-round weather not too different from that of Seattle in the winter—rainy and cold and nasty, but humanly bearable.

Around Arcturus, a mere 6.5 light years away from Mufrid but some 25 light-years from Earth, Wilson is a Cold Indonesia planet with just one habitable area—an island about the size of Borneo with the climate of Auckland, New Zealand. (There would be room for many more

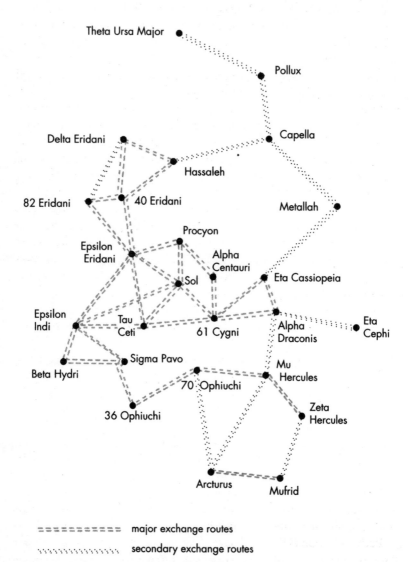

Map 1: Exchange routes, pre-FTL

colonies except that Wilson is almost devoid of land around the equator.) Besides the one large equatorial island, there are two polar continents, plus many Greenland-like islands in the temperate zones. Arcturus is much more massive and puts out more heat than Sol, but Wilson orbits so far away it gets only about half the insolation Earth does (much more of it is infrared, though—it's dim but warm). As a result, Wilson circles Arcturus at a distance of 7 AU, with a year of about 12 Earth-years.

Given its steep axial tilt, I created the following deliberately weird ecology for it: continental ice forms on the dark pole every winter but melts completely every summer, watering very fast-growing vegetation. Every fall the whole continent burns down. (This image may have to do with my having spent the last few years in Montana.)

The soot from the burning produces more rapid cooling in the fall hemisphere, but it also darkens the ice in the other hemisphere, thus accelerating the melt and hastening the warming there.

The result is that temperature differences between the hemispheres are large, and they reverse very rapidly. That's a formula for violent weather, so the folks in the single colony have to look out for good-sized hurricanes as a regular thing, a brief "nuclear fall" every six Terran years, and, about three years after each nuclear fall, spectacular hurricanes on a scale never seen on Earth.

On the other hand, between those, the weather's extremely nice, and the surfing is probably terrific. People might do a lot of hiking and camping on the continents or the other islands during their summer.

Now—what if we amplified the contrast between those two worlds by setting up cultures that differed drastically emotionally and psychologically? Suppose, for example, the icy, cloudy tropics of Nansen got a couple of dour, stern, puritanical groups ("we are not in this world for a good time"), and the warm sunny island on Wilson got a bunch of free-spirited, fun-loving romantics ("let the good times roll")? You might think of it as an exaggerated version of the difference between traditional New Hampshire and traditional New Orleans.

Now, what if someone who had long ago fled from one of Nansen's constricted, cold colonies for the warm tolerance of Wilson—had the chance to go back instantaneously?

Perhaps it sounds like he'd have to be crazy, but maybe there is something he really must do. And when people really have to do something they don't want to—there's the start of a story.

In developing that story, there's a whole other realm of economic and social models to be tackled—the dynamic/chaotic models that can generate a month by month picture of what happens on each planet the day after the turn on the transporter booth. Those are interesting too, but space doesn't allow tackling them this time out.

And somewhere along the way, of course, I still do have to write that story.

SUGGESTED SOURCES AND NIFTY READING

A Loose Guide to Finding More Good Tricks

Beenstock, Michael R. *The World Economy in Transition,* Unwin Hyman, 1984. Technical; a lot of good data.

Dewey, Edward R. *Cycles.* New York: Hawthorn, 1971. Out of print. Dewey's theories of the origins of cycles are mystical, and grossly out of date in the light of chaos theory, and he reports the coincidental and the ludicrous side by side with the well established, but there's much that's useful as well. Second edition edited by Og Mandino is even less accurate and useful.

Dunningan, James F. *How to Make War.* New York: William Morrow, 1983. All the basic information you'd need for near-future military simulations.

Flynn, Michael F. "An Introduction to Psychohistory," parts I and II. *Analog,* April and May 1988. Good coverage of many different regularities in social phenomena.

Gillett, Stephen L. "On Building an Earth-Like Planet." *Analog,* July 1989. Readable discussion of physical worldbuilding, plus a solid bibliography.

Goldstein, Joshua, S. "Kondratieff Waves as War Cycles." *International Studies Quarterly,* Spring 1985. Highly technical exploration of possible coupling. Some excellent tables of data.

Heidenheimer, Arnold J., Hugh Heclo, and Carolyn Teich Adams, *Comparative Public Policy: The Politics of Social Choice in Europe and America,* 2d ed., New York: St. Martin's Press, 1983. Many tables of interesting social data hard to find anywhere else. Also an excellent guide to what modern governments actually do and how they actually do it; a good antidote to some of what you'll find in SF.

Kennedy, Paul. *The Rise and Fall of the Great Powers.* New York: Random House, 1987. An excellent, highly readable discussion of many of the basic issues from a historical perspective.

Modelski, George. *Principles of World Politics.* New York: Free Press, 1972. *Long Cycles in World Politics.* Seattle: University of Washington Press, 1986. The basic texts on cyclic phenomena in international power relations. Highly technical. Good data.

Overseas Development Council. *The U.S. and World Development: Agenda for Action.* New York: Praeger. Published annually. The statistical appendix is invaluable.

Rosecrance, Richard. "Long Cycle Theory and International Relations," *International Organization,* Spring 1987. Review article on current issues in the field.

Samuelson, Paul A. *Economics.* New York: McGraw-Hill. So many editions it's hard to keep up, but anything from about the 10th (1976) forward should be fairly accurate. In my opinion, one of the best textbooks ever written on any subject.

Sundquist, James. *Dynamics of the Party System.* Washington, D.C.: Brookings Institution, 1973. The fundamental text on party realignment, the basic dynamic of American political change.

Van Duijn, J. J. *The Long Wave in Economic Life.* Unwin Hyman, 1983. Probably the closest thing to a classic in cyclic theory.

World Almanac. New York: Pharos. Published annually. There's no disgrace in using it; data you get here are usually reliable. Excellent for browsing for ideas if you're doing any statistical work yourself.

STOCHASM

When I submitted this story to the graduate fiction workshop at Montana, people got into an argument about which numbers and colors to assign to various fellow students and faculty, none of whom were in the room at the time. Nobody said much about the story. As you will note, in this one the other side won the Cold War; it was science fiction when I wrote it but I guess it's alternate history now.

Take any repeated similar events—traffic accidents, stock transactions, baseball games—count and categorize them, and you get trends. Trends in nature don't run without limit; the hitter who is improving doesn't eventually bat one thousand, the rising stock does not become worth more than the GNP, every car on the road doesn't hit every other one. Every trend reverses—watch long enough, and there's a pattern to the reversals . . . and where a lot of things reverse all at once, there's a cusp.

It had started out as a game three years ago, something to amuse him while he waited for a job to run or when he needed a break. Danny had kept track of every exchange he had with Karen, categorizing them into Social, Sexual, Household Business, Affectionate, or Competitive, and rating each one plus, zero, or minus. He had not thought it would ever mean anything, but, as he had known they must, the patterns had appeared. Now he was fascinated.

In the last four months, Sexual and Competitive had run increasingly positive, Affectionate and Social more and more negative. Household

Business had flexed up and down rapidly, the oscillations increasing in magnitude—the value of its first derivative was plunging down toward negative infinity. Based on past experience, every trend was due to reverse suddenly, any day now. Not that he could exactly talk about that to Karen.

He wondered if the upcoming social cusp had anything to do with it. Maybe everyone in the country was moving toward a personal cusp; maybe the whole weight of them added up to the social cusp. He pictured everyone moving along the curves, rolling along like marbles on a lumpy table top, all climbing up some big rise only to roll immediately off of it, colliding and scattering in random confusion.

The image was interesting enough to make him run through a fast set of calls on the net, finding an algebraic spreadsheet program; the telltale on the screen noted that he had committed himself for 1.49 newdollars. He flicked the approve key and quickly set up the marble model. Sure enough, if the number of marbles was large, and you knew their average speed and the shape off the lump, you could say how many marbles would roll off the lump in any one direction.

But of course you could never calculate which direction any particular marble would take. If he had taken the teaching job instead of going to work for the Bureau, this would have made a perfect classroom demonstration. And of course he'd have been classified mid-Thirties, and there wouldn't be this trouble with Karen. In fact, you could probably see that decision as another personal cusp . . . how would you model that? His fingers poised above the keys.

He heard the shower stop. He stored the results and logged off.

As Karen came out of the bathroom, the property line indicator pinged; someone was coming up the front path. Danny peered out the curtain.

"Oh my god, he's here."

"Isn't that just like a Russian?"

"No. Querry." Danny dropped the curtain. "It's not like him—usually he's right in the slot for everything."

"Well," Karen said, "he's *your* boss—you'll have to handle him. I'm not even dressed yet."

She hurried back to the bathroom, a smoky swirl of bright colors hanging over her arm, the smears of color on her back showing off her muscles. She was going to wear the Appearance tonight, he realized. For a Thirty-three, that was a bit pre-drift, but this *was* a pretty boho occasion—a lot of women would be wearing it. Still, he'd never seen Karen in it—that was vaguely exciting. "Hey," Danny said.

"What?" She turned around.

"You look spiv."

"I know. And the expression on the span nowadays, gospodin, is magno."

"Magno?"

"You got it. And thank you. Now see about your boss." She ducked into the bathroom as the doorbell rang.

When Danny opened the door, Querry was facing the other way. "I think there's a brushfire down on the canyon side of your yard," he said. Danny rushed past him to look. There was no smoke or flame anywhere. His boss caught his elbow. "Keep going. Let's walk down that way. Need to talk away from Uncle Mike."

Because he was a Twenty-four, Danny had a big yard; by walking slowly, they could talk quietly for a long time without looking odd. "Quite a gathering tonight," Querry said.

"Mostly Karen's boho friends. This composer, Merva, is a Forty-seven, and there's going to be a bunch of those. The only things to the right of a Thirty-three will be you, me, Kendergill, and the Russian."

"Should be lively. I could use a little variety."

The older man was always saying things like that; it made Danny nervous, considering where they both worked. Querry, after all, was an Eleven, almost the brownest of the brown. His avant-garde interests should have been min.

Querry grinned at him. "Surely I didn't shock you."

Danny shook his head.

"Good. Tell me, Danny, how do you feel about the SA?"

"Uh . . . I don't understand the question?"

"Good answer. Now, how would you feel about a withdrawal of the Supervisory Authority? Imagine you're being polled . . ."

"I think I'd like that."

"Wouldn't mind seeing some taterheads go home?"

Danny looked around. "Nope."

"Do you know how the great majority of Twenty-fours feel about the SA leaving?"

"Well, if we've got them classified right, probably the same as I do."

"Wrong. You're fringe five on this, Danny."

"Holy shit. I guess I'm really off drift. Where's the break?"

"At thirty-one. You're not even close. And you can imagine what it's like down at my end of the spectrum."

Danny nodded. It was only eight years since Reconstruction had ended and the Soviet troops had gone home. Officially, the Constitution had been restored, and the Supervisory Authority was only here "to prevent the development of a climate of militant anticommunism," but most bureaucrats still relied on the backup authority of SA. Almost nobody right of the Seventeens would be happy to see them go. "I guess people are used to them."

"Uh-hunh," Querry looked down, kicking the ground. "Now—second question: suppose we come up with a proposal to increase the number of classifications, say from the forty-six model to the one hundred three. How are you going to report out on that?"

Danny turned away. Something had caught the corner of his eye; he looked and saw a naked woman sunning herself on the rocks by the trail down in the canyon. He turned back to Querry. "Hmm. Speaking for the guys in Forecasting. I ought to love it. I suppose it might be a pain for Classification. How's it affect the subject we're talking about?"

"Good question. How do you think?"

"Well . . ." He scratched his head, stole another glance at the nude sunbather, let the equations and graphs dance in his mind a little, and then pulled his answer into shape. "Okay, I see it this way. Assuming you do a straight method split—just follow the procedures and take what you get, no detectable jiggering of the boundaries—you'll get a couple classifications that are, uh, livelier. People with, um, potato allergies, I guess you'd say, that reinforce each other that way. And some that like our Russian friends better, too. The whole thing will get more polarized, I guess."

"Which creates a demographic base for people who feel like we do. And of course with more classification interacting, everything gets more complex and less predictable in the long run, even though your short-run forecasts will be better. It won't be much, but it's a start." Querry turned back toward the house. "Time's getting on; the fire's out. Sorry I came so early—I saw the brushfire from the station. That was good work that you sent over, incidentally—I almost missed the train out here sending you your congratulations."

"Thanks. You can go on in and hang around in the living room—

Karen's dressed by now. I'd like to walk around out here and do a little thinking."

"Sure."

"Oh," Danny said, turning to face the canyon again, "is Kendergill in this?"

Querry leaned in close to his ear. "Out. Way out. I'm afraid he's a more typical Twenty-four than you are. I'll invite you over soon and we'll talk then."

"Sure. Thanks for your help with the brushfire."

"Anytime." Querry turned and went up toward the house.

Danny took the trail down over the broken rock, further into the canyon. He was thinking about his talk with Querry, and had half-convinced himself that he had imagined the sunbather; by the time he reached the rocks, he was actually startled to find her.

"Uh," he said.

"Hi." She rolled over onto her stomach and looked up at him.

"Hello."

"You must be Danny Parana. Right-light?"

"Yeah."

"I'm Merva. I was down here pulling in some feels before the big shosho. You're the tanno Karen's legaled to. Right-light?"

"You've got it."

"You read the talk pretty true."

"Part of my job. I'm in the DPB. You're talking stock high forties boho slang; I see it all the time. I'm a little less tanno than your standard Twenty-four."

"Still pretty down and brown for most of this crowd; half these Guy Jenas have never seen the brown side of thirty, not even their parents. That Green Jean was your boss?"

"Right again." Danny felt a little prickle on the back of his scalp; given Merva's classification, she was almost certain to be sympathetic, but once you got up over Forty-four people tended to be eccentric and unreliable. There was no telling what she might do or who she might talk to.

"So there's gonna be something beyond Forty-seven. And you're trying to get the breffs out."

"Not exactly beyond," Danny said, sitting down. "We'll probably re-split the whole system. It's high time anyway—the socioeconomic mix is a lot more complicated now than it was right after the war."

"And that's good for Forecasting and bad for Classification. I'm afraid I heard the whole thing." She smiled at his surprise. "You seem to ride the drift pretty true, like Karen said. I can speak straight English—hell, I have a masters in lit. I just wanted to know what I was dealing with before I talked too much." She rolled over again; she was about a shade darker brunette than Karen, but slimmer, and her skin was drier and looked older. She wasn't as pretty as Karen, but there really was something distinctive about the way she looked. "So how's a Twenty-four marry a Thirty-three?"

"She used to be a Twenty-eight. She's been shifting for some years."

"Lure of the boho, hunh?"

"I guess so. That and getting some use out of my rising income; after Thirty-one you don't work outside the home if you're a woman."

"*I* do." She stretched and yawned; Danny admired the way her muscles played under her skin.

"Yeah. Working outside starts again at Thirty-eight."

"You've really got the system down." She rolled over, sat up, and smiled at him. "What can you tell me about me?"

"Not much. Forty-seven's the catchall classification—"

"Right-light. See these here?" She lifted her breasts in her hands.

"Uh—"

"Stop staring, brownie, can't you afford to buy any dirty pictures?" She turned away, lying face down on the rock. He thought of saying something, maybe an apology, but it was obvious that she just wanted him to go away.

It was getting to be time for the guests to show up anyway; Danny went back up the trail. As he came around the bend up above her sun-bathing rock, he heard voices and looked back. She was talking to three men, all in very drifto drapes.

That explained it. Among high-forties, rep and conn-up were vital—fraternizing brownward was risky. He smiled to himself; if Kendergill or one of the other people from the office had turned up, he'd have been equally obnoxious.

When he got back to the house, Querry was talking with Johnny Kendergill in one corner, Karen was talking with two high-Thirties on the couch, and a Russian major was sitting quietly in the corner armchair, thumbing through the Thirty-three edition of *Time*. Danny headed for him; might as well get this over with.

"Danny Parana. Karen's husband."

"Hello. I am Major Vjarnyk. Quiet so far."

"Most of the crowd isn't here yet. It'll get livelier when some of the bohos show up."

"No doubt. Is there a quiet corner to which I can go?"

"Uh—"

"I don't like to intrude. If I can sit somewhere where I won't interfere—"

"Well, you *are* a guest—"

"By courtesy. I am trying to return it."

Karen joined them. "I see you've met our major-for-the-night. Found any common interests?"

"I think we share a taste in books," Vjarnyk said, gesturing at Danny's shelves.

"Oh, isn't that nice," Karen said. There was a long silence. "You know," she added, "we don't get to see many Russians, out here away from town."

Vjarnyk smiled. "You need not see much of me. I was hoping to arrange to be out of your way."

Danny found Vjarnyk a novel. "At least something is on track," he muttered to Karen as they went to the kitchen together.

"Ha. Typical breff. Now he's got himself established as a good guy."

Danny shrugged. "Yeah. But it's nice while it lasts."

"Try not to be seen with the breff too much. People think you're brown enough as it is." She handed him a bowl of green goo. "This goes next to the fried turnip sticks."

She seemed to be a little drunk already—she certainly smelled of gin. Danny decided not to say anything. The doorbell rang.

It was Merva, with her friends; Danny wasn't sure which was which, but their names were Plastic, Obsidian, Quagmire, Pontius Pilate, and Coathanger. One of them called him Bob.

At eight o'clock, when the city power was turned off, they lit the candelabra. By now Karen was dug in with a few of her high-Thirties friends in the corner; the men all had one-syllable names, like Ted, Jim, Cliff, Jake, Zach. Danny had never noticed that before; he said something to Johnny Kendergill about it.

"Oh, sure. Watkins and Tucker did a study on that. Too weak to have any predictive value. But it *is* there. What're your kids named?"

"I don't have any."

Kendergill shook his head. "And you're a Twenty-four, and more than thirty years old. Maybe you ought to reclass up a little—you're definite fringe five on that."

Danny let himself smile too widely, as if he were about to laugh. "Oh, I kind if enjoy the sensation."

"Seriously, Danny, I mean, that's why you ought to reclass. You want to fit, don't you?"

"What, and make it easy for you guys?"

Kendergill laughed nervously. "What's gotten into you?"

Well, he felt like bragging, and everyone would hear about it at the Wednesday weekly. "Can you keep a secret for a few days?"

It would have been more reassuring if Kendergill hadn't nodded so vigorously, but Danny told him anyway. "A whole gang of second derivatives—eighty-four of 'em—are within a standard deviation of zero right now. Almost a hundred more will pass through it within six weeks. The General Model's inflecting hard—a major cusp."

"Big?"

"Biggest one since the Occupation went home. Maybe even bigger— no good estimate yet, but it might be as big as the war itself, though probably not as visible—the first partial derivatives are all a lot smaller, so the cusp is more of a gradual hill than a sharp spike. But it sure is big, *and* close."

Kendergill whistled appreciatively; Danny imagined two lemmings talking about how the beach under their feet meant something was surely changing . . . the rattle of marbles on a lumpy tabletop. "Now, for six extra points," he added, "figure out what difference my telling you will make in the ultimate outcome."

"That's your job, Forecasting." Kendergill laughed a little to long and a little too hard.

Nobody actually turned and stared, but Danny realized his work partner was drunker than he should be. "Uh, Johnny, you want to get some fresh air?"

"Just getting nice in here. When's the music?"

"About another hour," Danny said. He looked around, but didn't see anyone free except Querry, heading for the bathroom, and of course Vjarnyk, happily engrossed in an old Eric Ambler.

"Hey, tanno, where y'pack the magno drool?" Merva said, behind Danny. "Need a little hot-loose-and-smooth just this immede." She threw an arm around him.

Kendergill winced and looked away; Danny led Merva to the kitchen. "Thanks for the rescue. How about Cafe Royale?"

"Perfect. That jean's pretty brown.

"You might say that. He's my partner on most projects—classification man. He's good—remembers every paper he's ever read."

"He's stock Twenty-four, isn't he? You don't like him."

"Yeah."

"Are you thinking of upclassing?" She put an arm around him again; the coffee was hot now, so they added the brandy. She stayed snuggled in close; he noticed that the Appearance really did feel like nothing. "Keep your hand off my ass," she whispered. "I just wanted to ask if there's any way I can help you and Mr. Green Jeans."

"Sorry." He moved his hand up to the small of her back. "It depends. You could let me know what you have in mind, but not here."

"Afraid of your legal?"

"You could say that. She's got nosy relatives. You never know where her Uncle Mike will turn up—the browner the household, the better he likes it."

She turned on the water and let it run hard and loud. "Better?"

"Yeah. I'm sure you can help." He swept her into his arms and breathed in her ear. "Tell Karen you like that rock for sunbathing. We're pretty sure it's not eared. I walk down there a lot."

"Good," she whispered back. Unexpectedly, she kissed him, then slipped out of his arms and through the door. He found himself facing Major Vjarnyk. "Uh, hi."

"I came for a glass of water." Danny handed him a glass. Vjarnyk turned the water down to half and filled it. "You have a good collection—Ambler, Fleming, Le Carré."

"You're welcome to borrow any of them."

"The one I am reading would be pleasant to finish. I am flying to Washington this week—I will mail it to you, probably from there."

"Fine." Danny knew he must sound a little nervous, but he already had a perfect cover for that. "I hope you're enjoying the evening. Have you tried any of the snacks?"

"A few. The little pieces of corn on the cob—"

"Yeah, it's a traditional American dish—"

"Yes. Very common in the USSR nowadays. Soldiers that serve with the Supervisory Authority bring it back—you can find it in most restaurants in Moskva." The major took a long sip of water. "You know, I have run into a certain strange notion among Americans; they are aware, I suppose, that corn on the cob was fed only to pigs among the people of, say, my father's generation. Some of them still have the notion that we are uncomfortable eating it." He drank again. "Yours is very tasty."

Danny leaned back against the sink. "Well, things change."

"Quite a bit." Vjarnyk gave him an unexpectedly broad grin. "You know, I have a son back home. I am divorced—he lives with his mother. She writes to tell me he is running with hooligans, *stilyagi*—only now they call themselves 'forty-sevens.'"

Without having to force it, Danny laughed.

"While we are talking about this system, there is one thing I would like to ask," Vjarnyk said. "Please do not answer if it is too personal." Danny nodded. "You and your wife are different classes. Classifications, I mean. Is that not odd?"

Danny nodded, sipping his drink. "We're both what we call fringe five—on the edge of our classifications. The household consumption pattern is basically Twenty-four and the opinion matrix is pretty close to stock Thirty-three. Yeah, my department doesn't like it much."

"I would not think that anyone would. The system, I mean."

"It has its advantages. You know who you are more now than you used to. Remember, we didn't create this structure—it was there before the war. We just discovered it and reinforced it." By now Danny's drink was cold, but he took a big gulp anyway.

"Discovered it how?"

"Something we call a Euclidean cluster algorithm."

Vjarnyk smiled again. "Sorry, that is not what I meant to ask. How do you know that there are only forty-seven kinds of people?"

"Oh. Um, well, let's see. If you have something—oh, let's say shoes. Some people like high heels a lot, some hate them, some are in between. Right? It forms a continuum; you could imagine it as a line, and everybody falls somewhere on it. Now, if you add another dimension— let's say feelings about property taxes—you could plot the two against each other. And presumably all people would fall somewhere on that graph. Well, it turns out that they aren't evenly distributed; they're in clumps. Those clumps—the clusters—are the 'natural' classifications that we look for. Of course we use many more than two dimensions, almost a thousand in fact. And we use a complicated statistical program, not eyeballing, to draw the cluster boundaries." He finished his drink and set it down. "I'm glad our books entertain you. I hope you'll enjoy the music." He glanced at his watch and turned back to the sink.

Vjarnyk nodded and went back out. Danny rinsed a couple of glasses. It wasn't Vjarnyk the man or even Vjarnyk the Russian that bothered him, he decided; it certainly wasn't Communism—he'd been happy enough to get his Party card, and he'd even been thinking of running for County Central Committee. Something else entirely . . .

Coming out of the kitchen, he almost collided with Cliff and Karen. "Danny! There you are. I think Merva needs some help setting up the keyboard ring."

"Sure."

"That is, if Ivan's done with his math lesson," Cliff added.

Karen giggled. As Danny turned away, he saw Cliff's hand slide under Karen's filmy Appearance skirt. The kitchen door swung shut.

Actually, Danny's help wasn't needed. Quagmire, a tall thin black man, had the keyboard rig up already; it was fun, though, to talk with him about it—there were some really clever tricks in there to make up for the unreliability of the batteries. Danny relaxed and began to enjoy himself; after a while, though, Plastic (or was it Obsidian?) came by and asked Quagmire if the brown was rubbing off on him.

"Well, fun talking with you, but I gotta get back to my own span or they'll cat my rep to shreds. K'neech, Danny.'

"Yeah, I gotta go brown-on myself," Danny said. "K'neech, Quag." He wandered off; as he drifted by Querry, his boss plucked his sleeve, nodding toward Quagmire and the rest of the bohos.

"You certainly work a lot closer to the field than I do."

"Yeah. Well, being married to Karen helps." She was still in the kitchen with Cliff.

"Yeah. What did that Russian talk with you about?"

"Work, a little. In real abstract terms. And he gave me the old standard Kremlin kiss-of-sympathy—you know, I eat corn on the cob, I have a wife and kid, I love dogs, baseball, and Kurt Vonnegut. All that."

"I checked his file out before I came. Nice enough guy, kind of gone native. Volunteered to stay here; dates some American girls—dates, I mean, not the usual."

"That's good."

"Yeah. Listen, when the uproar dies down you want to come to dinner next week? Maybe some poker too?"

"Sure."

Merva joined them. "Well, Quagmire gave you a good rep-out. How's my noisemover?"

"Real fine," Danny said. "Magno."

"Well, the feels are good—I want to get this little shosho going."

Danny nodded. "Hey, everybody. Showtime in just a few minutes. Pull up a chair if you can find one."

"Coathanger went out to fetch in Karen and Cliff," Merva added, quietly. Then, turning to Querry, she asked, "So do you read Boise Sound?"

"I love it," Queery said.

Merva shook her head and made a face. "Pretty soon, everyone's going to be a Forty-seven. Who's going to pay the taxes to support us?"

As Querry, Kendergill, and Danny sat down, Cliff and Karen came back in; Karen's body paint, under the Appearance veils, was smeared. Danny got up, vaguely thinking he might grab Cliff and start something, stepping over a couple sprawled bohos on his way to get to them. Karen caught his eye, seeming to dare him.

Behind him, there was a ripple of scales being run, first horns, then strings, then bass, finally all three woven together. Merva was already seated, running her fingers lightly over the keyboard. "Well, jeans, the feels are right—big sposs-bo for Quagmire and Danny—magno job on the rig." There was a splatter of clapping; Danny looked around, blinking. Everyone was looking at him. He went back to Querry and Kendergill and sat down.

Merva smiled, resting her hand on the keyboard. "This is a piece I've written under commission," she said. "I call it the Peace Suite—its concert debut is next year, on the fifteenth anniversary of the Treaty of Frankfurt. It's in five parts; I call them War, Peace, Truth, Lies, and Circular Rhythm and Blues."

Vjarnyk, still surprisingly courteous, had gotten up and come over to join the crowd.

To Danny's surprise, Merva's music was perfectly clear to him, not as drifto as he'd been dreading—"War" was a dark, thundering, threatening concise summary of three terrifying months when he had been seventeen.

"Peace" was mistitled—it was despair, defeat, ruin. Some of the Forty-sevens were openly in tears; Querry's face was rigid, and even Kendergill quit playing with his fingers and listened intently. Vjarnyk squirmed. Yet at the end of it there was a turn—an unexpectedly lighter, more hesitant last chord, a twist that apparently came from nowhere, still somehow implicit in all that preceded it.

A long, slow sigh from everyone broke the silence between the parts. "Truth" was almost doctor's office background music; Danny first thought that it wasn't as good as the others, then that it was good but didn't fit.

Vjarnyk stood up; he stood through the rest of "Truth."

Merva finished the part and sat without moving, staring at him. "Proceed, if you like," he said. "I am not a censor."

"Then why did you stand, breff?" Merva asked.

"Respect. Simple respect. I am sorry that it seemed a threat."

"What the hell else did you expect it to look like?" Merva said. "You knew what was in that piece. I saw that in your face. You're here in uniform, breff. What else could you mean?"

Vjarnyk started to speak, stopped, tried again. "I—I am sorry. I was moved. I understood. The inversion and the Boise counterpoint—they still did not hide that melody."

Querry snapped his fingers—and suddenly tears filled his eyes. "Hadn't heard *that* since the war. God, what were the words. . . ."

Vjarnyk turned to him. "I am not sure, but I remember seeing them once. In the British People's Republic it is a monarchist song, but here, I think, it is merely an expression of national culture—"

"But, since you heard it, the censors will never pass it," Merva said.

Vjarnyk flushed. "The board would have little choice—"

"I'm sure," she said. "Do you see any reason for me to go on with this?"

"I would like to hear. These people would like to hear. I will not intrude again. I apologize."

The room was quiet. Karen and Cliff were whispering to each other; her hand was on Cliff's thigh, brushing back and forth, teasing him. Danny could let Vjarnyk off the hook, but there was no special reason to save Karen's party.

"I apologize," Vjarnyk said again. "I cannot speak for your own broadcast censors; they are Americans like yourselves. But I do know that there is no law against anything of this kind in a private home. Please do go on." He looked around the room; Merva sat quietly, her fingers drumming on the top of the rig's CPU box. No one looked at him except Danny.

Then the Russian looked back at him without expression, directly into his eyes, and said softly. "This 'tradition' of having one of us at every gathering has gone on far too long. The war and Reconstruction, after all, are over. There is no law—only custom—that says I must be here."

For a long minute, his mind was blank. Finally, Danny stood up. "Get out of my house."

Almost smiling, Vjarnyk nodded and turned to go.

"Get out," Danny said again. "And since he's leaving, so is everyone else."

Vjarnyk stopped, not looking back. "I have just said that that is not necessary. Surely you will not spoil the evening—"

"It's spoiled already," Merva said. "You've been told to lift, breff. Make k'neech, Guy Jeans—Danny is right-light on this one."

As the guests grabbed their things, Vjarnyk approached Danny. "About the book—"

"Leave it here. I don't like you touching my stuff." Danny watched him out the door, up the path, till he disappeared in the shadows.

In a few minutes only Danny, Karen, Cliff, Querry, and Merva were left, carrying the plates and glasses into the kitchen and letting them rattle and bang at random into the sink. Danny threw in some soap powder and turned on the water; he jumped when they crashed again, sliding into a lower pile. Some suds had splashed onto his tunic. He dabbed at it with a towel, turned off the water, and went back out.

Merva and Querry were talking by the door; on the couch, Cliff was saying something to Karen. She looked up at Danny, her face pale and set. It was ruined for her, no matter what—she wouldn't get invited to anything on the span for some time. Danny waited until she met his eyes.

"Anyone want to walk down into the canyon, look at the moon or something?" He already knew his friends would accept; by the time he'd get back, Karen would be gone with Cliff.

There were still a few candles burning, and the front door was hanging open, when he returned to the house. After his talk with Querry and Merva, he was nervous and excited—doing the dishes might be a good way to unwind.

Karen had already done them; they were neatly arranged on the drying rack. Somewhere his mind counted off, two shelves of glasses, each five rows by eight columns, two slots empty, seventy-eight glasses. The average must have been almost exactly two glasses per person.

He peeped into the bedroom as quietly as he could; she was asleep on top of the covers, still in the Appearance, the makeup now blotched with sweat, staining the veils. He rocked back on his heels, looking down at the floor.

When he checked the bottles, consumed liquor worked out to very close to three drinks per person. Obviously that was an average, like the glasses. Almost before he knew it, he was sitting at the terminal, trying to work out a simple model that would account for those two almost-perfect integer ratios. He knew, of course, that there were other things, bigger things, he could be working on—but there was an elegance here in the small number of variables and the startling simplicity of the result. If he could express the process in just a few simple rules, perhaps only four or five equations, *that* would reveal the relevant dynamics behind the aggregate result.

His fingers slashed and pounded at the keys. He gazed into the screen, rejecting one, two, many models. It was getting later and later, but he knew he'd get it eventually.

Patterns can't be observed effectively from inside. Only from a distance, in time or space, can you really peg down what was going on. And what you find won't bear much resemblance to the view from inside the pattern—that, after all, is the whole fascination.

UNDER THE COVENANT STARS

I dictated most of this story on a long summer afternoon, while driving from Spokane to Missoula, past Lake Coeur d'Alene and over some high mountain passes. At the time, in 1986, it looked like the preachers were poised to take over the government of the United States. There's hardly any story of mine I'm happier to have become so dated.

Of course Brad, my brother—my half brother really but we never made that distinction—was famous, but when you're seven years old it doesn't occur to you that it's unusual to have a person in your family on the news every night, and to hear people talking about him even when they don't know who you are. So I never realized how strange it was that Brad always had time for me, even though I was seven and he was twenty-two. It didn't even surprise me that despite his schedule he had time to sit down in the basement and help me and Scott build a model. He just did it, just as Luella cleaned up the house, Mother went to her club meetings, and Dad went to the Senate.

Of course we were putting together a model of *Restoration*. Not one of those plastic kit models that they sold everywhere, either. Brad said that was too easy. You'd never learn to see the thing if you just stuck someone else's parts together.

We were working with cardboard and balsa and tissue paper and so on, trying to build it from the photos Brad had taken. Actually, Scott and I were watching Brad do it—our fingers weren't really up to the job—

and asking him questions while he did it, but he gave us the impression that we were all building it together.

"And here," Brad said, "newly completed, is our crew compartment. Not much smaller than the real one."

Scott looked at him funny. Scott was two years older than I was, but he had a lot of trouble telling when Brad was kidding, maybe because his parents were such serious people.

Brad grinned at him. "Not really. The crew cabin is actually about the size of a small bathroom—but five guys will be in it." I knew that they had planned on four, but a Reverend was going to come along and they'd had to squeeze a seat in for him. I wasn't supposed to talk about that, even though Brad had complained about it bitterly at the dinner table.

"Does that bother you?" Scott asked.

"Not really. We'll only be in there for two days." Brad squeezed the trigger on the bondgun, and the crew compartment was welded into place. "And to tell you the truth, I'd go if they had to cut my arms and legs off to squeeze me in."

That reassured Scott; he smiled and said, "Can I tell you something? I want to go into space like you. I mean when I grow up."

Brad nodded and said, "There should be a lot of chances to do that by then. How about you, Nehemiah? Do you want to be an astronaut too?"

My face got hot and the inside corners of my eyes stung. That had not been a good question, and Brad would have known if he'd given it a moment's thought. I looked down. He reached over and lifted my chin, looking into my eyes for a moment. I knew he was sorry and had not meant to say it, so he could have let it pass, but instead he said, "You know, being afraid to get on a hijump once doesn't mean anything."

I didn't know what to say, so I stood there and didn't say anything. The year before, I had frozen getting onto a hijump to Europe and had to ride in the baby compartment. Brad couldn't think of what to say next either, so we all got busy with the model again. A littler later, Dad came down and looked at the almost-completed model, pronouncing it "a good project and, unlike the real one, still under budget."

Scott had to go home for dinner, and it was almost time for ours. As we were going upstairs, Dad put an arm around Brad and whispered something in his ear; whatever it was, Brad didn't like it much and pulled a little away. I thought they would go off to talk about it privately, but just then Mother came home.

Her entrance was as big as always—big hug and kiss for Dad, same for me, and a peck on the cheek for Brad. Her body always stiffened when she did that, like she was trying not to touch Brad. That bothered me, and I asked him about it once, but he just said she was probably a little uncomfortable because she was only two years older than he was. I didn't see what difference that made, but it sounded like one of those grown-up answers that never make any sense anyway.

Luella, the servant, was an affy, and one of her little quirks was getting dinner done too early, so as usual, we all had to rush in to eat it in a hurry. Mother always muttered about there not being any good servants, but that was kind of stupid—most of my friends' parents had robots, which not only got the meal to the table when you wanted it, but could cook decently. Even at seven I had figured out that having a live servant, one of God's Afflicted, was purely a status matter and that Luella was here only to show the world that we could afford an affy on a live-in basis.

I shoveled down the beets, which were already a little cold but still the most tolerable things on the plate, and I listened. A lot of time Brad would talk about the mission preparations, or Dad would talk about who hated who in the Senate, or on the Space Committee or at USSA. I usually didn't understand much of it, but I tried to practice remembering it, because sometimes when I played with those people's children I could pick up something useful for Dad, the same way Mother heard things for him at the club.

Tonight, though, it didn't take any special effort to pay attention. Mother was not eating; she was clearly upset, but trying to draw her out never worked, so Brad and Dad made small talk. "You know the Trentons?" she asked abruptly, breaking into a joke Brad was telling.

The question was silly, but nobody pointed that out. The Trentons were Scott's parents and our neighbors across the backyard. Everyone waited. Finally, she said, "Their name came up this afternoon."

Dad raised an eyebrow. "What is there about them that would draw any attention."

"Martha's been doing some genealogy."

That was just scandalous enough to distract me for a moment. Martha was Mrs. Oldham, the wife of the Deputy Reverend General for DC, and for her to be linked to genies was really shocking—Mother had made Brad quit reading to me from the *Arabian Nights* because of the genies. But maybe grown-ups were different and they could get away with it. Or maybe the Trentons were in trouble because *they* had been dealing with genies.

"—thought I had made it clear that you need to keep those old busy-bodies away from the Project." Dad's voice was getting loud.

Mother got louder. "They aren't being 'busy-bodies.' They just want to see the Project succeed, the same as you do, the same as Father does." That was a bad sign. Whenever Mother mentioned Grandpa Hodge, they were getting close to a real fight. "And it isn't going to work without the Lord's help. If there's any trace of abomination—"

"Canadian ancestry is not an abomination." Dad was making his voice stay low. "We've talked about that. Esther, use your brain. You've got a good one. You've known Phil and Carol Trenton for six years, ever since they moved in behind us. Do you think they're doing anything—"

"It's not what they're doing or anything they've done. I like them. But if they're tainted then something has to be done." Mother sniffed hard—she was trying not to cry. "I report on these meetings to you. I never ask what you do with what I tell you. I even tell you everything about what Father says, and I never ask you what that's for. I'm just telling you what other people are saying. You said you wanted to know."

Then Dad was up and lumbering around the table to her, his big old belly making him awkward. He put his arms around her, whispering in her ear.

"No," she said softly. "But I'm all confused. Mother was there and she's been leaning on me about the Trentons all afternoon."

Dad nodded and kept holding her. "What else did they say at the meeting?" he asked.

I sat and ate quietly, and so did Brad. "They mentioned Nehemiah being around Scott."

Dad sighed. "So they can't even leave children alone." He put a finger on her mouth. "I know, I know, as the twig is bent and so forth. And we're going to end up with some badly bent twigs. I imagine they brought up Phil Trenton being a physicist."

Mother nodded, looking down at her plate.

"Esther." Dad's voice was gentle. I sneaked a look at Brad, who seemed to be engrossed in eating his diced carrots. "I am not mad at you. You have been of tremendous help."

"That sounds like something a senator would say," she said, looking up.

He laughed a little, but it came out more like a sigh. "Yeah. I guess it does. But it's true anyway. I'm just mad because we're only weeks from first launch, and now this comes up. I'm sorry I took it out on you."

She nodded and took a big bite of turkey steak. She had to chew it for a while, but she finally got it bolted down. "I'm sorry too. I don't know if I can do anything to get them off this. I'll do what I can, but they're already mad because Carol never joined the Women's League. I'm afraid they're going to push this one, especially because of the physics thing."

Brad cleared his throat. "I have a degree in physics."

Mother looked at him and nodded. "I know. They don't mind that. It's just that—"

"Phil Trenton is the only GS-13 on the Project who isn't a Reverend," Dad said. "He did a physics postdoc on his sabbatical a couple of years ago, when he had the chance to go to seminary. They haven't forgotten that, or forgiven it—they want their imprimatur everywhere on the Project. Same reason we had to cut the fuel margin down to zilch so you could take along a Reverend."

Brad nodded and wiped his mouth. "I see."

Mother looked down at her plate. "Except that the Lord build the house, they labor in vain that build it."

"Because the Lord gets the credit anyway," Dad said. There was a nasty challenge to his voice, and I was beginning to wonder how long it would be before they sent me upstairs. She sat with her hands folded in her lap, staring at her plate. "I don't know what we're going to do with Luella. This food is horrible."

"Maybe we'll all go out for a snack later," Dad said.

"Would you like to catch a movie, Nehemiah?" Brad asked.

"Sure." He got up and I followed him upstairs. We moved quickly because Mother didn't really approve of our supply of preRebirth movies upstairs. But tonight, trying to make peace, she would say nothing.

On the landing, I asked, "Brad, does Mother like Dad?"

"Oh, yeah. It would be easier for her if she didn't. I'm afraid they like each other a lot—that's what the problem is."

Often Brad made no more sense than any other grown-up, and this seemed to be one of those times. I sat down on the couch and Brad pulled out the old toy box, shifting the games on top to reveal the video cassettes underneath. I knew that Dad had had to marry Mother—it was some deal he worked out with the Reverends, so that he could stay in the Senate after the ReBirth Election, a few years ago. I didn't really understand that either, because people told me he had won the election; they said it was so the Senate would seat him, whatever that meant. And then for some reason or other they had had me.

Brad was lining up the cassettes in a row to let me pick. I said, "Sometimes Dad upsets Mother a lot."

Brad nodded. "But then again, getting upset is good for her. She's changed a lot from the way she was when she was nineteen. You do have to give her credit for that." It didn't really sound like he was talking to *me* anymore.

I sat back and looked at the tapes. "That one," I said, pointing.

He grinned. "You know, there's only so many lives to a movie tape. When this thing plays its last time, it will be awfully hard to replace until the next time Dad or I go to United Europe."

"We can play something else."

"Aw, now, don't be that way. I guess it's been a bad night for everyone. I'd like to see it again myself. Let's put it on." As he was sliding it into the machine, he turned and said, "Scott said he wanted to be an astronaut."

I nodded vigorously. "He says that to me all the time."

"That poor kid." He switched the machine on and sat down next to me, draping an arm around my shoulders. For the next couple of hours, we were off with Luke Skywalker. We got most of the way into the second movie before it was time for bed.

The next day they let Luella tell me. Dad would have done it, but he had to catch a zipper back home to Kansas early that morning, and wouldn't be back until ten in the evening. Mother had gone to the station to see him off, and then directly to a prayer breakfast, so she had told Luella, who had carefully written it down in her strange, blocky printing. While I ate my cereal, Luella read it to me, slowly, carefully, testing each word as her finger tapped it, then repeating it firmly. "You *you* mommy *mommy* say *say* you *you* not *not* spose *spose* play *play* with *with* Scott *Scott* no *no* more *more*." I'd seen other families' affys do it just that way, so it must have been some effect of the schools they sent them to after the operation. Affys went in with all different problems but they all came out alike; I thought that was spooky, and said so to Brad once. He told me not to speak of it to other people—"The Reverends provided the operation and the schools," he said. "People wouldn't like to hear you saying that."

Since I wasn't supervised much, and Scott lived just across the back hedge, we continued to see each other. It wasn't even any extra trouble, really; it just meant we couldn't be in each other's houses. The yards were big, and there were hedges and bushes everywhere.

It turned out, to my surprise, that Scott *knew* he was a Canadian. He had just not been allowed to tell people who didn't know. "There's nothing wrong with it," he said. "That's what my pop says. But he says that not everyone thinks so, and we have to stay real quiet about it."

"They said in Sunday School you made the Barrier," I said. "That's what wrecked all of Canada."

He nodded. "It's what made the Covenant Stars."

"The what?" I asked. I had never heard of them.

"It's in the Bible."

Bible Study was my best subject in school. "It's not," I said.

"Bet."

"Bet what? My folks don't want me to gamble. It's not Christian."

"I'll show you," he said. He ran into his house. I sat under the bush and thought. Dad always said that when you attack someone else's beliefs, you don't give him a choice—he can't really be your friend anymore because he has to choose between you and what he knows is true. I resolved that I would just listen; Scott was my best friend, so God probably wasn't going to send him to Hell anyway. And besides, I really wanted to know what he was talking about.

He came flying back across the lawn, a Bible clutched in his hand. "Right here," he said, scooting next to me. "Right here in Genesis. 'This is the token of the covenant which I make between me and you and every living creature that is with you for perpetual generations: I do set my bow in the cloud, and it shall be for a token of a covenant between me and the earth.'"

"That's for the rainbow," I said. "From the Flood."

"There are others here," he said. "We mark them in our Bibles. 'They that kindle the fire shall make restitution.' See? And America and the Russians had to stay out of space all this time. And here's 'Thou has set the borders of the earth.' That's what we did."

That last one was in Psalm 74, which I had learned by heart. "Maybe," I said. "But in Sunday School they say this part is about the Canadians." I pointed to it. "'They have cast fire into thy sanctuary'—that means heaven, which is the sky—'they have defiled by casting down the dwelling place of thy name to the ground.' That's about when the spaceship *America* got blown up." I was proud of myself; I knew the Bible a lot better than Scott did.

I had upset him, though, so I tried to change the subject and get him interested in a game. I was already feeling sorry for showing off; after all, if his parents were Canadians, they might have taught him all kinds of things wrong. He didn't want to play anything, but suddenly he brightened. "But what about the Covenant Stars?" he asked.

"I don't know what they are," I confessed.

"At night," he said. "You see them in the sky. What people call the Barrier. That's the sign of God's Covenant—'and your children shall not pass through fire.'"

"The shooting stars?"

"Yes!" He was very satisfied now. "Those are the sign that God won't let us blow ourselves up."

I knew about the Barrier, or course—out in the country, back home in Kansas, you'd still see a shooting star every four or five seconds. Dad said when he was little, right after the War, there were so many the light from them was like the light of the full moon, and it washed out the Milky Way. I had always thought they were pretty, even though I knew they were how the Canadians had denied America its destiny under God—I wasn't completely sure what a destiny was, but if God wanted us to have it the Canadians shouldn't have tried to stop Him. That they were hunted and persecuted simply proved God's curse was on them.

But Scott was my friend.

We played for a while longer that afternoon, but we parted eagerly. I went upstairs to the third floor to see if Brad had come home. He seemed as likely an authority as anyone else—I thought I'd like whatever answer I'd get from him better than what I'd get from other adults, anyway.

He was sitting on his bed, leaning on the headboard with his legs spraddled out. I knocked on his open door and he looked up from the sheets of computer printout in his lap. "Hi. Are you busy?"

"Naw, this is a set of rules and regs for other people's jobs. Low priority." He dumped the printout on the floor. "Come on in and have a seat." I sat down on the foot of his bed. "You look like something's on your mind," he said.

"Um. Yeah. Brad, I was wondering because—you know, the stuff about the Canadians Mother and Dad were talking about a couples nights ago?"

"Sure. What about it?"

"Well, what did the Canadians *really* do?" He folded his arms and opened his mouth; I was afraid he would try to brush me off with the Sunday school version. "I mean, some people say what they did wasn't an abdomination—"

"Abdomination?"

"Yeah. Some people say that really, they saved the world."

"Some people like Scott?"

"Um, like him, yeah."

"*Very much* like him. You need to be more careful. I can see that place between the hedges from these windows. Luella hardly ever gets up here, but if Dad or your mother sees you they'll have to make you stop." I was taking a little aback; I was never sure whether Brad was one of us or one of the grown-ups, and this didn't make it one bit clearer. "Promise to be more careful?" he asked.

"Sure. I promise," I said. He nodded and didn't say anything, so I asked again, "What about the Canadians?"

"Are you old enough to keep a secret? Like your friend Scott did, until he was sure it was all right to tell you?"

I nodded.

"You're sure?" He sat up in bed, leaning forward at me. "It would be real bad for me if someone found out I told you."

"I won't tell. I promise."

"Well, shit." He glanced at me; I'd never heard him swear before. "Yep, I swear and I corrupt little children and if I get half a chance I'm going up there to corrupt the rest of the universe. Sit up here next to me and I'll see if I can give it to you in simple terms." I slid in beside him.

"A long time ago, when Dad was younger than you are now, the two big countries in the world were the Soviet Union—the Russians—and the United States, and they didn't get along at all. They were racing against each other in space, to see who could be the first to get to the moon and the planets, and they were building weapons to fight each other on Earth.

"Do you know what a nuclear bomb is?"

"A great big one," I said. It was what my Sunday School teacher had told me. Besides, I had seen the Topeka Crater back in Kansas—Dad

spoke at the Memorial Park there sometimes, on holidays and so forth—
and I knew a nuclear bomb had done that.

"Good enough. Well, both sides had nuclear bombs on rockets, some
rockets on land and some in submarines, and they had some bombs on
airplanes too. All ready to go. And finally, one day, the War everyone had
been afraid of came.

"Now everyone thought the submarines couldn't be found under the
water, but that wasn't true. Special radar on the satellites could see all
the way down to the ocean floor. Both sides thought only they knew how
to do that—so they both thought they'd surprise the other side, and sink
all the submarines before they could launch their missiles. And when the
War started all the submarines on both sides were gone, first thing, and
none of them got a single rocket off.

"But both sides were launching their missiles from land, too, and
those were in fine shape. And if all of them had landed—instead of just
the few that actually did—it would have been the end of the world.

"But what no one knew was that the Canadians had something up
their sleeves. Since Canada lay between the US and the Soviet Union,
they knew that the War would be especially bad for Canada, because the
fallout—I guess you could say that's a kind of poison, Nehemiah—the
fallout would drift onto them, and the Russians would bomb them because they were America's friend. So they had made a plan.

"They knew that all the rockets would have to pass through one big
patch of sky. And they knew how to make nuclear bombs—though no
one realized they had actually made them. They built great big nuclear
bombs, and they had buried them deep in the ground, at the bottom of
long shafts filled with—"

"What's a shaft?"

"Kind of a hole. Like the kind in an oil well. Mostly they drilled into
the sides of mountains."

"So they drilled big holes and put the bombs at the bottom?"

"Actually, there were about twenty shafts leading down to every
bomb, fanned out in a circle so that the junk would go into lots of different orbits. And each bomb was surrounded by tons of ice, and all the
shafts were filled with a mixture of ice and junk."

"Junk?" I asked. "What kind of junk?"

"Almost anything you can think of," Brad said. "All ground up into
little pieces no bigger than a marble. Spools of old electrical cable. Broken up concrete. Gravel. Blast furnace slag. Broken glass. Old cars.

Sand. The kind of little glass marbles they make Fiberglass out of. Nails and screws and plumbing supplies. They didn't want the world to know about their trick, so they couldn't use too much of any one thing for fear someone would notice. They mixed all that with ice and put it in those shafts.

"When the War started, they set off the bombs—and all those shafts worked just like great big guns. The ice protected the junk for just the seconds it needed to get through the atmosphere, and then broke up from the heat and the strain. The junk scattered every which way, into all kinds of orbits, all criss-crossing through the part of space the rockets needed to go through. The Canadians set off two hundred of those bombs. That put five billion tons of stuff into orbit, all in only about twenty minutes."

He leaned back and looked at the ceiling. "And you know what happened?"

"It stopped the rockets."

"It sure did! Battered them to pieces. The Canadians had figured they wanted to hit everything an average of six times per square meter. That meant a few bombs got through intact and went off—like Topeka and El Paso and Minot—but most of them were too torn up to do any harm. Either they burned up from holes in their heat shielding, or the control circuits were smashed, or they were just too broken up to work. So only forty bombs went off in the whole world, and only nine of those on cities—the rest mostly blew up empty silos.

"The American President and the Soviet Premier didn't know what to do. The missiles they had in reserve were useless. The bombers were on the way, but it would be hours before they got there, and now that they were having time to think, they found out how scared they really were and didn't want to go through with it. So they worked out a deal, and brought their bombers back home, and signed a peace treaty. And they haven't come close to fighting since."

"So the Canadians did save the world." I was amazed. "Why does everyone hate them?"

"Everyone doesn't. Some of us think it's a good thing they did." Brad sighed, and his arm squeezed me a little tighter. "But the junk they filled the sky with made it impossible to send anything into space. Your grandfather—Dad's father, the one who died before you were born—remembered staying up all night to see men walk on the moon. Your father remembers when the men left for Mars, just before the War."

"That was the *America,* wasn't it? What happened to them?"

"They died up there, Nehemiah. When the War broke out they turned around and came back. Just to rematch orbits with Earth, in that unfavorable arrangement, took them months. But they thought they'd be able to think of a way to get down through the junk. They tried a lot of things, but nothing looked like it would work. When they finally ran out of time—supplies got low—they tried to just make it through on luck, but the junk tore their ship to pieces. Dad remembers seeing that—most of America did, because it was a clear night, and everyone went out to watch and pray, and the *America* made a huge fireball on re-entry. Even though the sky was lit up with shooting stars, brighter than the full moon, the *America*'s burn-up stood out in the sky. That was what really started the bitterness toward the Canadians, I think. People realized a whole set of dreams was canceled for at least fifty years. Sure, they were glad to be alive, but now that they were, they were walled into this little planet, just when they had all grown up thinking space was their future. And because of all that orbiting junk, no one has been to space ever since—until next month, when we're going."

I stared at him. "You're not going to die."

"I'm not planning on it." He looked straight into my eyes. "Every year more of the junk comes back down and burns up in the atmosphere. Less than six percent of it is left now."

I told him what Scott had said about the Covenant Stars.

"That's what the Diaspora Canadians believe," he said. "Or their church does anyway. There might be a little truth in it. The world's a lot better equipped for the space age now than it was then. We've got a UN that can really keep the peace out there now. Without a big arms race we have more money and scientific talent to apply to the problem. And because we spent twenty years designing, we know the ships are about as good as they can be."

"Why does the junk come down?" I asked.

"Well, every time a piece passes close to the Earth, it loses speed from passing through the upper atmosphere, and drops into a little lower orbit. When they get low enough they fall all the way into the atmosphere and burn up. And once they burn up they're no danger to anyone, of course." He leaned back against the headboard, looking up at the ceiling. "When I was your age you'd still see thousands every hour. But now so many have come down that it's safe to go up again. And that's why *Restoration* is going to fly next month."

"But some of it's still up there?" I had to know.

"Some. Not enough to be dangerous."

"Why don't they hit the hijumps?" I asked.

"Because the hijumps go up only forty or fifty miles. That's why they have to take hops—like remember we touched at Greenland?—instead of just one clean shot. Nowadays, they probably could just jump the whole way—the odds are really good they wouldn't get hit—but just to be on the safe side they stay low." He looked at me intently. "Was the Barrier what you were afraid of last year?"

I shook my head. I still hated to think about that. It had really just been excitement and tension; I had been so afraid of panicking that I had worked myself into a panic. But I couldn't tell that to Brad. "I don't know. Dad said we're going to take the hijump to see you land in Australia. I'm going to ride up front with the grownups this time."

He gave me a reassuring squeeze. "Good man."

He thought I was being brave, and I wasn't really, so I changed the subject by asking the first question that came to mind. "What if some of the junk hits you?"

"The odds are it won't."

"Well, what if it does?" I was old enough to know a half-truth when I heard it.

He smiled at me. "The ship is armored against the smaller pieces, and it's built so one hit won't be able to cripple it. Besides, for most of the trip we'll be above the Barrier—we just have to go through it going up and coming down." He noticed I hadn't smiled back, so he tried again. "To make it even safer, we'll be going through a low-density spot, taking off from Malvinas Station, and coming back through the same spot when it passes over Australia. We'll be okay."

"But what if you do get hit real hard, by some big ones?"

He sighed and held me close. "Well, if that happens, the ship might be destroyed and I might be killed. I'm sorry, Nehemiah, but that's what it would probably be."

I suddenly noticed my thumb was in my mouth, which was just for babies, so I pulled it out. But then I had to hang on to him real hard for a while. He didn't seem to mind.

"Why are you going?" I finally managed to ask. "You could stay here and be safe."

He sighed. "This will teach me to start answering questions. You never know where they might lead. I could say I just want to be the first.

That's true, but it's not the reason. Or maybe because I always won every contest I tried, and I want to try a bigger one.

"But really—well, it's like this. There's only so much to go around on Earth. Anything one person gets is something everyone else doesn't get. So we all try to get our hands on stuff and keep it away from other people, and we stick our noses in each others' business all the time."

"Like the Reverends?" I asked.

He laughed; it was good to hear that, and I hugged in close to his chest to listen. His armpit was sweating as if he'd been running. "Yes," he said, "like them, and—"

"Don't say so."

"Exactly. I can tell you have the family brains." He riffled through my hair with his fingers. "Yes, like the Reverends. And like all the rest of us squabbling down on this mudball trying to get the little good stuff there is. But out there—out there is everything we need. So people can grow up not fighting each other."

"Will we still be able to play Army?" I asked. I had been frightened at first, but Brad said it was all right, it was. Besides, I had been paying close attention for longer than I was used to, and I was getting tired.

"I guess so. If you want," he said. "But it will be just play. No one will get killed."

That sounded good to me. I said bye and headed for my room; I was working on building a model all by myself, and I wanted to get it done to show Brad before he left.

There was something a little funny to my right. I thought for a moment and then realized that the door into an unused bedroom had been closed when I had gone by before—or so I thought.

It didn't matter one way or the other, so I let it go, but it kept nagging at me all the way down the hall. Finally, just before I'd have gone down the stairs to my room, I turned around.

I saw Mother quietly emerge from the unused room and slip into Brad's room.

For a moment I thought I'd dreamed it. But I found myself slowly, carefully, avoiding all the loose, creaky boards, creeping on tip-toe back toward Brad's room. As I got nearer, I went slower, until finally I was taking long, careful balancing steps just barely touching my foot to the floor, then slowly shifting my weight and repeating the process. At last I reached the door Mother had come in. By now I could hear voices—

they were arguing. I slipped into the unused bedroom and pressed my ear to the wall to hear clearly.

"—To tell a child a thing like that!"

"Well," Brad said softly, "it *is* true."

She made an ugly, barking noise. "All facts, no truth. You didn't even mention God."

"I'm sorry. Was he Canadian?"

"Don't blaspheme. You made no mention of Revelations."

"What the hell does that have to do with World War III?"

"If you'd come to Sunday School, you might know!" I could hear that straining squeak that got into her voice when she was about to cry.

There was a long silence. I pictured Brad staring out the window. "Esther, I'm sorry if I've offended you. When he asked me for the truth, how could I tell him anything except what I thought was true? Dammit, I love the kid too."

"Please don't swear." I heard her sit down on the edge of the bed. "Brad, I try so hard but I just can't take this. You all act like you're giving me a big chance to grow out of my faith. And half the time the world really looks that way to me, anymore. But I believe what I believe, and I feel what I feel, and Nehemiah is my son. He should be given a chance to believe what I believe. He's mine."

There was a very long silence. "What do you want me to tell him?"

"The damage is done. I'll tell him about God's Mark on the Canadians, and the Fifty Years Penitence, and so forth, and show him the passages in Revelations. But it won't do much good now. You've given him your tight little smug everyday commonsense story, and that's what he'll believe. You are robbing that boy of the chance for faith."

Brad sighed again, loudly. "Esther, if telling the truth as I see it is going to keep Nehemiah away from God, then frankly it's a pretty lousy God."

"Oh, *The Truth!* How wonderful! That's why you told him you might get blown to pieces up there!" She sobbed, a sharp, wet, painful gasp. I could hear Brad shifting around, probably trying to get a hand onto her shoulder. "You know he worships you! You couldn't even remind him that God will be watching over you, or that nothing will happen with a Reverend aboard. You had to fill his mind with all this doubt and scare him half to death for nothing. What was that, the truth? Or just showing off?" I pulled back from the wall, not wanting to hear more, but by now they were both so loud I could hear perfectly anyway. I thought of leaving but I was afraid they might see me, since I hadn't heard Brad's door close.

"Esther, I'm sorry—"

"You show off all the time! You walk down the hall from the shower with just a towel on. What kind of sight is that for a Christian home? If Father knew, he'd *vomit.* Do you realize that could make Nehemiah start thinking about men—lusting for them? Are you trying to turn the boy into an abomination, just to show off all your hair and muscles? And now you pretend you might get blown up, just so he can see how brave you are. Don't touch me! I don't care if you're sorry—"

"Esther, I'm really trying to—"

"I don't care." She was crying harder, sharp painful hiccups breaking in among her words. "I can't live like this. You and your father always insulting the faith I was raised in. You act like my father was a witch doctor or something. And he acts like you're devils! Where does that leave *me?*"

There was a scraping noise that must have been Brad getting her a tissue, and then Mother blew her nose fiercely. "My father always says I love my family more than I love Jesus. And he's right about me. I can't help it. . . ."

"We love you too," Brad said. There was something funny in his voice. "Exactly as you are. Really."

"Bullshit. You won't even try. Either of you." She walked out into the hall; I pressed myself against the wall, afraid she'd come in. "I'm sorry I bothered you." She slammed his door and ran. A moment later she clattered down the stairs.

I waited to be sure Brad wasn't coming out, then crept down the hall and downstairs to my bedroom. Later, when Mother came up to talk to me, I pretended to be asleep, and she didn't wake me.

The next day, when I slipped out to see Scott, I was very careful to meet him in close to the hedge on our side, where none of the windows on my house were visible. I had brought along the model of the F66 electrostatic lift fighter, which I had built all by myself. Brad had said it was a very professional job. I wanted Scott to admire the care with which I had built the tiny lifters and shaped the sleek wings and wimshurst housing, but he seemed preoccupied, watching a big lilac bush in his yard. Suddenly his father, Dr. Trenton, came around the bush and walked quickly over to where we were seated, sitting down between us on the damp grass.

I was too astonished to think of anything to do. I was half afraid that we would both be punished right there. Even though I knew that I was forbidden to see Scott, and not vice versa, Dr. Trenton was a responsible adult, and I knew that ultimately they were all allied against children.

Dr. Trenton smiled at me nicely, though, looking at me over his reading glasses which he seemed to have absentmindedly worn into the yard. "I have something that your father or your brother—or both of them—absolutely must see," he said. "Can I trust you to take it to one of them? After that you can come back and play with Scott."

"Take it right now?" I asked.

"Yes."

"Sure." It was a plain manila envelope, sealed at the top, with my father and brother's names written on it. I took it and ran into the house, past Luella who was contentedly washing a window, on up the stairs to the solar. On warm mornings, Brad and Dad liked to take coffee there.

"Hey, Nehemiah, what's the panic?" Brad asked.

I held out the envelope. Dad took it from me and opened it. "It's from Phil Trenton," he said. "Must have been an idea he got after he, um, had to leave us."

"Let's have a look," Brad said.

They poured over it, ignoring me. I thought of going back to play with Scott, but this seemed more interesting.

Scott yelled out in the yard. My first thought was that someone needed to shush him or we'd both be in trouble. I bolted down the stairs, almost toppling Luella—which also woke her up, so that she finally moved to the next window.

There was no one by the hedge. My model lay on the dry crumby soil under a bush, undamaged. That seemed more like something that Dr. Trenton had done—the care was more like him than like Scott.

I heard Scott wail; the sound was from up near his house. Leaving the model under the bush, I ran forward to the second hedge and crawled through the scrubby spot to the other side.

A police car was pulling up in the driveway. Two policemen were hand cuffing Dr. Trenton, and I could hear the minister reading to him, "You have the right to the forgiveness of Jesus if you confess promptly. You have the right to avoid physical questioning by a prompt, full, and true confession. . . . "

It was just like TV. Scott was crying, sometimes screaming, and his mother was holding him back from running to his father.

I ran as hard as I could. I was winded now—it was my third trip across a very big yard—but I kept myself going and staggered up the stairs past Luella and into the solar again. Dad and Brad were engrossed in the papers from Dr. Trenton, and didn't even look up. "Dr. Trenton," I gasped out. "The police . . . at his house—"

"An arrest?" Brad said, standing up.

I nodded. Brad started past me. "Hold it," Dad said. "I can handle this from here." He reached for the phone.

"GUS Central," he said to the autodialer. A moment later he spoke his code phrase, and then he was through to a placer. "This is about a Federal arrest in my area," he said. "They've got a man I want released to my custody immediately." He paused a moment. "Check your board. I'm Rank Thirty-One. I have that privilege. . . . Yes, I'll be responsible for him." Another pause. "All right. His name is Dr. Philip Trenton. . . . yes, I know he was arrested for attempting a contact with me. It will not be necessary to handcuff him. Just bring him by, unhurt. And drop all charges. . . . If you ask me again if I think something is wise, I guarantee, young man, you will be working a manual switchboard at the Point Barrow Meteorological Station for the next twenty years. Is that clear? Thank you. Have him brought by as soon as possible. No, he won't need to be fingerprinted either."

Mother was standing in the doorway by now, trying to get Dad's attention.

"What do you mean? . . . Look, is there an order for his release on the way, or is there not? Let me give you a hint. The right answer is 'yes, there is, *sir*'—*No!* Don't rearrest him! I'll just—"

Mother had disappeared; in a moment she came back with Dr. Trenton. Dad looked up and made a face.

"One more time. Are the charges dropped? Good. Now don't touch anything, all right? I promise it's all okay." He listened for a moment, said "good" a couple of times, and hung up. "Phil, I'm sorry. Have a seat and we'll try to find you some coffee and a sweet roll. They must have been watching your house—I'll have surveillance pulled first thing. Did they hurt you?"

"Just my dignity. And they scared the hell out of my family."

Dad nodded, not looking up. His fingers drummed on the table. Mother came in again, this time with a fresh pot of coffee and some rolls.

"Scott would like to see you," she said. "He's downstairs. I'll get some juice for both of you."

I went down to join Scott. He had brought my model in and was looking at it carefully. "I don't think it got hurt," he said. "When my pop saw the cops coming he put it under that bush to be out of the way. Then he just walked up to them—he wasn't scared or anything."

"Thanks for taking good care of it," I said, and sat down next to him. "That must have been really scary."

Scott nodded. "Pop just walked up and asked them what they wanted. They didn't even tell him—they just grabbed him and dragged him back to the car. I was real scared, crying and everything."

I reached out and touched his shoulder; Mother came in just then. "Scott, I've got apple juice and apple turnovers here. Do I remember that those are your favorites?"

"Sure," he said. They were my favorites too, so we each had a couple of turnovers.

"That really is a good model," he said. "It looks just like the pictures. I want to try that too—making one from scratch."

"It's not easy," I cautioned. "It took me forever to get the damn landing gear to look right." I was feeling very adult and important—after all, I had been the messenger in all this—and thought I might try swearing.

"Yeah," he said flatly.

I could tell he was jealous—I was two years younger than he was and he hadn't built anything like this yet. "What are you going to build?" I asked. "I bet it will be neat."

"I don't know. I was thinking maybe an antique plane, like some kind of a de Havilland."

"What's a de Havlahan?"

"De Havilland. They were a Canadian airplane maker back in the nineteen hundreds."

"Like World War One?" I asked. "All those wires and struts to put on it? Wow. That's going to be tough but I bet it will look great."

He nodded. I thought he might have been embarrassed by my having seen him crying. We went upstairs to play Journey of Abraham—we always liked that one because if you got the right dice rolls you could make the other guy's Abraham take a wrong turn into Sodom or Gomorrah and get blasted.

After a while Scott seemed more like himself; I guessed he had gotten over his fright and embarrassment. "Brad told me what you said about the Covenant Stars was true," I said, "or most of it. Except—" I whispered—"I don't think he believes in God."

"Really?" Scott said. His eyes were big; we were both enjoying being wicked today, with the rules collapsing around us. "Does he think things just happen? Pop said some people think things just happen."

"I think so," I said, solemnly, since I didn't have any idea. We went back to the game.

"Die roll is a five," I said. "God said to Abraham, take Isaac up onto the mountain—and *tickle* him!"

Scott giggled and rolled his die. "Abraham obeys. He stays up there with Isaac, tickling him. They come down with the tablet of the Ten Hee-hee's." Now I giggled too; for a moment we were both helpless, but Scott got his composure back enough to squeak, "And because he obeyed, he gets to go five squares forward." He moved his Abraham that much closer to Canaan, and rolled again; it was his God roll, so if the number was higher than three he could give my Abraham a commandment. "Four." He grinned at me. "God says to Abraham, journey into Canaan duckwalking backwards."

My roll came up even, so Abraham was disobedient. "He says no, I gotta take a leak, and he goes four spaces back toward Ur." Scott whooped with laughter, rolling on the floor. I could hardly keep from shaking with laughter myself. I rolled the die and got a six; I could make a covenant. "God says to Abraham: this is our covenant." A mad thought seized me; instantly I was choking with laughter, but I managed to gasp out, "God says if Abraham never farts again, chocolate chip cookies will fall from Heaven every day."

That did it. We were helpless with laughter, rolling around, tears running out of our eyes, unable even to breathe.

I looked up to see my grandfather, the Reverend Hodge.

For a moment, we just lay there frozen. He smiled just a little and sat down on the rug beside us.

"It sounds like you boys were having a lot of fun," he said.

"Um, no. Yes." I said.

"Oh, of course you were," he said. His liver-spotted plump hand extended onto my board and set Abraham back up. "It was very funny, and you were laughing."

I nodded a couple of times. I felt like I was going to throw up—if I didn't know exactly what was coming, I knew near enough.

"You know why it's so funny?" He waited expectantly. I stole a glance at Scott; he was looking down at the floor. I didn't say anything, so finally Grandpa said, "It's funny because—" he dropped his voice like a conspirator "—*God is a stuffed shirt.*" He sat back looking at us. "Isn't he? He's *terribly* pompous. Always telling people what to do. Thou shalt and thou shalt not all the time.

"And do you know what's fun to do with pompous people? We make fun of them. We pretend they say silly things. . . ." He sat and waited for me to look up. Eventually I couldn't help myself.

His eyes locked onto mine. "Don't we?"

I nodded, unable to look away. My eyes were starting to water a little already.

"But God is *not* pompous, Nehemiah. He only seems that way to people who don't understand Him. God is not mocked. If you think you can make fun of Him, then you don't understand Him, even though your grandfather is a Reverend and your father is a senator and you go to expensive private schools. No matter how much your parents love you. No matter how many friends you have."

I could feel the tears starting to run down my face. I was about to blubber.

"You do want to believe, don't you?"

I nodded hard, miserably trying to keep from sobbing.

"You want Jesus to help you believe, don't you?"

"Stop it." Mother was standing in the doorway. "Father, leave him alone."

"I'm just—"

"I know what you're doing. You used to do it to me." Her face was slack, her voice toneless; she looked and sounded dead. "Leave him alone. It's not that serious, and you aren't helping him."

"I think I am," he said firmly. "I think that you know that what this boy needs—"

"I don't know that," she said. "It's not true."

His voice stayed low and mild; he never raised it. "But, Esther," he said, "if you'll just ask Jesus to guide you, I think you'll see. Just open your heart—remember how we did that when you were a little girl—"

"Yes, I do remember." Her voice was completely flat. "Now get out of here."

He swallowed hard. "Surely. It's your house." He got up. "Be careful, though. Remember I love you and I don't want things to happen to you. That's why I came over when I heard that—"

"I know," she said. "Now go."

Grandpa went down the stairs without looking back. I noticed how small and old he was. "Nehemiah, come with me," Mother said. "Scott, if you'll just wait here . . ."

I followed Mother down the hall, not sure what was going on. She led me into a spare bedroom and sat down on the bed. "Lie down on your stomach, across my lap," she said.

I did. Her wool skirt was rough against my face, and I could feel it absorbing the tears that were still there from when Grandpa had talked to me. I could feel her legs tense under me, and she sighed. "This is going to hurt."

Then she slapped me on the bottom, three times, fairly hard. It stung, though not very much. I was too surprised to be very upset.

"That," she said, "is for blasphemy, and for upsetting your grandfather. If you ever do that again, I will do this again. Is that clear?" She let me up off her lap. She didn't really sound very angry.

"Yes, ma'am," I agreed.

"Okay." She kissed me on the cheek. "Now it's all over. Go back and play." I stood there for a moment, getting my bearings. She laid a hand on my shoulder. "Nehemiah?"

"Yes, ma'am?" Until I got the new rules figured out, I wasn't taking any chances.

"Did that hurt?"

"A little bit," I said. It didn't seem like a good idea to lie just then, but I was hoping she wouldn't decide it hadn't worked and do it again.

"It was supposed to." She looked at me but seemed far away. "Nobody ever did that to me when I was little. Father just talked to me—you know, the way he was talking to you. I always thought I'd rather be spanked."

She seemed to feel bad, so I said I would rather be spanked too. It was probably true anyway. This seemed to take care of things, so I went back to play with Scott. Scott and Dr. Trenton stayed the rest of the day; Mrs. Trenton came over for dinner, too, which she and Mother cooked, giving Luella the night off. That meant not only the fun of having company, but good food for once. Everyone talked and laughed a lot, and Mother even had a couple of sips of wine and tried to learn to play bridge—that last was apparently *very* funny, from the way the adults were reacting, though Scott and I couldn't follow any of it.

It got pretty late before the Trentons went home. I think my parents had missed them. When they left, Dr. Trenton quietly said, "So you don't think there's anything to be done about it?"

Brad shook his head. "Anything we could do would hurt the Project worse than just taking the chance. I agree—we should fly the Putty Ball before sending up *Restoration*. But that's all under the bridge; we'll know soon enough anyway."

Dr. Trenton nodded. "Thank you for everything. We'll be in touch."

We all shook hands and hugged and kissed and everything, just as if they were going away forever instead of home around the block. When they were gone there was a strange quiet.

"Well, young man, it is definitely time for you to get to bed," Mother said.

"I'll tuck him in, if you're tired," Brad said.

They smiled at each other and agreed, and I was being whisked up the stairs before I had time to figure out whether I objected or not. Brad slung me up on his shoulder at the landing, like he did when I was little, and even though it was kind of babyish, it was fun and besides no one saw us.

As he helped me out of my shirt, I asked him. "What's the Putty Ball?"

"It's a kind of satellite we were going to send up, Nehemiah," he said. "Take off your shoes and socks." He turned to run water into the tub.

"Why didn't you?"

"Not enough money and nobody believed Doc Trenton. Except me and some other astronauts." He put his hand in the running water to check the temperature.

"I can take a bath by myself," I said.

"I know," he said. "Would you rather?"

I considered. "Will you wash my back?"

"Sure."

"And tell me about the Putty Ball?"

"All right. Get undressed, then." He sat on the edge of the tub. "You know we've already sent up several satellites, just to make sure the radiation belts and so forth are where they're supposed to be."

"We saw that on TV in school," I said.

"Okay. Into the water, and let's make sure the soap hits the back of your neck and under your jaw this time." He helped me in. "We don't know as much as we'd like to about what went up there in the first place. And therefore we don't know how any pieces of glass and brick and so forth are still up there. Radar can only count the metal pieces and photography can only find the ones that come down. The only way we can even guess how much is up there is to figure there's some ratio between the numbers of metallic and nonmetallic pieces—and the Canadians didn't record what all went down the holes so that ratio is just a guess itself. So we don't really *know* how much junk that doesn't show on radar is up there in the Barrier."

"Could there be a lot more than you thought?" I asked.

"There sure could," he said, soaping up my back, "and every piece moving many times as fast as a bullet. Doc Trenton thinks so, based on something called a spectral analysis of entry trails—never mind what that is or we'll be here all night."

He wet the cloth and rubbed my back firmly, working up a thick lather and rinsing it off thoroughly. "So what's the Putty Ball?" I asked.

"It was going to be a great big blob of a soft foam. It would all go up in a can, and then expand to maybe twenty meters across, surrounding the can. Then after it had been up for a few months, the can would poke a nozzle out through the foam and eject a second foam to cover the whole thing. The second foam would work as a heat shield; then a rocket nozzle would poke up and fire to slow the Putty Ball down, so the whole thing would tumble down out of space—because it wouldn't be very dense, it wouldn't land very hard, kind of like throwing a wad of paper off the roof. The idea was that we'd bring it back down, cut it apart, and see how much of what kind of stuff had gotten embedded in there. Then we'd know if Dr. Trenton was right or not."

"If he was right, would you still go?"

He held his hand out palm down, fingers spread, and waggled it from side to side.

"What was in the envelope?"

Brad shrugged. "More evidence that he's right. But even if he *is* right, there's still only about a one in a thousand chance of getting a serious hit while we cross the Barrier, let alone having anything go wrong from it. It's just it's not one in ten thousand like we thought. Really, there's just as good a chance of something going wrong with the machine itself . . . and that's not much of a chance. Now don't worry anymore."

I leaned back in the warm water, letting him wash my chest and shoulders too. He had taken off his shirt to avoid getting water on it, and I was looking at his hairy chest and wondering how long it would be before I grew hair like that. I hoped it would be a long time; I thought it looked weird.

Mother put her head in. "Oop, sorry."

"No harm done," he said, shrugging into his shirt while she looked politely away. "What can I do for you?"

"You can accept my apology for being so rude the other day."

"Decent now," he said, ramming his shirt down into his trousers.

She smiled at him. "You could probably be in six overcoats and a sleeping bag and still not be quite decent."

"I'm afraid so. Well, anyway, the apology's accepted. We've all been on edge with everything going on."

Mother smiled. "Thank you. I'll sleep better for that." She stepped inside; she was in her long bathrobe. "Here's for being a sweetheart." She put her arm around his shoulders and kissed him firmly on the cheek. She stood back from him for a moment, an odd expression on her face.

He grinned, leaned forward, and kissed her cheek. She stood there, blushing, and said, "I know you've both always tried to be nice to me." I thought she might laugh or cry or something, but finally she just said goodnight and went upstairs to Dad's room.

I had finished scrubbing myself and rinsing, so Brad toweled me off, got me into my pajamas, and heard my prayers. As I was getting into bed, I said. "Do you think things just happen?"

"Some things. Depends."

That seemed like a reasonable answer. I thought I had a lot to think about, and would never get to sleep, but in fact I barely remember getting into bed before being completely out.

The next morning, while we were eating breakfast, there was a loud knock on the door. Not bothering to call Luella, Mother went to get it. When she opened the door, there were two policemen standing there. "Sorry to bother you, ma'am, but if you could—"

"Oh, come in, come in. We're just having breakfast. Would you like a cup of coffee?"

"Uh, actually we just needed to check—"

"Are you sure? We have caffeineless too, and it's chilly this morning."

Mother was dithering like an affy. I expected Dad to go out into the front room and straighten things out, but he sat at the breakfast table quietly reading the newspaper, and so did Brad.

"Um, actually ma'am, we have an electronic record that shows that passports for Mrs. Senator Caron, Bradley Washington Caron, and Nehemiah Grace-of-God Caron were used at Moody Hijump Port early this morning."

"Oh, well, that's silly. We're all right here."

"Well, that's just the thing," the officer who seemed to be in charge said. "We were wondering if by any chance the passports might have been stolen from this house."

With a little squeal, which I'd never heard her make before, Mother got up and thrashed around frantically in the bureau drawers. I knew how carefully they were organized, and could have found the passports myself—third drawer down, important personal papers, under "I" for international—so I couldn't imagine what she was doing. Eventually, she said, "Now, I don't know wherever they could have gotten to. Brad, could you come out and help me look?"

"Look for what?" Brad called, not moving or looking up from his paper.

"Our passports."

"Are we going somewhere?"

She came in and explained it to him, even though he'd been sitting there listening. When he finally understood—which took quite a while—Brad went out and looked everywhere she had already looked. It took twice as long because so much stuff was on the floor. Then he volunteered to go upstairs and check the dressers. He invited me to come along, and we had a great time opening all the dresser drawers, empty and full, and feeling around. I had figured out by then that the one thing we didn't want to do was find the passports, so I was careful to check all the drawers thoroughly at least twice. It took Mother and Brad the better part of an hour to agree that they couldn't find their passports.

By now Dad had gotten into it too. Dr. Trenton and his family had disappeared the night before—apparently they hadn't even gone home from our house. Someone showing family Consecrated Privileges Passports for Brad, Mother, and me had gotten tickets at the last minute onto a hijump bound for Brussels. It had gone through Greenland Touchpoint before anyone had known anything, and was now en route to Brussels. If the police could get a warrant to the UN Ballistic Transit Authority before the Trentons got through the gate, they could have the Trentons arrested and brought back, but if the Trentons got out of the port, Brussels was the capital of United Europe, which had no extradition treaty with America. "They'd probably give them asylum," the policeman added. "We have a warning that says they're Canadians— maybe even secretly Church of Canada."

I understood that in about five minutes, but Dad took quite a while to get it, and wouldn't let the police go till they made it clear to him. Then he wanted to know about whether he could be charged with any crime, and whether he would have trouble getting replacement passports—the answer to both questions was no, but it took him a long time to understand it. "I'm not at my best in the morning," he said. "Haven't had enough coffee yet. You gentlemen care to join me?"

"No thanks, sir. Would you mind signing a complaint form here, stating you have reason to believe that the Trentons stole the passports?"

"Well," Dad said. "There have been a lot of people in here since the last time I saw the passports. I wouldn't want to make a mistake."

"All you have to say is that you have probable cause to think—"

"Now, don't lecture me on the law, officer. I'm an old country lawyer. I know these things."

They argued about it for quite a while; it took longer because Dad kept losing the point of the argument. Finally, one of the cops said to the other, "The hijump will have grounded and unloaded by now. They only take an hour to cross the Atlantic."

The two of them left, after refusing another offer of coffee. It took a while to get all the jumbled stuff back into place, but nobody minded much. Everyone seemed to be very happy—except me; I was missing Scott already.

That afternoon, when Brad was bringing me home from a ball game, he bought a bunch of roses for Mother. She seemed really overwhelmed when he handed them to her. "What are these for?"

"Either a great lady or a leading lady," Brad said.

She giggled; she really sounded like a girl. "Let me get these into water."

A week later, Mother pressed three of the wilted roses in her Bible. I don't think she ever knew that I saw that.

When it finally came time to get on the hijump at San Diego, I wasn't really scared at all. Partly I was a year older, and mostly I was just too excited by all that had happened in the past week. We had watched *Restoration* lift off from Malvinas, and spoken to Brad over the USSA radio link several times. And like everyone else, we had seen the pictures on TV. Earth looked a lot like it did in the new weather satellite photos of the last few years and in the old pictures from sixty years ago. But this was now—and people were seeing it with their own eyes.

I was on the hijump and strapped into my seat before I really knew what was happening. We took ten laps around the big circular track while the maglev brought us up to 650 mph, and then we were headed up the ramp, the strap-on engines thundering, and into the sky. The acceleration shoved us deep into our seats for what seemed like a long time; then the roar stopped with a whump as the strap-ons separated, and we were floating in silence.

Although Mother had thought it might make my fear worse, I had insisted on the window seat, and now I was glad I had. Because of the slight air resistance, it wasn't quite free fall, but I still felt almost weightless. Through the window, I could see the black sky over the curve of the Earth and the circular whorls of clouds far below. I could almost pretend we were going all the way to orbit.

Then we were over and shooting downward, weight returning as wind resistance brought us below free-fall velocity, the tips of the wings glowing orange. There was a strange pressure under our feet, and a faint rumble. "That's the maneuvering engine cutting in," Dad said, but I had already figured it out. The computer brought the ship onto the laser beacon and aligned it. We skimmed in over the water, Honolulu flashing briefly below us, and settled onto the maglev track at Maui Touchpoint. The first hop had taken only half an hour track to track.

We glided silently, an inch or so above the track, into the transfer station. As we slowed to a stop, carts carrying fresh strap-ons rolled up; I watched the crew attach them and connect the cables. They certainly knew what they were doing—the whole thing only took a couple of minutes, and we glided out onto the acceleration track to circle up to speed again.

This time, right after the strap-ons separated, Dad leaned across and said "Look that way." He pointed out the window.

There were two white arcs down below us. As I watched, the lines of white ended in bright orange blossoms. "Engine recovery," Dad said. "Those are our strap-ons, parachuting into the ocean. There are ships down there that pick them up."

We went through the Tarawa Touchpoint in the same way, and finally glided onto the Brisbane track, less than two hours after leaving San Diego. After declaration, the hijump transferred tracks and moved over to the regular zipper line to cruise into the downtown. It seemed strange to be riding in a hijump as if it were a plain old zipper, like the one we transferred to in Brisbane Central.

As we headed into the desert—Dad said it was called the Outback—I realized that the sun was setting, not rising as I had first thought. "Yep," Dad said. "Just about halfway round the world. We've overtaken the sun."

The only fly in the ointment for me was that, exciting as all this was, Brad would certainly be able to top me anyway.

The control room at the landing field was neat too. Everyone was very busy, and Dad and Mother both told me not to bother anyone. I was too interested in watching what the technicians were doing to do anything other than stare, anyway. Every so often I would get so excited that I'd go outside to the grandstand and jump around a little. The sky was quite dark now, and in the glare of the lights I couldn't see the stars—except for an occasional Covenant Star, flickering overhead. They reminded me that I still missed Scott, and I was getting cold all by myself out here, so I went back inside. It was almost time anyway—they had gone into their final orbit.

Everything was normal right up till they lost communication. Even then, no one worried at first because it was right on schedule. As Brad had explained to me, a re-entering spacecraft is surrounded by hot, ionized gas—while it lasts, it blocks radio completely.

But then the buzz of voices got louder, faster, and higher. The radar people didn't like what they were seeing; neither did anyone else. I kept hearing the word "tumbling"; somebody in one corner was chanting "Pull out pull out pull out" like it was a prayer. A fussy little man with a mustache who'd been guiding us around suddenly appeared and whisked us out onto the field. It was the wrong thing to do. In the black western sky out beyond the landing lights, in the terrible silence of shouting reporters and cameramen, a bright white streak had appeared. As we watched, the streak darkened to orange, like an incoming hijump, and then broke up as it turned red, scattering tiny lights that twinkled and sparkled much too much to be stars.

We stared at it until finally, mercifully, the glowing pieces of *Restoration* dimmed to invisibility. We sat down there, right on the runway, in what was supposed to be the reception area, and cried—all three of us. Behind us, the American MP's were seizing cameras and recorders. The Australian reporters wouldn't give theirs up, and it sounded like the Australian soldiers were coming in on their side; there was a lot of scuffling and shouting. I heard all that without thinking about it, just sitting there clinging to Dad and Mother.

Eventually a man came to ask for Senator Caron. Dad got up right away, wiping his eyes with the good handkerchief from his jacket pocket—I had never seen him use his good handkerchief for anything— and straightening his collar. I could see his muscles knot even through his suit, but he was under control, and he went in to talk to the reporters. Mother and I were guided to an old-fashioned ground car, the kind people drove for themselves with rubber tires, and the fussy little man drove us back to our room at the Landing Complex hotel. They gave us a bottle of sleeping pills, but we didn't take any right away. We just sat and waited for Dad. I fell asleep, sitting in a chair, my cheeks wet with tears and snot dribbling into my mouth. When I woke up, Dad was back. I didn't move, so they didn't know I could hear.

"You don't know that," Mother said. "It didn't have to be the Barrier at all. Maybe there's a design flaw."

"It doesn't matter," Dad said. "The program is dead." He slammed a hand against the hotel room wall. It sounded like it hurt. "Esther, you can't know. Thirty years of my life. When my friends kept their honor and went to jail, I made a bargain just so I could stay and fight for this. And now my son . . . and it doesn't matter. We'll never build and launch another one, not in my lifetime. Other countries will go; we'll ride along after it's safe. I got a call from the staff in Washington—they say half the votes I used to count on are gone." He leaned forward, covering his eyes with his hands and rubbing hard.

"That bargain you made to stay in the Senate," she said. "Was it such a bad one?"

He sat up and put an arm around her. "That was the only good thing to come out of it," he said.

"That and Nehemiah," she corrected. She sighed. "I want you to know, when we get there I'm going to collapse. But for right now I can kind of hold together. I've already packed."

"Packed? We're not going back to Washington tonight."

"Right," she said. "We're going to Jakarta. And maybe eventually to

Brussels. They can use somebody who knows a lot about the *Restoration* project."

He stared at her. "Defect?"

"That's the word. If we can catch the zipper within two hours, we can make the early morning hijump to Jakarta from Darwin. We don't dare call a car, but it's only about a mile and a half walk down the road, and the zipper station is automated. If we go out the back door it should be no problem—they're as confused as we are right now, and they won't be watching yet. Besides, once we're on the zipper we're in Australian territory."

I sat up slowly, but they didn't notice me. Mother looked sick, and Dad looked worse. "But we—" he began.

She sighed. "You used to be useful. The Reverends needed a space program to keep their image up, but not all of them were smart enough to know it. Father was smart enough, so he protected you to fight for it. Now that it's dead, he won't be able to. They'll retire him, but they'll jail you—if they don't declare you Afflicted. They don't need you anymore." She half smiled, but there were tears in her eyes again. "But I do. And there are other space programs that need to know what you know."

"But defecting—"

She took his hand and put it on a suitcase handle. "Pick it up. We can sort things out on our way."

"No." He glared at her, suddenly connecting in a way that he hadn't before. "I can't defect. I'm a senator. It's my country—"

"If you go back, you'll be a prisoner. Pick it up. Do you want this all to be for nothing?"

"That's not up to me. I have a duty to—"

"Who is it up to, then? God?" There was a strange tone in Mother's voice that I had never heard before. "Do you think Jehovah smote down *Restoration* because Brad mocked him? Or because the Reverend accidentally forgot a word in a prayer?"

He was staring at her.

"Do you?"

He shook his head.

"Well, neither do I. And if the people back home want to give up because of this—" she drew a long nervous breath "—*fuck* 'em. There are damn good people going into space everywhere. Those are the people you owe your loyalty to. Now are you going to go home, let them work on you until you confess to something, and then have them declare you Afflicted? Want a job cleaning the White House restrooms, trying to remember your own name? Or do you want to come with me and Nehemiah, and maybe get the human race back to space like you've been trying to do for thirty years?"

He sighed again, but he picked up the bag and his back was straightening. "We'll miss his memorial—we wouldn't dare to wait that long."

"Then we'll come up with a memorial of our own." Mother's hand strayed across the hotel room dresser, touching her Bible for a moment. She opened it, hesitating just a moment, then put it face down on the bed next to some loose clothing and a half-empty suitcase. "Looks more like we're planning to come back," she said. "Now let's go."

In a few minutes we were out a side door and walking through the cold desert night to the zipper station. "You'll need to be quiet," Dad said to me. "If you must say anything at all, whisper." I nodded and followed him and Mother, clutching my bag under my arm and holding the strap to my shoulder with my other hand. They were holding hands now and then, going quite slowly. I didn't have any trouble keeping up, but the icy dry air kept me gasping.

The landing field lights were off now, and above us there were endless stars. Every couple of breaths, a colored streak would tear across them, lasting perhaps as long as two of my steps. I thought of the Barrier coming down little by little till some night in the future when nobody would look up and remember; and of the sky becoming empty, as empty as I was, just trudging after my parents and putting one foot in front of the other, my clothes and things tugging at the strap in my hand.

FOR THE END

FINALITIES BESIDES THE GRAVE

This wasn't my first published story; it was the first one published that I still like. George Scithers bought it from me; it was about the thirty-fifth story I had sent to him. There are occasional sentences in here that go clang, and some other things I wish I could fix, but I still like the basic story.

When I saw the kids in gis headed toward me I did what anyone with any sense does, and crossed the street. That's the uniform of wallet-lifters and head-crackers, at least in Tucson. Trying to keep an eye on them and get around one of the bigger rubble heaps at the same time, I wasn't much watching where I was going, and I ran broadside into a dark-haired woman as she stepped up onto the curb. She almost fell, and as I steadied her I saw that she was slim and rather good-looking—even the norman didn't quite obscure that.

"Sorry," I explained. "I was trying to get away from those hitos across the street. You Americans make me nervous that way."

"It's all right." When her hand trailed off my arm, it was slow, and very soft and cool—I almost missed what she said next. "Are you British?"

"Australian."

She looked at me curiously. "I've never met a foreigner before. I'd heard accents like yours in old movies. What are you doing here?" She flushed. "I mean—"

"Quite all right. I'm over here to look at some supporting software systems for the Australian Air Force." I turned on all the charm I could come up with, not worrying too much about the accent—anything vaguely Ronald-Colman sounding would obviously work on this one, and though I'd been worried about some small slips in the cover persona in the last week, I'd been more worried about the creeping loneliness, what they call Monitor's Crazy, that desperate need to talk with somebody, be with somebody, with your guard *down*. I was starting to get fuzzy, I knew, careless about details, and I only had seventy-four days to go.

The conversation, with enough effort, adjourned from a hot dusty street to a relatively cool movie theater—a couple of the ceiling fans were working. Despite her being in the norman, she was pretty receptive to a little stroking and cuddling, and when I fired the autosyringe against her leg I don't think she even noticed. For the first time in a long time, things were working right.

One little detail almost did spoil it. The film was one of the Ben-Lithe-of-the-Moral-Guard series, and somewhere in the middle of it one of the pervert ring he was tracking down said, "Can you imagine the things they do in Tokyo?" For one second, I really thought I'd cry.

But I didn't, and by the time I got her up to the hotel room her face was flushed, and she was looking at me fixedly.

Usually after a couple of hours when the drug wears off they start screaming "What have I done" no matter how obvious it is, but this one just lay there for a while. I knew I ought to get her out the door before the effects wore off completely, but it was so damned nice to have company that I went ahead and took the chance of letting her stay. I thought idly that this must be another effect of the Crazy, breaking rules like this—which was odd, because events like this were supposed to ward it off. Seventy-four days, I thought, and here I am doing something risky.

She let out a little, sighing whimper, and I tensed for the scream. The incriminating hardware was all in the kit bag—I wasn't *that* careless, anyway. She sighed, slow and soft, a noise like snow falling would make if it made any. Her gray eyes looked happy, or contented anyway. "Let's do it again," she said, "a little slower this time."

I hugged her close, kissing her neck just where the damp, stray curls of hair touched it, trying to figure out what was going on but enjoying it too much to worry. This time it was a lot like I remembered it should be, like I imagined it would be again after Extensive Debriefing, and afterwards we both lay there, cuddling and stroking, agreeing it was great. I felt so unguarded I decided to give her the name I was staying under, breaking a few more regulations. "I'm John Hare, by the way. Introductions got rather lost in the middle there."

"Mary Lynn Burlman. Pleased to meet you." She giggled. "I do hope we meet socially sometime soon."

"I *am* sorry about the rate things happened at."

"That's okay. I didn't mind. You were so nice I felt like I knew you anyway. Most guys will take you somewhere and do it, but afterwards they start yelling 'slut,' and then the Noses come crashing up the stairs and it's out the window or take fifteen backzippers and lose my teaching certificate."

"You're a *teacher?*"

"Of course. For lesser mortals it's only five lashes."

"Well," I said, "you'll pardon my asking, but I thought that that job required all sorts of proof of morality—"

"The Moral Guard was quite properly impressed by my conversion at the age of seventeen. Actually I was just hanging up my gi to meet a better class of guy, but I really decided to go the whole way, and I made a good enough impression to get into the State Teachers' College. It was that or nursing school or home ec, and I hate sick people and babies." She wrinkled her nose; I thought I hadn't seen anything so pretty in ages. "They smell."

"What's home ec?"

"Home economics. What they call WT, wife training, now. Anyway, I'd been lucky—no immorality or deviance convictions, just two accessory-to-manslaughters and some assault charges. There're a lot of places where even the porkers just think of that as good, wholesome adolescent fun." She yawned and stretched; I put my head down to nuzzle her neck. It took me a minute to place the scent—it was baby powder, probably soaked in alcohol to extract the perfume, the poor girl's cologne. She pushed my head back up. "You're the first foreigner I've met, John. What are the women wearing in Tokyo these days?"

I shrugged. "Kind of a jerkin, I think, with a short skirt and a bustle. I'm afraid I'm a little out of date." Four years, almost exactly, out of date, and getting a little tired.

"It must be wonderful not having to wear a norman." She gestured vaguely at the crumpled pink heap on the floor. "They're so ugly. Knee-length and high-necked, and *ugly.* Besides, you can't walk in the stupid black pumps, and there's too much skirt to show off your ass." She stretched again and I admired the view; her face, I realized, must look older than she really was. "I'd love to see what you're talking about. Men are hopeless at descriptions. We haven't even seen photos in the past few years. What's Australia like?"

"Uh, the seasons are reversed?"

"Trust a schoolteacher to ask a question you can't answer." She rolled over and gave me a long, hard kiss, then snuggled up and went to sleep in the crook of my arm. For a long time I just lay there, taking slow deep breaths through her damp hair, running a hand up and down her arm. Once I got up and peeked through the musty gray curtains, but the street was its same old self, dusty and empty and dead, and for all the noise that Tucson made on a Saturday anymore we might as well be the only survivors. I looked at my watch—just past one, going on two; and at the mirror—twenty-nine going on forty and getting paunchy. There was plenty of time to spruce up for a four o'clock appointment, maybe even wash my hair—I like to feel fresh for those things. Maybe I'd even offer Mary Lynn some of the real shampoo that was the main privilege of this particular cover. (I had smelled the strong soap on her hair.) Then again, being in an air-conditioned room was probably a big treat for her.

I switched on the radio and let it play just loudly enough that words could still be made out. The station wasn't a GoodNews affiliate, but as no foreigner listens to those, no harm was done to my cover. It was one of the little FM stations that survives on ads from pizza places and funeral homes, playing old songs from the approved list, mostly sentimental love stuff and patriotics. After a few of the former I was feeling sad and lonely all over again, so I got back in bed and cuddled up next to Mary Lynn.

When I woke up it was pushing four and our bodies were stuck to the soggy sheets with our sweat. The air-conditioning was working badly as always, and I no longer had the time to wash my hair; in fact, I needed to start getting dressed right away.

Gently I disentangled myself from her and reached for my shorts. "Going to send out for the Noses?" she asked, not seriously.

"I'm afraid we foreigners lack the moral strength for that, Mary Lynn." I was buttoning my shirt, really wanting a shower now. "Maybe I should go to a Christian surgeon and have the right thing done for those of us with strong passions. Maybe it would stop me from spraying in the house."

The comb fighting with my hair was losing. With a mental sigh, I gave up—Redman would probably be in greasy overalls anyway. "I have some business to take care of before Sabbath," I explained, "so I'm going out about that. Can you get yourself out of the hotel without trouble?"

"Shouldn't be a problem."

"Would you like to have dinner tonight?"

"Sure." I suggested a place; she suggested a more intimate one; I agreed. With a last survey of the grubby little room that was the best Tucson had to offer, I gave her a nod and said, "Seven o'clock, meet you there," and was out the door. It occurred to me that I was whistling, and that crazy loneliness was somewhere way, way back in my mind. I liked it that way.

Redman started out with "Call me Dave," which was a bad sign to start with. I hate it when they're friendly. Furthermore, he wasn't the usual basement-lab-troll type, the kind that spend several years on end working on the Gadget, whichever of the several it might turn out to be. He did have thick glasses, his jeans and T-shirt did need washing, and his short, sandy hair looked like it had been gradually shellacked into place with his sweat, but he just didn't have that hard fanatic glint in his eye that years of scrounging parts and money produce. Actually, during the before-business small talk, he had come across as a bit of a Renaissance man, well-read as much as an American can be legally, an amateur painter, and a one-time athlete.

As we went out to the Q-hut behind his house, I found myself hoping that he didn't really have anything.

It didn't seem likely, though.

He was talking at a fast gallop the whole time, in that odd, high, light voice that didn't go with the Texas drawl. I asked where he was from; it turned out to be Beaumont, which explained the accent and all those paintings of Jesus hanging in his house. "Learned a lot there, more on my own since, didn't make engineering school but I think I'm about caught up. That garden there's organic, drip-irrigated, learned that from Dad—cheapest way to do things for the home and beats the daylights out of supermarket prices. Not much work, either—the old rugging there keeps the weeds down. I just walk out there and pick what the Good, Sweet Savior gives me for dinner, and he gives me pretty good since I make it easy for him. I guess that's usually about the way of things.

"Now, right in here is where it is, this Quonset hut, I guess you fig-ured. The biggest problem I had was getting a large, superhard vacuum tube for the electron-positron collision vortex. That superconducting set of focusing magnets was no piece-a-cake to get ahold of either— eventually I ended up stripping it off an old military space shuttle and spent two years rehabbing it."

There was absolutely no question, I thought glumly. He had a work-ing MAM power plant built around a Yamanaka Positron Emitter. I asked where he'd gotten that particular item.

"Smuggler from Mexico. Hate to have any money making its way to the yellow Jesus-haters, but they had these things and we didn't. Get a few of these running, though, and Old Satan will find he's in lots of good pure grade-one American-made trouble."

I found myself thinking of Dad, somewhere a few hundred miles west, lying with God knows how many others in a bulldozed trench, and all of a sudden the loneliness was back. For a minute I thought I'd lose everything, but then something snapped into place.

Redman was a nut-lop job, and probably had had the Christian oper-ation done when he was in his late teens. Beaumont was an early center of the Church of Sweet Purity back when it was merely an aberration and not the law of the land. He must have been among the first few.

Usually that gives them a hell of an emotional commitment to what it was done in the name of. There was very little chance he'd take the bait, and I'd be fully justified in just taking care of him now, but—I had started to like him, so I might as well dangle it, anyway. "Mr. Redman, as you might be aware, I'm not authorized to buy your device just immedi-ately. What I am authorized to do is to offer you a considerable sum of money and a salary to come to Australia and work for my firm, develop-ing this. You could have a fully-equipped lab, and all the parts you need. . . ."

He shook his head. "This was built by an American, for Americans. I like to think it may be Jesus' instrument to make us great again."

I knew I ought to just deal with him then and there, but an image kept swimming up in my mind of him working there far into the night, setting each thing just so to get it perfectly right, fussing over every single part, soldering with more care than a surgeon takes because each chip was so precious . . . an odd little picture of him lying there on the cot beside the work bench, exhausted, sweat-drenched, and clammy. I just didn't want to do it, so I tried again. "Perhaps I didn't make myself clear, Dave. We already have these devices in the outside world. Once cheap, efficient positron generation is available, the rest of the system follows very quickly. I'm offering you a position because your engineering and innovative talents appear to be far in excess of what you'd be able to use in this country. You would find a matter-antimatter power system impossible to make and market here anyway—by mutual agreement between the central banks, finance wouldn't be available here, and in any case the UN wouldn't allow the YPE to be sold in America."

He grinned triumphantly, pointing to a set of graphics-machine printouts on the wall. "Got it about nine-tenths doped out how they work, myself."

He was right. Anyone, of course, can X-ray one and draw the parts, but he'd actually figured out all the materials involved. "Laser and vortex for inefficient fusion," he said, going on like the kid who got the alarm clock back together. "Neutrons from the fusion drift to the film here; and the big positive charge on the film, plus the magnet, pushes emitted positrons out on the hard-vacuum side. Took me a while to figure out what combination of materials would be strong enough, gastight enough, and still be a good positron emitter after neutron addition; but I did it."

"Brilliant," I said, meaning it. I looked around the room once, nodding. The careful tidiness, the deliberate care taken in working drawings for his eyes only . . . and the stubbornness. I wanted to have about ten old friends to get good and drunk with. If I could just not hear this harsh, jolting English—more than anything I wanted to be through the Extensive Debriefing and *home.*

I took a slow breath. No question. Monitor's Crazy was getting me. Still, if I could hold off on getting maudlin, I had a dinner date tonight; and besides, this was a relatively simple problem. I suspected that everything was in this beat-up old Q-hut, but I'd do the house too to be sure.

I pulled out my pocket recorder. "I'm sorry you feel that way, Dave," I said, and pushed the hidden button. The little tracer dot from the low-powered laser was right in the middle of his forehead. He almost had time to gasp, staring at the red beam shining in the light dust in the air, before I punched the second button and gave him a burst of microwaves. The clot formed instantly, big as a golf ball, right between the frontal lobes. He was dead before he even started to sway, and he crumpled rather than fell. Usually you don't get a clean shot like that.

Of course it doesn't take much effort to get a fire going in a workshop or lab. For that I could use almost anything on hand. The hard part was disabling the homemade automatic extinguisher—the software in it was damned clever, including a couple of sabotage detectors to make parts of it lie low for a few minutes just in case someone tried to do what I did. Fortunately the pocket reader spotted the odd blocks of code, and after I recorded them for later study I just wiped the whole works. An astute arson-man might have figured that out; but Gomez wouldn't, if my dossier on him was accurate.

I opened everything flammable and kicked it over, then hotwired round the transformer on the MAM and fed in direct 120V AC, more to make sure that no one else picked up the YPE than anything else. After the two big vacuum tubes ruptured and the resistors were smoldering, I pitched it against a drooling can of solvent. It went up with a roar and I got out quick.

The house was a bit trickier—he turned out to have a safe that was supposed to be good to 500° C. Fortunately he hadn't invested in one that was blast-proof, and I got the door blown—I guess he was only afraid of fire.

There were copies of all the working drawings in there, in a couple of cardboard boxes that almost filled it. I took those upstairs, and put them on the bed, then got the curtains lit. Flames were beginning to lick out one window of the Q-hut, I saw, so I got going.

I was most of the way downstairs when I heard a little yowl. The old slogan is, "If they were innocent, they wouldn't be bystanders," and by and large we do work that way, so what I did next was professionally inexcusable.

I trotted back up the stairs. The bedroom was going to go up in a hurry, the bed and some stuff on top of the dresser already caught, some little places on the carpet near the window about to go.

Right in the middle of it was a mother cat—she must have been Redman's—trying to get her kitten out.

I jumped in. I knew I was losing time and that firemen and porkers could be here any minute, but I couldn't leave them like that. She seemed to know I didn't mean any harm when I scooped them up. Probably she had just always been able to trust people, I thought as I ran down the stairs with them—strange idea.

I just wanted to let them out the door, but she started to struggle as soon as we got downstairs. I got her out the door anyway, despite some scratches from what felt like eight little razors on her back feet, and started to close it.

She left the kitten and raced back in. Where there's one kitten, there's several, I realized.

I went back up after her—I know that's crazy. Redman was out in the Q-hut, dead, and I hadn't been that worked up about that routine part of the job, but here I was saving his cats.

By the time I got back to the bedroom she was standing at the door and wailing. The heat was more of a solid, painful presence than anything else. I squinted, eyes watering, took a deep breath in the hall, and went in. I hope I had guessed right that they'd be under the bed.

The flames from the bed were a foot high in places, and the covers were on fire right down to the floor. I had never been anywhere so hot before. I knelt on the floor, noting abstractedly that it was hot enough to scorch my knees, not a real burn, just like a sunburn. This had better be my last trip.

Mother Cat was still at the door, meowing; the little ones were at the end of the bed, right where I was looking, unable to come out on the hot floor and being slow-cooked by the burning bed over them. I scooped them up in my arms, counting five, and got up. My scalp was itching and my knees and the soles of my feet hurt—I had the eerie feeling that my hair was on fire, but my arms were too full of cats to check.

Eyes almost shut, I made it out the door and down the stairs, Mother Cat following and mewing the whole way. I kicked the door open and set all the kittens down on the stoop.

The mother was looking up at me, and I reached down and stroked her. She should have plenty of time to get them moved somewhere, I thought; but, just in case, I moved the whole crew down to the driveway culvert. She seemed to appreciate it—I got purred at for my trouble—but I had really overstayed my welcome and a half dozen neighbors could well have seen me. I was six blocks away before the sirens started, but that's cutting it a lot closer than I like to.

I kept thinking about that mother cat. Maybe it was some effect of the Crazy, but her expression—well, I know it sounds dumb, but she looked a lot like my mother had when the Blue Berets suddenly burst into Camp St. Paul, with a couple weeks to spare—for us.

On my way back to the hotel, I slipped into the bathroom at an ice cream stand and changed into the clothes from my kit bag. I carried the ones I'd been wearing for the Redman job a couple more blocks and threw them into the back seat of an abandoned car—not orthodox procedure, but effective enough for the few days I had to avoid detection. I went up the back way to my room. It took a lot of washing and an impromptu haircut before I felt ready for my date.

The place she'd picked for dinner was a nice open-air place. The sun had just set; and, power being expensive, the stars were unbelievably sharp and clear. For the occasion I wore a summer norman—light blue ice-cream suit with white shirt, red tie, and straw boater. She was in pretty much a copy of what she'd worn that afternoon.

The food wasn't much—synthosugar is a big Arizona product controlling a high percentage of jobs and an even higher percentage of state legislators, so it was all miserably sweet. On the other hand, the dancing shadows from the amber glass-jar candles made the little place seem almost as romantic as it was supposed to be, and I was definitely not lonely; the evening was a success before it began as far as I was concerned.

"How long will you be in Tucson, John?"

"Another week, maybe. Our Air Force wants me to look over a couple of new fighter-control programs; we're taking a bigger share of peacekeeping in the next UN Five Year Plan. You'll be starting school again in September?"

"Yeah."

The conversation lagged through most of the meal, allowing me to concentrate on the wilted salad and spotty potatoes more than I wanted to. There's always that fear in any public place that there's a bug around, or maybe your waiter is a Nose. Mary Lynn probably didn't know enough to be afraid in a hotel room; since I had swept mine regularly, I wasn't worried. The bugspotter hadn't found anything much above random numbers in weeks.

Dessert came, orange gelatin with whipped cream, and I was still working on the safe small talk. "Do you like children?"

"I don't know. A lot of them in my class are very polite, really well-trained." She let her voice drop. "Here's hoping when they hit puberty they go at it like bunnies."

"Sorry—I forgot you deal with them professionally."

"I'd love to have some of my own." She had slipped one shoe off; I felt a warm, clean touch as she ran her foot up into my pant leg. She was smiling.

"Well, not in the restaurant, certainly." I was about to whisper that she ought to be more careful, but she held a finger up. "This place has been bugswept," she said. "They do put a lot of plainclothes boys in here all the time but no one's close enough to hear us. And as for this," and her foot slid up and down my shin like an agitated gerbil, "unmarried schoolteachers have to worry about getting fingered as lesbians. This will go down on my record, if anyone's watching, as regrettable but harmless and healthy."

The band was starting up; most of the dances of the last seventy years were illegal, so I brushed up on my foxtrot and waltz that night. Afterwards, there wasn't much hope of smuggling her up into my hotel at night, and she lived with three other girls, so I just walked her home. We held hands and talked about her childhood. I didn't talk about mine.

"How did you know the place was bugswept?" I asked suddenly, keeping it casual as we got to one lonely corner.

"Same way I know you're a Monitor. I know what to look for."

Denying it wouldn't do much good. And I could hardly kill her on a public street, even a deserted one—too many potential eyes around. "How did you arrive at that conclusion?" I asked.

"You carry an autosyringe with an aphrodisiac. That's not exactly a drugstore staple around here."

It's also not general knowledge, so what I had here was either a porker or a Nose, and one pretty well up in the hierarchy.

"By the way," she added, "don't let me alarm you." I braced, waiting for the hand on my shoulder. "I'm not with the government; I command Resistance activities in the Tucson area."

Well, at least that explained that. Assuming she wasn't just a Nose with a good story for getting information. I gave her a hug and a kiss. "Your place is a couple of blocks up, isn't it?"

Mary Lynn nodded, and the soft curls falling around her face bobbed gently. For a second I wanted to be anywhere, anywhen, anyone else, or at least just alone, really alone, with her on this deserted street in the desert. "Still going to take me home?" she asked.

"Yeah. I'll be back in touch in a day or two, though."

I was lying, of course; it's routine in a situation like that. There had been a drinking buddy in Magnitogorsk who was in some sort of Marxist revival group, and I'd had to lose that contact too. Aiding the Resistance is not our job. As long as the fanatic governments of the world are in no position to threaten the authority of the UN, we stay out. That's what "respect for sovereignty" is supposed to mean, anyway.

Besides, there was one way to be reasonably sure she wasn't a Nose. If I could walk away unrestrained and unfollowed from her door, she either wasn't one or she was much more subtle than they usually get.

At the door I held her once again, enjoying the heavy, warm feel of her body through the crisp cleanness of the norman. Then I kissed her goodbye and left.

She passed the test.

I had to take a few precautions, anyway; that night I switched hotels and cover ID, including hair and eye color. The next day, early, I got through the phone modems to the files at Tucson airport and got my old ID onto a flight and created a new record of my arrival.

Still, it almost seemed a waste. One more ID change for one more day—all I had to do in Tucson was see Harriman. But caution counts, and I'd hate to get caught with just seventy-three days left to go.

Harriman's office was stereotypical for an American businessman today—completely afunctional, a little puddle of luxury behind a solid wood door. The carpet felt like grass, the walls were decorated with good, imported holos, and the desk looked to stretch a block in either direction. Most of it, of course, was basically a bar anyway. Behind him there were two big glass sliding doors, a brilliantly green landscaped balcony, and a brown expanse of mobile home courts, probably about thirty-five years old.

Harriman himself was going bald, but not badly, and had a big shock of silver hair that was probably blond some years back. His suit was visibly London cut—probably from London at that, despite the American tags he'd no doubt had sewn in. There were a few too many rings on his fingers for my taste, and his tan was deep and rich; a lifetime of those tans had given him skin like old leather, well-oiled and tough. The bright blue eyes, my information said, got to be that color the same way mine did—one more high-cost illegal-but-tolerated import.

For once I was looking forward to one of these things. Not that they're ordinarily that bad—get the information, make arrangements, forward information, get out of town, easy. Just usually they're both boring and risky at the same time, which is a bad combination. Today, though, I wanted to spend my time doing exclusively things I'd done a hundred times before.

"Come in, come in," he said. "I have what you need here. Would you like a drink?" The only decent liquor in the United States hides under executive desks, so I said yes.

"Right here." He handed me the standard list, the one that told me who had phoned or written St. Peter's Motors with technological ideas in the last month. Even though the Treaty of Halifax's secret provisions kept the number of places in engineering school drastically low, there was enough free-floating technical information for any basement tinkerer to cook up all kinds of things. Especially nowadays, when cheap, sophisticated components were making a renaissance of bicycle-shop engineering everywhere in the world.

About half the list was cranks—pills to turn water into gasoline, perpetual-motion machines, and so one. Another third was trivial, bag-of-tricks stuff that hurt nobody. That last one in six, though, was serious high technology with military potential. The Quarantined powers had been disarmed of nuclear weapons and banned from space—but that wasn't enough. The world had almost blown to hell. . . .

"What do you do with that anyway?" he asked as I photographed it.

"What do you think?" Damn it, they *know*. There must be someone who can put things like this together with things like Redman.

"I just wondered why this guy Wilson is still around. That's a real threat. The one with the electric grease—that could cut into our market for machine part sensors."

"He's barking up the wrong tree. Using a piezoelectric effect in a thin fluid film isn't economically possible across any reasonable range of constraints, according to the evaluation team. He's bright—so we'd rather he kept chasing wild geese."

"Why don't you just, hmm, deal with him anyway? He's close enough to some of the stuff we import—"

"Kill him? Not for your markets. As long as it won't help your government break Quarantine, we have no quarrel. We may be your sole source of products, and you may be our biggest distributor in the United States, but you're still a drop in the bucket compared with the world market."

He drummed his fingers on the desk, the rings giving a little castanet effect. "Maybe," he said, "and mind you I'm not religious and I wish we could still call ourselves *General* Motors—maybe someone else ought to run the world. It doesn't seem right that the two countries with the greatest potential—"

"When you did run it, what did you do with it?"

There was an awkward silence. "If the Resistance was better funded or better armed—" I began.

He shook his head. "We've talked about it. Too many of our executives have a sweet deal going; free enterprise is more fun with no competitors. We could never get the consensus—or the guts—to do it." He stared out the window.

Maybe starting to like people was a symptom of Monitor's Crazy. Hastily I got the conversation back to business. "Two firms were caught in Utah last week. You'd better tighten security."

He nodded. "We already have. Those guys were caught by the porkers who got the bright idea of following all the trucks to see what got loaded and unloaded. We move all our imports around in-plant, with no separate warehouses. We should be okay."

"What about worker blackmail?"

"Everyone in a sensitive job is part gook. If we get turned in, they'll have to run for their lives."

It went back to small talk, harmless small talk. The deal was going to be the same as long as conditions were the same; names for us, imported parts for them. Meanwhile, Harriman and I could have a good drink together. Strictly routine.

But I was getting close to tears by the end of it, though I don't think he saw.

I knew I wasn't being followed, and Mary Lynn's place wasn't staked out; that's the total of mitigating circumstances I can offer.

She'd mentioned, sometime last night, that she was the only one with a bedroom to herself. I found her window and rapped on it. She rolled out of bed, drew a gun from the table, and had me covered in one smooth movement that I had to admire. I raised my hands.

"John Hare, with a little editing, Mary Lynn," I said.

She pulled up the sash. "Come on in, stranger. Sorry about the hardware. My roommates will keep quiet—we can talk."

I climbed in. We stood there hugging for a while; as far as I was concerned, a hundred years would have been short for it.

It was a little room; the bed and dresser took up two thirds of it, and the ceiling was a bare seven feet. To judge from the pressed-board moldings, it wasn't much more than sixty years old. The walls were hung with bland landscapes, plus a couple of religious posters that conspicuously faced the window.

Several glasses turned out to be hiding in her top dresser drawer; we got two of them out. She carefully unpinned the JESUS WILL MAKE IT ANEW poster to reveal a real honest-to-God prewar pre-Repro bottle of Wild Turkey, less than half gone. Good liquor twice in a day; not bad, not bad at all. We settled back to do some cuddling and sipping. "Celebration," Mary Lynn explained. "I figured you were gone for good."

"I would have been if I'd been following rules."

"Yeah. Rules." She took a sip and sighed. "I get so tired of handing out 'Restore the Bill of Rights' pamphlets to be left on the shelves in public restrooms. The least they could do is allow us some assassinations and church bombings." She pushed her tangled hair up onto her head, then let it fall, shaking it from her eyes. "I wish I could leave with you. How soon do you go?"

"Some months. I wish you could too." I decided to switch over to my revelation story, the one we tell when people find out we're Monitors. At least it was closer to the truth. I settled back, looking up at the ceiling and sliding an arm under her. "You asked about Tokyo. Well, to tell the truth, I was born in the States. When I was two, my mother ran off with a Japanese businessman." (Actually, we only ran to San Bernadino; Dad was an attorney, and a sansei.) I grew up in a big, clean, healthy city, one that wasn't falling apart. I'd love to show it to you."

She turned her head. I could feel her breath on my neck and smell the strong soap on her hair—I remembered that I had meant to give her the shampoo, which wouldn't fit my next cover anyway. Her lips grazed the skin of my neck for a moment before she asked, "What would we do there?"

"Maybe a long walk down one of the malls, first, with a stop in a *kisaten* for tea and pastry."

"There's a film I have to show the kids. It shows Tokyo jammed with people, crowded and miserable. Everyone wears old clothes."

"Sure they do. That footage is older than either of us. Forty years ago, say in the midseventies, a lot of working people in Tokyo were sleeping several to a room. But now it's the garden city of Japan—Ohira's Legacy is what we call it—wide malls and parks, lots of trees and open air, and *quiet*—everything moves on maglev within city limits."

"What am I wearing? One of those jerkin-and-skirt things?"

"Definitely. You have great legs."

"You have an evil mind. What do we do that night?"

"Well—"

"Evil mind!" She giggled.

"Okay, we go to a play or the movies. After that we go to some little cafe where the band plays the Tsukuba Sound."

"What's that?"

"It started out in the artists' community that grew up in Tsukuba, the science city. It's jazz, descended from some things Brubeck did with impressionism, but with a more explicit blues base, and some heavy Japanese influence, of course."

"I don't know anything about jazz."

"Even better. We go to a cafe to hear a good group, and stay there till two in the morning while I tell you all about it. Then we go home and party with the band and a couple of poets I knew in school. For breakfast I fix huge plates of eggs and ham and we all sit around wolfing it down and talking music and literature and politics. Everybody except the band is late to work, but it's Friday and that's normally a half day anyway, when nobody gets much of anything accomplished. That night we do it all again."

I looked over at her; she was near tears. I suddenly felt terrible, having run on like that. After all, for me there was the Extensive Debriefing, the period of intensive psychotherapy that would hopefully get the worst of the experience behind me, and then the whole rest of my life in the outside world. What did she have to look forward to?

I almost missed what she said next. "Could I come if I married you?"

At the time it seemed a perfectly reasonable question. "I don't know. They might get sticky about it, but if I completed my mission they wouldn't fuss much. If the UN is so worried about what happens in the Quarantined countries, I'm sure they can find somebody else to look into it for them." I stretched. "Anyway, how could you get permission to marry a foreigner?"

"If you promised to convert and become a missionary—"

"My papers wouldn't pass for that. They didn't back-cover me for the years before I 'existed.'"

She nodded, seeming to accept it. "What's your real name?"

The Crazy had me, all right; I told her. "John Yamada. I took my adoptive stepfather's name."

She giggled. "Wanted, John Yamada, tall Japanese, currently blue-eyed. Alert Christians can spot the yellow Jesus-hater by his hissing accent."

My teeth clamped. A wave of nausea rolled over me. "There used to be a lot of Americans with names like Yamada, Mary Lynn. Where are they now? We don't even have an accurate count of the deaths. If the UN troops hadn't turned up when they did, I'd be among them because of my mother's connection."

Dad, I thought of you then, the crazy thing—maybe the Crazy thing—was that it was baseball I thought of—sitting on the couch with you watching the A's, out in the backyard where you taught me shortstop—your old position for UC-Irvine.

I was squeezing the mattress edge hard. I took a breath and relaxed. "I'm sorry, but that wasn't funny."

She got very quiet.

"Look," I said, "I lost my temper. I'm sorry. If we do find a way to get you to Japan, though, you'll hear worse, even with political refugee status."

"What about Australia?"

"It's a nice place, but it's not home." Not that Japan had been much of one, either, when I got there knowing only "arigato" and "sayonara."

"I guess you could get there eventually."

"I suppose I'd have to. Would you really marry me to get me out of here?"

"If you can figure out a way." I finished my glass. "Maybe I should just slip out like a gentleman."

"Would your papers stand up to a paternity suit if you gave in and married me quick?"

"Paternity suit?"

"You know the rule is use-it-or-lose-it. There're fertility drugs in the drinking water. I have abortifacients, but I haven't taken any yet."

"Mary Lynn," I said slowly, "I've had a vasectomy." She didn't know what that was; it had been illegal too long. I told her, and added that we were required to have them. She started out looking disappointed, twisting her hand in her lap.

She shook her head slowly. "Every goddam male in the world is castrated."

I started to explain, but she slapped me. I spread my hands, not knowing what to say or do. She hissed, low and fast, "If the UN is so goddam worried about the preachers and the mess they're making of this country, why don't you send the Blue Berets to straighten it out? Some of us are dying, and some of us might as well be dead, and all you can send is a few castrated spies!"

I could have talked all about respect for sovereignty and so forth, but since she was screaming at me, I didn't think she was in the mood. Her roommates might wake up and not understand, and she hadn't told me if her neighbors were okay. I left in a hurry; she threw a glass after me.

I didn't even get to give her the shampoo.

The next day I was Robert Angus, businessman from Indianapolis, trying to establish some contacts in Missoula. His hair was brown and his eyes were green. I settled in at the hotel I'm in now.

I came to this country to find myself, but all I've found out is I'm not here. They're all pretty crazy, too. If you lived in this loneliness all your life, well, you can imagine.

RESTRICTED TO THE NECESSARY

This story got more angry letters than anything I ever published, including Kaleidoscope Century. *Apparently psychopathic killers are a little disturbing and all that, but many more people are just not ready for gay wolf sex.*

FROM: Captain Rwanda Goodall, TNS *Boaz*
TO: Admiral Taildancer, Western Spiral Arm Command
SUBJECT: Routine copy of onship misdemeanor court martial—3rd Lt. Pyotr Nakasone, TN. Confession transcript w/ decision attached. Cf. documents pertaining to Eric Pastiglio case, transmitted previously.
ACTION REQUESTED: Routine approval.
DATE: 5/4/3496

They tell me that this is pretty much routine; in fact the skipper said if it was up to her, she'd just let it go, but it's there in the camera record, so they have to either investigate me or have me confess. If I confess, the worst I can get is five jolts. Maybe I'll get less, maybe just a reprimand. I'm hoping.

That doesn't sound real professional, but they said if I just let it all dump out, then Doc Sealeater can evaluate it easier, and of course I am a little bit worked up—it's pretty upsetting to get your permanent commission at ten hundred and be up on a charge at fourteen hundred. Anyway, if I can get this done by fifteen hundred, Captain Goodall says we can get the sentence carried out before dinner, so at least it will all be over.

I *am* pretty upset. I've known Eric—I guess that's I *had known* Eric, but it's still hard to think of him being gone—like I say, I'd known him for a long time. We roomed together in the primates' dorm at the Academy for all four years, and senior year we took a first medal in human doubles tennis. We'd been through all the usual stuff together, I guess, and crammed for every test together, and in a lot of ways we were like brothers.

That was good for Eric because he didn't have much of a gift for making friends. Eric was a nice guy, but shy, so he just hung around me most of the time, and then after a while people would get to know him. [TRANSCRIPT EDIT INSERT FROM EXAMINER: Note that Eric Pastiglio {Manifest #22, Pro. Com. 4/5/3496, deceased 5/2/3496} according to Academy record showed distinct preferences for primate company, but that introductions by Pyotr Nakasone {Manifest #20, Pro. Com. 4/5/3496, Per. Com. 5/2/3496} show no such pattern. In conformance with hypothesis of no contagion of Anti-Doctrinal ideas. Signature Cmdr. Sealeater, MD, TN. END INSERT; RESUME TRANSCRIPT EDIT] One thing I will say—he never talked about his home world much. I knew Scyros had only been under the Doctrine for about 150 years, but I never saw anything in Eric's behavior to suggest anything wrong.

At least not till today. God, that's a morbid thing to say about a friend. [TRANSCRIPT EDIT INSERT FROM EXAMINER: Actually part of a normal shock/grief response. Self-evaluation is excessively harsh, but not pathologically so. Signature Cmdr. Sealeater, MD, TN. END INSERT; RESUME TRANSCRIPT EDIT]

So, anyway, we survived the last semester of Jaynesian psychomechanics together too—for once I was the good student and he had trouble—and just when we thought it was good-bye for ten years or so, berths got reshuffled and we both ended up on the *Boaz* for our first mission. I'm sure it was a relief to Eric to have a friend aboard, but it was a relief to me too, and besides, I had worried a little about Eric's being able to make friends with me not around. Even with me there, he seemed uncomfortable around Thickmane, the other provisional commission on board, and that was strange because Thickmane is a great guy. But I put it down to the quirky moodiness that came over Eric a lot.

All three of us provisional commissions had been working since we lifted, of course, on our final xenoethnographic problem. Hardly anyone ever flunks the FXEP if he works at all, but the problem itself was so challenging that "anyone with a modicum of intellectual curiosity would feel compelled to work his tail off on it," as Thickmane put it. "Of course, you guys seem to have done that already."

I set a bowl of standard chow down for him, then got one for myself and sat down with it in my lap. "I must have misplaced mine," I said. "They made us check them at the door in the primates' dorm. Makes it easier to sit down."

Thickmane grinned at us and ate. Eric was quiet as always, so I asked, "How's yours going?"

He shrugged. "I thought I had a good answer before and just had to write it up. I kind of got hit with an idea for a completely different answer, one I'd rather use, so I want to work on that."

"That'll be tough," Thickmane said, licking his chops. "You want to talk about it, Eric? We're allowed to compare notes, you know, as long as what we give is basically our own answer."

He shook his head. "It's a really strange idea, and I think I need to work on it awhile to really understand it myself. Like I said, I already have an answer, and if this doesn't pan out by twenty-one hundred, I'll just write up what I have. Thanks for the offer, though, Thickmane. I might call you in later."

"Feel free. How's it going with you, Pyotr?"

I shrugged. "Think I've got it. If you wouldn't mind taking a look—"

"Sure. In exchange for a good brushing." He scratched his ear with his back paw.

"Happy to," I said. "Sure you don't want to compare notes, Eric?"

"Not just yet. See you guys." He went to his cabin; Thickmane and I went to mine.

Thickmane, of course, had his answer in perfect order. He was third in XE in our class, anyway. "But yours is really good, Pyotr. Best thing I've ever seen you do—this'll pass you with no trouble at all. Now, if you don't mind using that opposable thumb of yours—"

I picked up the brush. "You've got it. Head, back, or belly first?"

"Start with the head." He winked and wagged his tail significantly. "If we finish up with the belly, maybe something will happen. If you'll help me slip off this voder—"

I unsnapped it and pulled the harness off over his head. Without the voder, of course, he wouldn't be able to speak, but it was pretty clear we wouldn't be talking much, and the things *are* awkward up close.

I tugged his ears a little, just to flirt, and started to brush out his shaggy mane. I've always been a little partial to wolves anyway, and

Thickmane is the most beautiful wolf I've ever seen. As I ran the brush along his back, I nuzzled his face; he turned and licked my nipples, his hot, strong breath blowing in my face.

That was all I could stand. I set the brush down and turned around to bring my face between the big, shaggy legs. The big wolf lay down beside me, the soft fur on his snout brushing my thigh, and then we were lost in making love. It was incredible—I'm not sure that belongs in a Navy report, but it was, and the doc did say everything. As I've said, I like wolves anyway, and Thickmane is a terrific lover.

I asked Captain Goodall if she thought my feelings about wolves were weird before I started this confession. She said that's just in the range of normal preference—in fact she said she'd always had a big thing for dolphins, which is awkward because few of them like gorillas, supposedly because the body hair gets soggy, wet, and cold. After that business with Eric, I guess we'll all be feeling weird for a while. It feels kind of creepy to think of him up there all alone in his cabin, working on *that,* while we were rolling on the mat.

The main reason I mentioned that, though, is that Thickmane's been feeling guilty, and I want to get it on the record that I don't think there was anything we could have done. Eric stayed in his cabin with the door curtain pulled the whole time. Even if Thickmane and I had been around, chances are Eric wouldn't have talked to us about it. I think Thickmane's problem is that he feels responsible for everything.

Of course, part of the reason he's so much fun on a mat is that he's so dominant . . . but I suppose that doesn't belong in a record of this kind, either. [TRANSCRIPT EDIT INSERT FROM EXAMINER: Note significance: attribution of pattern of behavior is to individual personality. Tends to confirm no transference from Eric Pastiglio {Manifest #22, Pro. Com. 4/5/3496, deceased 5/2/3496}. Signature Cmdr. Sealeater, MD, TN. END INSERT; RESUME TRANSCRIPT EDIT]

I do remember that we talked about him for a while, lying there in the afterglow. "I don't know, just kind of an odd talent," I said. "He's great at deducible math. A thousand years ago, when living organisms were still doing physics, he'd have been top of the class."

"If he's so good at math, why did he have such a bad time in Jaynesian psychomechanics?" Thickmane asked. He rolled over closer; I scratched his mane affectionately.

"Well," I said, feeling a little disloyal, "he isn't really very good at math. He's good at deducible—if you can get an answer by doing it step by step, Eric will get it. But Jaynesian is all adeducible—no pathway to the answer, by definition, right? And he doesn't seem to have any intuition. He does all the routines—memorizes the relations, visualizes, meditates—and still nothing pops, and if it does, it's wrong. Certainly, he doesn't have your gift."

"Lucky guesses."

"Once is luck. Two hundred times back to back is talent." I pressed the tip of his ear between my lips.

"Mmm. Scratch behind that one, will you? Yeah. I suppose I do have a gift that way. You're not such a slouch yourself." He wiggled against me, that warm wolf smell strong on my face, the soft hair of his underside brushing my thighs and belly.

I thought of starting something, but it was close to dinner. "Well," I admitted, "I guess so. Part of his problem, though, isn't really the math at all. He just doesn't find any of the stuff obvious. He even had trouble with Krendl's Theorem. And that should be obvious as soon as you look around and notice that none of the intelligent species averages any smarter than any other."

"Wasn't he from—"

If it had been anyone but Thickmane, I'd have snapped at them out of habit. I was used to defending Eric—it certainly wasn't his fault where he was from. But somehow the question wasn't so personal this time. "Yeah. He's from Scyros. One of the last Anti-doctrinal worlds to fall. But his family's been Inner Doctrine for a century."

Thickmane shrugged. "I didn't mean he'd picked anything up. I just meant he hadn't seen many intelligent beings other than humans before he came to the Academy—Scyros is what, ninety-eight percent human? You or I have always met plenty of minds like our own wearing different bodies, so for us Jaynesian stuff is obvious. If a brain is big and complex enough for a mind to run in it, we expect a mind to be there. Eric knows that, but he hasn't experienced it to the extent we have."

Looking back now—that was only about twenty-four hours—I can't believe how close we were to the truth. I guess Thickmane isn't the only one who feels bad, at that.

Anyway, Thickmane and I started talking about other things, and then we went down to dinner. We were planning to ask Eric sometime— it seemed interesting to have grown up around just one sapient species—but not especially soon. Like I said, we had no idea. [TRAN-SCRIPT EDIT INSERT FROM EXAMINER: Note again that causality is attrib-

uted to environment. Tends to confirm no contagion from Eric Pastiglio
{Manifest #22, Pro. Com. 4/5/3496, deceased 5/2/3496}. Signature
Cmdr. Sealeater, MD, TN. END INSERT; RESUME TRANSCRIPT EDIT]

Eric didn't even eat supper in procos' mess; he just popped in,
grabbed a field ration, and turned to go. He looked kind of haunted,
and we asked, but he shrugged and smiled. "I still don't know. I'm
thinking of taking a stimtab and just staying up all night."

Thickmane shook his furry head. "Not a good idea—you lose mental
efficiency—"

"Not that much. First forty-eight hours you're still at ninety-five percent. That should be good enough. And I need those hours."

Did riding a stim all the way to the next morning put him over the
edge? I guess Thickmane and I will always wonder if we should have argued harder. But we wished him luck, and that was the last we saw of
him till the next morning.

In practice, the FXEP is an oral; after all the calculations and notes and
graphs, they give you three minutes to get your basic idea across, and
then refer to your written work only if there's some question. It had to
be given, of course, in the ship's commons because that was the only
place everyone could meet—we have an officer corps of one gorilla, two
orangs, a dolphin, two orcas, and an elephant.

As we lined up to go in, Eric grinned at us. "I think it paid off," he
said. "I have a really different solution, but one that's *so* elegant . . ."

"That's good," I said.

"It should be interesting," Thickmane added.

Eric didn't say anything; I guess it was clear we didn't want to hear
what we'd be hearing soon enough.

We sat and stared at the wall for a while; I was getting more and more
wound up. They give you the permanent commission the moment you
pass, so chances were that within the hour we'd all be celebrating, but
meanwhile it was nerve-wracking.

After a long time, the door opened and Chief Engineer Kipling
poked his head out the door, his snout fiddling with his voder as it always is. I think he's just never happy with his voice. "Follow me, please,"
he said.

Eric flashed a quick thumbs-up, Thickmane wagged his tail, and we
followed Kipling through the door. For a moment I wondered how
dolphins and orcas handled this, then I realized they probably just

waited at the mouth of the swimming tube that leads into the commons.

He led us to the front of the room, where we could face the entire gathering, including the doc, the pilot, and the second engineer in the tank. "As chief scientist, I will state the problem," Klarman said, hooking his legs over the table and stroking his orange beard. He picked up a card and read:

"'The hypothetical world for the FXEP has two sapient species, both already past the Jaynesian transformation. Species **A** herds Species **B** for meat. The **B**s are also used as tutors for the **A**s' children. There is no record of any act of violence against the **A**s by the **B**s, even in cases where, for example, a long-time family tutor is slaughtered for the table on the whim of a child, or where **B**s are ordered to slaughter their own children or parents.'

"You were asked to identify a specific step you would take toward rendering the data intelligible."

Captain Goodall rose, resting on her knuckles, and said, "By tradition, we proceed in order of Academy class standing, so we'll begin with Provisional Commission Thickmane. What is a specific step you would take to make the data intelligible?"

Thickmane sat straight and proud; I had done a good job of brushing him that morning. "I would tend to doubt the given data. There's a good chance that some kind of rebellion, probably symbolic, actually *does* happen frequently and is being punished by killing and eating the rebels—but it's not apparent to outsiders. So I'd start by interviewing **A**s who had owned two different groups of **B**s—one group that had been slaughtered and one group that had died of natural causes. Differences in testimony might well tell me what behavior by the **B**s constituted a hidden rebellion."

There was a general murmur of voders in the room. Klarman nodded. "That's genuinely excellent. You've passed the exam."

Captain Goodall came forward. "Stand to attention." She drew a third lieutenant's badge on a clip from her pocket belt, removed the proco's badge from Thickmane's collar, and hung the new badge in its place. "Welcome to the permanent crew, as second scientist. As juniormost member so far today, take your seat there." She pointed.

Thickmane got up and padded over to the spot; I noticed they had already put a rug down there, and that there were two empty chairs next to it.

There was a brief burst of applause from the officers; Captain Goodall nodded, and they were quiet. "Provisional commission Pyotr Nakasone, please state your answer."

I swallowed hard. I knew abstractly that there were always many thousands of possible answers to a xenoethnographic problem, but Thickmane's had been so well received that I felt intimidated. "Well," I began, "I would suggest examining the religious texts and legends of the **B**s and comparing them with the traditional recipes of the **A**s, to see if similar rituals are prescribed. One working hypothesis is that the **B**s are able to rationalize the situation by regarding the **A**s as divine. This seems particularly likely because of some information in the supplementary packet: the main **B** civilization was destroyed four centuries ago by technologically superior **A**s in a surprise attack. There is some analogy to the American human civilizations under the Iberian conquest. I think it possible that the **B**s have been trained to regard being cooked as a high honor."

Everyone, including Thickmane, nodded. It was very quiet. Then Lieutenant Sunsplash, the pilot, slapped her tail hard on the surface, and everyone applauded. "Good job," the skipper said. She came forward quickly. "Stand to attention. Welcome to the permanent crew, as third pilot." She reached out and unclipped the proco insignia from my shirt, and attached the new third lieutenant's insignia. Everyone applauded again.

"Have a seat," she said, pointing to the chair next to Thickmane. I went and sat next to him, and now only Eric was left up in front.

There was something strange about the way Eric leaned forward—a bit too eagerly. Captain Goodall didn't seem to notice, though; she simply said, "Provisional Commission Eric Pastiglio, please state your answer."

"I also found my answer in the supplementary information," Eric said. "I think there's a genetic determination involved. The **A** species is descended from solitary predators—similar to terrestrial big cats or tyrannosaurs. The **B**s are descended from herbivores, herd animals, kind of like kangaroos. A lot of herbivore species have a definite pecking order, a 'bull of the herd' system. I think that quite possibly the **B**s have a genetic predisposition for being dominated."

There was a shocked silence. My head was buzzing and I wanted to vomit. Even through the voder, the skipper's voice was strangled and ill. "Did you ever hear such an idea before?"

"No, I—it came to me. If you consider the evidence—"

Captain Goodall's voder whistled arrest-at-once; we all grabbed Eric. His confident smile collapsed; he was limp. "What did I do?"

The captain started to answer but couldn't find any words. Over the speakers, Doc Sealeater began, "The pattern of thought—shows certain tendencies—" and faded out.

Klarman took a deep breath. "You may as well hear this, since your classmates will, anyway. It has taken us a thousand years since the Age of Awakening to establish the Inner Doctrine. And yet you contradicted its First Principle: The nature of a sapient's consciousness is determined only by itself. In other words, you were given that the species were both sapient; their physical attributes should have been of no interest to you. There are at least fifty possible solutions, like those of your classmates, that would deal only with relations, messages, beliefs, training—and you came to none of those. If you can arrive at the conclusion you did, then your education is a complete failure because the one thing that we know for sure is that the shape of the body has nothing—*nothing!*—to do with the mind that it houses."

Eric was well-trained; I'll give him that. He bowed his head in quiet submission and said, "I understand. I flunked. But why am I under arrest?"

Klarman looked as sick as I felt, but he gritted his teeth and explained, quoting the Book of the Great Peace. "'The moment that the shape of the body is presumed to determine the character of the soul, you have begun the irreversible fall into speciesism; therefore, brothers, never presume to know the individual in the absence of individual data.'" He gestured at the triangle on the wall. "*They* were the victims of your kind of thinking. Not one of them was ever awakened before the last one was gone; what they might have told us of the world around us died with them."

Eric stared up at the equilateral triangle, into the eyes of the blue whale, the pygmy gorilla, and the Siberian tiger. Tears gushed from his eyes.

As we started to move him, he stiffened and fought, but of course the skipper and the two orangs were much too strong for him. The rest of us were only needed to keep him from getting a handhold or grabbing something he could use as a weapon.

We dragged him down the corridor as he punched out at us, sobbing and moaning; I hope I never hear that sound again in my worst nightmare. I think it wasn't until the last moment that he knew what was happening to him. Certainly, Thickmane and I were just helping the crew; we'd heard rumors in the Academy, of course, but I don't think any of us remembered them just then. I hope Eric didn't, anyway.

When we got to the airlock, he grabbed the inside doorframe, down low, and held on. Without thinking much, I kicked his hand two—no, three, definitely three—times, finally grinding the hard little lumps of his fingers under my heel until he let go. [TRANSCRIPT EDIT INSERT FROM EXAMINER: Camera record shows that Nakasone kicked three times but hit the fingers only twice. Note the basic concern for truth even when dealing with recent high-stress memory, indicative that there has been no permanent injury. Signature Cmdr. Sealeater, MD, TN. END INSERT; RESUME TRANSCRIPT EDIT] They dragged him in, throwing him against the back wall; the captain drew her knife and covered him as the rest of us got out of the airlock. Then she backed out and threw the door-close lever.

That ought to complete my confession, which is supposed to be for maltreatment of a prisoner. I guess this is beside the point. But I feel like I should include it for some reason, and Doc Sealeater seems to think so too: just before the door slammed shut, Eric started yelling something about being the original—I didn't get the original what—and then screamed, *"Animals! Animals! Animals!"*

Just like that. Three times. I don't know what he meant: the orcas, wolves, and dolphins on board eat dry food like the rest of us—on a little exploration ship like this, there's no room for livestock or pets—so there weren't any animals on board. But then, considering how sick poor Eric was, I suppose that it didn't really mean anything.

I could still hear him screaming and pounding on the door for a second, but then Lieutenant Sunsplash dropped the ship out of hyper. We were suddenly weightless as we reentered normal space. Captain Goodall cycled the airlock; the exterior valves opened into space with a heavy, thudding sound. She hit the eject button, and we heard the unloader trip. Something bumped against the exterior door.

The exterior door slid closed, the air hissed back in, and it was quiet. The warning bell rang, and then weight came back as we returned to hyper.

I feel terrible. Sure, he was absolutely Anti-Doctrinal, and we had to get rid of him, but there was no excuse for kicking and stamping on his hand. We'd have gotten him out the door eventually without that. Dangerous as he potentially was, none of that was his fault. He had been raised on a planet full of weird ideas, and somehow one of them soaked in too deep to be washed out again. We only needed to get rid of him— not to hurt him.

That's a thought. When he screamed "Animals!" he probably meant me.

[FILE WITH: 1. Verdict (misdemeanor guilty). 2. Record of Reprimand. CLOSE FILE: AUTHORIZATION FOR ACTION: Cptn. Rwanda Goodall, TNS *Boaz*.]

ENRICO FERMI AND THE DEAD CAT

Here's another story that never found a home. Enrico Fermi is remembered for many things, such as the nuclear reactor and the atomic bomb, but one of the smaller ones was something he apparently posed in a lunch discussion group, the so-called Fermi Paradox—given how many habitable worlds there must be, and how long the odds are against our being the first civilization in the galaxy, where is everybody? Why aren't they already here?

From pole to pole, about five centimeters deep, the green scum covered the fourth planet from the red star. It floated on the oceans, raining down forever into their depths. It lay across the continents in thin green sheets, leaving only the highest mountaintops bare. It washed down rivers; at their mouths it clung to piers unused for a hundred thousand years. It blew on the wind against piles of rubble that were no longer buildings, stuck to the naked rock on plains that had once been deep in topsoil.

And the green film was all there was.

Each year there was less of it, for no circulating ecology fed it. It bled away to the ocean floor, or on the wind to the glaciers and mountaintops, each time losing forever some of the carbon and nitrogen fixed by the planet's former ecology.

Faintly at first, radio signals fell on the planet. Ancient genes woke from disuse and responded.

The green film coalesced and organized. Cells specialized; the film transformed itself into a single planetwide organism.

Mighty stalks of cellulose fiber, kilometers high, grew up in less than a decade. Long filaments ran over beaches and rocky coasts down into the sea, and membranes at their ends filtered in silver, gold, aluminum, and copper, which traveled a molecule at a time up the filaments to coat the outsides of the stalks. At the top of the stalks, leaves grew. Other organs grew deep into the ground, taking energy captured by the leaves and binding it into separated metals and great chambers filled with acid.

It took thirty years to finish growing. By then the signals were strong and clear, with one great dip in strength for ten twenty-fourths of each long cycle that might have suggested—had there been a mind to suggest it to—a world with its radio stations concentrated on two thirds of its lines of latitude.

The final phase of the genetic program activated. Great currents pulsed along the stalks in the shape of incoming signals, interrupted in a pattern read from the genes themselves.

After barely two years of this, the energy reserve exhausted, most of the few remaining bioavailable trace elements of the planet squandered, the great organism reverted within hours to green scum. It devoured its own towers and filaments and batteries, subsiding first into a thin remnant of the green film, then, over millennia, into mere spores.

The spores waited while ammonia and methane replaced free oxygen in the atmosphere, while rain and wind scoured the continents bare. Occasionally something flickered toward life, perhaps once in fifty thousand years; always it met a spore, and shortly became a spore itself. Eventually the sun went out.

Suddenly, among the normal static and background noise, there were bits of pieces of fifty-year-old television programs. Occasionally stray blips flickered in and out on older radars.

Then the EuroEar on the back side of the moon started getting it, and before anyone really had time to ask any questions, dozens of ground-based radio telescopes, even home-made ones, were picking it up.

So there was no hope of keeping the transmissions secret. Within a week almost all newspapers were printing copies of the message, showing that the stops always fell in pairs and that the pattern of stops repeated identically every few hours, regardless of what old broadcast it had been superimposed on. Some used bars, some used Morse Code notation, but all offered prizes for the best "decoding."

Within two weeks the prizes were all claimed. Any number of biologists had noted that the four possible pair values—short-short, short-long, long-short, and long-long—could be assigned to the four nucleosides on a strand of DNA. And when the translation was set to

thymine=short-short
adenine=short-long
cytosine=long-short
guanine=long-long,

the DNA resembled that of several terrestrial viruses.

There were a few nut letters in the papers, of course, and one religious publisher brought out a confusing, badly written and badly printed book, *Satan's Spawn from Space,* but mostly people just watched to see whose laboratory would actually produce the organism first. Every dime the respective governments could scrape together poured into the labs, and there were fresh scandals in grant diversion every week.

Ohio State, something of a dark horse, won, producing a virus from the DNA.

Triumph was sweet for several months, until it became clear that the stuff didn't do anything. It seemed to be so alien that no living thing on Earth made antibodies to it. It replicated freely enough inside cells, but after making a few copies of itself it did nothing there, diffusing lazily through organisms without affecting them at all. Its only other notable feature was that all of the descendants of OSU's first virus replicated simultaneously, at intervals of 4052.88 seconds, as if they all carried copies of the same clock.

The message from space died out after two years, fading to nothing across a few days. Within a few years the virus was no more than a curiosity. Inevitably, as its harmlessness became apparent, precautions became lax, and it escaped into the environment.

Papers were published arguing that there had been no message—that some sort of accident or fluke accounted for the stuttering fifty-year echoes. Others claimed that the message had been written in a four-letter alphabet, and that the resemblance to a DNA sequence had been purely accidental. Three scholarly journals devoted themselves to the interpretation and discussion of the signals, and on most college campuses there were one or two exosignalists.

The mystery virus itself found minor niches in science. Because it was ubiquitous, safe, and rather large, high school students did science-fair projects with it. A Japanese company patented a process for converting it to edible protein. Ecologists studied its spread, finding it in insects in the Antarctic dry valleys, among the first lichens on a new volcanic island in the South Pacific, and in fungus in a cave deep within K2.

Most people forgot about it most of the time.

Probably, in the two hours of agony as the world ended one day, no one even thought about the virus. Every living thing with a voice was screaming; everything that could tear tore at itself, ripping out sickly green hunks from its own flesh.

Within a few years, the green scum spread over the surface of Earth, in an even layer about five centimeters deep.

It waited for a radio signal, one with a recognizable pattern. Had it been capable of speech, and of disappointment, it would have said that it had never been disappointed anywhere in the galaxy.

EMPTY SKY

Yet another orphan in my parade of orphans; this one has been seen by many editors, and has been through a lot of changes too. I doubt that the religious offensiveness is really the problem.

Past two A.M., and the last drunks were on their way out, taking all the time they could because the town was cold and mean: no late diner, no after-hours, nowhere else for them to go. Every trip up from the walk-in, getting cases of beer up into the coolers behind the bar for the day crew, I let a few more drunks out into the February drizzle.

Irv, the owner, came downstairs from his apartment, and asked me, "How was the evening, Eddie?"

"'Bout the usual."

Maybe Irv showing up before all the customers were gone meant a lesson tonight. Two more trips to the walk-in to go.

As I slammed the last case of Bud into the cooler—it was the kind of town that had no local beer—I looked up to see Irv letting the last guy out, the one who had been trying to pick up Kristin, the bartender. I'd marked that one down as maybe a problem—one of those lost-puppy-dog-eyed guys who can't quite keep a mustache in order, who hangs around till the last minute because he hopes the girl with bleached-blonde mall hair, Wonderbra, and bright blue contact lenses likes him—but he went quietly enough.

Trouble that didn't happen was typical of Irv's. Being door man for Irv was a soft job because there were almost no fights, never any serious ones. The worst I ever saw there was a car salesman and a bank branch office manager pushing each other around. My job wasn't so much to break up fights as to keep middle-aged men who were pushing each other from falling, twisting an ankle, and having a chance to sue Irv.

I switched out the outside lights, yanked the front grating closed, and locked it. When I turned back Kristin had just finished wiping down the bar.

Irv said, "All right, first exam tonight."

My blood froze solid. Six months of memorizing that Latin verse and learning which phases of the moon went with which herbs went with which body parts went with which words of the Old Tongue. Six months learning how to burn what when and what to say while you did it and what it was for. Six months and not one word about our having to take a test. I'd kept up my practice, but anyone who's been to school is afraid of a pop quiz.

Kristin's throat jerked in a little spasm; she didn't like this either.

Irv smiled a tiny bit. It was nothing like that big phony grin he gave customers, still less like the happy grin on nights when, instead of launching into a new lesson, we'd just sit around, pulling down beers out of the cooler, and ask him questions about the Lesser Way. "Now, don't panic. This is nothing you could have studied for. Just a matter of finding out whether your hard work and attention is getting you any-where."

Kristin sat down on one of the bar stools, tugged the Suede Miniskirt that Sold a Thousand Beers into place, and said, "I don't s'pose Eddie and me could, like, wait till next week and take the makeup?"

Irv shook his head. "It's not that kind of exam. It's more like a med-ical. Just seeing what kind of shape you're in, so to speak. Eddie, you're on deck first. Tell me about spells you've used, for yourself, more than once."

"Well, let's see. There's the minor healing for others, minor healing for self, and—uh"—I was blushing—"uh, that is, I also—"

"You've been using the seduction spell, right, Eddie?" Kristin's grin was big and toothy as a shark's, except that a shark doesn't usually have pink lipstick on one incisor.

"Yeah."

"Let *him* say it. How's it all worked out for you, Eddie?"

"Well." I tried to pull together all my feelings and memories about the months since June 21, when I had started on the job that I got by an-swering one of the strangest ads I'd ever seen. That was a lot of time with a lot of events in it. "Um, like you say, the thing that makes it the Lesser Way is that you can never be sure the things that it makes happen wouldn't have happened anyway. It's statistical, sort of, you do it just right every time and it works more often than it should, maybe every time if you knew everything about how to do it, but you never do."

"How often did they all work for you?" Irv asked. "No modesty, no bragging, no shading. Just the truth."

"Oh, well, every time, but all the same . . ."

Kristin stared and shivered. "You're way ahead of me."

"Me too at the same stage," Irv said. "So every time you tried to heal a cold or a paper cut, it worked, and every time you put the seduction casting on someone—"

Kristin laughed. "I can vouch for that. Thursday you got Tracy to walk out from between a guy talking about his Beemer and that big bodybuilder who never says anything, straight over to you, ten minutes to closing. *And* she went home with you."

My face was burning. I didn't think Kristin had noticed me doing any of that.

She wasn't letting up any, either. "So how long did it take you to bone the chick?" She also knew that, stupid as it is in this day and age, I get embarrassed by girls talking like guys. "You lay some pipe into her?" She made sure I knew she was doing it to bother me.

I was hoping Irv would shut her up, but he must've thought it was a good question, because he nodded and gestured for me to answer.

"Uh, actually, the first time was, um—well, the spell must have really took, because I didn't get my car started in the parking lot before she was—you know, all ready and um—"

Irv nodded the way I remember the chem teacher did when you did something right. "All right, so your success rate is pretty clearly one hundred percent. You're already bordering on crossing over from the Lesser Way."

Kristin winked at me. "Next time we have lunch together, Eddie-buddy, I want every detail. Every single one. You nailed the biggest tease in the place. I hope she turns out to be the type that begs and screams and says 'Oh, baby'—the girls that come in on Thursdays would *love* to hear something like that about her."

One reason I'd never even thought about trying with Kristin was that she was so comfortable talking about stuff that embarrassed the hell out of me. Also, I really didn't feel good about what had happened. Tracy was an all-right human being, as far as I was concerned, actually. She was just a pretty girl who loved attention, the way some of them do if they're insecure or were ugly ducklings when they were younger or something, and therefore she tended to flirt and tease a lot. Sometimes guys misunderstood, especially because she liked to dress dramatically. Besides that, since the only thing she really liked or cared about was male attention, Tracy usually ignored other women, and that's a sure formula for annoying them. They radiated hate at her so thick you couldn't've cut it with an ax.

Tracy hadn't been back to Irv's since that night—which had gone to dawn, and she really had screamed some things that I don't think were usually her style at all—and when I'd phoned her a couple of times she'd been very cold and distant. I figured she was humiliated, and probably she thought there was something wrong with her that had made her act like that. I hadn't been able to think of any way to make her feel better; it didn't seem like the truth was going to help, especially not if she believed it.

Irv cleared his throat. "And what exactly have you found out from these experiences?"

Kristin snorted. "He probably found out that she's just as stuck up and shallow whether she's teasing or fucking."

Irv silenced her with a glance. "I mean about the Lesser Way," he said.

"Well . . . it's like you said. All you can do is move things around. If I take somebody's cold away I have to give it to somebody else; if I heal a paper cut on my finger, I have to make some of my hair fall out. And the seduction spell—well, it's harder to explain. I guess what happens is that every time I use that, I feel, uh, colder. I see the world more as a place for using the seduction spell and less as a place for . . . um. Um. Finding love. Having friends. Taking care of other people. You know." I did not grow up as a guy who says things like that. "So I kind of have been cutting back on it, 'cause I don't like what it feels like it's doing to me."

When I looked up, Kristin looked worried and Irv was sitting quietly. Finally, he said, "You know, of course, that the more you use it the more effective it will become. Eventually you would be able to cause any person of any age and either sex to come straight to you and offer herself, or himself, sexually."

I tried to make a joke out of it. "Yeah, but I can't do Bill with all the Secret Service watching."

He raised an eyebrow. "You could get them all to join in. But how would you feel about that power?"

"Um." Damn, why hadn't I stuck to curing colds? "Uh, actually, tonight, I was trying to get somewhere with Deb, that tall girl with the red hair, and I could have used the spell any time, but . . . I just wanted to see—"

Irv raised a finger at me. There was something pretty spooky in the way the dim fluorescent lights over the bar reflected from the crevices and lines in his face, like out of a movie or something. What was even spookier was that I knew at once what he meant.

"Well, okay, that's not true. I, um—I really like Deb. I didn't want to make her do anything she wouldn't naturally do, and I really didn't want to hurt her and humiliate her the way I did Tracy. So I just wanted Deb to do it—uh, that is, do whatever she wanted to do—um, just because she liked me."

Irv's lips pursed. "Good enough. I think you'll find your way into the universe as a power we can all live with. Maybe as a very great power. Now, Kristin, what have you used?"

She smiled. "Oh, let's see. I've tried the spells for discouraging love. Those are a big help at the end of the night. But—I kind of thought the point of what you were asking Eddie about was that things have costs, and somehow or other I haven't seen any costs to using those. I smile at the guy, I make the Knot That Unbinds in the bar towel and say

> *te adligavi*
> *te adlaxo*
> *numquam ligaberis*

under my breath, and in a minute or two he gets up and goes—and he always seems happier, and I know I'm happier. Seems like everyone is gaining in that situation."

Irv nodded. "That's a good question. What do you think, Eddie?"

"Hmm. Well, maybe . . ." I realized. "Oh, I see. As long as they're hanging around fantasizing about Kristin, they're protected from other kinds of pain, at least for the moment. When Kristin turns them loose, they wander off looking for more of what they really need and less of their fantasies. So the relief they get, and Kristin gets, is balanced by the pain they're likely to meet out there—in fact it's overbalanced, because if they go looking for what they really want, failing to get it will hurt a lot more than not being able to pick up the cute chick behind the bar."

Kristin flashed a pout at me, like she was going to try to make a joke out of it. Irv held up a finger. Finally she said, "Okay, I see what you mean, but it seems like the pain they're getting exposed to is *good* for them, like they need it."

Irv nodded at her. "That's it exactly."

"But doesn't that make the pain another benefit?"

"Doesn't it still hurt? It's got nothing to do, you see, with whether the pain is beneficial or harmful, only that it hurts, and therefore you'd rather avoid it if you could. If you strain your back, it's going to hurt, and it doesn't matter whether you strained it stealing a television, or carrying canned goods into a shelter for the homeless. It hurts either way." Irv leaned back. "Anything else?"

"Well," she said, grinning, "I nicked my finger in the kitchen and drew a little blood, so I used the pain to lighten my hair and make it easier to keep nice. I guess that's pretty obvious about the costs. And I tried zapping Eddie with the seduction spell, but it only sort of worked—he followed me with his eyes all night but he took some other blonde home."

I blushed all over.

"Why do you suppose it didn't work?" Irv asked.

"Oh, maybe I said the words not quite right, maybe I liked Eddie too much to get cold about him the way Eddie does about the women he gets."

Irv got up and said, "I think you had both better come on up to my apartment. You pass, by the way, since it's clear that at least you have developed a habit of counting the cost first. You won't get into too much trouble if you do that."

"Is there a Greater Way? Do we start learning how to do that tonight?" Kristin asked.

He turned around at the door. The red and blue from the Bud sign shot multicolored shadows deep into the creases of his face. "The Greater Way is not exactly something you do," he said. "It's somewhere you go."

It was like something out of the kind of slick-covered fantasy novel I'd read lots of on Amtrack and Greyhound. We walked through a slightly dirty full-length mirror in Irv's small bedroom, as if we were diving into a vertical pool of mercury, and came out on the other side onto a dirt road. I looked back and saw no mirror, and certainly no bedroom, behind us.

It had been past three when we stepped through the mirror, so I was *way* too tired for midday sun just then. Kristin flipped the shades out of her purse and onto her face; that and the heavy-duty makeup that she usually wore for work pretty much erased her expression.

Irv said, "We'll only stay a few minutes this time. I've deliberately come into some of the back country so that we're less likely to run into trouble. I just wanted to make sure you understood that this is real, that if you've been holding back any belief—"

"Whoo, boy, not anymore," Kristin said. "What's the castle over there?"

"They use the word *caer* locally for those," Irv said, "and it's not really a castle, at least not in the sense of a fort. More like a big country house. The owner is probably around somewhere but he and I are *not* friends, so you might want to stick close in case we have to go back real fast."

"Do you have any friends here?" I asked, looking around. The forest behind was like a painting—everything was just as arranged as a Japanese garden, and every object looked as if it were cut into the ground or sky with a razor knife, so that outlines shone as if backlit.

I thought of some of the trivia I'd picked up dropping in and out of college so many times. Blake had written that madmen drew lines around things, and later that wise men drew lines around things. Here the lines were real and something or somebody had put things inside them.

All that vividness was tough to look at, even for a short time. I could feel the gritty sand of needed sleep under my eyelids, and the thick blue of the sky, like a painting a kid would do in kindergarten, was getting to me. I was about to suggest that maybe our few minutes were up when Kristin jumped backwards against me; I caught her automatically with one arm.

What came out of the hole in the hillside made me wish there had been a bigger person around, for *me* to hide behind. Though it looked fairly human, it was eight feet tall, at least, with lots of extra body hair on its body where it shouldn't have, and its face looked like the way a really bad burn victim might look without any surgery, as if the bones underneath had melted and run in some hideously painful heat, crushing the cheekbones, slumping the lower jaw far forward, curling the nose into a snout—yet somehow left the soft, furry skin unscarred.

"Rarving," it said, and its mouth split into the widest grin I'd ever seen—nobody else I knew had a mouth that went all the way back to a pair of floppy bat-ears. "Smee. Fido. Dint tink you'd be on dis side, longtimes, unh-unh."

Irving, it's me, I thought, as if translating. Did he actually say his name was Fido? Anyway, he seemed to be a friend—

"It was just going to be a pop-in with two new ones, Fido," Irv said, "but I'm glad to see you anyway. What's the news here in the Ostmark? Is Theosten Theorsen still the local heat?"

"Elf bastid. He still is. Yunno we can't do nuttin' yet, mur'cle I ain't got caught 't'dis post. Still-a warst Mock'f'em all. Can't be he'ped, we do it one of dese years, slit ev'ry damn e'f t'roat."

He advanced slowly toward us. He was naked, and had fur everywhere. The fur on his face was soft and thin, like a puppy's. But despite his talk about slitting throats, there was something in the big dark eyes that reassured me that any quarrel I might have with him would be my fault, not his.

Irving nodded. "You keep your watch—*shit.*"

An arrow socked into Fido's chest and he fell backwards, arms whirling around. The arrow was less real than anything else I had seen there, purely a golden burning outline of an arrow, surrounding a void. Nevertheless blood gushed onto Fido's fur, and the shocked pain in those eyes, so like a dying dog beside the highway—

I was bending over him, Kristin beside me, when the fiery cold of the noose settled around my throat, burning and freezing at the same time. I heard Irv shouting something, and it got very dark—just time to realize my fingers were burning, dropping off as I pulled at that noose—

I fell onto Irving's bedroom floor, gasping in the dusty warm air. Kristin fell across my back and lay still. I was staring at my charred, ruined hands—I seemed to have lost all my fingers except my left thumb—

Fido, the arrow gone, but blood pouring from his chest, fell backwards into Irv's nightstand and knocked a lamp over.

When I looked back, for the first time I noticed Kristin's outstretched leg in front of me, blood splashed on the white hose and the cowboy boot. I felt her cough once, a wet gurgle, against my back.

I found enough energy and attention to say "Uh."

Just as I passed out, the most beautiful woman I'd ever seen, naked except for the platinum hair that fell to her waist, flew backwards away from me, screaming, and hit the wall. The comforting dark descended, along with one other thought: *My hands hurt.*

As I woke up, my hands seemed to be on fire, but I had all my fingers to feel the pain with. I was lying in Irv's bedroom, to judge by the nightstand in my field of view. That meant I must be in his double bed, and that the warm thing beside me was Kristin. From the feel of the sheets I knew I was naked, but Kristin seemed to be asleep, so I wasn't quite embarrassed yet. I tried to turn over to see if she was okay, but the moment I tried to press with my hands, pain shot through my arms as if I had stuck them back between that noose and my throat, so the best I could do was to turn a little sideways and look at the part of her face that stuck out of the covers facing me.

Dark roots were showing in her hair—not a lot, but since she was one of those bleached blondes who are careful about that, it meant we'd been asleep some days. Someone had cleaned off all her makeup, and her face was pink and a little uneven in color, and from the angle I could just see faint hints of dark mustache—she must wax that, usually, I thought distractedly.

As a matter of fact, Kristin was downright plain, up close and without all the special effects. Not having much else to think about till someone showed up, I spent a little time wondering why I hadn't really seen it before, and got as far as figuring that maybe she hadn't wanted me to see it.

"Anybody awake in here?" Irv's voice said, softly.

I gave my voice a try and found I could say, "I just woke up some minutes ago."

"Looks like you turned yourself as well," Irv said. He sounded tired, old, and sick. "Can you turn yourself back away from Kristin? After Fido, I only had the energy for the one spell on the bed, so you're both in there naked."

Good old Irv. Old-fashioned and polite to the last. I flipped myself over. My hands felt like I'd put them down on a hot grill and leaned on it.

As he came into view, I saw that he looked terrible, at least as bad as two of the regulars that had come down with AIDS.

Standing next to Irv, holding him up, was . . . Mr. Clean.

At least that's what I first thought he looked like. It was an ugly sort of guy, muscled like a god and near seven feet tall, totally bald, and with one big, prominent earring. He guided Irv gently into a chair beside the bed, and then went around and turned Kristin over.

At first I was a little bugged—so apparently I couldn't be trusted to be a gentleman, but this stranger could?—and then I realized that the "stranger" could be trusted exactly because he wasn't a gentleman, or a man of any kind. "Fido?" I asked.

"Ya got it, Mac," Fido said, coming around and sitting on the floor, which still put his eyes well above mine. "How do you like the new palate and speech center? I can practically make myself understood, know what I mean?"

The eyes were the same, and after a moment I realized that if I looked hard I could see him—not under, but through—whatever Irving had put over him. "You look great to me," I said. "Irv, what's the matter with you? Did you get hit with nerve gas or something over there?"

He coughed, a hideous sound full of wet flesh rubbing together, and then said, "I had three people badly hurt—did you see Kristin take the arrow through her back? Went straight into a kidney and slashed her colon in half—and since you were all unconscious, no one else to be the pain source. The glamour I cast over Fido, so he could do shopping and help out downstairs and so forth, cost something, too. You all were too out of it to feel your pain, not to mention the risk of losing you to shock, so I couldn't use any of your pain for healing, and I needed a lot of pain to do the job. So I worked a minor self-reinforcing spell on myself, to give me something to work with. At the moment I've still got lung cancer complicated with a hearty case of pneumonia, bowel cancer, and the nasty beginning stages of spinal tuberculosis. But I'm really feeling a lot better since Fido's been awake—drawing on the pain in his chest, I've gotten rid of a lot of what I had. In fact, if you don't mind—"

"Go right ahead," I said. I pressed my hands against the mattress, sending screaming pain shooting up my arms till I thought I might throw up or pass out, feeling my skin get icy and clammy. When I couldn't take it one more second, I looked up to see Irv, still not looking well, but clearly better and stronger.

"That was a lot, Eddie; you don't have to give me that much—"

"You gave me back my hands, and you probably gave my friends back their lives," I said. From the startled look, and then the smile, on Fido's face, I guess being called my friend was big news to him. Hell, when you've been through one of those things together, what else can you be but friends? At least that was my excuse for about half the friends I had. And if I had just made a friend of Fido, he probably wouldn't be the worst-behaved one I had, or even the ugliest.

Kristin stirred behind me and whispered, "Eddie?"

"Right here."

"Christ, did we have a *really* great first night, or is my nightmare what really happened?"

I laughed but even that much was enough to set my hands on fire again; seeing Irv draw an easy breath, I clenched my hands against each other for a second, giving him another jolt. We all got it explained to her, sort of, but by the time that was done she and I were both exhausted. I had gathered that Fido was holding down my old job as door man for Irv's bar—I bet there was *no* trouble now—and Irv was somehow managing to tend his own bar. As soon as I knew that the not-quite-as-real-as-I-had-thought world was being taken care of, that little release from responsibility was all it took to send me into a deep sleep.

The next time we woke, to judge by the light, must have been almost a full day later, and by now the healing spell on the bed had managed to fix my hands up pretty well; they tingled like bad athlete's foot, but they were all there, the fingers were new and pink, and I could wriggle them, though it stung and they were stiff. I seemed to be well on my way to a set of Fu Manchu fingernails as well.

Kristin, hurt far worse than I had been, was still in real pain, but no longer dopey from it. Irv sat over next to her and seemed to lose years of age and suffering every few minutes, which told me what she must be feeling like. Being Kristin, she wasn't going to let me know if she could help it, but since I did know, she didn't mind holding my hand. Every so often she'd forget and give it a hard squeeze; I'd gulp and Irv would drop another year.

The spelled bed was doing everything, I realized; my old high school football shoulder separation had cleared up, so that I could comfortably put my left hand over my head for the first time in years. My old broken toe had straightened and I would probably not be able to forecast rain by it. The red rose tattoo on Kristin's shoulder, and the Grateful Dead skull on her thigh, were fading too; Irv was puzzled by that and thought there was something wrong with the healing bed he had made, until she said that she had gotten each of them for long-gone boyfriends and had wanted to get rid of them for a long time. "But is there a way to concentrate it on the places where I'm really hurt? It just seems unfair to be using the bed for things like that when you're so ill, Irv."

"I'm not that ill anymore. Last of the cancer went this morning, and the TB is about gone. I saved the pneumonia for last because it's a pretty good pain source without being quite so debilitating. And I don't power the bed, honey, I made it and now it just keeps doing what it does. Like if you ever made an electromagnet for science fair with bell wire and a nail—after a while the nail gets magnetized and you no longer need the current. The thing I really apologize for is putting you both in it together—I wouldn't have done that if I'd had a choice. The bed has been steadily healing any division between you two, which is to say it's probably more effective than any love spell I know how to cast."

I looked over at Kristin and she looked back at me; she had her old grin, which I adored, but there was a slight shyness to it. "I don't object much," I said. "Might've taken me years to get around to it otherwise." The grin widened and I knew I'd said exactly the right thing.

I also realized I was likely to say exactly the right thing for Kristin from then on, and she for me, and suddenly I wasn't sure how I felt about that.

The bed had had more time to work, and her stiff pale hair had turned back to its natural color and texture, not just the roots but the whole thing, so that she now had a mass of thick, soft, light brown hair that fell in untidy waves around her head.

She was smiling at me, still. "Hey, it fixed your broken nose," she said.

Irv cleared his throat, and just then Fido came in with a huge platter of scrambled eggs, toast, and fried potatoes; Kristin wasn't quite up for more than the toast yet, but I compensated for her.

After Kristin fell back asleep, Irv and Fido helped me up from the bed and into one of Irv's old bathrobes. "I'll go over to your place and get you some real clothing tomorrow," Irv said. "We've just been so busy trying to keep things from falling to pieces."

I followed them into Irv's kitchen and sat down at the table with them. As I looked at Fido now, in the warm sunlight, I was fascinated. It seemed as if I could see his real face underneath his appearance, not like a disguise poking through a mask, but more like a video ghost constantly threatening to merge into the real image.

"Hmm. The bed seems to have strengthened your sight, as well," Irv said. I knew he didn't mean the kind you get from your eyes. He sat down where he could look at me closely. "You're penetrating the glamour I've thrown on Fido, aren't you?"

"A little," I said. "If I didn't know what Fido really looked like, though, I wouldn't be able to say more than that he didn't quite seem to be what he looked like. Irv, where were we and what was going on? And did I hallucinate that somebody else came through with us?"

The memory of the blonde girl I had barely glimpsed was a razor cut in my heart.

Irv sighed. "Well, that's part of why I needed a little council of war here. Frankly I wish Kristin were healing faster, because we need her too, but I'm afraid she didn't have one clean hole through her lungs and heart like Fido, or just massive physical mutilation like you had, Eddie. She was ripped right through the guts, and coming back to this side the barbed head on the arrow swung around inside her, and on top of everything else the elves smear their war arrows with dung from the goblin pens; it was only because Fido took the first shot, with a hunting arrow, that I was able to save both of them."

"Is she going to be okay?"

Irv grinned. "Not to worry, Eddie. If I do say so myself, making the healing bed was one of the most remarkable pieces of magework done in the last few centuries. Most especially on this side of the Barrier. Once the word leaks out that it exists, they'll be questing for it in a dozen universes for generations to come. She's going to be a whole lot better than okay.

"What we *do* need to talk about is a little situation we've got downtown, and what's to be done about that. But first question; if I told you that there were real elves, and real goblins—"

"You already have," I pointed out. "Fido's a goblin, aren't you, Fido? Then how come he's a nice guy?"

"It's all a matter of PR," Irv said. "The elves are better at it. And to be fussy, elves and goblins are the same thing. Best way to say it is that goblins are ugly on the outside—"

"Hey."

"—sorry, Fido, I should say by humanocentric standards—and elves are ugly on the inside." Irv sighed. "It might be easier if I started at the beginning, but we're short on time, so guess I should begin in the middle and just let you ask about anything you can't guess from context. The elf and goblin world is the world that is one step more spiritual than ours on the Great Chain. That is, magic works more and is stronger over there, and consequently, since physical matter is sort of the jamming noise in magic—think how many spells work on information systems like brains, immune systems, and so forth, and how few work on purely material objects—the elves and the goblins react a lot more strongly to having a physical component than anyone on this side does. Most of us have nothing more than an occasional feeling that the world isn't what it seems or what it might be, and maybe a vague feeling now and then of our bodies being in the way.

"One level below us it's practically pure matter—nice place to visit but hard to get back from because there's barely anything to power the magic. But one level up from us, where the elves and goblins live, there's a constant sense that the idea is real and the matter is an inadequate filling for the shape of the idea. That's why everything seems to have an outline. And the beings of that plane feel a constant discomfort from the presence of the material world.

"If they learn to embrace and trust the physical—like the goblins do—then it shapes them, alters them, exaggerates itself, and they end up looking like Fido, become mortal, and eventually die. If they are brought up hating their bodies, hating everything connected with physical existence—then they live forever and they look like Alanareia."

"The blonde woman I saw come through with us?"

"Unh-hunh. Piece of her Creator's handiwork."

"I don't quite understand."

Fido sighed. "Some universes, like this one, have no Creator. We call those the Free Places, and most of us in the other universes want to get into them, even if like this one they only have life on one tiny orbiting rock. In the Free Places things are partly random, partly the operation of natural laws, partly the free will of the inhabitants. There's no poetic justice and no one is constantly converting what happens to people into the raw material of stories. Unfortunately, many of the other universes, planes, whatever you call them, have Creators."

"Gods?"

"Close enough. And a Creator, by nature, is a rotten bastard; the only reason to go to all the trouble of making a universe is to have billions of things that are inferior to yourself. The one for Faerie was a real stinker. You can be beautiful and immortal like the elves if you hold yourself out of everything warm and physical and real, or, if you insist on love and friendship and so forth, you can look like us goblins, feel all your higher functions slowly deteriorate, and have your soul turn back to nothing when you die. Only choice our Creator gave us.

"Ever hear of Gawain and the Green Knight, or babies stolen by elves, or any of that? A lot of the people in Faerie used to come and play in your world all the time; we could be ourselves without changing here. The problem was that what we goblins looked like sort of automatically set off all your human xenophobia. Awfully tough to make friends with anyone other than children. And what the elves liked to do was to tease you, get all that hopeless devotion and love from you humans, and then vanish back to the other side, leaving all sorts of mess in their wake. I suppose I can't really blame them for it. They were just acting like perfect images of their Creator.

"That's why your last big mage—the one you knew under the aliases of Merlin, Paracelsus, Roger Bacon, and Leonardo—made the barrier between the worlds that you could cross but we couldn't. Something about a thing that happened when he was still a kid, half a dozen human warriors he needed badly for some war or other went chasing off after magic cups and 'beautiful princesses' that were just elf bitches playing on local superstition. I don't blame your mage at all, despite the fact that it closed the border and took away our main way of escape. The messes the elves like to make are bad enough where the elves are."

"But the immediate problem," Irv said, "is that Alanaeira is not just an elf out doing a little slumming and making some misery, like they usually would. She's a full-rank mage herself, and way out of my league; you're a pretty big wild talent, Eddie, bigger than I can judge or evaluate, but chances are she's even bigger than you. And now she's on this side—she chose to jump when she saw me open the gate."

"What's she doing here?" I asked, "if she's not doing what an elf usually does here?"

Irv sighed and put his feet up on the table. "Well, that's what this little council, possibly of war, is all about. We've now got an elf mage hanging out among the street people downtown, loading up on pain—great place to do it, no?—and getting ready, real soon, to blow a hole in Merlin's Wall. After which there will be practically an invasion."

It had all come at me pretty fast; I sat back, thought for some long minutes, and finally sighed. "So, uh, if it's an invasion, what will they do to us? And what can we do about what's-her-name?" I knew perfectly well it was Alanareia, but for reasons that I felt rather than could have named, I wanted to pretend that I hadn't paid that much attention, and besides I wanted to hear her name again. . . .

"Oh, they'll do to us what they did before. 'And the sons of god looked on the daughters of men . . .' and vice versa. Look, how do you make a *human* with a perfect surface? You make it all surface. You make it hate its own insides. Well, hey, presto, that's how they make elf kids proof against turning into goblins, which is what they would naturally do at puberty."

"Not *naturally*." Fido seemed almost to growl. "Not that at all. This"—he gestured toward his body, and it seemed as if the glamour opened like a curtain for an instant and revealed his lumpy, misshapen, impractical body—"this is what the Creator does. Asshole. He had the power so he decided to torture us, and he made us as ugly as he could manage to keep us home, and to make us enemies of anyone that might give us a little friendship."

"I'm your friend," I said, "no matter what you look like." It just popped out, and I had no idea why I'd said it, though it was true.

Fido beamed at me, so happy he seemed half-crazy, and Irv dropped me a wink that probably meant I'd said something good.

"Anyway," Fido said, "it's only over in these beautiful Free Places that you get a choice. Over here you can be whatever you turn out to be; back in Faerie we are what the Creator decides, and he decided to make us all ugly, inside or out, to prove he could, I suppose. He was never big on explanations, and nowadays he mostly sits around revising the early history of our universe to make it more flattering toward himself. So *nothing* over there is 'natural,' which is why I jumped on Irving about it. Everything over there is 'supernatural'—things don't just happen, they're *made* to happen. With malice."

"Are you really going to kill all the elves someday?"

Fido sighed. "Could happen. You heard Irv mention the 'goblin pens'? An elf's idea of a good time is watching us publicly tortured. And"—he leaned forward—"and, and, you know, they *eat* us."

Irv nodded slowly. "Every so often a gang of goblins will manage to catch an elf alone and—well, it's understandable, but that's horrible too. And the reprisals are always at a hundred goblins for one elf. With the hearty approval of the Creator. By now the magic has woken in you enough so that surely you know how some objects sing and speak a little, about where they've been and what they've done?"

I thought a moment. "Yeah. I have a pocket knife I've had since I was a kid. It talks about all the traveling we've done together and all the stuff we've had to fix. Sometimes I wish it would shut up about the little piece of metal it lost off one edge when we were getting a doorknob back onto a door."

"Exactly. Ever read *The Lord of the Rings?* There's a sword in there whose name translates to 'Goblin-cleaver.' Tolkien must have heard some rumors, or maybe some of his writers' group were more than they seemed. I suppose Tolkien himself might even have been. Anyway, 'Goblin-cleaver' wasn't just a pure invention. I've met the original; and what it whispers about is a time when some Mighty Elf Warrior or other found a valley where there were a few hundred very old goblins—remember, their brains deteriorate the more affection and love they get, too, so that after a few decades of all that goblinly hugging and cuddling, all of them were pretty well what we'd call retarded and absolutely helpless—and butchered them all, killing the best-loved ones first."

"Okay, you've convinced me we don't want them here," I said, not convinced at all if I thought about Alanareia, but dead sure as long as I kept my mind on what Irv and Fido had been telling me. "So how do we deal with this elf chick?"

"There's the problem," Irving said. "The simplest thing we could do about it is kill her, but frankly I don't think we have the power. If we could I'd rather get her to voluntarily return to Faerie, which she quite naturally doesn't want to do since she's a talented mage herself, and if she can open the gateway she'll be Boss Elf and the Beloved Goblin Eater and any other title she wants to give herself. That would be best, since we'd avoid having bodies to explain and we wouldn't have to have a duel of magics with her which we might very well lose, but I can't imagine her cooperating. So what we need to do is reconnoiter—and I can't handle the exertion and she recognizes me anyway, and she'll see right through Fido's glamour, whereas a single guy in a car—"

"*That's* what she's doing?"

"It's a good way to meet guys in pain. And a lot of the people who work around her have a variety of medical problems—which she's making worse, I'm sure—to supply more pain. I'm sure it's just temporary till she has the combination of money and magic that she needs for moving up in the world."

"She won't recognize me?"

Fido gave a bitter laugh. "You're mortal. She never looked at you. Trust me."

"You seem awful sure."

"I know her. She's my sister."

The town was cold and nasty. Finding a streetwalker was no problem. It was finding the right one that was hard.

You took a turn off the freeway where somebody from out of town with money would and started to circle through side streets and there you were—a dozen long coats open in the February chill, and girls, some not much more than children, some looking like they ought to be grandmothers, turned to face the traffic, thumbs out as if hitchhiking, letting those long coats fall open to reveal all sorts of outfits. The little Oriental girl, who looked about twelve, in the cheerleader outfit, I decided, took my personal award for best reason why I needed to move to another town soon.

You could spot the vice cop cars too, because the girls could spot them and they'd whip the coats closed and fade into alleys about three cars before the cops got there, then re-emerge practically backlit by the taillights of the cops. Pretty clearly the game was the game; I figured the cops probably collected in either cash or tail a few times a night and otherwise the driving was a way to burn off extra energy from the donuts.

A vice cop was two cars in front of me, so I was getting less lead time than I really needed to look for Alanaeira, and was thinking of taking a side trip onto the faster streets for a block or two to change my place in the traffic flow. Cold rain was beginning to spatter down in little gusts, leaving greasy tracks on the windshield behind the wipers, and making the job that much more complicated; the more elaborate puffed-up hair out there was wilting, and a lot of the girls were packing up under awnings and next to buildings. No doubt prices were probably coming down as well.

The car in front of me stopped, the brake lights turning the water on my windshield red, and a tall black woman got out and strode away in her leather coat and spike-heeled boots. Another happy customer, I suppose; the car whipped out of traffic at the next light and was gone. Since he'd made a couple of circuits in front of me, either negotiations had gone on for a while, or whatever he'd wanted from her had been something she could do while he drove.

Shit, it felt cold in my car. It's a huge rusting old Cadillac, thirty-seven years old in September if the door plate can be believed, with a hyperactive heater that keeps it roasting hot all winter, but it wasn't putting a dent in the chill of this night. I found myself thinking a lot about Kristin, back at Irv's, asleep under the covers in a soft mane of warm hair and sleepy breath, and about a couple of twenty-four-hour restaurants out on the interstate toward the edge of town that were just remote enough from the town to have some warmth and friendliness to them, and maybe even a little bit about home, fifteen years ago, back before the old man started to drink a lot.

The trouble with shopping when you don't intend to buy is that everything on display, after a while, starts to remind you of everything else you'd rather be doing. The beat-up looking woman, brown hair smeared flat to her head with icy rain, makeup smeared to a blue bandit's mask, opening her coat to reveal running shorts and a pair of thigh-high boots, looked like somebody I'd like to drop off with Rose, who ran one of those diners, with a note pinned to her that said "Please give this woman a shower and a job and treat her kindly for a year or two." There were a couple of kids barely into puberty that I thought Kristin and I ought to adopt and get into some square meals and school. Probably none of them would have appreciated it. Probably I told myself that so that I wouldn't have to get serious about doing it.

I rounded the corner and the black woman with the coat and the boots was the only one on the street as the rain started to thunder down, scattering the girls into god knew what holes for shelter (suddenly every pay phone for blocks had someone at it, probably begging her pimp to pick her up). The cars were scattering too, including finally Mr. Vice Cop Sir. I figured, give it one more trip around the stroll and call it a night; maybe Alanaeira wasn't working tonight, or more likely she had found something that was taking all night.

There was nothing to look at—except drenched, freezing girls standing at phones—and in very short order I had completed the trip, so that the black woman had only gotten about half a block before I was coming up behind her again.

In about two seconds she lost half a foot of height and a yard of platinum hair cascaded over her collar as she put up a big yellow umbrella. She turned and opened her coat at me, and it was Alanaeira, no problem with identifying that. She had on a one-piece bathing suit, high on the hips and low on the chest, a bright smear of fluorescent blue stretched over her astonishing body. Her breasts stuck straight out, her waist arced in, impossibly slender, and her hips flared just enough so that you knew she had a taut little bottom. The spike-heeled boots and the leather coat still fit her, so they were clearly being affected by the same glamour she was casting.

She stuck out her thumb and smiled hopefully at me; something about it suggested, more than anything else, that she was looking for some nice man who would take care of her, that everyone tonight had brutalized her but she was counting on me to make it all better.

I deliberately did not think about why I pulled over and took the turn into the dark part of an alley. She strutted up to my window as I rolled it down. I felt her mind probe mine, slip over the false surface Irv had prepared, slide into the planted pathway that was supposed to lead her past everything that might make her suspicious.

She didn't seem to trip over any rough spots; maybe she was intent on extracting the next load of pain. She leaned in the window. "Hi, babe. You a cop? You want to go out for something?"

"No, I'm not a cop. Sure. Get in."

She smiled and winked at me. "Come on, now, babe, I got to be sure you're not a cop. And you know I'm not a hooker or anything, I'm just looking for a man who wants to have fun . . . come on, touch me where it's good and show me your thing and then we can talk."

It had been a long time since I'd resorted to anything like this, and never in this town, but the ritual's the same everywhere; there are things cops aren't allowed to do, or at least don't want to have to testify in court that they did. I yanked down my fly and dragged my warm penis out into the cold draft from the window; she reached in to take it in her blood-red nails, and I reached out to tug the crotch of her suit to the side and slide a finger into her. From the feel of things, business had been brisk tonight.

Her hand on my penis closed gently and stroked once, and I was abruptly rigid. "Oh, babe, oh it's so nice," she said, with a wry little wink that seemed to indicate a lot of depth and intelligence, as if she were laughing at the silliness of the ritual; I could feel the false mind that Irv had planted in me being convinced that she was a very unusual woman, this was just temporary for her, I was the guy to save her from it. "Okay, babe." She tossed her hair back and I saw the delicate sweep of the high arcs of her cheekbones. "Love to be with you. Suck it for thirty, give you the whole thing for eighty, in the car, or take me home for the night for two hundred and do me as much as you can." She'd spotted the eighty bucks Irv had put in my wallet, and how much was in my bank account, and she still hadn't noticed the barriers. It was as Fido said; she was only looking at what interested her, and not seeing the rest.

The trouble was, knowing all that did me no good, because I was about as vulnerable to her as any other human male.

"In the car," I said. My voice was high and scared, not like mine at all. We'd figured it might be the simplest thing to just get her into the car, peel out onto the freeway, and drive like hell till I got to the next exit where Irv and Fido were waiting.

None of that had figured on the effect she would have on me. I handed her the eighty and she said "Pull around the corner and there's a nice little alley that has a streetlight; you're going to want to see this."

The car didn't get cold or uncomfortable for the whole time it was going on. She was out of the suit the moment the car stopped, a body like every fifteen-year-old boy's fantasies displayed in nothing but the spike-heeled boots, and in what seemed only another moment she had me down to my socks.

You'd expect a streetwalker to know how to please men, and as I thrust into her and her thighs wrapped around me, she gave me the best act I'd ever seen, her butt lifting off the seat to meet me, head thrown back and crying out like a cat in rut. But that was nothing compared to what a telepathic streetwalker could do; she gave me, literally, every-thing I had imagined, said the right words at the right time, did things I hadn't known I wanted exactly the way I wanted them. . . .

Somewhere about my fourth orgasm—she was doing something or other so that I didn't even have to stop between—I began to wonder whether she was actually going to fuck me to death. Around the seventh I began to look forward to it. I sat back, and her head immediately plunged down onto my penis, sucking eagerly. She turned in the street-light coming through the car window to show off her body and hair to best advantage.

I let a long, slow breath out. The pleasure was overwhelming, and I relaxed into it like a warm bath.

The streetlight shining through the fire escape cast slotted shadows on the dark red bricks, and something in it held my attention. She found a fantasy or a thought to bring forward from somewhere back there, when I'd been about fourteen, already thinking of running away, had gone to a school dance because there was nothing else to do, walked home with some neighbor girl that I was being too cool to talk to. . . .

I felt Alaneira's mind closing around mine, probing gently into the memories, and they started to blur. . . .

My eyes locked on that shadow again. Hard, straight edges, broken by the roughness of the brick, a dark red that was almost gray in the blue streetlight.

I'd done something petty and mean, actually. The girl had drained my wallet, made me look gooney in front of her friends, flirted a lot with older guys so that I felt out of my league. So when I went to kiss her goodnight, I'd grabbed up under her sweater, yanked her bra down, and squeezed her breasts hard. Startled and in pain, she'd half-screamed against my mouth; her porch lights came on then, and I'd let go of her as I said, "See you in school. Nice tits," and disappeared into the darkness, half-running home.

It was the kind of jerky, rotten thing teenage boys do; not exactly intending to hurt her, just not caring whether I did or not, more interested in what it felt like to have that power over her. I imagine that when she went inside either no one noticed her or else somebody saw the bunched mess of her sweater and slapped her and called her a slut; that's what would have happened to my sister. It was that kind of neighborhood.

But I could feel two images being transmitted from Alanaeira, delicately floating around the memory, finding an angle to edge it out . . . one in which the girl responded eagerly, loved it, wanted more, and the porch light broke us apart just as she was pulling her skirt up . . . another in which I saw the shock and hurt in her eyes, tenderly took her into my arms and made it all right. . . .

Actually when I got home, of all things—it was only about midnight—my mom had been baking cookies. I think because the old man liked them and she was trying to keep him distracted or something; but anyway, I ended up sitting there at the kitchen table two minutes later having milk and cookies, my hands still smelling of the cheap cologne from the girl and my mind still replaying the touch of her body. The old man was sleeping in front of the TV and none of us—my brother, my sister, me, my mother—were going to wake him up. We sat at the table and had cookies and there was a lot of smiling, even from me. . . .

Alanaeira closed on that memory and I found her trying on revisions, one where I talked with Mom about what had happened and ended up being dragged back and apologizing to the neighbor girl, saving her from the brutal father who was about to beat the hell out of her, taking her punishment myself—*why can't I remember her name?* one part of me asked myself—and another where the whole family sort of settled into a Leave It to Beaver fadeout and late at night I secretly wept for the girl as if I'd been a young poet.

I focused on the hard edges of the shadow. Alanaeira sucked hard and deep, body undulating, and I felt my hands twitch to reach out and hurt her breasts, slap them till they were black and blue, teach her to enjoy it like I had the neighborhood slut—I took a deep breath.

The shadow lay on the rough red brick. The droplets of water on the windshield were cold and dirty. The streetlight was harsh and glaring.

The car was freezing cold and I ached all over, but in particular my testicles had been handled so roughly that they felt like they'd been kneed, and my penis felt raw and sore. I was sitting in a slimy, ice-cold pool of goo, practically stuck to the seat of my car. Alanaeira stank of sweat, a lack of bathing, and stale semen from god knew how many men, and the moaning and thrashing she was doing wouldn't have fooled anyone. I grabbed her hair to hold her still, pulled my penis out of her mouth, and probed her deeply with the sight. To my great relief she didn't have AIDS.

With a cry she sat up; there was horror in the way she stared at me, and she lunged for the door, but my hand stabbed out and locked it, and I used her terror and pain to make a spell that would keep her inside the car till I released her.

I started the engine—thank god for once it started promptly in the cold, and jesus it was cold in here—and put the car in motion. Unable to work the door, she slapped at me and screamed. I whipped the car backwards around the corner and shot down the alley.

I don't recommend naked freeway driving, especially not while fending off someone who is slapping and screaming at you, and most especially not on roads slick with freezing rain. It was a good thing it was about four in the morning, because I was all over the road, but luckily there wasn't much ice at the exit, and I managed to get the car down there, whip into the little dark parking area where Irv and Fido were still waiting, hit the brakes and open the door. I fell, still naked, out of the blast of the heater and into inch-deep freezing water and sharp gravel, and if it woke me up at all I don't remember.

* * *

I was back in the healing bed, with Kristin, when I woke up. I felt considerably better, though also a lot like an idiot. Kristin's eyes were open and she had a painfully sad smile.

"I'm sorry," I said, figuring that she either knew everything or was going to.

She nodded, and I could feel the bed working; the distance between us closed considerably. "You were up against more than you could handle."

"I'm still sorry."

"Can't be helped." She pulled me closer, and the little twinge of pain in my heart seemed to add some force to the bed; I knew, deep down, then, that not only was it going to be all right, she would forgive me, but I would be able to accept the forgiveness.

Voices from the other room began to penetrate my consciousness; I could hear Irving's voice chanting something, and urgent whispering from Fido.

Carefully I pushed myself out of the bed and crept toward the door; this time I'd been provided with a set of pajama bottoms, I noted with gratitude.

Alanaeira was weeping quietly; what Fido was saying, over and over, was "You're going to be all right. You're going to be all right. . . ."

I looked through the crack of the door, and froze.

All that beautiful hair lay in a pile on the floor, and she was naked, tied into a chair. Irving was chanting over her, standing behind the chair, and Fido was kneeling in front of the chair, holding her gently, his hands resting on her arms.

And her bones and body were melting and twisting slowly, rendering her hideous. A third breast was growing on her sternum as I watched; the fingers of one hand were elongating and adding joints; one cheekbone was sagging and running like butter in a hot frying pan, and her jaw and chin were slowly merging into the underside of a squared-off muzzle.

She wept, and clearly she knew what was happening, but she didn't ask them to stop.

I let the door close softly; I don't think they saw me. I realized then that Kristin had been peering in around me, as well.

Something in Irving's voice sounded like finality, and then I heard him say, "Now you've got to try the mirror. This will be bad. . . ."

Her voice sounded like a grunting sow. "Me try. Me try. Got see."

The wail that followed was horrible; if it had lasted longer than the second or so it did, I could not have borne it.

Something heavy and damp hit the door, and then Fido was screaming. We shoved the door open—it was hard work—and what was blocking it was Irving's headless body. There was blood everywhere, and in the middle of it sat Fido, beating his hands on the empty chair where Alanaeira had been.

The room was thick with the smell of fresh blood, dripping from everywhere.

And all around, thrown on the walls, were bits of mirror. In each of them, looking into the room, eyes staring wide with terror, was Alaneira's face, not as we had last seen it, but her elf-face. Irv's head lay on the floor, staring up at the ceiling, the tongue protruding and black.

"The bed? . . ." Kristin suggested.

"Only works on the living," I whispered. I heard her turning away to upchuck on the floor.

Fido was now battering the chair to pieces, and I was glad in a distracted way that we had no neighbors who might hear. I made myself lurch over to the chair where Irv, or someone, had left clothes for me, and got myself dressed, yanking things into place without attention, just getting into condition to go. I peeked out the window, saw the Cadillac parked down below, found my keys on the dresser.

Kristin had thrown up everything she had, and was tearing off the old sweatshirt she'd been wearing, running into the little sink-and-toilet bathroom to splash cold water on herself.

"You need to get dressed," I said to her. "We have to get out of here. And we have to get Fido to come with us."

Kristin nodded. "All that . . ." She gestured at the other room.

"We're disappearing. They can look for us as members of a Satanic cult or something." I reached out, took her hand, and concentrated, feeling her fingerprints change, along with mine. Her eyes got wide and she stared at me; maybe that minor parlor trick was bringing her out of the stupor, or the fact that I was using her headache to do it with. "Wish we could take the bed—it was Irv's masterpiece—but there's no time," I added. "See if Fido will come with us—uh, dress first."

She pulled on some clothes and, bracing herself, stepped through the kitchen door.

"She's still in there," Fido said, dully. "Look at her. Look what it's doing."

From every fragment of mirror, Alanaeira stared out, face wide in horror, lips contorting.

"What happened?" I whispered.

"She'd been an elf too long, I suppose," Fido said, his voice thick with despair. He dipped a finger in Irv's blood and marked a mirror fragment. Alaneira's screaming face vanished as the fragment turned black and lumpy, like a piece of broken coal. "But . . ." He started to sob. "But, Eddie, you saw, she wanted to stop, you saw that, didn't you? She was trying to become a goblin and accept it. . . ."

"I saw," I said. "The blood—that will free her?"

Fido nodded, his tears running all over his face, glamour tears on the glamour face crossing tracks with real tears on the real face. I dipped my finger in Irv's blood, nodded a thanks to his sightless eyes, and began marking the mirror fragments. There were a lot of them, and Kristin was helping shortly after. She didn't seem to need to ask what we were doing or why.

"She's trapped in them," Fido explained, "caught betwixt and between—can't bear the ugliness of being a goblin or the coldness of being an elf. All we can do now is release her."

"You were close," Kristin said, prompting him.

"As children, yes, she was my big sister. We were elf raised. She was the only one who'd defend me against the other elf kids. . . . I guess everyone knew I was headed for the pens, except maybe me." He started to cry again. "And the only reason she could defend me . . ."

I turned and saw Alanaeira's face in dozens of places; she was weeping too, from the remaining fragments. I hesitated a moment before marking the blood on the piece—she looked straight into my eyes and nodded for me to do it.

Irv's blood was cooling and congealing as we continued the job, and it stuck coldly to my fingers as I made the mark, but it still did what it had to and the mirror fragment turned to a black mass that reflected nothing.

"She could defend you because she was tougher and meaner than the other elves," Kristin said.

"Yes." Fido was sobbing now. "And she . . . she let me get away . . . when I got the change and they were hunting me, she . . . let me get away."

"That seems like a pretty tender, affectionate feeling to me," I said, marking yet another fragment. There were so many, most no bigger than a quarter. "Why didn't she . . ."

"Because, because, because . . ." and now Fido was sobbing so hard that Kristin got up and threw her arms around him.

We didn't get to find out right then.. There was a roar and a flash, and something was coming out of all the mirror fragments. Not like smoke or flame, not a physical substance at all, but a sort of shimmer in the air, a feeling, a force—the way when you're a kid you imagine that there's something you can almost see between the magnet and the piece of metal.

The wall flew up behind me and clobbered my shoulders; I barely had time to duck my head. Kristin looked like she'd been hit on the skull—she slid down the wall in front of me like a doll in three pieces under its clothes. Irv's house shook savagely. To my right, Fido crouched in the corner, clutching the carpet as if trying to dig through it.

Irv's headless body bounced and jumped as if it might stand up, and suddenly his head turned on the stalk of its severed neck and spoke. "Blessed are you, for you have made a doorway for me—"

Fido wailed and clutched his face and ears.

"And as for you, Accursed One, though this sacrifice had to be, it would have been better for you never to have been than for it to have happened through you—"

I was pissed. I kicked Irv's head, figuring it wasn't Irv anymore. It flipped over and threw the Sight at me.

I threw it back. The head withered, shrank to the size of an apple, and burst open. Whatever it was, it flew out the window and was gone.

"He'll be back after me," Fido said.

"Good," I said, "because I'm after him." I . . . *looked*. I was beginning to realize I'd picked up some skills from the process. "Let's get Kristin into the bed. She's still alive."

"We did. "I'm going to have to amplify it," I told Fido, "and I need a lot of pain to do that with. I guess I can do it all myself—"

"Nope, Eddie. I'd rather be the one. Let's hit 'em."

I seated Fido on the edge of the bed, near Kristin, and raised my arms. I was realizing how much I knew how to do.

The jagged bits of mirror flew out of the other room and assembled on the wall facing Fido. Alanaeira stood there, screaming, trapped. "Speak the truth," I commanded.

"I stayed beautiful because I just used you, Fido," she said. Her voice was high and sweet, what you'd expect of an elf. "God made me that way, you know. I could force other elf kids to be nice to you even though it made them want to throw up. I could protect you from them but they couldn't protect their goblin brothers and sisters from me. You were just something to wave in their faces. You're just an animal to me, nothing more than a scary pet that I used to hurt the other beautiful children."

The burst of pain from Fido was exquisite material; I poured it into the bed and felt Kristin's spine rejoin and straighten, felt her become herself again completely, felt her move onward. . . .

I turned back to the mirror. Fido was in hysterics, which I had expected; I was giving him his worst fears, and just hoping he could forgive the cruelty of it later. I let him watch Alanaeira being eaten alive by ants; they started on the soft pretty places first, and the mixture of horror, shame, lust, and fury from Fido let me complete the healing bed and make it even more Irv's masterpiece.

I shoved Fido down onto the healing bed, to let it fix him in whatever way was needed.

Then, as the bed took the goblin and remade him, I scooped up a handful of Irv's blood from where the stump of his neck was draining his torso, and hurled it onto the mirror. It went black. I felt Alaneira's moment of peace and release, and realized that not long ago it would have mattered a great deal to me; now it was just something that happened. She didn't deserve her peace any more than Fido deserved her misery.

An instant too late, the God of Faerie shot back into the window, heading for the mirror, an idea moving like a streak of light. I had him.

Gods die when confronted by reality. Lose the connection to the shadowy other worlds that they inhabit, and they die. Get them into a physical body and kill it, and they die.

I was stronger and faster than he was. Therefore he perished. In his death I heard a great shout from the other side, as so much magic fell apart, and contacted all the myriad things that had needed doing for so long, happening all at once. I savored one place where goblins, being fattened for the feast, burst the no-longer-magic corral and fell upon an elven choir in its crystal hall. I rejoiced as the elf poets looked up from poring over the immense collection of preserved works in their libraries, and saw the advancing mob of goblins, and laughed with the goblins as poets thirty thousand years old were hurled into the flames of the million-year-old library. Everywhere the crystal shattered; everywhere the songs became screams; the stake, the noose, the rock, and the torch swept away the elven civilization. There was a great crushing of perfect faces and shattering of symmetric beauty, and voices of perfect purity shrieked once in pain and were gone.

A universe of pain poured across the barrier toward me, and I lapped it up. I looked back at Irv and saw what a good guy he had been, with his little power; I wasn't as good a guy, but I had a lot more power, and I could at least try to be like Irv.

I felt something sweet and hot stir in my blood, and copying Irv's bed spell, the thing he had labored through ten lifetimes to make himself able to do, I reached out and went him far better; I used most of the elf pain to remake Faerie into one vast healing bed. The fires would burn low; the elf bodies would rot; grass would grow where the shining cities had been. And the next generation, loved and cherished by its goblin parents, would be neither elves nor goblins; just children, with a world full of magic to play in. Some day, in a couple of centuries, I would have to take a vacation there.

Meanwhile there was enough leftover pain and energy to complete reworking myself, and plenty to do on the plane in which I had been born. I let myself retake my mortal form.

"The police will arrive sometime tomorrow," I said to Kristin, as she sat up in bed. Beside her, Fido groaned and sat up. Both looked remarkably well.

Kristin nodded distractedly.

"Fido, are you all right?"

He nodded slowly. "Is my glamour going to fade?"

"Never again. The bed has fixed it on you. Do either of you remember what happened?"

They shook their heads. Time enough for them to find out later; I could tell them this evening, when we had time to talk. For right now there was no good reason to use more magic than needed; we could get away well enough without having to mess any further with the natural order of things. I gently talked Kristin and Fido out the door and into my Cadillac.

Once I had Kristin sleeping in the front seat, and Fido sprawled across the back, I went back into Irv's apartment, checked his desk and found his car keys and his business insurance. The insurance went on the front seat of his car, as if he had been thinking about it, and then I went back upstairs. I finally let myself look at my friend and teacher and feel that I would not see him again until I myself crossed over, millennia hence; the pain and grief let me put his crushed head back into some sort of order and reattach it to his body. I made the blood in the room flow back in through his nose and lungs and into his circulatory system; it was a poor copy but good enough to fool any coroner who had no reason to be suspicious. Finally, with it all done, I thanked Irv again, poured a bunch of paint thinner around, and tossed a match in. Probably he wouldn't care, being dead, if he got framed for arson or suicide. "Bye," I said, "I'll try to be good."

Very distantly I heard his soul responding; he seemed pretty pleased, not to mention very calm about it for a guy who had just had his head torn off. I got a sense that he wanted me to try really hard, but the Realms of the Dead aren't easily penetrated, and maybe I just imagined that part. Anyway, I was sure I caught a little glimmer of pride that his work had been the basis for my changing Faerie over into a Free Place.

There wasn't much in my apartment that was any good to us; I had a coffeemaker and supplies, and I sent Fido around the corner for some beer, hot dogs, and buns. We cooked up the hot dogs and ate them, had a few beers, and then switched to coffee for conversation. I told them what had happened; I was glad that they didn't seem to treat me any differently than they had before the big changes, because I knew I was going to need friends from now on, and it would be harder to make them.

"So what now?" Kristin finally asked. "I never really even knew whether we had training to complete, or whether we were pretty well done—"

"Depends on what you mean by done," I said.

She brushed her long brown hair back; it was a mess. "Damn bed. Three years of hair in two weeks. And most of the time I wasn't awake to keep it combed."

"It's more your color," I said, "and besides, even without the healing bed's effect on me, I'd have to say it's really beautiful and your best feature. You look a lot less like a doll and a lot more like a woman than you have since I've known you. That ought to count for something."

"Well, it won't do me much good for bar work, but then I can feel that aside from what it did to my appearance, the bed made me over into somebody not fit for bar work either. I suppose that's another way that it makes us into what we should be. I guess what I should be, if I can judge from the effect it had, is some kind of generous spirit who makes everything around me bloom. I think that might even be the destiny that brought me to this town; I'll have to work a few spells to make money flow my way, and then open up a coffee house or something of the sort for sensitive young artists, or bright students, or something I can be gentle to. The kind of place that hasn't existed in this town before." She took a long sip of coffee, glanced sideways at Fido, saw that he was just sitting morosely looking down at the beer in his hand. I felt her decide to finish the conversation about us first. "Eddie, can you train me? I can feel I have some distance to go, before I can make my little place more the center of magic that it needs to be."

"No, I wish I could, but I've no gift as a teacher. I'm sort of a wild talent; I can do all that stuff and understand it intuitively, but I couldn't teach you to save my life. If you want to know more, you'll have to find another magician like Irving. I suspect you'll find one pretty easily— probably he'll drop by right after you open your place."

I stood up, stretched, looked around. Now that I *saw,* I understood a little of why the town was cold and mean, enough to know that for Kristin this was the perfect place, because she could heal it, but for me there were better places to work from.

"So—what are you going to do?"

"Move to somewhere else, settle into something to pay the rent, and do a little exploring on my own. Now that I've got the ability, I don't feel any need to be under anyone's wing—if there's a Wizards' Union or something, I'm not joining." There was, in many planes, but I wasn't joining. I wanted to tell her why. Someday I might. Meanwhile better she didn't know. "I'll see you again."

She smiled at me, a nice warm smile. "Now that we're bonded like this I don't suppose we have much choice about staying in touch. And I guess I've made it clear enough that I'd like to. If, uh, you don't exactly feel the same way, then maybe you'll—um—"

I stretched, hands out and open as if she had me at gunpoint. "I like you too. But there's a little project of my own that's going to take up a lot of time. I'll visit every couple of months or so—I'm not planning to move far." Already I knew there was a town, not far up the road, where people tended to paint their houses and to smile at each other on the street; where spring brought a little more sun, and fall a little more color; and where when people did things they shouldn't, they did them for pleasure, and not just because they shouldn't. It seemed to me as if the whole earth were laid out in a vast grid, with some places getting more of the good, some more of the bad, and most about what they'd have been otherwise.

To learn magic, I had come to one of the coldest and meanest places on the planet; now I could go somewhere warmer and safer.

Maybe, if things went better than I expected, I could bring Kristin along later. Or maybe she would eventually remake this town into a place where I could live. When you're both going to live a few hundred years in young, strong bodies, there's a lot more ways to where you're going, and you don't care as much which one you take.

Meanwhile she'd be okay here, given her awakening gifts . . . and anyway, I had told her the truth. I really didn't know crap about training other magicians.

It actually took me a couple of days to get my affairs in order, dump most of my possessions at the Goodwill, and get the little that remained into the car. In that time, Kristin and I finally found time to make love, which was very pleasant, and that also gave me a chance to leave my soul between the pages of her high school yearbook. It would be a long time before anyone knew where to look for it, and as long as she didn't know she had it, Kristin should be safe enough.

I wasn't sure where Fido was; he had left that evening without saying much. Probably he had some private grieving to do, and after that he would be getting a job someplace. A goblin would rather live on this side of the Barrier if he could, and with his permanent glamour he would pass for human easily enough.

The morning that I left, Kristin dropped by to kiss me goodbye and make me promise to stay in touch; she'd placed a couple of ads in the personals that she figured would draw a real wizard out of the woodwork sooner or later, and found herself a job waiting tables at Rose's coffee shop, out by the highway, for the interim, just to get the feel of such places. Her plan was to have four or five medium-sized windfalls in the next few months, enough to let her set up the sort of place she wanted; shortly after the windfalls the right location would go up for sale at a low rate, and that would take a bit more magic. Her gifts were more than adequate.

Kristin smelled and felt wonderful in my arms, and I wished that I could stick around, but I had things to do and so did she.

On my way to the interstate, someone practically stepped into the road in front of me, raising a thumb. It was Fido. I let him in, and as we continued he said, "We going anywhere special?"

"Just to a nicer town." I noticed he had bought some new clothes and looked nearly respectable. "I have some things to get done."

"Need a partner?"

"Depends. Do you want to know what I'll be doing?"

"Something to do with . . . all this that happened, am I right?"

"You're right."

We drove for half an hour without speaking. It would have seemed like a coincidence to me, once, that as we went under one underpass the sun suddenly came out. Finally Fido asked, "Is it okay if I ask what you have in mind?"

"You know how some planes have Creators and some don't?"

"Unh-hunh. I was the one who told you about them in the first place, remember?"

"Well, I *saw* something in the middle of all the fighting and uproar. Something interesting. Creators can die, and then their planes become Free Places . . . gradually and over time. Eventually the process puts an end to magic, of course, across a few thousand years; magic doesn't work all that well here, for example, since we bagged our Creator almost two thousand years ago."

"Thought that was a story. In fact a story that was a lot older than two thousand years."

"I did too. But I did a little investigating, and it turns out the story had more truth than you might think. Humanity was looking forward to it for a long time, so there were lots of versions of it; when it finally happened, everybody, even the Creator, had their script down cold.

"But the best part is that one part wasn't true. He didn't come back. We set ourselves free. Well, seems to me . . . well, look at the guy we had, for example. Made a world where everyone was born with an evil streak and then punished anyone who exercised it. Created us in his image—sneaky and malevolent—and then created a hell to send us to for having been like him, because he hated himself. Sort of a more twisted version of what your Creator did when he made everything important in your universe revolve around beauty and ugliness, and then punished you for it. And those are far from the nastiest Creators out there—there are a lot of them that didn't even offer false hope to the miserable creatures they made.

"So my thinking is, if they can die . . . well, it would take some figuring to find out how, of course, and it wouldn't all be easy, and sooner or later I guess one of them is going to get lucky before we do. Want to come along?"

"Oh, yeah," the goblin in the seat beside me said, and there was something wonderful in his smile. "I'm up for it."

By now the sun was all the way out, and it was becoming a nice early spring day, a month before it was due. There were no other cars on the highway, so I made a hard right turn, not on or into the ground, not into the sky, but another direction entirely, and we rolled onto a winding highway in another kind of world.

"Are we looking for anyone here?" Fido asked.

I felt the power surge and ooze across this plane and said, "Oh, yeah, definitely." The sky was an elaborate sweeping dome of delicate, planned crystal here, the trees curved elegantly, and every hill was alive with things it seemed about to say. It reminded me of a Ming vase I saw once in a museum.

I thought of bricks and baseball bats.

"We'll be back," I told Fido. Then we turned hard left, back the way we'd come, and we were on the interstate again. The sky was wonderfully empty.

LET US SPEND SOME TIME

WHY THE STARS ARE ALWAYS SO BRIGHT FROM COUSIN SID'S FARM

*I absolutely refuse to justify this story. If you have half as much
fun reading it as I did writing it, I will have had twice as much
fun as you did.*

Getting the president to the presentation, and bringing his whole Cabinet and all those advisors, was the hardest part of the whole business. A modern president in peacetime cannot disappear for several days as easily as John Quincy Adams, or even Calvin Coolidge, could.

They took all the obvious measures. They did it in August, when Washington nearly closes down. For the past five years, four decoy facilities, ominously code named Brooklyn, Queens, Bronx, and Staten Island, had been operated in remote areas to draw off reporters and foreign agents, and the president was seen boarding military flights to each of them in the last week before they actually did it.

There were other diversions. The oldest reporter in the capital could not remember an August when so much news broke so suddenly, and no one in the press had a moment to think as they rushed from story to story. The Chief Justice, saying privately to the president that "the fate of the nation outweighs my reputation—hey, that rhymes," arranged to be caught in a motel room with five naked underage girls and a life-size anatomically correct inflatable Satan. The Navy called in the media and announced that they could not find the carrier *Nimitz*, which was discovered in San Diego the next day flying the Canadian flag, with the name on its bow covered by a hastily painted "RCS *Chucky Beaver*"; the Navy promptly issued denials that it had ever happened. Phone lines to the West Coast mysteriously went down for a few hours after a story broke that the governor of Oregon, an old and close friend of the president, was holed up with a rifle on top of a TV tower in Salem, shooting at anything that moved and vowing not to be taken alive. The lines came back up, and the story turned out not to be true, just as the last planeload of reporters left the runway at Dulles.

And even with all that, the president was photographed getting into an unmarked van behind the White House by the vacationing editor of the Squarepeg, Ohio, *Daily Equivocater.* Luckily, he waited to run it until after he got home four days later; by then no one at the AP was interested.

So ultimately it did work. Somewhere in central Idaho, a vectored thrust transport of a type that did not yet officially exist settled onto the steel planks of a landing pad. Camouflage netting was immediately thrown over the plane, and the presidential party emerged from the jet and raced to a concealed opening, following a long tunnel down into the immense facility under the mountain that, when it was necessary to speak of it at all, was known simply as "The Big Place."

It was a good name. For nearly thirty years, more than half of all the supposed cost overruns and accounting errors had gone into this complex. Over two hundred thousand workers, in many cases with their whole families, were officially listed as dead. The managing director, on the rare occasions when there was anyone to give a tour to, had been heard to say that the Big Place had the only McDonald's in the country where all employees were cleared for Top Secret.

He would have liked to show this party around, but there was no time; instead, he stood in the corner of the main assembly hall and let the Chief Scientific Director speak. The CSD would be followed by seven other directors and managers; the next day all of them would help the president and his advisors examine the options.

The CSD cleared his throat. "I see we're all here. We may as well begin.

"I'm told that most of you have no particular acquaintance with modern physics. The explanation I am about to give you is necessarily grossly oversimplified." He seemed to wait for someone to demand a full and complicated explanation, but when no one did, he went on. "You might have heard of 'wave-particle duality' in mathematical physics: any 'wave' phenomenon can be treated as the action of 'particles,' and vice versa, with valid results. The obvious example is light, which is both photons—particles—and a wave in an electromagnetic field."

The Secretary of Commerce, who read several large slick science magazines every month, raised her hand. "Aren't some things really just particles or just waves? Like sound, which is just waves in matter—"

"I'm glad you picked that example." The CSD smiled; at least the first of the necessary planted questions had come right on cue. "When we mathematically treat sound as a particle phenomenon, we get a beautifully behaved and explanatory little guy called the 'phonon'. That might seem like a purely abstract, arbitrary trick, but a lot of modern acoustic equipment works only because phonons are in some sense 'real'—in defiance of common sense, if you wish.

"This laboratory was founded because, many years ago, a group of grad students got drunk together and played with the reverse process— taking something that we usually think of as a particle phenomenon and describing it as a wave one. The 'particles' they studied were *thoughts*— which had all the required nature of particles for a perfectly conventional analysis."

"Wait a minute, sir," said the Director of Central Intelligence. Good—that was the second one, right on cue. "You mean they were studying their thoughts about particles—"

"They were treating thoughts *as* particles—we called the particles of thought 'thinkons.' Thoughts combine, split, alter each other, cancel out, and in general interact in describable ways; it's quite easy to define a seven-dimensional space in which thinkons do that, with three dimensions corresponding to our spatial ones and one to our time. Now, having defined thinkons, we proceeded to treat them as wave phenomena, beginning from an old expression—"

"Excuse me, you said 'we'?" An unplanned question from a tall man in a bow tie.

The president spoke for the first time since they had arrived. "I have been reliably informed that the four men and two women of the original group have each done at least three major pieces of work that in more ordinary times would lead to a Nobel Prize. As it is, their very existence is so secret that their families believe them to be dead, all killed in a car wreck en route to a convention many years ago. These people have given a great deal for the nation."

Someone in the back of the room clapped; then everyone did, and it was a long time before the CSD, overcome with emotion, could speak again.

"As I said, we began from the old expression 'brain wave.' We used standard procedures to convert the particle properties to a wavelength and frequency.

"Now, in any high school physics class you learn that wavelength times frequency gives wave velocity. Imagine our surprise, gentlemen and ladies, when it appeared that the wave velocity was slightly over one billion c."

Most of them stared blankly, except for the Secretary of Commerce. She whistled loudly—another unplanned interruption.

"c is the speed of light," the CSD explained, awkwardly getting off script. "According to all the physics we thought we knew, from Einstein forward, nothing could go faster than that. And yet thinkons were going not just faster, but a billion times faster."

There was a stunned silence. Two dozen lifelong politicians had just found themselves to be standing at a great moment in history; every one of them was painfully aware that a stupidity uttered now would be quoted longer and with more relish than even Coolidge's celebrated comment on unemployment.

"Fortunately, the first person we showed it to was the department chairman, who had done some work for the NSA. This facility was started shortly after—and now, after years of work, gentlemen and ladies—*thinkon physics works!*

"And we won't make the mistake of earlier generations of military planners by introducing thinkon-based technology piecemeal. No, we are ready within a few months to begin building, in industrial quantities, weapons and equipment with capabilities absolutely undreamed of across the board. If you can imagine George Washington suddenly equipped with working machine guns, tanks, submarines, airplanes, radios, and computers, you have some idea of the leap we contemplate. Within one year we can achieve a security never known before by any power in history.

"But before I turn you over to the people who will explain these things in detail, let me lay out a few basic principles of thinkon physics, so that you will have some idea of how such devices are possible.

"Thinkons have many properties which are inversions or reversals of the ordinary physical ones. For example, just as mass emits the graviton, the exchange particle for gravity, and thus creates what we perceive as a 'gravitational field,' the thinkon is the exchange particle for what we dubbed a 'field of study.'

"Study is a remarkable force, a curious mirror image of gravity. It repels matter with a force proportional to thinkon emission and to mass as in gravity, but directly—not inversely—proportional to the square of distance. In other words, the farther away it is, the harder a thinkon emitter shoves it away. One of our cosmologists believes this can eventually be shown to account for the familiar phenomenon of the expanding universe.

"Thinkons are produced every time information is handled or copied; the more coherent, precise, and novel the thought, the more thinkons are emitted.

"Thinkons can also be polarized into a coherent beam—"

A Great Crash in Everyone's Mind All At Once!

*ATTENTION.
*YOUR CIVILIZATION HAS BEEN REVIEWED BY THE SPATIAL PROTECTIVE AGENCY OF THE INTERGALACTIC... UMM... UMMM... FEDERATION. YOUR THINKON PRODUCTION IN YOUR LAST FEW... DON'T HELP ME... GENERATIONS HAS REACHED INTOLERABLE LEVELS, CAUSING RELOCATION OF MANY—WHATCHAMAJIGGERS... GALAXIES, AND OTHER DISRUPTIONS IN THE FRAMEWORK OF REALITY. HAND ME THE CARD, BR'ZX'PH, I'M GOING TO HAVE TO READ IT—YOU WIN THE BET. SINCE YOU HAVE FAILED TO CORRECT THIS SITUATION THROUGH YOUR OWN EFFORTS, THINKON SUPPRESSION IS BEING IMPOSED THROUGHOUT YOUR SOLAR SYSTEM TO PREVENT EMISSIONS EXCEEDING STANDARDS. THIS IS A ROUTINE PROCEDURE INVOKED AGAINST ANY CIVILIZATION WHICH EXCEEDS THINKON EMISSION STANDARDS AND IT IS UNLAWFUL TO BELIEVE THAT YOU ARE BEING DISCRIMINATED AGAINST.
*WE REGRET ANY INCONVENIENCE.
*HAVE A NICE DAY.

"Um, I forgot what I was saying," the CSD confessed.

"Well," the president said, "it's late in the afternoon already. Let's send out for some pizzas and see what's on the tube."

The CSD remembered—there would be planted questions. This must be one, because he knew the answer. "We can get pizza from the commissary," he said. "They ought to give it to us, I mean we pay taxes and all. And we have a satellite antenna—*Gilligan*'s on in twenty minutes, and then pro wrestling—"

Afterwards, everyone agreed it was the bestest meeting they had ever went to.

THAT STYLE THINGIE

Read over your compositions, and where ever you meet with
a passage which you think is particularly fine, strike it out.
—DR. SAMUEL JOHNSON

A couple years ago I got stuck teaching a creative writing class, in one of
the sorts of academic deals that get cut between department chairs and
that usually involve photographs of each other naked with farm animals,
and gigantic shipments of heroin distributed to schoolchildren. I never
did find out what the exact nature of the evil deal between Jim and
Sandy was, but there I was with a bunch of college students who
thought they wanted to write short stories.

Actually I cleared out about ten of them immediately by declaring
that since this was a college class at the junior level, I would read all written work until enough spelling and grammatical errors had accumulated
so that a professional editor would have tossed it aside, then draw a line
and not read farther. If I drew the line at all, the paper would get an F. I
also told them they'd be writing one bona fide short story per week for
the first three weeks, and quite a few people decided there were easier
places to fulfill a general education requirement for "expressive arts."

That got me down to seventeen people who had some business being
in a creative writing class, including two who have now had professional
publication, and a few more if they would get going and write and submit something. (If you're reading this, guys, that's a hint.) By the fourth
week, everyone had produced at least one thing that could be identified

as a short story—not always well written, not always successfully plotted, often populated by cardboard or incomprehensible characters, sometimes not even interesting, but the lifeless object that lay on my desk was a lifeless short story, as opposed to a lifeless personal confession, vignette, or student essay.

Somewhere around that time, a young woman who was one of the better writers in the class dropped by my office to discuss an A she had gotten (A's were scarce) on a short story. She was surprised at the A, and bemused that several students in the class, who were used to getting A's for their writing, had so far not reached above a C. So I talked about her story, and what made it a good story, and at the end of the conversation—still not really persuaded that she deserved an A—she said, "So you don't take off points for that style thingie."

A little further conversation revealed that most of her life as a writer—this was one of those people you pray for in a class like that, someone who filled up notebooks just for the hell of it from the moment she could hold a crayon—had been filled with admonitions: "use college words," "can't you find a better way to say it, something dramatic and exciting?", "learn to love words," and "it's okay but there's no poetry in it."

Having received just that kind of complaint from my own English teachers for many years, I cheerfully told her that, no, I didn't take points off for that style thingie. In fact, I slammed the hell out of papers that attempted that style thingie. The words she used were simple, clear, and arranged in ordinary sentences; that was good. Her job as fiction writer was not to impress me with her vocabulary, or make me sit back and exclaim about her splendid sentences, but to tell me a damn story, and that was what she had done.

She went on her way convinced that I was an eccentric, but then that's what happens to most students who come to my office.

One of the stranger things in the whole strange field of science fiction is a passionate belief in Beautiful Writing—lots and lots of extraspecial exciting words thrown no *hurled* no CASCADED upon the reader in a shimmering shower of precious verbal gleaming gleanings and a singing pillar of righteous fiery syntactic spinach.

The only thing any good in that sentence was the spinach, and to hell with it.

Whatever its dubious literary parentage, science fiction as we know it today grew out of the pulps, where writing was paid for by the word, and the excitement of the story was what mattered. In such an environment, some good writers flourished, as did some bad writers, and a whole vast array of mediocre writers. Style was freer then than it has ever been since; a writer could write practically any way that got the story told (though on the other side of the coin, an editor also felt free to do just about anything to what the writer wrote). Hence, because it wasn't stamped out in time, the wordstorm, the paragraph or six of showing off, of the kind found in writers as diverse as Harlan Ellison and Ray Bradbury, became one of the common tools of our fictional trade, and some of the fans have, for some horrible reason, come to love it.

By now there's another kind of reader and writer who is nodding his head in agreement, and about to get thwacked on the backstroke. There's also the tradition of supposedly transparent prose, that of Orwell and Twain, of "just get on with the story" and "a plain tale plainly told." In older science fiction you see it in writers like Asimov or Brunner (before he abruptly began wordstorming in the mid-60's). It's a school that lends itself to a different kind of parody: "He went to his father's funeral. Somebody shot his brother there. It was cold and rainy all day, and when he got out of the police station, after answering a lot of questions, he felt sad and cold. He got a cup of coffee but he still felt sad and cold. He went home. Later that night there was an explosion." That is, it's all reportage and flat affect, a Jack Webb delivery that is in many ways as fake as the wordstorm.

Well, then, what ought style to be? I will venture just two thoughts here, and then see if they hold up with a few examples from writers known for their style.

The first is that an effect that is not gotten by the action of the story should not be attempted with the words; that is, if what is happening is dull, or ineffable, or involves people we don't care about, it cannot be made more exciting, effed, or engaging by hurling abstract nouns, metaphoric verbs, and overnumerous adjectives at it. That is sentimentality, as much as the great waves of violins in a movie that tell us that we ought to feel something for two young lovers who have in fact been boring us stiff. There are people who are suckers for it, and they are welcome to it, but it's not style—it's kitsch.

The second thought is a bit more subtle: style is a habitual pattern of choices that can be abstracted from the personality, period, genre, movement, or rhetoric in which they were first noticed; therefore, although a bogus and silly style is independent of the reader and writer (it is bogus and silly to anyone who knows what they are looking at), a strong and definite style is a matter of taste between any two good readers. That is, where there is style, there is something that can be done a number of ways, and it is clearly chosen, more often than not, to do it in a particular way. Furthermore, that set of choices might first have been noticed in the works of a particular writer (Hemingway's short sentences, Chandler's deliberately strained metaphors), in a period (the slow beginnings of most early Romantic novels), in a genre (the matter-of-fact reporting of violent death in hardboiled novels), in a movement (the sudden violent outbursts and the lengthy harangues in expressionist plays), or in a particular rhetoric (the pathetic suffering of children in social-realist novels)—but wherever they were first noticed, they are portable; they could be used by someone else in some other text and still be recognizable, which is another very long way round of saying that they are truly choices, whether conscious or not.

Now, what I am saying about these abstractable choice-patterns (and what a horrible phrase *that* is), is that where they are sentimental, in the sense of reaching for an unjustified effect, or affected, pretty nearly any competent reader can see this and reject it. But by nature, a pattern that is strong and effective—i.e., one that helps rather than hurts the story, enhances rather than detracts from the reading experience—is truly a matter of individual taste.

Or, put briefly: bad style is objective. Good style is subjective.

I'm going to try this out on the works of four writers grabbed off my shelf, all still practicing, all of whom get regular praise for their style. This is a paragraph pulled out of the middle of each novel by opening it blindly and pointing; I've modified my choice by picking the nearest paragraphs of "characteristic length," i.e., about as long as the median length on the page (so that a writer who mostly writes short paragraphs is judged on a short one, for example).

> His arms came up suddenly, wildly, knocking the cloth backward out of Kivrin's hand, and then he was sitting up, flailing at her with both his hands, kicking out with his feet. His fist caught her on the side of her leg, buckling her knees so that she almost toppled onto the bed. (Connie Willis, *Doomsday Book*)

The first observation here is that Willis gets a lot of active and specific verbs into one short paragraph. She likes adverbs a bit better than I do.

She uses "and then" correctly—i.e., to link discrete parts of a continuous action. This impresses me because it's a point of fussy precision. Many writers don't use "and then" correctly, thus producing stories that read as if a five-year-old child were summarizing them—"And then we went to the woods. And then we picked berries. And then a man jumped out of the bushes." This is so obnoxious that some writers have sworn off "and then" entirely and will cross it out everywhere they find it. But it does have a use, and here it is used exactly right—the action is continuous, but one part of it happens before the other, not simultaneously with it.

The most interesting thing here, by far, though, is that Willis has really structured the events in a completely moment-to-moment fashion. Each noun and verb appears in the paragraph in exactly the order that Kivrin, the viewpoint character, would encounter them. Reread it and see—it's done very well: the arm, the cloth, the hand—she sees it coming, her attention shifts to the object being knocked, she feels it in her hand. This kind of unity between word and action is hard to do, and while it may not have been conscious, it cannot have been an accident.

The style here gives us a direct, strong hook to the action; there's not an ounce of falseness or sentimentality to it. The style is strong and effective. I prefer plainer verbs to more specific ones; but now we're in the realm of taste, that second part of my argument. The flailing, buckling, and toppling would be hard to take over time—I'd rather see more hitting, bending, and falling—but this is very much a matter of taste, and for all that it's not what I'd like best, it's a real style, not a fake. I could reasonably wish that I wrote things to my own taste as well as Willis writes to hers.

> They crossed the river by Blackfriars Bridge, neither of them saying much, though the old man seemed to be as pleased as a child on Christmas morning who, now that everybody is home from Mass, is finally allowed go to into the room where the presents are. He led Doyle down Great Surrey Street and then to the left down one of the narrower streets and finally to a high brick wall that completely enclosed one fairly large lot. There was a stout-looking door in the wall, and with a grin and a horrible raising of both eye-

brows, the old man held up a brass key. (Tim Powers, *The Anubis Gates*)

First observations should be obvious, and the first observation is that Powers is a lot more free-spending with words than Willis is. Some parts of this are hard to picture: I'm not sure what there is about raising eyebrows that can be horrible, what the difference is between large and fairly large, or whether they spoke or not or about what. There are certainly more qualifiers, adjectives, and adverbs than I like.

But the biggest problem here seems to be that the strongest part of the paragraph is that kid being kept out of the Christmas room. That's a whole story, right there, in that sentence, and it's far more interesting than watching Doyle and the unpleasant old guy go to a hidden door. Indeed, the emotional impact of the moment seems to be coming mostly from what is borrowed from the Christmas story, and very little from the old man himself.

It's almost the perfect case of getting the effect from something other than the actions themselves; take away that poor kid who is being kept from his presents, and you have a walk described in excessive detail, and a happy old man whom the viewpoint character experiences as unpleasant. Powers has certainly written better paragraphs elsewhere, but I'll stick to a gun here: too often, as if he doesn't quite trust his material, he gives it a paint job with a striking image, a mini-story, an arresting phrase, that for a moment takes us right out of the story. This is one place where the good Dr. Johnson, quoted at the beginning of this piece, is absolutely right. Strike out the fine parts; make the story do its job.

> There is a knock and Katie Wilson enters. Tucker's wife, frizzy-blond and sharp-featured, at first might be mistaken for an aging cocktail waitress with little on her mind, but then one would notice the sharp intelligence and alert sensitivity behind the heavy makeup and southern drawl. "Richard?" she says, "I'm glad you're back." (Dan Simmons, *Phases of Gravity*)

There's a tough problem here, though it's a common one; a new character is being introduced, and presumably something ought to be known of her to keep the story interesting and the people in it real. Yet what she's doing is not much more than saying "hello" at this point. So the three sentences Simmons gives us divide up the job: 1. Get Katie into the scene. 2. Tell us something about her, and 3. Have her perform one (small at this point) function. Of these, only number 2 can carry any emotional freight or do anything interesting.

"There is" is a phrase that can often be gotten rid of; it's a verbal tick created by the need for the viewpoint character suddenly to become aware of a thing. Here it preserves the exact order of action and should probably be tolerated; it's not an especially graceful choice but probably a prudent one. Similarly, not much could be done to the last sentence; one could move or discard "she says," but again this is more a matter of taste.

But that second sentence is something else again. Science fiction writers, forever struggling with huge quantities of exposition, are always overstuffing sentences, and this one is about to explode. The action doesn't really provide time for Richard to think these things during the place in the action that the sentence occupies; it's not part of the action, but an interruption.

As an interruption, it is a set of stage directions that serves mainly to claim that Richard has learned to disregard Katie's appearance—at the same time that it seems to make him dwell on it. It is interesting, too, that the favorable terms are mostly abstract, the negative terms altogether too concrete; it wouldn't be much of a caricature to say that the message here is that she's pretty smart for a white trash bimbo. The sentence seems in part to try to avoid saying that—and not to succeed in its avoidance—by the use of many specifics and a loose construction of oppositions. This long excursion around a hard uncomfortable kernel is another case of a bogus style, but it's bogus in the opposite direction from Powers—not trying to add punch, but to soften offense.

In fiction, offense should not be softened; deleted yes, but softened never. The view expressed in that windy sentence may be Richard's—in which case the reader should be made more succinctly aware of Richard's class bigotry. Or it may be Simmons's—in which case he perhaps was expressing something unconscious that he did not really want to say (and should cut it), or perhaps was expressing his real feeling (and should jam it up the reader's nose).

This last is almost cheating:

> Angie called pause again, rose from the bed, went to the window. She felt an elation, an unexpected sense of strength and

inner unity. She'd felt this way seven years earlier, in New Jersey, learning that the others knew the ones who came to her in dreams, called them the loa, Divine Horsemen, named them and summoned them and bargained with them for favor. (William Gibson, *Mona Lisa Overdrive*)

The reason it's almost cheating is that it's cyberpunk, and the cyberpunks caught a bad case of wordstorm early on in the development of their movement. This paragraph features a reasonably controlled mini-wordstorm; that second sentence in which we learn that the way she's feeling is a set of vague abstractions. We are then told that she's felt this way before. At that point, anyway, I'm lost, but since the point of the action seems to be that she's taking a break, feels pretty good, and is reminded of an important incident in the past, I'm not *terribly* lost. Still, a specific here, a pinned-down nebulosity there, and this could have been a much stronger paragraph; words like "inner unity" are being summoned to do the work that the actions should do.

I would absolutely have to say, then, that of the four selections, it is Connie Willis who has the strongest style, by far. But I selected these four books for a reason: I enjoyed the Powers, the Gibson, and the Simmons very much, and I haven't been able to force myself through the Willis. Objectively she writes a lot better than all three of them; but finally she just doesn't tell a kind of tale that will hold my interest. When you come right down to it, I just don't seem to give very many points for that style thingie.

DELICATE STUFF

This story takes place in the universe of Orbital Resonance *and* Kaleidoscope Century, *about twelve years after the events of* Orbital Resonance. *I had originally intended to do a bunch of closely linked short stories; this was the first, and then I sat down to write a five-thousand-word story about Melpomene Murray and it turned into a novel (and now two novels, with two more to follow).*

All the graphics were wobbling around in the center of their clean-and-green ranges, none falling to yellow or rising to red. Homer Bizet always loved the last hour of shaping, riding herd on the intricate patterns of thousands of rising and falling bars. There was no window into the tank, of course—some of the bacteria were photosensitive—but after nine years of this, Homer could "see" the left lower exhaust nozzle as clearly as if it were actually growing in front of him, visualize the dance of the depositor bacteria as they laid down the complex alloy lattice on the surface, knotting hexes and octagons of fourteen different elements together to form the new part.

One bar dropped abruptly toward yellow. In G/8/7, a parabolic section near the throat, cobalt concentration was falling toward minimum. Homer patched in a flow line and fed more cobalt; the beryllium and terbium bars immediately shot upward toward red. Probably the cobalt had inhibited their depositors. He cut back their flow gently and shot in a little extra metabolite for all three depositors. The bars fluxed wildly for a second or two, then settled back into steady, slow pulsing. He exhaled, relaxing—this was what made the job interesting, but it had been close for a moment.

The faint ping warned him that someone was approaching in the corridor. Finished grown metal was many times stronger for its weight and thickness than any cast or machined alloy, but grown-metal work was so delicate that nothing startling could be allowed to happen in the tank room.

Carol softly cleared her throat and emerged from the entry way in front of him. "It's almost your shift end," she said.

That annoyed him a little; he had forgotten to check his clock. A glance upward showed the blue remaining almost entirely eaten up by the yellow completed. "Right," he said, "thanks."

All the bars were behaving, still clean-and-green. Technically, running any one bar seven per cent of the time in the yellow and eleven in the red was acceptable if total time out of green on all gauges was no more than nine per cent—Homer had been shop steward a couple of years ago and knew the standards. But he liked to stay tight in green, and this was his third straight day without a yellow, fifth without a red. . . .

Homer had let his mind drift, and now C/6/6 moly was shooting up toward red. He dumped metabolite in fast, pulling the activity as high as he dared, and the bar plunged. But he had overcompensated, and before he could inject more molybdenum, the graphic had flickered yellow.

The momentary low was meaningless—it took several seconds off concentration before the probability of misshaping the sites rose above .0001—but he still wished his long clean run hadn't been spoiled.

Nothing more happened for the next couple of minutes. Then the bell sounded and the computer injected the tank with killers, bringing the process to an instant halt. Behind the wall, the grapple clanked faintly as it lifted the mostly complete nozzle from the stand and transferred it to the deionizing bath for fixing. Homer leaned back and stretched, trying not to blame Carol for the spoiled run.

Although she *had* disturbed him just before it happened.

"Well," he said, "that's it for today. If you don't mind, I want to see what the holo says before I go."

"Sure," she said. "I brought the mail. There was some stuff I thought you might want to get a chance to look at before Enoch had a chance to call."

"A response?" He wasn't sure whether he wanted it to be or not.

"All three. The postmarks are within an hour of each other." Her arms slipped around him in a hug. "Probably they're all locked in a bidding war over the best grown-metal tech in the solar system."

"Moose shit," he said, trying not to smile. "You know most likely they've *all* turned me down."

"But at least you've *applied.*"

The holo came back then, and he delayed opening the mail to look at the screen. Completion had gone from under eighty-six to almost eighty-nine per cent. Even allowing for the slowness of final surfacing, within ten working days he would be done, and this was the last of the nozzles. It would be interesting, finally, to get started on the major structural members.

"Just over three per cent," Carol said. "That's really good at this point, isn't it?"

"Yeah."

"Well, then they'll just have to take you. Now open the letters, Homer, before one of us explodes."

He smiled in spite of himself, kissed her lightly on the cheek, and took the mail from her. The addresses on the envelopes were a little dark and blurry—he wished again that there was money for a better faxer, and for half a dozen other things. Well, maybe there would be money—

He opened the envelope from Global Hydrogen. His father had worked three years, twenty years ago, with the teams hanging the Quito Geosync Cable, so he had a slight leg up . . . but not enough of one, according to the letter. Should he wish to retrain, of course . . .

The envelope from Tsiolkovskigrad Station Maintenance contained a polite form rejection assuring him that his name had been added to the list but that the company's orbital operations seldom needed custom grown-metal parts. There was a list of their suppliers that he might wish to submit résumés to. Every firm on the list had had a no-hire notice out for at least two years.

That left NLPF. Nihon Libration Point Facility did not want him for the slot to be filled in eight months time because two persons senior to him in experience, one of them with a better overall record, had also applied. He had come in third amount 450 applicants.

But there *was* an immediate opening, nonvested, straight wage, indefinite term.

Wordlessly, he passed all three letters to Carol. She flipped through the first two more quickly than he had; the NLPF offer stayed in her hand for a long time. Finally she said, "Well, it's immediate, but maybe you can buck them back a year—"

He shook his head. "I'll ask them, but this is 2036, and with the Moratorium on, they can offer it to another guy tomorrow, and he'll take it and ship up the next day."

She nodded, her face expressionless. "And there's no vesting. It's strictly for wages."

"That's right." At least she appreciated that it mattered to him. "Here I'm fully vested."

"With no paycheck." She looked away. "I'm sorry, but you seem to forget that sometimes."

"I bring in money," he said, "enough to pay my share and keep us living. We can keep going on our Dolework, and that's not going to go away. Besides, I'm the last grown-metal tech on the Deepstar Project. If I leave without a replacement, the project folds and I lose all the profit rights from my vesting. It would mean my last two years were for nothing—"

"And if it folds anyway, what do you have? That vesting won't be worth anything. And as for the Dolework . . ." She bit her lip and swallowed hard.

"Go ahead," he said.

She looked down at the ground. "I don't want to. I'd just say something I don't really mean."

"Very *Christian* of you," he said. "Extra points in heaven for this little girl."

"Homer, stop it." Her tears were dripping from her face onto her shirt. She did not look up. "I don't want to have a fight."

"Well, maybe I do." He hated the ugly sound of his voice, but Carol had started this whole thing. She had whined until he started shipping out résumés to what few openings there were, and she had built it up in her mind into the thing that would save them from the "shame" of the Dole—a shame that was entirely in her mind, thanks to her parents. "Maybe I want to have a fight," he said, "did you think of that? So why don't you go ahead and say it? The only work I get paid for is the Dole, working on Enoch's crew, and I'm never home because I work two jobs, and Moddy and Abe think they don't have a father. Come on, let's say the whole thing. And you don't see why I have to do this. . . ."

She had turned away, looking down at the sterile white tank room floor.

"Let me tell you something." His hands squeezed each other painfully; he could feel himself trembling. "*This* is my job. This is what I do. I'm growing the critical parts for the first crewed starship here. I'm going to own a great big piece of the Public Services Contract. And if you're about to ask if that means more to me than you or the kids—well, it does."

She was still silent, not moving, sulking as always. The pit of his stomach felt cold and heavy, but he went on. "I thought you got past all of that a long time ago, but I guess I was wrong. I know your parents taught you that every Dolework fiver has Satan's hoofmarks on it, but I was raised in the twenty-first, and I'll take the Dole or worse to stay here with Deepstar. If you can't stand that, maybe it's time for a nice unChristian divorce."

"Homer," she said, after a long silence, my mother sent me this note. She's coming out for a visit. I can try to tell her no, but you know she'll probably just turn up anyway."

He turned and left then, not giving her a chance to say anything more, fleeing down the corridor to the Deepstar main entrance and into the crowded malls of Spokane Dome. He hoped they would notice that she was in the tank room without him and give her a hard time.

Not really looking where he was going, he automatically started for home. He realized that Carol would go there too, and wished they could avoid each other longer, but neither of them had anywhere else to be.

His wristcom whined like an angry mosquito. When Homer touched the acknowledge, Enoch Velasquez's face filled the tiny screen. "Heya, Homer. One of my regular Tuesday swampers is down sick. Time and a half if you want it."

"What's my return time?"

"Oh six-thirty is the ET. Could flex a little one way or another. You still get twelve hours at one-point-five pay even if we're back early—and your full time at that rate if we run late."

"Well, I'm tempted, but that's only half an hour before I'm due back on the tank, and I need to be up and green for that."

"Sleep during your out-and-back and catch some catnaps," Enoch urged. "I can't make you take it, and god knows you're entitled to some downtime on your Dolework—you've got a great record—but it's going to be a long haul, and I need a full crew, and a good, reliable one too. All I can say is I'd be grateful."

Enoch had been more then generous in the difficult years after the

Moratorium, when Deepstar had stopped paying anything at all and the temp market had virtually shut down. He was a good boss, as generous as a Dole contractor could afford to be.

Unfortunately, as long as the Moratorium was still on, that wasn't particularly generous. When the run on the banks and the stock market had started two years before, the government computer models had shown no bottom—if allowed to run its course, the depression would become permanent. The economy had simply gotten too interlocked to revive in a bootstrap start.

So they has passed the Moratorium; Homer remembered how relieved he had felt when it was announced. You couldn't be laid off or fired, your vesting kept accumulating, and you and your pension fund would continue to accumulate IOU's. Theoretically, some day it would all be paid off.

Meanwhile, to meet the bills, there was Dolework—work for Public Services Contractors, at minimum wage because the low bid got the contract. As long as you took every offer, it would feed, clothe, and house a family, though not in style. An extra night's Dolework right now might mean a birthday present for Modesty, even dinner out with Carol. . . .

Homer knew what would happen if he stayed home this evening: they would shout at each other until his nerves were shattered and he was guaranteed to be short of sleep for his next stint at the tank. Then they would agree that he would apply for more jobs, that Carol's mother would come for a month, and that he would keep working on Deepstar—for despite Carol's hopes there were really not many jobs anyway, and as long as he stayed with Deepstar, he could at least keep his skills current.

Of course, she'd always have the NLPF offer to throw in his face from now on. "I'll take the job," he said to Enoch.

"Good man! Your pickup's at Berth 631A in twenty-five. See you there then." Enoch clicked off.

631A was on the other side of Spokane Dome, so Homer dropped two dollar coins into a gliderail car, got his change, and keyed in the address. The little car rose and sped down the track. He stared at the dime in his hand for a moment. In better times, they had simply thrown dimes in an old jar; now that jar was all the savings they had.

Ordinarily, he liked to look at the falls in the center of the dome, foaming and thundering below the big green swath of Riverfront Park, but this time he would need all the sleep he could get. With regret, he set the windows to dark and reclined his seat.

At Berth 631A, everyone except Enoch was already waiting by the diskster. Ulysses Hayakawa, a Dolebird by preference who actually liked being a swamper, leaned against the sloping side of the disk where sunlight from one of the windows was hitting it. "Heya, partner."

"Heya, Ulysses." Usually, on Homer's regular Monday and Thursday shifts, they worked together; Homer wanted to get it done and get home, and Ulysses wanted to do it well, which meant quickly.

The two younger members, Cato and Naomi, sat on the deck rolling dice and poring over a copy of *Surfaces in Opposition*. Naomi had converted to cybertao a few years back—a lot of people had taken up the Stochastic Faith lately—and since Cato was crazy about her, he was studying it. Ulysses had once said that it was a good thing that Naomi had not taken up "gravitic correction," the current fad for hour-long headstands, because if she had, Cato would have caved in his head.

Homer was still hoping this would be a simple fishing run up to Flathead Lake, but he knew it was going to be game—otherwise why such a long trip with such a big crew? And it wasn't any season for fish anyway, and Billings Dome had been less and less willing to sublease Flathead fishing rights to Spokane lately.

Going after animals always bothered him. There was more wildlife of all kinds in North America than at any time since 1700, and he certainly liked venison and elk as well as anyone else, but he just hated killing things.

Sure enough, when Enoch arrived and let them into the diskster, the inside was stocked with woods suits, light amps, dart guns, and fletch-rifles. Game for sure.

Homer stretched out in a jump bunk aft; harvesting disksters were built for silence and maneuverability, not speed, and they would be running more than 500 km up toward Glacier, a two-hour trip along the old highways. The charged impeller needles popped out and started the ionized airflow over the disk surface, lifting the craft and shoving it forward. The comfortable routine seemed to wipe his worries away; before Spokane Dome had even gone from the rearview screen, he was asleep.

When he woke again, they were about fifteen minutes from their first stop. Naomi was continuing her long-running argument with Enoch; Cato, as usual, was sitting next to her and patting her arm every time it sounded to him as if she'd carried the point.

"But there's nothing spiritual to it," Enoch said. "It's plain common sense that a complex ecology like wilderness produces more biomass and raw protein than a simple ecology like ranches and farms. You get so many more cross-feeds, and there's virtually no waste. That's sophomore college ecology, not the Immanent God."

"Science is how the Immanent God makes himself known to us," Naomi said firmly. Cato touched her arm. She ignored it and continued, "Within sixty years of the Copy Diffusion of Turing, Gödel, and von Neumann, the global ecosystem began to roll back to its natural and proper complexity. Could that just be coincidence?"

"No," Enoch said, "that's economics. We finally got cheap, fast information-processing capability to make full use of the natural system without damaging it. The reason for land agriculture wasn't that it produced more food per acre, but that it produced food on predictable acres and simplified your tracking. You always knew where the corn or the cow was. It wasn't till we got cheap satellites and computers that we could harvest wild food at acceptable cost and keep our harvesting from unbalancing the ecosystem."

"Then you admit my point," she said. "We got those things right after the Copy Diffusion of the First Triad—it was purely a coincidence."

Homer knew enough Cybertao doctrine, having gone to a couple of lectures years ago and even read *Forks in Time,* to know that coincidence was supposed to be how the Immanent God consciously evolved toward his upcoming birth. Not only did it all make a certain peculiar sense, it made it almost impossible to argue with a cybertaoist.

Ulysses grunted awake next to him. "What's she going to do if Enoch ever converts?" he asked.

"Start on us, I guess."

"Go, Enoch."

Homer nodded agreement. Ulysses sat up on the jump bunk and looked at the screen. "Well, that's nice and restful. First call is bison, open country, flat ground. Piece of cake if we don't spook 'em."

"Yeah." They moved cautiously forward to the suit locker; Enoch sometimes took turns suddenly without much warning. Homer passed Ulysses his suit, then pulled his own on. The lightweight covering always made him feel better, as if he were armored against the dirt and bugs of wild country.

A few minutes later, guided by the satellite, they left the old road and crossed three kilometers of open ground toward the target herd. The satellite showed no wolves or humans in the area, so there was little chance of the bison spooking.

The diskster settled without a sound onto the summer-dry ground downwind of the herd. The cabin lights dimmed. Homer flipped on his light amp, setting it for spectral compression so that infrareds would show as red-to-orange and ultraviolets as blue-to-violet.

They emerged from the glowing red cabin to see the herd of bison half a kilom away. The moon glowed bright green in the amp's eyepieces; the deep green grasslands were as quiet as they had been before Columbus.

Enoch's subvoke crackled in their ears. "Ulysses and Homer go right; Naomi, me, and Cato will go left. It's a clear night, so wait for the designator; we want one clean hit on each."

"Brain shots again, boss?" Ulysses asked.

"Yeah. Still nobody wants the thinking part. It says something about modern times. Let's go."

Silently, they closed in on the herd. The bison glowed crimson in the lenses of the amp, oblivious in the warmth and plentiful food of summer—happier, Homer thought, than he was ever likely to be.

They stood in their positions for a long time while Enoch talked to the satellite. Finally, the purple lines of the designator lasers stabbed down from the star-filled sky above, pointing out bison.

"Ready on the right," Ulysses subvoked.

"Go ahead," Enoch responded.

Ulysses shot one immediately, and the purple designator switched off as if it had somehow drawn its power from the living beast. Homer sighted his fletch-rifle, placing the laser spot on the right place on the skull for a clean brain shot, and squeezed the trigger.

The fletch, no bigger than a grain of sand but moving at four km/sec, slammed into the center of the laser spot, penetrating the bison's skull before the binary agents in its structure collapsed together under the impact to form the unstable neurotoxin. In an instant, driven by the force of impact, the deadly stuff had diffused throughout the big animal's brain, and the bison died before it fell. Within less than a minute the toxin would decay to harmlessness, though to be on the safe side the brain would be discarded.

Purple lines from the sky selected two more fat cows and a yearling; Ulysses and Homer brought them down.

As the last one crashed to the ground, something finally alerted the herd, or perhaps it was just time to wander a few hundred meters more upwind. They walked away quickly, not even sniffing at the bodies.

"Tidy little job," Ulysses said. "The way I like them." They walked forward to wrap the monomyl lifting slings around the carcasses.

As he tightened one sling, Homer caught a glimpse of the big, sad eyes of the bison. He hated to admit it to himself, but he was bothered. Getting fish or edible fungus or wild berries was different—even pleasant when the weather was good. This always felt like murder, even though he liked a good bison steak as much as anyone.

They had barely tightened the last sling when Enoch brought the diskster up, extended the crane, and began to load the carcasses into the cryohold. Homer and Ulysses quietly climbed in, leaving their suits on but pushing their light amps up onto their foreheads and carefully racking the fletch-rifles.

In a few minutes, the four bison Cato and Naomi had bagged were also loaded in. "Dressed out, this haul ought to make eight tonnes, maybe ten," Enoch commented.

"Next call tonight, boss?" Ulysses asked.

"Waterfowl," Enoch said. "Hope you feel up to some wading."

It was almost an hour before they reached the old upcountry slough, a place where a beaver pond had silted up and spilled over into the low part of a meadow. The ride was smooth enough, but Homer had trouble getting to sleep. He could not get his mind off Carol.

He didn't know why he was always blowing up at her. In her situation he'd have been much more obnoxious than she ever was. Was it that he could "hear" what *he* would have been thinking? Maybe she didn't think that way at all. After all, she'd grown up in a born-again indocom, thoroughly sheltered, scheduled to become a Homemaker. Maybe, in fact, she didn't even *care* that he was rude, that they lived on Dolework, or that the kids couldn't go to an acadenhanced DC—

Of course she cared. She wasn't a little nit straight out of the indocom. She had run away from home as soon as she was old enough to claim citizen's protection against her parents. And Carol wasn't stupid—no more than she was ugly. He remembered her hugging him, and thought of her right now, sleeping alone in their bed.

Homer was lonely, but it was pleasant somehow. He still could not get to sleep, not even with the help of Enoch and Naomi endlessly bickering about cybertao. Even Cato fell asleep after a while.

He watched the mountains and trees roll by, and finally drifted off to sleep, but he seemed to wake up almost immediately. Looking at the clock, he saw that he had actually picked up twenty-five minutes of sleep, which was better than none, anyway.

They were off the road, winding through clearings and along old, half-overgrown logging roads, occasionally skimming a creek or river for a while. It would be nearly daylight before they got to the slough, but the two-meter-tall new pines in the old logging road prevented their going faster.

"This job is going to be impossible in twenty years," Enoch said, "once the old forest grows back."

"Job didn't exist twenty years ago," Homer pointed out. He remembered that when the Youth Orientation Program had taken the refugee children from Labrador Camp on a tour of this part of the country, the level ground had been all wheat, the hills dotted with cattle, and only the distant mountains forested. He had been eleven then; he was thirty-four now, and in that time the grasslands and bison had come back.

At last they set down in a broad meadow. To their east, bands of red streaked the gray wash of the sun rising over the Mission Range.

"Your suits are wadables," Enoch said, "so if you keep the water at your chest or below, you should stay dry. We have dart guns for these guys, with a string trace so you can just pull them in. The ducks are too small for the satellite to designate, so I've set a monitor to let me know when we've fired fifty combined. And when we have, I better see fifty ducks in the bags."

Again, Homer worked the far side with Ulysses. The flock had not yet roused. Over and over, he pointed the heat-seeking dart at the sleeping duck, fired it, reeled in the paralyzed bird, and threw it into his bag.

Homer had twelve and Ulysses seventeen when Naomi slipped on a submerged log and fell backward into half a meter of water. The ducks rose squawking and shot off in all directions.

Cato, short on his bag as always, took a shot at a duck in the air. Fathers exploded from it; with a croaking scream, the duck veered away. It had lost most of a leg, but the dart had not penetrated the body to inject its paralytic venom. They heard it crash into the water somewhere out of sight.

"Nice job," Enoch said. "Real nice job. We needed four more ducks for our total bag, and this had to happen."

"Got a wounded one, boss," Homer said. "I better go after him."

"Shit." Enoch spat on the water in disgust. "We'll still be three short."

"Sorry, boss," Naomi said quietly.

"These things happen." Enoch sounded as if he would like to kill her. "It's not really anyone's fault." He sat down on a rock; faintly, they could hear him checking with the satellite controllers. "No other flock nearby we're authorized to touch. Looks like that's a day."

"We really should go in and get that duck, boss," Homer said. "It'll bleed to death or die of shock."

"Yeah." Enoch grunted unhappily. He glared at Homer, who finally realized that all this was going onto audio record for Public Services review, and the rules forbade leaving wounded game to die. If he had not mentioned it—well, it was water under the bridge, and the poor thing *was* hurt. "Yeah. Why don't *you* go get it, then, Homer? The rest of us will wait here."

Homer ignored Enoch's tone. "Sure." He turned, lurching and crashing through the thick cattails in the direction the duck had gone, quietly switching off his transmitter to leave himself free to mutter.

"I'll go with you," Ulysses said, following him.

A hundred meters farther along the pond shoreline, blood floated on the water. "Poor thing," Ulysses said, clicking off his own transmitter. "And Enoch was just going to leave it to die."

"Yeah." Homer knelt to look at the floating clump of blood. "Does this tell you anything?"

"Do I look like the Old Indian Guide? For all I know it contains his fax address and contact code if you read it right."

Homer snorted agreement. They kept working slowly around the outside of the slough. Finally, half an hour later, they found it floating in the middle of a deep pool, its head underwater, surrounded by floating blobs of blood. By now the sun was fully up over the Missions, and the first lazy flies were circling the dead duck. "Might as well go and get it," Homer said, and waded out.

He was swimming before he had gone two meters, unable to keep the neckline of his suit above water. He dragged the soggy bird back with him, the cold water oozing over his chest into his crotch and down his legs. The suit "breathed," so the water would squeeze out or evaporate sooner or later, but meanwhile it was cold misery against his skin.

"Let's go," he said, stuffing the bird into his bag. He flipped to mic and called Enoch. "Boss, we got him. If you've got a fix, we'd appreciate a ride."

"You got it, ETA five," Enoch replied, and clicked off. He didn't sound angry anymore; one of the things that made him a good boss was that he couldn't stay angry.

"Well," Ulysses said, "that made it a little more interesting, but I still feel sorry for the duck."

"Me too." Homer did some knee bends experimentally, hoping to either work the water out or warm it up. "At least he went pretty quickly. Would have been worse to find him thrashing around and hard to get a shot at."

"Yeah." Ulysses stretched and yawned. "Say, Homer, you've been pretty quiet this trip."

Ulysses Hayakawa was as much of a friend as he had anymore; it would really feel good to unload the whole mess on a sympathetic shoulder . . . but could he trust himself to be fair to Carol? "Well, things haven't been so good at Deepstar. The UN's not so sure it wants to go ahead with a Public Service Contract on a crewed starship. So they might let it lapse with a one-time payment. Uh, that should stay under your hat."

"Sure." Ulysses turned to look at the sun rising red over the Missions. "Storm for sure before noon out here. Glad we're going to be back in the Dome—though we might run into it coming in. Hell of a night, wasn't it?" He yawned and stretched. "I love this job. I even take my three weeks Free Dole every year hiking and camping up here. I can't imagine what it would be like to have to worry about getting the work I want."

"It's not easy," Homer said.

The diskster came up to them, floating half a meter off the water, air whispering over it. The smell of ozone from the impellers cut through the wet early morning air like a driven nail. The big craft glided slowly past them and settled onto the meadow in a soft sigh of crushed grass. The front hatch slid open, and Ulysses and Homer climbed in, slinging their bags into the chute to the cryohold.

He had planned to sleep on the way back, but could not. Naomi had recovered from her drenching enough to argue with Enoch again, which reminded him that he was angry with her, so the normal squabbling was louder and more shrill than usual. Further, the water that had gotten into Homer's woods suit had soaked his clothes so that they now clung to him in an icy hug.

To pass the time, he mentally wrote letters to Carol. In the first years they had been married, they had often left notes for each other after a fight—somehow it was easier to write apologies than to speak them. Once, after Carol's parents had visited, Homer and Carol had traded letters four times before they could speak to each other again, even though they were sleeping in the same bed. They hadn't written notes like that in the last few years, but maybe he would today.

He curled tighter on the jump bunk, trying to tuck up small enough to stay warm. The extra half hour retrieving the duck had virtually shot his time margin; he would not be able to start the premix as early as he usually did. It would be an hour into shift before he could begin injecting the bacteria and starting to grow metal, and in these delicate last stages, he would be lucky to pick up one percentage point toward completion today.

Of course, as long as they didn't actually put the piece in or inject the bacteria, anybody could handle the premix. He fingered his com, trying to think of who he could ask to start premix for him.

Deepstar Corporation itself was down to three execs, all working for vestment alone. There were fewer than thirty workers left on the whole project, and he knew none of them well. Everyone else in his department had left; there was really no one he could call.

Unless Carol—

There was no mirror but he made a face at himself anyway. Carol was certainly not going to hand Moddy and Abe over to DC an hour early and then run over to Deepstar to start the tank for him. And being honest with himself, he had to say it served him right. He would have to wait and just take the time penalty.

He wished he could talk to Carol; he began to imagine writing the letter again. He tried to invent good excuses she might accept, but none of them was close to the truth. It wasn't just that *Deepstar* would be a name in history, like *Santa Maria, Half Moon, Discovery, Apollo 11,* or *Justice 9*. No one remembered who built those either.

And it wasn't the challenge of a difficult, intricate job. From a pure technical standpoint this project was actually pretty easy. He had gotten fussy about staying totally clean-and-green mostly as a way to stay awake.

He watched the riverbank roll by. Enoch had decided to bring them down the Clark Fork instead of along old 90; they would probably rejoin the highway somewhere around where the Blackfoot came in.

Well, start a new "letter" . . . he couldn't sleep anyway. He might actually be getting a little warmer and drier.

He felt no particular dedication to his children or grandchildren. If *Deepstar* left on schedule, by the time it finished its trip through eight Sol-similar systems, his youngest possible grandchild would be ninety years old. Homer had no desire to go. Within a few years message lag would stretch communication to collapse—anyone who left on such a voyage was as good as dead to the people he left behind.

He just wished Carol could see it his way. Deepstar was *his*. When his parents had fled Europe in the wake of the Unification War, they had lost everything. As a child in Labrador Camp, he had not even owned his shoes or shirt—both were UNRRA property, hand-me-downs destined for more handing down. Now he owned his furniture, his clothes—and his vesting in Deepstar. Something he could pass on to Abe and Moddy, something that could not be taken from him—made worthless, but not taken away.

Why was something so simple so hard to say to her? Since the Panic of '34 and the Moratorium that followed, new jobs with vesting had been nearly nonexistent. There were straight-wage jobs, and of course there was always Dolework, but a real job, one where you could come to own part of it, get real voting power—those were gone. If he left Deepstar, abandoning his accumulated vesting before he had enough service to make it permanent, he was back to start, owning just some clothing and furniture.

And although just now it was only the Moratorium that forced Deepstar to keep its employees on at all, and kept the creditors from seizing the corporate assets, owning a piece of humanity's first starship at least looked like it had some potential. This was the equivalent of owning Wright stock in 1902—

He knew what she would say. Plenty of people had tried and failed to build an airplane, and their stock would have been worth nothing.

The disktser banked sharply, climbing up over the riverbank and running across a grassy field to old 90, just before Missoula Ruin. They were now only a little over three hundred kiloms from home, and he still hadn't gotten any sleep. The disktser settled into high-level flight a meter above the old road.

The screen showed the mountains in the distance; ordinarily, Homer enjoyed these early morning trips. Eagles soared on thermals above the abandoned towns, and bears fed on the wild berries in the old ditches. Once, just as they crossed Fourth of July Pass, he had seen a bighorn sheep calmly staring at the passing diskster from the top of an old ramp.

Now, however, he just wanted to get back to sleep, to be functional during his tank shift.

"You awake?" Ulysses asked.

"Yeah. Can't sleep."

"Me either. Too excited. That finding the duck was about as close to real hunting as I've ever gotten. I felt sorry for the poor bird, but still— ever done real fishing? With a rod and line and everything?"

"No."

"There's nothing like it. No satellite to tell you what to do, no designator to tell you what to hit. You're out there on your own, just you and the woods." Ulysses sighed. "I don't think they'll ever license private hunting again—private hunters would screw things up too much too often for the harvest. But still . . ."

Homer grunted. "I'm afraid I'm a pure city kid. I'd rather they just domed North America and fed us all on battery potatoes—"

Both of them know that Homer didn't really feel that way, but they enjoyed the argument. Actually, last year Homer had brought Carol and the kids out to the resort dome on Flathead during their Free Dole, and they'd all had a great time hiking in the hills and trying to master the old-fashioned sailboats. That had been a good time. It seemed long ago.

The argument with Ulysses fizzled without every really starting. Homer dozed a little then, finally. He woke up, still tired, as the top edge of Spokane Dome came into sight across Lake Coeur d'Alene. Within minutes the diskster grounded in its berth. "Looks like we beat the storm by a good hour, anyway, so we did something right," Enoch said. "At least most of us stayed dry."

Homer grinned a little, said good-bye, and caught a gliderail car for home. He still didn't know what he would say to Carol.

She was gone. A note said only that the kids were at DC. He checked the clock: he was already beginning to run late on his shift at Deepstar. Still, he couldn't quite go yet, somehow . . .

He looked around again. Modesty's favorite pajamas were wadded into a ball by the kids' room door, as if she had been dressed in haste;

Abe had gone to DC without Glump, his stuffed tiger. An empty glass lay on its side on the kitchen table.

He checked the wastebasket. There were several wadded pieces of paper.

Homer pulled them out and smoothed them. All of them began "Dear Homer"—two went on no further. Another followed up with "I'm angry" before being wadded; one added "You Europig Dolebird, they should have sent you back." A last one, torn in three pieces, read "I love you, but I just can't stand this anymore, so I'm going to" and then trailed off in a dozen completely illegible cross-outs.

What had she decided to do and then decided not to tell him about?

He imagined her at the table that morning. Abe and Moddy would have been wolfing breakfast, spilling everywhere (splashes of milk and oatmeal at Abe's place, not mopped up—another strangeness), shouting, "Guess what!" Carol would be bent over the note, trying to force it out—the letters looked as if they had been slashed and burned into the page—half-blind with tears, mumbling, furious, trying not to shout at the kids. Then she had decided something.

If she had any sense, it was to get rid of Homer.

He sat down, breathing hard. He wanted to find her and apologize right now. He wanted to just sit there and feel sorry for himself.

The comlog. If she had called on the house terminal and not on her wristcom, then—

She had. His clumsy fingers stubbing on the keys, he called up the record. After putting the kids into the glidecar to the DC, she had dialed up a car to take her from here to Deepstar.

He stared at it, baffled. Then he knew.

Grown metal is delicate stuff, woven to the precise shape of an atom-by-atom spec. She need not know anything more than what she had picked up from him. If she were just to lower the partly grown piece into the tank and dump in all the salts, metabolites, and bacteria together, in half an hour the smooth perfection would be irrecoverably buried in a formless lump of metal. Weeks of work gone, now, when the Deepstar Project was in danger already.

Especially if she also threw in the finished parts still sitting on the racks. A year's work and more . . . and she was in the tank room with it right now.

Carol could kill Deepstar. She had every reason to want to, and she would *know* that she could do it, if she gave it even half a moment's thought. She wasn't stupid, after all.

He had to redial twice for the glidecar because his hands were shaking. He splurged on an Express Priority—his car would take precedence over all but emergency traffic.

The glidecar was standing in front of the apartment when he opened his door. He pushed the close button behind him, jumped into the car, and hit the destination confirm. The car lifted and shot into the express lane, swinging through service tunnels to take short cuts authorized by his priority. Pipes and cables flashed by him, then express lanes, then more service tunnels—

In less than three minutes, the car slid to a gentle stop and settled to the track in front of the Deepstar complex entrance. He jumped out, slapped the dismiss on the outside of the car, and ran inside.

The tank room corridor entrance was three hundred meters down the main tunnel within Deepstar. He ran as hard as he could, the guard gaping at him but—thankfully—not stopping him. Of course he wouldn't have stopped Carol either. . . .

Homer ran as hard as he could, his breath knifing in and out and the blood pounding in his head.

The telltale light at the entry to the tank room corridor was flashing red—someone was in there, and the tank was active.

He stopped a moment, hands braced against the wall. He had to quiet his panting. It was thirty meters down the corridor to the tank room. The ping would tell her he was coming, but if he got there fast enough, he could catch her in the act.

Kids or no, he would testify. She would go to a labor brigade for years to work this off.

His breath was back. He checked his pulse. It was racing, but it didn't feel like it would slow any time soon. On his toes, he dashed down the corridor, holding his breath, trying to make no sound, almost falling into the room as he came to the door.

Carol was sitting in the observer's chair. Automatically, he glanced at the boards. They glowed impossible steady green—they were only that steady when—

"Did you get hung up out there?" she asked. "Your clothes are wet—"

"You did the premix," he said, staring at the board. "The tank's ready to go."

"It's not that hard," she said. "I just selected default preset for today's date. I hope that was right."

"Yeah. It sure was." His knees trembled and his tongue seemed to swell, making it impossible to breathe. "Why did you—I mean—?"

"It matters to you a lot, I guess. Maybe I just wanted to see what you'd do. Anyway, I checked the registration and found out you were delayed, and it was my day off from Dolework."

His eyes stung. He walked slowly to her, his legs still numb and clumsy and held her.

"Was it real bad?" she asked. "Did they make you kill animals again?"

"A duck got wounded and I had to go after it," he explained lamely. He let go of her and sat down. "I'm really tired, I have a lot of sick time—I won't lose a day's vesting if I make this just a half-day. . . ."

He felt like a fool. He thought of how she must have hurried to get here. "So take a seat," he said. "It'll help my concentration to talk through this, and afterward we'll go get the kids and maybe spend the afternoon at Riverfront."

He explained deposition rates and maximally probable lattice surfaces and metabolites and inhibitors. He showed her all the fluxes and tricks of the graphics, letting the bands ride into red and fall into yellow for emphasis. "It's sloppy but well within tolerance," he apologized.

Carol said little; Homer's voice got hoarse, but he kept explaining, as if, when he stopped, she would quietly vanish forever. He surprised himself by getting eight tenths of a percentage point in three hours.

"That's really good," she said.

He let the grapples lift the exhaust nozzle from the tank and return it to the deionized wash. He could feel nothing inside anymore. "I could go home and call NLPF," he said finally, as he shut the last of the boards down.

"There's no vesting and no security. They could fire you after two weeks. Better to stay here and protect what you've got."

Although he took her in his arms to keep her from seeing the tears on his face, she pushed his head back gently and saw them anyway. And he saw hers.

DEEP IN THE HEART OF GENRE

There are a lot of writers, of science fiction and everything else, who say they don't pay any attention to the critics. There's even a term for such writers. They are called liars.

It is unlikely that there is anyone else on Earth who has read as many reviews of my work as I have. To read a review is a pleasure that at best is like masturbating—intense pleasure while accomplishing nothing— and at worst is like picking scabs—it may not feel very good but it's hard to resist once you start.

Though most reviews are favorable, one can't help noticing patterns, and the pattern I notice most is that, according to nearly all reviewers, I'm unoriginal. This is usually said with a tone of faint apology by the positive reviewer, and as a triumphant unmasking by the negative reviewer. Generally it's true, as far as I can tell; I would be hard-pressed to think of a gadget, character, situation, or plot device in anything I write that hasn't been done by somebody else somewhere before. (Even the ones I make up display an alarming tendency to turn up in older books that I read later.)

My feelings of guilt about this amount to occasional twinges from what I think of as the Romantic Hangover: eight or so generations after the Romantics, we're still much too frequently behaving according to their scripts, and one of their sillier ideas is that there's something special or wonderful about doing a new thing, or doing it in a new way.

It is often harder to do something good than something original; ask any ballroom dancer or figure skater. It is often more rewarding to the audience to see something done well than to see something new; I'd far rather see a fairly traditional performance of a Restoration comedy, done well, than a new performance of anything by Christopher Durang. But an endless stream of stories about artists, ranging from comic books ("Nobody sees I am a genius but I will *make* them *see!*") to public school teachers ("Nobody saw that he was a genius, but he had good self-esteem, and a positive attitude, and eventually they saw that he was a well-adjusted member of society who contributed significantly in his own way"), has continued to hammer the idea that art is about the shock of the new, the one true making, and all that other nonsense.

There are times when something new comes into being. Generally it arrives as something crude and energetic—think of jazz or rock in their early years, of newspaper comic strips before 1930, or of the hardboiled detective novel for examples. A generation or more later, somebody sees potential in it and makes it rise above its crude-and-energetic origins, showing that there's such a thing as doing it well. Blind Lemon Jefferson gives way to Duke Ellington, Chuck Berry to John Lennon, *Mutt and Jeff* to *Krazy Kat, Red Harvest* to *Double Indemnity.*

Both of these phases are already thoroughly accomplished in science fiction. It's time to admit that all that remains is the third phase: craft and virtuosity. There's not much of anything that's new to say, and the job now is merely to say it well.

For there to be something new to say in science fiction, there would have to be a new future that someone, somewhere particularly cared to imagine. Roughly from Lindbergh to the moon landing, there was a possibility, which grew ever more remote as the actual physical limits manifested themselves, that there might be some kind of adventurous life, open to many, in space. Not all SF was about rocketships and other planets, but that was where the core was, and the exploration of that core was what energized everything else.

As the core collapsed—as it became more and more apparent that space travel was going to be expensive, difficult, and restricted to a very small number of people for a very long time—it left behind an interesting group of freestanding ruins. A large number of readers had been trained to read for a certain kind of awe, and to elaborately construct the backstory from tiny clues in the text. Hence such things as time travel and alternate history stories, once a small branch off SF, expanded to take up some of the slack; hence the gentle humanist stories of regret and loss in futures that didn't turn out to be what had been promised; hence cyberpunk, where the existing world gets more wild and dangerous and the shiny technologies now being made by boring Silicon Valley drones for the use of boring Wall Street drones somehow acquire the romance and danger of guns, whores, and heroin.

The old SF vision of 1940–1970 or so was often childish but it had one thing going for it—the anchor that there really were rockets being built, and some of them were really going to go into space. The space age was where those writers located their dreams, and if the dreams were sometimes childish fairy tales or simple adolescent power fantasy, there was also room there for everything else we find in literature, and plenty of extraordinarily fine writers worked that vein.

What they did defined SF for the foreseeable future, like it or not. This is why practically everything genuinely original published since then gets denounced by older SF fans as "not really SF." This is also why the truly biggest "movement" of the last thirty years, dwarfing humanists and cyberpunks combined, is the retro movement—the writers who write old-style space opera just as if none of the scientific, technical, cultural, or artistic changes of the last few decades had happened.

To some extent this is because the market for the new is always smaller than we think it is. When SF was a new, vigorous, fresh injection into general culture, it was the taste of a small number of bright cranks. Now that it has become the common fodder of Hollywood, video games, and all the rest—so that to a great extent it *is* general culture—only a small number of bright cranks within the readership and viewership are looking for anything new.

So why, getting personal again, do I not supply the bright cranks, who I like and respect very much, with what they say they want? Admittedly they are probably the most interesting readers to write for, but that's not the kind of artist I am, and, as a Sufi proverb I'm fond of says, you can only spend what is in your purse. I imitate, I rework, I see what might be done a bit better this time than was done last time, or what cliché can be stood on its head to reveal something slightly more true. When I set out to write a science fiction story, I write somewhere near the heart of the genre, and all I try to do is to do it well.

I like the work—the scribbled calculations, the discovery that some cliché isn't quite right, reading the popular science press to stay at least sort of current and use the concepts in a reasonably correct way, tweaking sentences here and there to get things down into simple declaratives and scrape off all those names for emotions, thus to eliminate the sort of lumbering, blundering "poetry" and Beautiful Writing that passes for good prose in SF. The pleasure, for me, comes from the craft: it's like playing a familiar song that your fingers know perfectly, like acting Shakespeare, like directing Feydeau, like doing a simple life drawing; the idea is not to do the first one, but merely to see how well you can do, this time. It's enough.

BANG ON!

Here's another never-before-published story. I think it suffered from timing more than anything else. Jerry Oltion and I were batting ideas around on a very long drive, and this one sort of grabbed me. By the time I wrote it, though, and had it in submission, it was 1992 and the world was drowning in alternate Columbus stories. Also, a lot of alt-history folks seem to take the subject more seriously than I can manage to make myself do. It always seemed to me that historical figures who got caught in somebody's alternate history damned well ought to resent being pushed around and made to accommodate a twentieth-century writer's idea of what's interesting; but then, maybe I'm just forcing them to feel a resentment they otherwise wouldn't.

"Excellency," the minister said, "the man is an obvious lunatic. In fact, an obvious Italian lunatic. In point of fact, an obvious *Genoese* lunatic."

Ferdinand nodded. "This much is obvious. But it is also trivial. There are several considerations more important than whether or not this fellow is a brick or two shy of a load."

There was a long, long pause. The next person to speak was the Papal Envoy, who said, "Excellency, did you hear what you just said?"

"It didn't sound much like fifteenth-century Castilian, did it?" Ferdinand complained. "Someone—or something—trying to make me sound colloquial and rough, just because I spent my teenage years at war instead of school. And for that matter, why are we speaking English?"

There was another profound silence. Once again, King Ferdinand had grasped the obvious, and once again his grasp had exceeded every reach in the room. At last he spoke again. "Well, I suppose we all realize by now what this means. And after all, I do get to be the King and beat the Moors and wear a crown and everything—"

"And you are married to the most beautiful and virtuous lady in Christendom," said the minister, who had been Isabella's most favored courtier before Ferdinand had noticed his brains and ability and borrowed him.

"Now *that*," Ferdinand said, "is an intolerably drastic meddling with history."

"But very much what I really would have said," the minister protested.

"True. Shall we then pretend that I said, in response, that you must be averaging the two and that, alas, it is the virtue which pulls her score up?"

The minister nodded. "And then proceed from there."

"Very well," Ferdinand said, and turning to speak to the Papal Envoy, he added, "Now, hear me out on this one." He scratched furiously under his nylon tights—just as soon as he could get the time he was going to give the Royal Alchemist holy hell over how itchy and hot his new "miracle material" was. "Now that Granada has been disposed of, it is time to undertake new ventures. And there are three factors to weigh into all this. First of all, however crazy this project of firing a cannon so big that the ball never comes down may be, it is not one bit madder than the notion of sailing to China across what the Royal Astronomer estimates to be 16,000 miles of ocean, and with his looks and wit our Genoese lunatic had practically charmed Isabella into *that* silly venture. Secondly, for those of us who have an interest in seeing the royal power consolidated, there is the fact that a large project like this will serve admirably at pulling the kingdom together. And finally, unlike the project of losing three caravels and crews to no good end, this creation of gigantic canon will still do us some considerable good, even when it fails—to wit, we will be able to use them to blow the living crap out of the Moorish cities in Africa."

The minister winced at the "blow the living crap," especially in front of the Papal Envoy, but consoled himself with the thought that Ferdinand was an old soldier, after all, with twenty years of warfare behind him. And besides, he had not really said it, at least not in English.

The envoy, on the other hand, showed absolutely no sign of concern at the King's language. Rather, he seemed to enjoy it. "I think," he said, in his whispery, raspy tone, which he had cultivated for decades because it made him sound sinister and thus powerful, "that the project would seem to have great merit. Indeed, it might be the greatest achievement yet of the Materialist Brotherhood, surpassing even their invention of suffocating gases for use against the infidel."

The minister, who had a hard time controlling his reactions, shuddered, remembering what he had seen during the triumphal parade into the dead city of Malaga, where all the inhabitants had perished within a matter of scant minutes.

"Consider the following." The envoy got up and walked slowly toward the window. The early evening sun gleamed from the rayon of his white stole and turned the qiana of his robe into a thousand subtle shades of deep crimson. The reflected light filled the deep shadows the direct sun made in his face, setting it in bold relief without harshness, so that the total effect was one of wonderfully deep wisdom and piety.

He snapped his fingers, and his private portraitist, who had been sitting quietly in the corner, rushed forward to find an angle, seat himself on his folding stool, and begin sketching.

"For all the great benefits that the Materialist Brotherhood has brought us, the schism which has grown out of them has been the most serious threat, by far, that the Church has ever faced. The great majority of Materialists, of course, are content merely to learn the intricacies of the Creator's handiwork in these new and wonderful substances they find, to the benefit of all of us.

"Alas, the ones who are not interested in *what* is so, but *why* it is so— these preachers of a 'Dialect with the Creator'"—he spoke the name of the banned book as if it soiled his mouth—"these are the great attackers of sound doctrine in our age. How we can be provided with so many advantages for Christendom out of the same font that brings us such foul heresy is indeed a deep mystery."

"Ahhh!" sighed the portraitist, drawing as quickly as he could. "Once more, please?"

"'—is indeed a deep mystery,'" the envoy said again, overdoing it this time, naturally, but thus making it possible for the portraitist to emphasize the wise, as opposed to the cunning, aspects of the planes of the face. The Envoy heaved a deep sigh and went on. "Now, no doubt with the time you have been spending on disposing of the infidels—"

The minister shuddered again. He did not want to think either of the gas chambers or of the bodies rendered to make explosives and fertilizer, but, to his horror, realized that he must think of such things frequently enough for those who would read his thoughts to understand clearly. How many more times would he have to picture the Moors, screaming and struggling, forced into the squat concrete buildings from which none emerged alive, passing under the sprinkler system that sprayed a hundred gallons of holy water an hour as the crew of chanting priests baptized them en masse, and at last—but his attention was drawn back to the room, where Ferdinand was waiting impatiently for a chance to talk some more, the portraitist was still sketching furiously, and the envoy was finishing a major (to him) but trivial (to any other observer) disquisition on the nature of heresy.

"—and yet, even after having burned over two hundred heretics, the Dialectical tendency in the Materialist Brotherhood continues to be a thorn in the side of the Church, and anyone would think from the way they continue to grow that these executions had been genuine martyrdoms. Why, only yesterday I received a letter that described how the Chief Pharmacist at the Vatican—a man responsible for thousands of visions of the Blessed Virgin, or I should say co-responsible with the Blessed Virgin herself—was discovered not only attempting to arrange the chemical elements into a chart of categories, but inventing some sort of number system for them that could only mean that the man was engaged in full-fledged dialectic."

"They burned him, of course," Ferdinand said, politely.

"Not yet. Alas, he knows so many formulae that he is able to dribble out a few at a time as they work on him for the improvement of his soul, and of course each must be tested by doctrinally sound Materialist Brothers and confirmed before it can be accepted . . . they may still be working on him at Christmas."

"Maybe I'll be in Rome when they burn him," His Most Catholic Majesty added, an odd glint in his eye.

The minister, who was beginning to resent not having been named, became so irritated that if it had been up to him, he would have stormed forth from the room, for he knew that no such tendency had ever been detected in the real Ferdinand of Aragon, and that to extrapolate a love of suffering from a successful military career was absolutely unjust. But like it or not, the minister was stuck here to supply a viewpoint and maintain reminders that the subject under discussion was Christopher Columbus's proposal for an artificial earth satellite to be launched by a

giant cannon. Not a pleasant job, especially in the harsh glare of attention repeatedly focused on him, but someone had to do it, and the minister was nothing if not dutiful.

"Therefore," the Envoy said, summing up, "what we must do is turn
the methods of the Dialecticals against them. Their latest heresy is that
the Earth somehow circles the Sun, all the time whirling like a top, and
there have been rumors that an idea growing among them is that the explanation for how so absurd a state of affairs can be occurring is precisely that given by this fellow Columbus—that is, the idea that the same
force which causes objects to fall is the force that holds the stars in their
courses."

"Ahem," said the portraitist.

"'Force that holds the stars in their courses.' Would it help if I gazed
up at the rising Venus?"

"It's evening, sir. Venus can't be rising," the portraitist said. "Just
hold the angle you have." There was a long pause in which he drew but
the story did not advance. "Thank you, I have enough now." He continued to draw, but attention was not drawn to him again for a long time.

"Indeed, one might suspect that Columbus himself is a Dialectical,
either secretly and actually, or in an intention of which he himself is not
yet fully aware," the envoy continued. The bitterness in his voice might
have been due either to his feelings about heresy, or to the fact that only
fragments of his longest speech were being reported. "We need, more
than anything else, a demonstration—*by this method they call 'experiment'*—that the crystal spheres are still there as they have always been.
And what better way to show this than to have the impious shot ricochet
from the lowest sphere?

"Or, if by chance they manage to aim low enough to miss the lowest
sphere, there can be no question that the shot—contra the Genoese lunatic—will fall to Earth anyway, for there is nothing to keep it in motion,
and Aristotle clearly teaches us that it must therefore come to rest.

"And in either case the most important thing of all is that it will be a
very large and public event. The absolute and abject failure of Captain
Columbus will provide overwhelming evidence—in the Dialecticals'
own terms—of their folly."

"But, er"—the minister suddenly realized that he was being called
upon to voice the sort of question that could get a man up in front of the
Inquisition, and so was very careful indeed in how he phrased it—"but

what if the Adversary should somehow contrive to make the experiment work as Columbus says it will?"

The envoy beamed at him, and the minister realized his phrasing had been perfect, and that he could look forward to life continuing. "There is no cause for concern," the envoy said. "The Church will bless every object connected with Projectus Lunarum Novarum repeatedly and if need be continuously. The Adversary will be allowed no chance for entry. And in any case"—he waggled a finger in a way intended to suggest the stern but warm papa, a bit of practice against the day he might become Pope, which unfortunately looked more as if he were trying to shake a disagreeable object off of his finger and onto the minister—"the experiment *will fail.* Have no doubt of that."

The minister, knowing how narrow his escape had been, resolved to have no doubts at all—thus ensuring that he would be bedeviled by doubts for the remainder of all time. But even as he realized this, the envoy was turning to the King. "And so, Excellency, I must say that the Church will look very favorably upon your funding of this Projectus Novarum Lunarum."

"And we can always use it to blow the living crap out of the Moors over in Africa," Ferdinand said, nodding emphatically. His grasp of the principal issue, the minister realized, was rapidly turning into a stranglehold. "Besides, if I give him the money, he'll stop asking for it, and that will get Izzy off my case."

The minister was so appalled at the abuse of history and of language that he finally found the strength of leave the chamber and stalk off to prepare for his next scene. The envoy, with a great, sweeping bow, did likewise, but rather than leaving the palace he proceeded to distant chambers by pathways that were known only to himself, a few other priests, and the Materialist architects who had laid the palace out. The portraitist, shrugging at the failing of the light, folded up his kit and accepted Ferdinand's invitation to accompany the King and "head down to the kitchen, get a snack, and check out the new serving wenches." The austere colors he used the next day, because they bothered his full-blown hangover less, created a wonderfully ascetic effect in his portrait of the Envoy, and from that day his career was made, so that he passed from attention in rather better shape than almost anyone else.

When the envoy reached Father Lope's chamber, the confessor— who was also the Vatican's chief secret agent at the Court of Castile, as everyone knew—was expecting him. He listened carefully to the envoy's account, and agreed at once with his private conclusion. "You're quite right, of course. If you will just have a word or two with the appropriate people in the Materialist Brotherhood, I'm sure we can ensure that the shot will break up somewhere over the Atlantic. God, after all, helps Man best when Man does his share." He smiled warmly, and the envoy thought for just one moment that he might escape without another confession, but then Father Lope turned and placed a soft wax cylinder on the machine, and brought the great ear of the recorder up to the grille of the confessional. "May I tell you that—unofficially—your confessions are being greatly enjoyed in Rome? And that I have been instructed that we must investigate, ever more deeply, this temptation toward sin that you have been experiencing, because you are felt to be absolutely vital to the Cause of the Church, and thus the purification of your soul matters so much more than most others?"

The envoy, who was not a fool, knew immediately what this must mean; whatever pleasures were being derived when the vinyl copies of his confessions reached Rome, there was also material in them to destroy him utterly if the occasion for that should arise. Only his continuing successes here at the Court ensured that the confessions would continue to be consumed for pleasure, not for evidence against him.

With a mental sigh that he never allowed to reach anywhere near the physical realm, he launched into an elaborate confession in which he was troubled with fantasies of angel-faced novices, just fully developed, with immense buttocks, who tore off their habits, revealing great billows of red hair and voluptuous young bodies, and begged to do foul things to him. He was unusually inventive this time, but after all, the Pope was a Borgia, noted for being easily jaded.

The Wazir had been happily unaware of the sense in which he was a counterpart to the minister until it was pointed out. It gave him pause; he wondered if somehow times had become so modern that the whole story would be about the doings of flunkies. But of course there was no way for him to know, so after pausing for a moment to straighten his robes, he continued down the long corridor, his feet padding softly in his beautifully made slippers.

At the door, he paused. He wished this were someone else, but he had little choice. Most of the ruling family of Granada had perished in the dreadful gas attacks. Many of the survivors had converted to the dirty Christ-faith to keep their lands and property. The young man on the other side of the door was, to put it bluntly, the best of the survivors.

Unfortunately he showed every single one of the tendencies toward pleasure of his great-uncle, the old sultan, the last undisputed and the last to die at peace in *al-Andalus*. From the giggles and screams coming from inside the room, the Wazir knew more or less what he would find. He just hoped his young master and charge could bring some concentration to bear.

The moment he entered, he realized that if he had waited five minutes matters would have been much better. Unfortunately his interruption had now transformed the situation utterly. The plump slave girl scuttled off to the side, away from the desperately frustrated nominal heir to the throne of Granada—indeed, of all of *al-Andalus*, if—*inshallah*—it could ever be won back by *jihad*. "Well?" the prince said, not even covering himself, let along bothering to dress.

"There is excellent news, my lord. All of the coast of Africa, perhaps as far away from us as the Mameluke lands in Egypt, is about to be devastated by a new Christian weapon which Ferdinand and Isabella—accursed be their names and may dogs gnaw the genitals from their rotting corpses—are at this moment building. The situation is utterly dire and desperate—and thus could not be better for us."

The prince rose, quietly pulling garments around him. "This is one of those riddles you are so fond of putting to me. Could you not train my mind by just telling me what is going on, as most Wazirs do for their princes?"

"I could, but up until today the most likely function you would find for yourself was as Wazir to some prince, and as such it was important you learn these skills."

"Up until today . . ." The young prince was obviously beginning to think, which was what the Wazir had hoped would happen. "Then what you are saying is that this new threat of Ferdinand and Isabella's might furnish a reason for our old North African allies to assist me in retaking Granada. Or even *al-Andalus,* which might be possible if we found a way to get the Turks involved."

"Precisely."

"The intelligence reports?"

"Right here."

As the prince scanned them, his fingers began to trace the pattern of the script. Every so often he would look up and stare into space. The

Wazir knew that the prince did not actually do this while thinking; he did it so that people could see him thinking, and therefore would not interrupt him while he thought. He had no idea whether or not the prince knew that.

"They are building it well to the north and west," the prince said, finally. "Our chances of taking it by direct assault are zero—unless somehow we were to get the Turks involved, which is not only unlikely but would merely put a Turk on the throne. And a gun of that size—do you realize it could drop a mass of many tons onto one of our cities? Might it be that they intend to make that mass hollow?"

"Hollow?" the Wazir asked. "But why would they want it . . . God be merciful!"

"Yes, you see it too," the Prince said. "They could wreck our cities with a gun one-fifth that size, taking only a month or so per city. But if they were to use a big shell filled with their damnable poison gas—a single shot might accomplish their purpose."

The Wazir bowed low. It had been the dying wish of this young man's father that his son grow up with a tough mind, one thoroughly receptive to fact and willing to face it no matter how unpleasant, and that he master the skills of perception expected in a Wazir. It was clear that he had exceeded even the greatest hopes for him.

As he remained in his bow, however, the thought also crossed the Wazir's mind that perhaps, given a tendency toward heavy-handed irony noticeable thus far, what might actually be happening was that some reversal was being set up. He considered the thought for a long breath, but since it was untestable, he dismissed it from his mind. It was that ability to ignore the unknowable that had made him a success as a Wazir in that long period before anyone had heard of him. He just hoped it would be of some help now that he was in the middle of things.

Captain Columbus was less than pleased, and he told them so. "Of *course* it has to be built in sections! We can't *cast* a gun two thirds of a mile long! And *of course* it has to be aimed permanently in one direction! We have to bury it in the ground just so it will hold together!"

The King's representatives nodded sagely, doing their best to appear to understand what they were being told. What they were primarily understanding was that Columbus's gun could not be "swung around and test fired against *al-Hoceima*" as the King had suggested, and now they would have to go back and tell him that. This was not going to be easy, for once Ferdinand locked onto an idea it took a long time to cure him of it, and he had seemed very attached to this one.

Meanwhile, Diego was kicking Columbus under the table, reminding him of who the funding source was and therefore of who needed to stay pleased.

More gently, and with less table-thumping, Columbus explained, "What must be remembered here is that to do what it is to do, the gun must contain a discharge of thousands of tons of modern high explosives. Without the new steels that were originally developed to contain the new explosives, this would be completely impossible—as it is, we are straining the far limits of the possible. If I may coin a term"—some strong suggestion invaded Columbus's mind, urging him to call it "spin-off," but that was so clearly an illiteracy that he rejected it at once—"er, collateral benefits are what will make this of benefit to Castile. Good grade cannon steel was made at rates of perhaps twenty tons per year, and high explosives at perhaps five hundred, during the peak war year of 1491. Yet orders of Projectus Lunarum Novarum alone total two hundred and fifty times the steel and two hundred times the high explosives, allowing for a few follow-on shots. Once that capacity is built, it is at Their Most Catholic Majesties' disposal—and for practical purposes it will be the whole modern armaments industry of Christian Europe."

One of them nodded and wrote something on a pad; it was actually a note to himself to remember to change his linens before going to see the King, but the one who was seated next to him, whose memory was good enough not to require notes, had carefully memorized Columbus's argument. Still, talking to Ferdinand was going to be much like taking candy from a child by promising it more candy later. . . .

The third representative had a brief flash of an idea and asked about it. "So, Captain Columbus, you are saying that if we did wish to build smaller versions of this gun for long-range bombardment, we would probably have to build one gun per target? And we could not correct its aim once built?"

Diego kicked Columbus twice, harder, just to be sure he realized that they were up against the worst of all possible questions.

"I would have to—*ouch!*—say that—*ooph!*—yes, that's true." Columbus stood up, hastily, and moved down the table.

"And the gun would presumably continue to hit one target, over and over?"

Diego nearly fell from his stool, but his captain was now out of reach.

"Not at all." Columbus, who knew perfectly well why he had been kicked, was delighted to get a question of the kind. "There is considerable random scatter coming out of the gun. In consequence the shots would gradually level a whole city, provided only that the gun is aimed correctly in the first place. Let me show you—"

Diego, who had been through a few demonstrations with his captain, groaned inwardly, but there was nothing he could do as Columbus strode to the window. "You see this basket of eggs, gentlemen?"

They had crowded around him, and, sure enough, once he mentioned that it was there, they saw it. The painter, who had unaccountably been doing a still life in that room, was at lunch, so that the basket of eggs was quite unattended.

"Now, let me see—a length of pipe would be ideal—"

"Well," Diego said, "if we suppose that there was a plumber in here, working on a sink, perhaps because he was a close friend of the painter—"

"No good," Columbus said. "Fifteenth-century Spain, remember? No indoor plumbing. But there might be a piece of rain guttering—"

Sure enough, there in the corner, there was. "Now," Columbus said, "we place one end on the back of a chair, here, and the other just over the windowsill, and we roll the eggs down it one at a time, and watch what happens in the courtyard below. You will see that even though the eggs are going through an identical physical process, they will form a scattered pattern of overlapping splashes in the courtyard. In the same way, over the course of many shots, the gun would hit an area, rather than one single spot."

They all nodded sagely and Columbus began to roll eggs down the piece of guttering; as she had said, the eggs spattered in an irregular pattern, on the ground below.

"Can I do one?" asked one of the representatives.

Magnanimously, Columbus stepped to the side, and soon the representatives were all rolling eggs down the piece of gutter. When the eggs were all gone, they were in a much better mood; two of them knew that Ferdinand would enjoy smashing eggs and therefore could be mollified, and the third had apprehended something rather like the Central Limit Theorem. As he was departing, he asked, "So it's all a matter of correct aim to begin with. And might I ask how we are to achieve this correct aim without having fired the gun and without being able to see the target?"

"Well," Columbus said, "that would depend on very accurate surveying, I would imagine."

The representative nodded, and followed the others from the room.

Diego sighed. "I think you sold the idea to them again, Captain. It amazes me that we've been able to get this far."

Columbus shrugged. "We'll get the rest of the way. Any response to the letter, yet?"

"No, sir. And I think you're an idiot to be corresponding with a Dialectical under any circumstances, no matter what you need to know. Let the Church get hold of that and you'll be on a stake in no time."

Because he knew it was true, and he didn't like the idea much, Columbus was a bit put out by that. "We have to consider it. If they're right, and the world is really rotating, then firing the gun east to west is going to lose us quite a lot of speed. Perhaps enough to prevent it from working."

Diego shrugged. "So overcharge the gun. What difference does it make if it blows on the first shot, as long as the ball goes where you want it to?"

Irritated by a supporting character having all the sensible suggestions, Columbus snapped at his old and trusted subordinate. "I don't know why I'm spending all this time talking to you. There's no basis for you in history. I wish I were out at sea again instead of meddling in all this endless politics and funding!"

Diego, who realized how frayed his commander's nerves were, ignored the slight, and gently led Captain Columbus off to a too-long-delayed lunch. The room remained as it was for a long time. Then a painter, who was still trying to remember why he had been working in this room, came in. He stopped at his canvas and turned toward the arrangement—where was the basket of eggs? The basket was now on the table, but it was empty.

He had the vague impression that if he could just find his friend, the plumber, all of this would become clear.

"Heavier objects fall faster. It's right there in Aristotle," the abbot pointed out. "If we do things to structurally weaken this projectile, so that it will break up, the pieces will stay up longer. Is that what you want?"

"They will still come down, though," the envoy pointed out.

"Yes, and more widely scattered, and probably impossible to find.

But I did want to point out that if perchance this notion of a body falling around the world should happen to be—"

The envoy raised a single finger, one that said only that matters were getting dangerous here; the abbot nodded. "I see. Well, I had thought that perhaps, since we were, er, assisting the natural failure of the experiment here—"

The envoy smiled. "Precisely. But is it really a good thing for the Pope's servant to hear the details? It is my task to feel, and to declare, my faith in God—not to see how God *gets* things done, but just to see that they *are* done." He swept out of the room.

The abbot leaned back and thought hard. There were three things they had to do: make sure that the ceramic jacket would crack, make sure that the insides would fall apart, and somehow keep the density of the insides exactly the same as it would have been if it were all made of the requested steel. Creating a jacket that would crack was easy—they had plenty of failed formulae for heat-resistant ceramics that looked like the real thing. For the other . . . if the slug were made up of steel plates, tied to each other with some dense material—such as lead, which melted at low temperatures—he had it.

He had thought briefly that he might turn out to be a secret Dialectical, or even a saboteur, but he realized that he had just had as much of a scene as he was going to have, so with a sigh he went down to dinner. He had liked to think he might have had a talent for intrigue or mystery, but he was never to find out.

"Surveyors," the Wazir said. "According to our spies they are training hundreds of them. And strangely enough, the gun itself is not aimed directly at us."

"The accounts of it—" the prince began, and cleared his throat. Two plump young girls got up from the low couch and exited silently; the Wazir had noted with approval that since this affair had begun, the Prince had been more and more willing to be interrupted. "The accounts of it are obviously exaggerated. Our mathematicians calculate that if a gun that size were actually built and fired that it would literally miss the Earth. But why am I telling you this? You have read the same reports I have."

The Wazir nodded, appreciating the Prince's courtesy, and said, "That is out of our hands, of course. Just as I am now supposed to mention that our work on a big gun of our own, thanks to a generous loan from the Mamelukes, is progressing rapidly—even though you have also read those reports. Whatever the Christian dogs intend with theirs, ours will be ready almost as soon, because it is a smaller project—all we need is something with which to hit them, as a response to their shot. And God be praised, their techniques of building in sections and of burying it in the ground were quite applicable to our problem as well."

The Prince sighed. "If all we are to meet for is to say what we already know, then perhaps I should add the only piece of real news. The messenger was sent with our threat this morning. If they should fire off that monster of theirs, we will retaliate at once, regardless of who it may be aimed at."

The Wazir nodded. It was harsh, it was an ultimatum without alternative, and it was simple. It was the only way to communicate with people like Ferdinand and Isabella.

Ferdinand had never been much of a scholar, but he was trying hard to follow what the Genoese lunatic was saying, and much to his surprise, succeeding pretty well. "So then it is really a matter of geometry?"

"Yes, indeed," Columbus said. "We draw the round earth. We draw an extension of the path of the ball for one brief time—let us say one minute—and then the distance it will fall toward the round earth's center in that same time. We set the arrows head to tail, connect the ball to the last arrowhead, and—ha!—here is the new position of the ball. And as you can see, it is just as far above the earth's center as it was before.

"In actual practice, of course, we use something much larger than my drafting table will accommodate, and indeed we draw the pathway down to the second. By working at the larger scale our measurements become extremely accurate. So if we do not hit the correct height and speed on the first shot, we will surely get it on the second or third, just by varying the charge."

Ferdinand nodded. "It seems a shame that there is no more accurate way of calculating; you are limited by the accuracy of the lines you can draw with your straightedge and compass."

The Papal Envoy shuddered involuntarily. A man had been burned at the stake the year before for proposing just such a method, which, absurdly enough, had involved the heretical notion of dividing by zero, though cleverly disguised by claiming that it was a number "infinitely close" to zero. He wished that the Pope would prohibit the use of zero, a number of infidel origin anyway. To conceal his distaste, he leaned forward and looked carefully at the chart. "But what about the tendency of a body to slow down and stop?"

Captain Columbus smiled at him, which gave the Papal Envoy a sinking sense of being used as a foil. "Oh, eventually, it will. Over a period of weeks. But we have determined through experiment that that tendency is caused by the air, and if your Materialist Brotherhood has estimated correctly, at the height we are firing to there will be very little of that."

The Envoy relaxed. If this man acknowledged that bodies must come to rest, he was still correctly Aristotelian and therefore not a Dialectical. He even permitted himself to say, "It is indeed a pity that there are no better means of calculation available than to draw the picture ever larger."

Diego, who had been sitting quietly in the corner, looked up and said, "Almost, one can imagine, that if the advance of science had begun later, instead of being endowed heavily by the blessed Eleanor of Aquitane— or if it had begun with studying the motions of bodies rather than the nature of substance—" He shook his head. "What am I talking about? Why am I saying these things?"

Ferdinand sighed. "I am afraid it's obvious."

Realizing what the King had implied, they all felt the icy hand of another intervention grip them, and none of them cared to remain in the room. Ferdinand hurried off to a long day's hunting; Columbus and Diego spent much of the day riding from workplace to workplace within the project, hastening everything onward as much as they could; and the Papal Envoy went to confession, where he confessed to the most graphic fantasy—this time involving not only the young novice, but several of her sisters both spiritual and temporal—that he had yet imagined. He could not deduce whether Father Lope looked pleased because more of this sort of thing was wanted in Rome, or because this, at last, was sufficient to have the envoy recalled and executed. Tired, discouraged, and frightened as he was, the envoy did not really care.

The messenger from *al-Hoceima* had had ominous feelings ever since he crossed the Mediterranean. Despite what he carried, they had been unwilling to give him an escort or guard, and because the King and Queen were both far off, where the big cannon was being built, he had already had to ride much too long. Now, his precious dispatch bag slapping his thigh, he had just time to realize that he had all the marks of an expendable character when the man stepped unexpectedly onto the road in front of him. The messenger tried to ride around, and received a bullet in the brain.

They secured a dozen gold coins from his wallet.

Eventually the message was used for toilet paper.

God be praised, the prince had stuck to his declaration. As no word, not even the courtesy of defiance, came back from the King of Aragon or the Queen of Castile, he had pushed on, getting the gun completed and loaded. True, the ball was mere iron, unlike the sophisticated ceramic-jacketed projectile that the spies said that the Spanish were building, but it should be more than adequate to the purpose. The Wazir was over-joyed—here was a man it would be worth following anywhere.

When the bright flash lit the northern sky, the Prince and the Wazir had been sitting out upon a pleasant balcony, sharing coffee. They knew at once what the long red column of fire must mean, and in moments they were shouting for horses, riding out to the great gun in the side of the mountain. It would take them half an hour to get there, and then the final load-and-fire might take an hour, but they would manage somehow. That shot must be answered tonight.

High above the Atlantic, the shot, where no one saw it, began to split open; in a moment, the last breaths of the atmosphere had torn the peeling ceramic off, and the steel underneath had grown red hot, so that the lead holding it together melted and ran like water. A moment later and the projectile was tumbling, dumping great slugs of steel out into the high atmosphere, plunging back to Earth far sooner than it should have because of far greater wind resistance.

In the real world, there was of course no reason for a chunk of steel to come down in one place or another. Indeed there was very little reason for the chunks of steel to be anywhere at all. But in a world where nothing happened without meaning, it could hardly be avoided that the twelve-year-old heir to the Aztec throne, being borne on a litter through the capital, should be killed instantly when the blow struck from the sky, thus ending one lineage and presaging the ascension of Cacama the Great.

It was a jaguar priest, looking across the ruined part of Tenochtitlan, who gulped hard and realized what was implied by the death of Montezuma in this fashion; since it could have little to do with the present story, it must imply an impending sequel. There would be little enough time to get ready for that—he hurried to arrange an audience with the Aztec himself.

He thought with some sympathy for a moment of the others, across the Atlantic, who had not yet realized the situation they were all in, but after all they would learn soon enough.

The Wazir had to admit that the Prince's reasoning had been impeccable: "if we are to send them such an ultimatum, we must be prepared to follow through on it, but if—*inshallah*—it should prove that their big gun is in fact aimed at some other faction of Christians, we want only to tell them that we have the same tools to our hands, and not to start a war. Too, we and they both should see the effects of this new weapon before we too lightly embrace it. And finally, they have provided us with a perfect target—something they stole which we can now deprive them of. So our first target is chosen by them—*their* first target, where they first used suffocating gas. And, not incidentally, which our navigation charts have located with great precision. Our target is Malaga!"

The explanation was very precise, but the Wazir was from Malaga, and cunning and brutal though his job compelled him to be, he was not a jealous man; he loved his native city deeply, and he did not want to see it destroyed merely because he could no longer live there. But he knew that such touches were given him to make him seem human, and he knew that after the brutality of the Castilian conquest of Granada, there was little room left for humanity in the world.

Still, there was surely room for a momentary feeling of regret.

So he indulged it, felt a deep sadness wash over him, and gave the order.

The biggest technical problem had been to find a way to fire off so large a mass of explosive all at once. A single touchhole at the breech would have resulted in large quantities of the soupy mix of nitroglycerin and sawdust squirting out the barrel unignited, thus absorbing rather than adding to the force of the explosion. Instead, each of the first ten sections of the monstrous device was punctured by a dozen touchholes, and each touchhole primed with a sizable charge of black powder.

It had been Ibrahim b. Hassan's inspiration that had led to a way of igniting all the black powder primers simultaneously. Examining the ruins after one storage shed had been destroyed by a lightning strike, he had noted that the witnesses had said the building was not hit by lightning but had blown up just afterwards; wondering whether lightning could have jumped through the ground, he had hit on the similarity to sparks; experiments on a much smaller scale had confirmed that sparks were quite effective at igniting black powder.

More importantly, perhaps, he had found a way to keep the spark-stuff in a jar. Thus there were twenty slaves working the cranks on the great chain of glass balls that spun up to speed, the soft felt rubbing up a fury of sparks, the jars crackling and making their unpleasant smell as they filled with sparkstuff. From one side of the chain of jars, a heavy copper chain wrapped in linen led down to where the bare copper was wrapped around the monster cannon. From the other, a short chain led to a copper bar on a hinge, currently vertical, waiting to be pulled by a rope so that it would fall onto the copper plate from which hundreds of thinner chains snaked down to what Ibrahim referred to as "spark plugs," a logical name that seemed to be catching on for the ceramic plug with a wire at its center that stuck into the touchhole.

Two minutes after the Wazir's signal, they received the signal back from the slavemaster—the jars were now filled with sparkstuff and the slaves turning the cranks could now only keep them full, not fill them fuller. The prince put a gentle hand on the Wazir's shoulder, perhaps even to say to him that he knew how painful this occasion must be, and then yanked the rope that pulled a copper bar over so that it fell against the plate.

The roar was beyond belief.

When they got back to their feet, they were bleeding from ears and noses, shouting to each other to be heard at all. But there was no question it had worked.

If only Ibrahim could have been here to see this. Alas, he had continued to wonder whether lightning was made of sparkstuff, and while flying a kite in a thunderstorm, had gone to Paradise with a swiftness and cleanliness that could only indicate that God was pleased with his courage, if not with his piety or common sense. They had found the charged jar next to his remains, confirming his notion; but an idea, however useful and correct, was really only one idea, and the man who could come up with more ideas was far more to be missed.

Poor Ibrahim. The Wazir sighed. They had had such hopes for him—not only had he had a name, but he had been working on something that showed promise of significance for a sequel. One would have thought that, if anyone were to survive—

But it did not do to question the ways of God. As his hearing came back, he could hear the cheering and shouting.

"It certainly made a big enough noise," Ferdinand said.

"Eh?" Columbus asked. He had had to be very close to it; the complicated works that dumped burning coals down shafts to the gun had required his and Diego's immediate close supervision.

Poor Diego. Located farther up the gun than Columbus, he had been too near one of only three shafts that had blown through. And with a name of his own . . . anyone would have thought . . .

His captain would miss him bitterly, but for right now, just as soon as he could hear them, he needed to get out and face the cheering throng.

The Papal Envoy had been quite unsure whether the summons to Rome was for reward or punishment, and he knew that that was intentional and the way things normally were. Normally he would have embarked at Valencia or Alicante, but word had reached him of a comfortable, fast, modern ship at the harbor at Malaga.

He knew what sort of luck this was; something that would bring him to wherever he was going. The truth was, he was exhausted and ready to go along with anything.

He never felt or saw it coming. There was just one moment in the bishop's palace (formerly the Wazir's family home) in Malaga, and then another when he woke abruptly and discovered, to his disgust, that certain heretics he had ordered burned had been absolutely right—God was simply too nice to send anyone to hell, and so they were all here in heaven.

He was even more upset to discover that the Muslims had gotten another part of it right . . . or he was upset until the red-haired novice began to undress him, and then discovered a broad-mindedness in himself which he had never noted in life. His next to last thought ever of earthly things was that, having been killed by an infidel weapon, he would probably be beatified, but his case for sainthood would surely never make it unless there were good political reasons. It all mattered astonishingly little.

His absolute last thought, before he lost himself in the novice's tender embraces, was that he was almost certainly not going to be in the sequel, and that mattered a great deal. "Let's go, honey," he whispered. "We've got something to celebrate."

* * *

"So our shot landed in Malaga," Captain Columbus said. "I'm afraid it does reveal that my calculations were quite wrong. The world really is about as big as the Royal Astronomer says it is. This will mean a somewhat larger gun, and starting over from scratch—"

Ferdinand, one ear still bandaged, dismissed the Genoan's carefully planned speech with a wave of his hand. "Man, you don't realize what you've already achieved. Didn't you see the size of the crater it made in Malaga? You've invented the ultimate weapon, for heaven's sake! You can hardly expect us to worry about details when we've so much to get done; why, there are fifty giant guns to get built within the next few years." He turned to the minister, who was waiting with the already-cut orders. "I'm afraid we are going to have to turn all of Projectus Lunarum Novarum over to the army, at once. But we are certainly not unaware that your services were indispensable—and so we've decided to reward you. Not only are we going to finance you to sail to China, westward, but we're going to allow you to build the vessels you'll do it in. Anything you want, within reason."

"But—" Columbus sputtered, "Your Excellency, surely you are aware that—if the calculations are at all accurate—"

"Yes, I know, it's excessively generous. You get not only a virtually unlimited right to draw on the royal treasury, but in addition you will be setting the record that can never be broken by sailing two-thirds of the way around the earth, and thus I suspect your name will live a good deal longer than mine. But what's the point of being a King if I can't do big favors for my friends?"

The royal entourage swept out so swiftly that Columbus could do little more than bow. When they were gone, he rose and scratched his head. He missed Diego a great deal. Right now it would be very helpful to have someone to talk to, especially someone given to brilliant ideas, because he needed several.

As the King and the minister walked down the corridor, the minister said, "Do you think it will work, Excellency?"

"Oh, admirably. We'll be rid of him for sure this time. If he tries to sale across sixteen thousand miles of open ocean, he'll die out there, as surely as you like. If his own crew doesn't hang him from the yardarm, or whatever it is they hang them from. But he's far too stubborn not to try."

King Ferdinand continued to walk down the corridor, but the minister stood stock-still. His dignity had endured much in the last few weeks, but now there was a new horror to be faced: a way had been left open for a sequel.

A small man was tugging at his robe, "Sir, I was just asking—"

"I'm sorry," the minister said, for he was a kind man and did not blame others for his recently acquired deafness. "What were you asking?"

"Have you seen a friend of mine, a plumber? He's been missing for weeks—"

"What is a plumber?" the minister asked, but we cannot be sure whether or not he ever received an answer.

HOPE AGAINST HOPE

It's pretty much normal in a seven-year-old to hope to play major league baseball, be a victorious admiral, go to Mars as a famous scientist, and be elected president; it's even normal to hope for all of the above. By the teen years, you've learned to pick a few hopes instead of all of them; and at age forty, my present age, it's not particularly reasonable to hope for things of that kind unless you have already had more success than most people ever do.

I've taken no surveys, and this is not a scientific essay, so you are quite free to disbelieve me here. But without any hard proof at all, I would conjecture that many of us can remember the details of our childhood fantasies about "when I grow up" much more easily than we can recall a similar level of detail about our last work week. We imagined them at a time when we had many fewer things to do and a much poorer grasp of the possible. We lived there mentally much more than we ever could in any fantasy now.

Rationally, as adults, we hope only for things that lie at the end of some credible, continuous, feasible pathway into the future—that is, there's a way of reaching our hopes that we can imagine taking, in which each step prepares us for the next, and in which no step is impossible from the previous one. These are the reasonable hopes, and they are the hopes of happy adults.

A surprising number of the genuinely happy people I've known have had no more gift than the ability to place their hearts mostly on reasonable hopes. Perhaps it would be best if we all could. But this essay is going into a volume that will be read by the science fiction community, and one distinguishing characteristic of that community is that unreasonable hopes—those hopes of childhood—are harbored far into adulthood, generally by converting them to pleasant dreams, but occasionally just as if the hoper were still seven years old.

It's one of my favorite things about the science fiction community, and it's also one of the things that sometimes makes me feel like working my way through a WorldCon with a chainsaw and a hockey mask—except that that would be a futile attempt to fulfill one of *my* unreasonable hopes. Good or bad, it is very much the way we are, and ultimately it's difficult to sincerely wish oneself out of existence.

It occurs to me, though, that unreasonable hopes may be the clue to why the science fiction community, which was always divided into a web of tiny cliques anyway, has reached the point where most people seem not to be aware of anything but their own corner of the web. It is argued, often, that this is a matter of sheer size, but a little thought will show that although it's true that much more is published than any one person can read, most of that is media tie-ins and continuing series, and the subgroups of readers who follow those things generally manage without having to read all of it.

Take out the media-related books and the continuations of series that one does not personally care for, and the number drops by around two thirds. Take the remaining third of science fiction and group it, and there's still a lot, but it organizes into perhaps a dozen "schools" or "subgenres," not more—no one of which produces more than three to four "must read" books in a year. A lot of our sharper critics do manage to stay on top of things, and while they may occasionally miss an individual pearl, by and large they can give a pretty good picture of what is out there in the oyster bed. Moreover, since absolutely nobody can make a living writing SF criticism alone, it is also a safe bet that most of them are holding down other jobs (perhaps writing fiction themselves, but that's a full-time job as much as flipping burgers, writing manuals, or painting houses).

So, in short, I think the size of the field is an excuse, not a reason, for the increasing fragmentation of science fiction and fantasy.

If people always fought and disagreed, how do I know the fragmentation is increasing? Mainly because there was an older canon—the stuff from roughly the Campbell *Astounding* through the end of the New Wave—that everyone in the field read, whether they liked it or not, and to this day in a room full of arguing science fiction fans, you are more likely to get nods of recognition if you refer to a short story from 1953 than one published in 1995—or even ten years ago, to allow for dispersal time. What I'm asking is why people don't read each other's stuff anymore, and I would say it can't be purely a matter of volume; that explains why people don't read everything, but it hardly explains why every faction and clique seems to read so intensively within the group.

My guess is that what has happened is that what was once a reasonable hope has become unreasonable, and hence moved into the realm of dreams and impossibilities. The fan community no longer has any single reasonable hope to anchor itself in; all that are left are the unreasonable ones, and about these there can be nothing but conflict.

Consider: when you are eighteen, you might be very well coordinated and extremely good at some sport, and also bright but not exceptionally bright. So you might reasonably hope to become an Olympic athlete, or you might reasonably hope to become a medical doctor, in either case by dint of a lot of hard work. Hoping to become both simultaneously, with no sacrifices or conflicts, would be unreasonable; but, for example, you can hope to spend a few years training and trying, and then, regardless of whether you make it to the Olympics, enter college and pursue a course of studies leading into medicine. You can reasonably decide that being one or the other matters more to you, and pursue that hope exclusively. You can reasonably hope to pursue both and wait until the clash becomes unavoidable, at which time you hope to make a reasonable decision.

Now: your two unreasonable hopes are to become a Catholic bishop and to become an astronaut. You are fifty years old, you are not a priest, you have led a spectacularly decadent life, and you have inoperable cancer and are not expected to live out the year. Either career would require a miracle; chances are you don't really plan to achieve either. But your vision of yourself as bishop—and your vision of yourself as astronaut—may be important to your sense of who you are. And if they are, they are incompatible.

How do you resolve the difference? You don't, because you don't have to. You let one or the other take over your fantasy life for a while at a time, enjoying them seriatim, like Walter Mitty.

But what if you belonged to the "fantasy you" club, in which everybody in the club had to have the same hope, and you had to pick one? You can't be both the bishop and the astronaut; the qualities you would develop for one are not the qualities you would develop for the other.

Another way of looking at our unreasonable hopes is that each of them is a vision of what we would be if the world were our way, and what the world would be if our better selves were part of it. It's an expression of our feelings about the way things are supposed to be, and the way that we wish we were—not to mention the way that we wish other people were.

In the first thirty years of science fiction, the promise of rocket flight, and later the early space program, supplied part of a coherent and reasonable hope. Other parts of the hope, of course, were shaped by the promise of unending prosperity, the consumer revolution, and a variety social forces ranging from progressive education to the atom bomb. We might disagree about the details of the trail to the hope, and there were those among us—Alfred Bester and Philip K. Dick, to mention two prominent ones—who argued that the hope was a bad thing to hope for, but it seemed reasonable to look forward to a world in which there would be a frontier in space, a comfortable life at home, an end to many of humanity's ancient follies and evils, and a meaningful existence for practically everyone.

By about 1970 at latest, that hope was becoming just as unreasonable as all the ones that lurked in the fringes of science fiction—hopes like the hope that one would be able to step into a time machine and help the Allies win the war against Hitler, or that one might be secretly an elf left behind after the elves departed this plane of existence.

We've had a whole generation in which there were only a couple of reasonable hopes, and both of those were quite small hopes—the humanist hope that we might all at least be gracious about it and remember the good as the world fell apart, and the cyberpunk hope that in a nasty, violent, dangerous, but functional world, we might get through with a great deal of style. Neither has the kind of centrality that the old rockets-robots-rayguns reasonable hope once did (and that old hope, now that it's unreasonable, still hangs around like a childhood ambition to play professional baseball in a man who is thirty years old and sixty pounds overweight).

That, I submit, is where the SF world splintered, perhaps irrevocably, perhaps only until we turn up another Doc Smith or John W. Campbell to weld another big, enduring reasonable hope together. Unreasonable hopes clash with each other; they cannot merge or reconcile, and those who harbor them have very little reason to refine or modify unreasonable hopes. (If you're going to hope to be an elf-princess, you might as well hope to be a beautiful and intelligent elf-princess and one hell of a swordsperson too, while you're at it.) That is, unreasonable hopes don't process into discourse because they give us nothing to talk about; they pull us off into corners where we talk to ourselves, instead of dragging us into the center of the room to talk to each other.

Is it reasonable to hope that sometime soon, somebody will write a book or story to reignite reasonable hope?

TALKING TO PEOPLE
WHO AREN'T THERE

INFORMATION AND UNFICTIONABLE SCIENCE

This article was originally a speech to the American Library Association.

Ever since the Enlightenment, when it became clear that from now on significant change would occur within a single human life span, we have tended to see change as originating more in some parts of society than in others—that is, to see some things as drivers or engines of change. These perceived drivers of change, especially when they have been technological, have tended to become (depending on what we think the world is changing into, and how we feel about that) objects of either fear or hope.

Usually the technologies that threaten or promise drastic change appear in fiction as objects of both fear and hope simultaneously. In the 1940s and 1950s as it became clear that space travel would shortly be a reality, there was a great flock of novels in which space would be the new frontier, providing us spiritual redemption, as Americans expect any good frontier to do. The limitless resources and opportunities for adventure would reshape us into a species which was both happy and comfortable and hardy and adventurous, solving both the problem of want and the problem of prosperity. But at the same time there was an abundance of tales of alien invaders, and stories of brutal colonial empires in the stars.

Turn back two decades and you will find the nightmare of aerial massacres of whole cities imagined in Robert Sherwood's *Idiot's Delight* appearing on the stage in the same year that the League of Airmen were bringing us permanent peace and prosperity on the screen, in *Things to Come*.

Turn back to industrialization, and the gentle utopia of *Looking Backward* shares image space with Blake's dark satanic mills. Reach back to the Renaissance—and the exuberant dreams of Leonardo and Kepler have more than a little to do with Marlowe's *Doctor Faustus* and Hobbes's *Leviathan*.

Thus it is no accident that in our present day, when SF writers look at information technologies, we look with a similar mixture of hope and fear. The past fifteen years have seen the rise of cyberpunk stories in which the technology of information becomes the mutual weapon of criminals and tyrants—and yet also the dream of nanotech, of information rich environments in which everyone's wishes are fulfilled. As always, utopia and dystopia draw from exactly the same well.

Theodore Sturgeon once pointed out that the "science" in "science fiction" is really knowledge—that fundamentally science fiction is about knowing things and the difference that knowing things makes. I would emphasize that it is *fiction about* science—that is, that it is by definition not science, but stories we make up to surround our constructed or inherited images of science.

It's been a truism for at least fifty years that we really only know a few stories and we tell them over and over. The story of fear is generally this one: some dreadful menace, separate from our innocent selves, menaces the world. A Freudian would say that's a projected id, a Frankfurt School Marxist would say that's bourgeois hegemony, a Christian would say that's evil, an existentialist would say that's the surrender to not-being, but whatever it is, its most important attributes are first that it's Out There and second that it's threatening the good person In Here. Everything is terrible—due to this single force—and in fact if we investigate we will only find that things are worse than we thought, because the forces of evil are more pervasive than we thought.

Fortunately, a stranger comes over the hill—standing in for the ego, working class, impartial intellectual, Christian, alienated but responsible man, whatever your outlook puts its trust in. The stranger cleans the bad guy's clock and restores freedom—roughly defined as freedom from the dread of the Bad Thing From Out There. At which point, rather than become a tyrant himself, the stranger takes off to whatever part of Out There strangers come from.

The story of hope is as simple and as familiar. The world is unrecognizably better because the root of all evil was defeated some time back. But it begins to creep back in, and our hero, this time, will be tempted by it, discover the truth, turn to fight it, and restore Happy Valley to its happiness.

Now what does this have to do with information? I suggest that the picture of the "information age" currently forming in pop culture—most especially in science fiction—owes a lot more to fiction than it does to science.

What do we fear? Drugs, organized crime, the all-powerful state, shadowy forces of conspiracy, malevolent corporations, the gradual decay of the social infrastructure . . . and what does information become to the cyberpunks? An extremely valuable commodity that makes you feel like a god, struggled over by organized crime, alternately suppressed and exploited by the all-powerful state in its battle with forces that have no names, secretly made and distributed by huge faceless corporations which can nonetheless be brought down by it, grabbed on to and exploited by every bright person trapped under the social rubble—in short, information as something combining the major perceived aspects of drugs, illicit influence, intelligence secrets, crime, and opportunity.

We fear, in short, that the new information technologies might be the means by which the people on top ensnare and control everyone else; information becomes the metaphor for everything malevolent that moves in secret, and merges into the stream of stories that runs from Oedipus to Hamlet to Frankenstein, Dr. Jekyll, Conrad's Kurtz, and finally into Chandler, to Freud's case studies, to every story in which a buried secret turns out to have given birth to a monster. What do we fear? We fear the past—we fear that it will come oozing into our future, unredeemed, unredeemable, thick with the poison that it produces from lying in the dark. And because it is our handling of information that is changing rapidly, we focus that fear—that the past is not over with—on information.

What do we hope for? I suppose we hope that we will either conquer or fulfill the past, that either it will turn out that we are free to be better from now on, or that all the evil of memory will turn out to have been for some purpose good enough to justify it. And because conflict is basic to every story, we then find a way to raise the fear again and put it back in the closet . . . so that it can jump out at us again. We know, deep down, that we have the material means to make Earth a paradise—we have had them since the 1920s or so—we know that we have neither reason nor excuse for the poverty and misery in which most of the Earth's population lives, and that the bulk of reasons why so many of our species' young males spend their days waiting for the cue to begin murdering each other are reasons that could be dropped and forgotten in a heartbeat if we had the will. We sense that real determination on the part of everyone—acting on our hopes and not on our fears—could change the world drastically and for the better overnight. And once again, we fictionalize the new information technologies to imagine Vernor Vinge's singularity or K. Eric Drexler's nanotech—we have the information technology do for us what we want so much but cannot quite bring ourselves to do.

But hope and fear, if they are indeed the roots of science fiction, have practically nothing to do with reality. The space age has not led to a new frontier in any of the senses once hoped for, because it costs a small fortune to get a tiny number of people even to the edge of the frontier, because what is in the immediate neighborhood is mainly of interest to specialists, and because our notion of the "frontier" forgets that after all it took 150 years to push the settlement line a couple of hundred miles inland in North America. Frontiers move too slowly to be exciting on a daily basis. Daniel Boone spent a lot of time chopping wood and Meriwether Lewis complained of boredom in his diary. Nor, of course, did the space age lead to vast new colonial empires—of rock and vacuum?—and one definite result of the planetary program is that we now know that any possible invaders have a very long way to come.

The images we find in science fiction always come more from the fiction than from the science—more from what we want than from what we know.

This in part is why we SF writers are notorious for not living up to our own propaganda. I know that for decades we've been telling parents, teachers, librarians (and anybody else that might keep our books out of the grubby fists of teenagers) that we help prepare kids to live in the future. But I think we were lying. At least I don't recall any studies that showed that habitual science fiction readers were immune from all those mass fainting spells that accompanied the landing on the moon, the personal computer, or the use of genetic alteration in medicine. Experience would seem to show that the young deal with the future pretty well—they go charging right into it at one second per second, then settle down and live there, without much fuss, whether or not they read science fiction. And our sorry record for prediction speaks for itself—it's

1995, folks. Where's the helicopter in my backyard, why doesn't the sidewalk move, and when does the Chicago to Luna City rocket depart, anyway?

If we make the dubious move of deducing what a thing is for from what it seems to do, then the purpose of science fiction—aside from killing a dull afternoon in a small town, which is certainly the major purpose I had for it—is not to prepare us for the future but to assure us that the future will be familiar, that the rescuing stranger, the hometown hero, and the spunky gal will still be there to defeat the dark lord, the omnipotent conspiracy, and the Thing That Crawled Out of the Past.

We are not about promoting wonder, but about containing it, in the sense that NATO contained Communism and a corral contains horses. And in this function we are not only successful, but we actually *do* tell the truth. Our children will not live among wonders. Nobody will, because when the future gets here, it is always just the place where we live.

It will not be wondrous to them, but it will still be outside the farthest reaches of our fiction. As too many people have pointed out, the future is generally stranger than we *can* imagine. The solar system that we now live in—thanks to the Mariners, Vikings, Pioneers, and Voyagers—is far wilder than what was in the SF of the thirties and forties, which was a mere expanded Earth—or expanded group of Hollywood sets. The human immune system is vastly more complex and interesting than what Crichton described in *The Andromeda Strain,* and the problem of global pollution and ecosystem deterioration is astonishingly more tangled and difficult in the real world than in *The Sheep Look Up, No Blade of Grass,* or *The End of the Dream.*

Our science fiction assured us that the future would be strange and filled with wonders. Now that we are here, by the standards of that time, it is unrecognizable. Our SF is revealed as the reassuring fairy tale that allowed us to believe the future would limit itself to being strange and filled with wonders.

I do think information science is going to drive the next march into the future. But forecasts are as premature as always. The serious study of information as a subject is very much in its infancy. Issues like redundancy, self-reference, entropy, signal-to-noise, intelligence, chaos, holographic constructs, and recursivity—which, if the people studying the questions are on the right track, are essential to even naming the problem—are still floating around with multiple not-apparently-compatible definitions. The central questions about perception, creativity, knowledge, communication, thought, consciousness, and all the other aggregate phenomena that seem to arise when a group of organisms, cells, devices, or beings start exchanging and copying messages, are still so badly phrased that we probably wouldn't recognize answers to them right now, even if we were handed them. We do, however, face an increasing realization that the answers to those questions are fundamental to our finding answers that will satisfy us for those nagging older questions—questions like who are we? why are we here? is there any sense in which "why" is a question that matters?

So what we can be fairly sure of is that the future information-based society will resemble neither our hopes nor our fears, and hence will not much resemble science fiction or any other fiction. To point out only the most obvious differences, information will not be like drugs—there's too much of it relative to demand, not too little; often you can resell it after you use it; and sometimes the most effective way to exploit it is to give it away. Neither will information be like magic that allows us to get what we want effortlessly. In the first place there's the problem that "what we want" is itself a message subject to all the ills that information is heir to, and more importantly thermodynamics will demand that the more the product is to be like the statement of what we want, the more we will have to expend energy on that statement. New technologies will let us hear messages from all over the world but we can't guarantee that any of them is what we want or need to hear. We will be able to fill information storage beyond our wildest dreams, but as the storage gets fuller, it gets more like the universe it depicts: the information you want is all there but you can't be sure you can find it in a reasonable time.

One thing that does seem likely is that our concept of truth will do some shifting. As the techniques of replication and modification become better, the authentication of information (in the sense we know it today) will become impossible—and yet people will keep right on going on with their lives, in ways we can't easily imagine. Does it matter if there are six different people on the news who all say they're the President of the United States, as long as there's bread at the corner store? If we never reach beyond the moon, will it matter if everyone can live in a world too various ever to be explored? If you have the option of living entirely among people who agree with you, so that you need not ever be aware of dissension, will the people who live next door (but electronically in another universe) in the Village of Unending Contention ever have a reason to knock on your door? And if there's no longer a common reality to which to refer, if we can't believe the world around us, it seems unlikely that we will have much room either for cold, comforting fact or for the willing suspension of disbelief.

And if we get to any of those worlds of competing realities and informational overloads, will the "we" that gets there even think those are questions? This is what we sneak up on every time we sit down to tell lies about the future. You will get there and you will experience it as more of the same. But will you be the same?

The reassuring message of science fiction is in the prevention of wonder. We assure you that the companions who people your imagination—the cynical tough scarred good guy, the cackling mad scientist, the captive princess, the comic sidekick, the corrupt plutocrat, all the rest of them—will be there with you, and even if the six-gun turns out to be a neural disrupter, the knight's armor is made of cellular automata, the lady with a past is only virtually real, and the secret Nazi stronghold is an orbiting computer the size of a Ping-Pong ball, finally it will all be the same. It's okay to go to the future because we can all be tourists in the country of wonder, reassured that just behind all that frightening newness there is going to be the same old, and therefore we can point and gawk and say "gee whiz" and enjoy the sense of the world's exoticness and our adventurousness.

It is not the job of the storyteller, but of reality, to slam the gate behind all us travelers to the future and lock us up, stranded in time, in an unfamiliar future, to deal with it as best we can. But once we find ourselves in the future, we hardly hear the gate slam at all. By the time we get there it has become home.

The deepest truth behind science fiction is this: we always live at the edge of wonder and it's never wonder once we cross that edge. The transcendence for which we reach is like a childhood surgery: you're scared, but you'll feel just fine afterwards, and you'll hardly remember what happened at all.

BETWEEN SHEPHERDS AND KINGS

Brad and Dafydd really did do some arm-twisting to get this story out of me. This caused many people to assume that it's autobiographical. I've never dated a real estate lady in my life.

When we are tired, we are attacked by ideas we conquered long ago.

—FRIEDRICH NIETZSCHE

The day the invitation came for the *Free Space* anthology, Ray Terani left it on his kitchen table, where it stayed for months. That, he thinks, was his real undoing. Unfortunately it was still sitting there, unopened, this afternoon when Dafydd and Brad dropped in on him, and since he had told them before that he "loved the concept" and was "almost done" with the story, now he's out of stalling room. He'll probably have to write the sucker within the next day.

Not that having read the guidelines would make much difference. Ray is a pro, one of those guys that people call to fill out an anthology in a hurry or to whack out a cheapie novel to fill a hole in a publishing schedule. And he knows perfectly well that although worldbuilding detail changes, all hard SF is basically the same. Memorize a dozen details and usually you're ready to go; as he sits here with the sheet in front of him and Brad trying to explain it, he's already memorized most of the details he will need.

Ray has been arguing in a quiet sort of way with Dafydd and Brad, not so much about the story that he's going to write—and he will write it, make no mistake of that, not just out of friendship or for the money, neither of which is reason enough to keep going on a story, but because he has something to say, he thinks. The argument is more about whether it's possible to write the story Ray wants to write; Ray is saying he can't figure out how, and that it's impossible to figure out how, while they're trying to prove to him that the problem can be solved and the story can be written.

Ray is only mildly handicapped by the embarrassment of being caught not having even opened the guidelines. Embarrassment rarely even slows him down. He just isn't embarrassed by the long delay he has caused by promising them a story and then not delivering, nor even by the way in which other people waiting for his story are being embarrassed by him.

Nothing, after all, could be as embarrassing as having a story in a book like this in the first place, he thinks, as Dafydd elaborates on some point or other with footnotes by Brad, *and the whole reason I want a story in it is because it's embarrassing. Because it will make all my left-wing friends go "Yuck, how could you be published in* this*?" And by doing that I won't feel like I've sold out intellectually to them, but since it's a very lefty idea, I won't feel like I sold out to Dafydd and Brad either. I can feel like I'm really my own person, at the center of my complex set of relationships.*

Ray prides himself on his complexity.

As Ray listens to Dafydd, he opens another beer, quietly saying to himself that he's really just having all this beer to relax his damned aching back. He spent the morning running—one way to stay off beer till after noon, something he's been trying to do—and there must be something wrong with his running shoes because after every step, after the first mile, Ray had a miserable stabbing pain in the middle of his back, right at the small, right where each little shock seemed to merge with each other shock.

Maybe the beer will even relax him enough to write his idea into a story.

Not likely though, because if it were going to help it should have already. Right now he's so relaxed he's practically comatose. The problem has been all along that the idea won't go into a story. He can feel in his bones that it won't.

While he sits there, sinking into the feeling that this job can't be done, half another beer goes down, though he notes that neither of the other guys has taken more than a sip. Well, they're talking more than he is, after all. Ray's mostly listening. Several times he has raised a point or two only to be told that the point was irrational; if he felt that way he shouldn't.

He draws a big smiley face with his finger in the little puddle of beer on his kitchen counter top. He'll have to clean up before Leslie comes over this evening.

He starts his mental process to get the story done. He imagines space. What was called outer space till we got there. Cold, empty, lonely, vast, more clichés, and more clichés.

He visualizes the usual muscular white American man (UMWAM, he abbreviates it) posturing in front of that huge and lonely backdrop. The backdrop is *there* for the UMWAM to posture against. Sometimes the usual muscular white American men have breasts and vaginas, or dark skins, or for that matter breathe methane and live on pure thought energy, but they are still UMWAMs. They brag about achievements and all that, hey, they think the purpose of freedom is so that achievement can happen, but what they do isn't really about achievement, it's about that moment of standing against the stars.

And why do they stand against the stars? Always up close, so they won't look so tiny against all the blank that's really there. Space is 99.999. . . . % empty with so many nines in that last string that the last digits wouldn't be distinguishable from the error in most experiments. All that empty black indifferent clichéd void. The realer you write it the scarier it gets; mostly there's nothing at all in the universe, and the little that there is, is a thin scum sticking to the immense dark vacuum. The way a cliff without a guardrail attracts you and scares you at the same time, that void is what pulls the reader toward hard SF and what will scare him away if you're not careful.

So you stick an UMWAM between the void and the reader. You have to make that UMWAM stand close so that he subtends a lot of visual angle. Even then the lightless uncaring vacancy just kind of leaks in around the UMWAM, so you never really feel safe.

Oh, well. Ray gets up and gets another round of beers out of the fridge. He's drinking about three to the other guys' two. Have to start sobering up in about an hour; gotta be straight for Leslie. Straight and ideally hard. She's starting to suspect, a little, that maybe he isn't all that turned on by her, and he's not, and furthermore she suspects that maybe he doesn't like her much, and he doesn't, and Ray can't have that because he's convinced she needs him. He likes touching her body but the truth is her age lines bother him, he hates all the excess makeup, the heavy tan seems weird to him, her bleached-blonde hair is coarse and rough to his touch, and he wishes he could just be around her and take care of things for her, and he didn't have to listen to her or have sex with her.

Ray also prides himself on his honesty.

The next step in getting this story to be a story, Ray thinks, is to give the UMWAM a name, a job, and something that goes wrong with the job. Ray can't quite concentrate enough to do that so he tells Dafydd and Brad that they've got to hear a new CD he just got, even though he didn't think much of it, just so he can slap it on and that way they'll be quiet while he thinks.

Story must have hero. Hero must have problem. Hero must solve problem.

Problem is that for the *Free Space* anthology, the problem is supposed to be about freedom, and control, and all that, in a starfaring future.

And that's what's silly. Freedom *is* the problem. Control *is* the problem. And there will be no starfaring future.

Start again. Okay, we want hero to learn better. Heinlein said that, Brunner explained it, must be true. Only three kinds of stories, *one:* boy meets girl, *two:* brave little tailor, *three:* man who learns better. If our boy is a freedom-obsessed UMWAM With A Problem and he is introduced to a girl who has no freedom neurosis, people will just agree with the UMWAM, even if the girl wins on logic and on story outcome; no challenge to the damn stupid idea. Brave little tailor *defines* Hero With A Problem and that plot line really requires freedom; if the brave little tailor doesn't really choose to carry Sauron's Ring to the top of the glass hill where he can shoot it out with Grendel at the OK Corral, well, then why does he deserve to get to be a swan at the end? No freedom no hero . . . So no boy meets girl and no brave little tailor.

Man who learns better it is.

Ray's pretty drunk now—one of many reasons Brad and Dafydd are his friends is that they're very tolerant of a fat balding slob whose sentences often wander far away into the ether. Nobody who wasn't could be Ray's friend. But he outlines his argument, and Brad listens, and Dafydd picks through the logic, and then Brad sums up for Dafydd, and by the time they're done, they've agreed that he should write about a man who learns better, and another beer is gone.

One of them, maybe Ray himself, suggests that the UMWAM should be from a warship, no a privateer . . . Ray begins to giggle. He was trying to think of something innovative and here he is back with every damned cliché of historical romance. Mighty ships between the stars, so huge and mighty that they seem to challenge that vast empty dark cliché, freighters and merchantmen and battleships and a huge array of boy toys. And now *privateering?* An institution extinct on our world for generations, because it fundamentally didn't work once mass democracy and the steam engine came in, is supposed to get revived in the era of electronic democracy and FTL?

Stop giggling, Ray tells himself. The other two aren't as drunk as he is and maybe he didn't explain to them clearly enough why the privateer is such a silly idea. Maybe even if he were sober he couldn't. Maybe he isn't trying.

Nonetheless the UMWAM is a privateer, all the same. It will make the story work. When the story works the idea will get into it comfortably. Once the idea is in it comfortably the story can get written. Better yet once it's comfortable in there people can read the story, pretend they're thinking about the idea, and feel nice and safe, protected from the big bad idea.

So the UMWAM builds a house of bricks to keep the big bad idea away.

No. This isn't that kind of story. The mighty UMWAM and Stander Against The Stars is a privateer out there in Capitalist Space. Out robbing bad-guy spaceships. Teaching them all about freedom by taking their cargo for free and forcing their crews into freedom. Ray is having a lot of trouble feeling attracted to the UMWAM at this point, and he tries to say so, but since he started talking over the CD, so did Dafydd and Brad, and now they're all really loud, and he can't seem to form the idea he wants to say, that a privateer is the wrong hero, that at least he can start his UMWAM off in something less sleazy than being a hired gun for the State—that's the phrase, it got Dafydd nodding along—

Maybe, Ray thinks, he could write from the viewpoint of the merchant carrying the goods?

The phone rings. Mercifully Brad kills the CD; Ray staggers into the bedroom, through the corny little mock-Mexican archway, slipping on the cruddy hardwood floor. Gotta clean this place someday. Leslie would like that. Hell, Ray would like that. But when you get up at noon to write and knock off at six and start drinking or hanging with the guys or go out with Leslie, well, when is there time to clean? He hears his mother saying, *"So for the love of God Ray get a maid,"* in his mind's ear, just before he picks up the phone and discovers it's her. She stole a quarter from a nurse's purse or something and has phoned him again; she wants to ask him about something from when he was a kid, some ball game or something his dad (now six years dead) took him to, how his first wife (divorced seventeen years ago) is doing and does she know about his second (divorced five years ago), whether Ray could get some of her clothes for her from her house (sold three years ago), and all that. Finally after ten minutes he hears the nurse come up behind his mother and say that she has to get back to the area where she is allowed to be, and his mother says "I have to go now, Ray-ee."

Ray-ee. Always cracked him up that she could make a diminutive out of that.

"Ray-ee," she says, "I haven't said this before but you know I can tell when you're drunk. And you are. And it's working hours, not drinking time at all. Ray-ee I love you and you know you were raised better than that."

"I love you too, Mom," he says, ashamed to say it in front of Dafydd and Brad, infuriated at himself for being ashamed. He catches them looking away, and he knows that hearing him go through this bothered them, and he knows they're still his friends and they're there with him. Suddenly he loves them very much too, or is the love coming out of the beer bottle? Does it matter? "Bye," he adds.

"Bye, Ray-ee. Come see me," his mother says, and then the phone slams down. Probably the nurse grabbed it out of her hand and did that. Ray thinks of the novel, neglected in the next room while he talks with his friends, his third horror quickie this year and the one that will pay for taxes and Christmas. He decides that since the Mangler has to get someone in the next chapter, it will be a nurse from an old folk's home, a cruel nurse, a nurse that the Mangler will cut the breasts off of and then force them into her throat till she chokes. *Great image,* he thinks, and walks into the other room and scribbles a note to himself. His friends put up with that too. He loves them. He really is going to write a great story for *Free Space* one way or another, as a reward to them for being such great guys.

When he gets back out of his bedroom they have moved to his living room; silently Dafydd hands him the guidelines, again, and goes back to arguing some picky point with Brad. Ray can't follow the thread of what they are talking about with his head this way so he sits down in his favorite armchair, noting that they've opened a beer and set it there for him, and thinks about the whole problem some more.

So the UMWAM works on a privateer ship. He doesn't have to be the captain or anything, it can be just his job, he can be kind of morally unaware at the beginning of the story and thus it will be easier for him to learn better. From somebody on the merchant ship they capture. The merchant whose goods the privateers are going to take—merchant? goods?

That was the question he had almost thought of before. *What* merchant? *What* goods? The only reason there could be a merchant with goods in this story is because the guidelines have been set up to create them; there's nothing less natural than a free market so there has to be all sorts of jiggering with physics to make a free market happen as anything other than a brief historical accident. They had to come up with a magic dingus to prevent molecular-computer technology because if stuff got too abundant capitalism would collapse—markets run on scarcity. They had to come up with FTL to get to the stars at all and then make their FTL even less plausible for there to be interstellar trade.

There's an energy associated with a body in orbit around one star, and an energy associated with a body in orbit around another star, and to get between them, there's a transition energy—the difference between the two that somehow has to be made up, out of fuel carried on the ship or some other source. That magic dingus in their FTL must be making use of at least as much energy as the transition energy (probably more, if entropy gets into it). A little doodling with plain old $E=mc^2$ shows that whatever you're shipping, it would be cheaper to stay home and transmute the same mass, by a series of nuclear fusions, out of hydrogen. With energy sources of the magnitude needed to get from star to star, why not just stay home and make the damned stuff yourself, whatever it might be?

Ray's gaze crawls down the page in front of him. No explanation offered in the guidelines. Maybe the magic wish-fulfillment dingus they've made up takes advantage of some kind of low energy of transition in some bogus other dimension between points . . . but if the energy of transition, star to star, is so low in that dimension, wouldn't quantum effects dictate that a lot of stuff would be constantly appearing and disappearing in space, enough to be detectable?

Back out of all such considerations, as quickly as you can, if you want to write hard SF. Thinking about that kind of thing leads to noticing the puppeteer pulling the strings, seeing the man behind the curtain, noticing that the stars are tiny holes in thick black felt hanging forty feet away in a dark space. *Don't* see that. You can't write about freedom if you start noticing unfreedom, it might lead to awkward questions, and there's a story to get done.

Ray thinks, I will get over this. I will start my story now, in my head, while my friends argue, and then when they go I will write a page or two, then shower and change for my date with Leslie.

The privateer captures a merchant ship—no, better, a mid-21st-century generation ship, a slow-moving space colony intended to get to its destination across a period of many generations. And the people on that ship stopped worrying about getting to the destination a long time ago, because living anywhere other than the ship no longer seemed attractive. It no longer seemed attractive because on the ship there is now a unique society. One without freedom or control, one that is no longer haunted by one and obsessed by the other (or vice versa).

Ray, thinking the story, there in the armchair in his living room, looks at that idea and says, okay, but now it has to be entertaining, and that means my UMWAM with a problem will have to be standing somewhere physical, so that I can describe his exact experiences moment to moment and the happy reader can hallucinate being there, thereby ignoring more of the words and visualizing more of what the reader wants. Well, then, let's put this UMWAM at the helm, because surely ships have helms.

Ray pauses a long time trying to think of what controls would be on such a helm. A steering wheel seems singularly inappropriate, as does a throttle, a stick, or a tiller.

So what exactly does the control panel on a ship—that works on a physical principle made up entirely to preserve capitalism far beyond any point in history when it is possible for it to exist—look like? Well, don't put him at the helm. Put him in a boarding party.

Stop giggling at FTL ships with boarding parties. The UMWAM's in the boarding party because he's not high enough ranking to ring the bells, he has too much experience to shovel the coal, and he doesn't have the skill to trim the sails, okay? Ray says to himself, angry at the way that he keeps blocking instead of flowing on this. *And give the poor bastard a name. He's a finagled UMWAM. Finn Agled Umwam. Finn Agledum Wam. Fin Edumwa. Good enough. He's Finn Edumwa.*

Well, great, then, so the privateer takes over this old generation ship and sends it off on a course where a prize claim party can pick it up later. So Finn Edumwa is left there to force the people on the generation ship to follow orders. Finn is now the absolute monarch over all these people who have neither the concept of freedom nor of control. What concept do they have instead? Wrong question. What do non-Japanese have instead of giri and gimu? What did people fall into before romantic love? Where is your lap while you are standing up? What is the point of this thought?

Ray sighs, thinking hard. Dafydd asks him hopefully if he has an idea, and Ray says that he does. His idea is that tonight he will talk with Leslie about getting her into real estate school. Lots of fortyish bimbos do well in real estate. Or at least lots of them are in it. And he'll take her someplace and get her a nice dinner. He hasn't taken her out in public in a couple of weeks and he knows she's afraid that he doesn't want to be seen with her, when the truth is, he doesn't want to have people realize that he no longer cares what he's seen with. And it's not her fading tarted-up beauty, either, it's the huge gobs of random word assemblage that passes for her conversation, the high-speed spew of self-centered psychobabble . . . all the stuff that gives away the sad fact that Ray Terani no longer listens to the woman he dates, he just wants to cuddle and fuck and not be alone.

Some kind of signal passes between his friends, and Dafydd and Brad excuse themselves and head out the door, into the LA sunlight, down the peeling-painted steps to the steep little driveway and their cars. They want to leave him alone so he will be able to write his story.

Ray sits down and types eight fast paragraphs of violence, the boarding of the generation ship, the seizure and securing (good place to work in awesome details like that a generation ship would have to be kilometers long). Then he hits the point where he has Finn meeting a beautiful girl who is willing to take a job as his assistant during the long six months until the tow truck—uh, the FTL ship to tow the prize—arrives.

Finn is now the undisputed monarch of a generation ship with, oh, say, four thousand people on an indefinite voyage to nowhere. They don't have the idea of freedom so they won't rebel. They don't have the idea of control so they won't obey. They ignore him. He threatens their lives. They do what he says till his back is turned. He takes hostages. That will get the next six pages done, and with room to spare for Finn to argue with the girl and fall in love with her.

Dumb little irony. So the guy from the freedom-side ship is going to end up a tyrant. *That doesn't get me out of freedom and control, does it?* Ray thinks. It explains how freedom and control could be created in an environment without them—and thus saves Ray from describing that environment. Which was the whole point in the first place.

Maybe Finn should be converted to their way of thinking.

What was that way of thinking? Oh, yeah. The one that can't be described.

Maybe Ray is having all this trouble because Finn comes from the "freedom" side of that dichotomy.

Okay, so make him from the controlling side. Not the Federation, they're too pure a case. Let him be a—what's the silly term? A Jeffie. A New Confederate. Strange that someone would pick as an emblem for freedom a name that most of the possible readers associate with slavery (or loudly pretend that they don't associate with slavery). As if that weren't really the whole purpose anyway.

The defenders of freedom always tell you that what matters is freedom for ideas that are hated; everything else is regarded as too easy or trivial. Sort of the cold shower approach to freedom; you must have freedom so that you can listen to ideas that you don't like.

"If nobody objects," the freedom addicts say, "you don't need freedom."

But, Ray thinks—and he must remember this to annoy Dafydd with—that logically implies that if you do need freedom it's because somebody wants to do something objectionable. His fingers fly over the keys:

"This is why anyone who spends a lot of time talking about freedom—Sophocles, Socrates, Kleon, Seneca, Hobbes, Locke, Rousseau, Paine, Jefferson, Danton, Marat, Proudhon, Marx—is an obnoxious pain in the ass with no social skills. Their greatest fear is that someone might make them pay for their random assaults on people around them; they want to be free, meaning that they want it to be costless for them to annoy others. Freedom is the ability to hurt without being hurt, and as such the ultimate free lunch."

Ray decides that's a manifesto and takes it out of the story. If you want to send a union, call a messy westerner, or something. Besides Ray's still a little too drunk to know whether or not he agrees with what he's written.

Drunk and getting horny—the creative process does that—and that's a good thing too, because it seems to reassure Leslie that Ray will sometimes make really crude passes at her the moment she comes in the door, like it proves she's attractive rather than that he's just horny. Or maybe getting horny this way is his way of loving the poor deluded aging tart. He can't decide that either. He really isn't functioning too well mentally—might as well write, then. No need to be functional to write this stuff.

So, then, Ray will grant them that the name, the New Confederates, works for this future, because these are the new people who demand the freedom to rob and enslave whoever they can.

So if Finn is a Jeffie, a New Confederate, a freedom fraud, whatever, the question is, is he really, at his core, true to his espoused principles— or to his society's actual behavior? A nineteenth-century white plantation owner could be either really a believer in all the liberty stuff (but then why hadn't he manumitted the slaves?) or in what he was actually doing (which was more usual). So does Finn *really* believe in freedom or order? He's got to be the man who learns better, but from which of the positions can he learn better better? Could a control freak learn to see reasons to just let things go by? Could a freedom addict learn to see freedom as a cause of unnecessary pain? *And could either of them learn to change into something besides each other?*

Well, now, that's what the story is about. And that's why Ray has sat here half an hour staring at the screen.

His mind drifts; idly, he strokes his half-erection. He'll do Leslie as soon as she gets here; she likes to think he likes her that much that way. He needs it anyway. And tomorrow he'll drive out and see Mom, third time this week, but it seems to cheer her up so much. Tonight after he's had sex with Leslie, right there in the front hall, as fast and as hard as he can because he's scared to death that he'll start to look at her overtanned skin and cracking makeup and lose his erection, she'll smooth her dress back down and they'll go out for dinner, instead of Chinese and videos here, and he'll let her babble on about being actuated and crystals and what some producer who almost cast her said fifteen years ago. And then they'll share his bed and he'll wake up not lonely and feeling okay; tomorrow that should be good for a day without beer, and if he's sober he can go see Mom without feeling ashamed (though after his visit to her usually he'll drink and cry a while).

The thing he wants to say is, he's not choosing to do these things, these are what he is. At the end of *Barbarella,* the angel saves the bad girl as well as Barbarella, and when Barbarella complains, he explains, "An angel does not love. An angel is love." The Sufis say you can only spend what's in your purse. Ray doesn't choose, he just takes care of it, does what he can for people, even when his feelings really aren't up to it. Nor do the people he does these things for force him to do them. They don't have that much power over his life. If he dumped Leslie he'd forget her by next month; when Mom dies he'll be sad but really she was gone long ago, the wrinkled thing in perpetual care is a stray wandering whispering bag of memories from the far past. The chains that hold him are not even threads.

He is not forced, he does not choose. That's what he wanted to tell his friends, he thinks, and even though it means still being a little drunk when Leslie gets here, goes to the fridge, opens one more beer, sits back down, and looks into the screen. It is blank, blank as the real sky, blanker than the crowded space of *Free Space*—the screen, defined as a screen, contains nothing at all, just as the universe, defined as a place for matter and energy, contains almost nothing.

Ray stares into that bottomless cliché, gaping void, blankness, and imagines a ship, immense and silent, slipping through it faster than he could see or think. Then he tries to think of a place where no one expects him to obey stern freedom, no one expects him to fit into a cold and lonely slot in an all-embracing order. He stares and stares but he just can't see it, not yet.

THAT KID WATCHING HIS SHOES

There are more kinds of escapes than most people let themselves be aware of. It would be fair to say that when I was a teenager, I was a pretty miserable one, and I read science fiction to escape. But I'm not sure at all that when I say that, I mean the same things other people do.

I did pretty well at school, mostly netting the sort of teacher comments that said, one way or another, "The kid is sort of weird and he appears to be goofing off a lot," or "The kid is badly socialized and bright, and I wish he'd get it together." I had a decent number of friends, was disliked by about as many people as I disliked, was sometimes bullied (usually physically), was sometimes the bully (usually psychologically), and if I wasn't exactly in the middle of the normality bell curve, you could still see it from where I was. I had an unpleasant home life and therefore had to be selective about which school friends I brought home, but this is not exactly the stuff of which martyrdom is made, either.

Probably the best description of me was voiced by a guy a couple of years older, who happened to have a locker across the hall from me at Bowling Green Junior High School; he referred to me as "That kid who's always watching his shoes."

Now, looking at your feet is not the natural way of doing things. You bump into stuff and you miss most of the scenery. The reason I was doing it was that I was trying to be alone with my thoughts, and those thoughts were pretty much what you'd expect in a middle-class adolescent male: I wished I knew how to behave in public so that I wouldn't look like a goon, I wished to be fabulously successful at something so that I wouldn't look like a goon, and I wished that my face would clear up and I could get contact lenses so that I wouldn't look like a goon.

The standard take on why I liked SF so much in those years would be that it gave me a chance to identify with characters who had clear skin, perfect vision, fabulous success, and a bale of social skills, or at least acquired them before the final chapter. The same thing might be expected from most of the bad pop lit that literate adolescents scarf down, from Westerns through romances to everything else (except in those occasional dreary and miserable books, beloved of school librarians, in which the ugly unpopular kid learns to accept being ugly and unpopular—the kind of stupid and cruel lie you need an Ed.D. to think of foisting upon the young). But, whatever the other kids who read were getting out of their reading, at least as I recall, I didn't find much *comfort* in the exploits of Lance Squarejaw (whether as Captain Squarejaw of the Federation Starship *Admirable,* or Sheriff Squarejaw of Lizard Flats, or Sergeant-Major Mâchoire-Carrée of the Foreign Legion). What I found was distraction. The idea of fitting in to my society, acquiring respect, or doing anything of any importance at all well seemed about as probable as flying by flapping my arms—maybe less probable, come to think of it. I read all that stuff and enjoyed a lot of it, because adolescence is the great waiting room of life, and like all waiting rooms it's filled with reading material that you can drop in an instant if anything else comes up.

The escape that science fiction gave me was of an altogether different kind. You open a page of science fiction and somewhere along the way someone says, "It would be nice to have a dog for this," and the other one says, "You're old enough to remember dogs?" and for an instant you stop dead.

The story is set in a world in which dogs are extinct. Ten pages later you see a character who is an old man, and he has pictures of all the dogs he once owned on his wall. He tells the small girl about each of them, and she has trouble understanding why anyone wants a pet that licks your face and chews up your property. He sighs and says everything was better before the war.

You have to have held the first anomaly in mind long enough to attach the second anomaly to it, all in the hopes that sooner or later there will be a third anomaly that makes things a little clearer. Meanwhile there are twenty more anomalies, similarly suspended; it's a whole world that needs figuring out.

Which is a pretty good description of adolescence. The world makes no sense to adolescents because they were born yesterday, for all practical purposes; their consciousness has just become something like an adult's, and vivid as their memories of childhood may be, they were remembered by someone who thinks differently than they do now. Now there are all sorts of signals about what to do, what not to do, what's appropriate and what isn't, and so forth, pouring in on the kid. The first natural reaction is to try to simplify it: get it reduced to clothes and boys, or sports, or music, or anything at all that can be made into a simple set of rules. Defy everything else and declare that it doesn't make any sense or that it's all stupid. Anything to control the intolerable swarm of input.

And what did I do besides watch my shoes? I suppose I practiced, a little, in a very safe environment. It didn't matter in the slightest whether I ever figured out how to relate to an Asimov robot; it was a consuming puzzle, but not a matter of life or death. Unlike, for example, figuring out how to relate to a girl. The rules of family versus friends versus adult community were complex and only hinted at; but the rules of a Philip K. Dick paranoid society could be figured out (and the real world resembles them, perhaps, more than it cares to admit). It was even better that while trying to figure out what was going on in the world of a book, I wasn't thinking about myself as much, and anything that gets an adolescent's attention off himself has to be a good thing.

Lately, I am told, publishers claim that much of the old science fiction audience is now reading "media tie-ins"—those novels about the further adventures of television or movie characters, or about what they were supposed to have been doing between episodes or movies. Affluent adolescents have been hiding in books for a couple of hundred years, at least, and these new books are where they are choosing to hide.

I just wonder about the kid of today, watching his shoes. He knows what Han Solo looks like, she knows the whole history of the Federation, they know the background and the story-thus-far for everything they read. There isn't nearly as much of the figure-out-the-world game; now it's just a matter of figuring out which standard plot you're going to be walked through.

Is he, or she, getting enough practice figuring stuff out? Does the process require *enough* thought to get kids' attention away from themselves?

I hope so. The teenage years can seem like a century. It can be a long, long time before you're ready to look up and look around. I would hate to think that the escape hatch that I got out through isn't there anymore.

DIGRESSIONS FROM THE SECOND-PERSON FUTURE

My father calls this "that mouse story" and has told me it's his favorite. Maybe I should mention that he's not exactly like the father in the story; he's more like the mouse. And I never did get him interested in "Inna Gadda Da Vida," either.

I cannot begin with "you will be" without raising questions. How do I know? Who are you?

It is possible that I won't answer them.

You will be a mammal. You will have, relative to the other creatures around you, a big brain; you will have forepaws that can grasp and hold.

You will be descended from something now alive. Perhaps me. Perhaps Henry, my white mouse who escaped when I was twelve. I never did find Henry, despite a thorough search. But then again, my father may have set a trap, killed Henry, and disposed of the body without my knowing. It would be like him.

At any rate, you will be this mammal. You will be less than a half-day's easy walk from home—your word for it, of course, will not be "home." Your eyes will scan the meadow in front of you, waiting for something slow and stupid you can kill with the piece of broken glass you hold in your forepaw. You will turn often to look and hear behind you; sometimes you will sniff the wind, unaware of how little you can smell now, compared with what your ancestors could before the brain gave up its old marriage to the nose and took up with the word.

By the sun, it will be past noon. Around you, gold mottles of sunlight will swim in the shadows; one length of your body in front of you, the shadows of the trees will disappear at a sharp line, and beyond that line the yellow and green of the meadow will begin. Flies and grasshoppers, familiar to you and me and the dinosaurs, will circle over the meadow—and, in pursuit of them, something larger and smarter, a bat or a winged lizard, jaws snapping.

There are two ways nature handles information—genes and brains. Bugs picked genes. A couple of phone calls back, I argued at length with my father that the bugs were right, and that their unthinkably longer unchanged survival proves it. He enjoys arguments like that.

When you look down at the forepaw clutching the glass knife, the forepaw will be hairy and scarred, the glass shaped and sharpened by forepaws before yours, by so many so long before that you do not know all the names that went with the forepaws. You won't look down long. Some older one of your kind, a parent or mentor, will have taught you that such absorption in a nearby, unimportant object, away from home, is dangerous and foolish.

When you look up the beast will be crossing the field, huge, scaly, muscular, blundering, and stupid. I might notice that it is many tons of meat; because it will be utterly inaccessible, you will ignore it.

When the big scaly thing is halfway across the meadow, there will be a great roar, fire will come up from the ground, and a wave of pressure will pound against your face like a dense wad of old leaves. When you look back up, you will see the big thing dead, a whole leg torn off, blood puddling under it from torn arteries, the head turned sideways on the broken neck, exposing the charred and blackened underjaw.

From when I write, I could say that the big reptile will have stepped on a long-buried tank of gasoline, the finally-corroded aluminum giving way and sending sparks into the separated, self-jellied fuel, or I could say he will have stepped on an unimaginably old land mine, or a buried truckload of ammonia fertilizer or dynamite. But by the rules I can say no such thing to you. Despite my faith that you will be able to understand brush, grass, trees, home, sun, and any number of other things, I cannot believe that you will understand anything that I might consider a plausible cause of the explosion. But physical plausibility matters to me—my father's influence, I suppose—so I'll settle on the ammonia fertilizer.

It's funny how so many little clues you notice without making sense of them can swarm back at you later, forcing you to a conclusion years afterward. I think in all probability Dad did set a trap for Henry.

And of course he would not tell me.

Henry was all right with Dad as long as he lived in his cage in my room. I fed him, gave him water, changed his litter—did all the things that adults give children pets for when they decide that the child in question should learn responsibility. I also talked to Henry a lot while I held and petted him. To be honest, I never did learn to like the spidery creepiness of his little paws on my palm, or that slick snaky tail, or the snotty-wet probing of his pink nose. I am sure Henry liked me even less—I knew that even then—but it didn't matter. I needed someone to talk to; he was physically dependent on me. If it wasn't friendship, it was still something.

I think my father understood some of that. I remember one of his infrequent visits to my room. He had come home earlier than usual one night, while I was still awake. When he came into my room, he made a big point of saying hello to Henry. I was eleven—much too old to believe that Henry cared whether people talked to him, but a little too young to recognize my father's awkward overture. I had been wondering about my own sanity—for godsakes every serious conversation I was having was with a *mouse*—and my first thought was that Dad, hard-pressed as he always was with work, was really losing it.

After the clumsy start, though, we just talked about what I was finding in the drop of pondwater I had under the microscope. He loved that kind of thing; I even taught him the names of a couple of paramecia I had identified from library books. He was really interested—on the road all the time as a tech sales rep, he spent a lot of time in Motel Sixes and Howard Johnson's with *Scientific American, Popular Mechanics,* and so on. He'd talk about things he'd read over the big family dinners on the weekends—I thought that was neat.

I had forgotten; it sort of came back with Henry, who was supposed to be just a way of personifying one of your possibly rodent ancestors. I know it's supremely unlikely that you will be descended from Henry.

Too bad for you, too, because for a mouse, he was pretty smart, almost human.

At any rate, you will be where I left you, staring at the still-smoking but mostly edible remains of that huge reptile, the probable descendant of a crocodile. You will not exactly think—surely not in words, no more than I would. You will just rush forward to the fallen reptile, skirting burning clumps of grass, hardly aware of what you are doing. You will jump and scramble up the scaly belly of the huge thing, standing in a moment on the side of its rib cage.

From a crude skin bag slung like a bandolier over your shoulder—you will not have any idea of what a bandolier might be, and your shoulders will be less square than mine so that the bag often slides down—from that bag you will pull something else, a thing I would recognize as a glass bottle with the bottom broken off and the broken edges rubbed smooth with quartz, and raise it to your lips, and blow on it like a trumpet. You will blow again and again until at last faint, similar sounds come back to you.

When you look down you will see the carrion-eaters gathering around you. Your mental inventory will take no more than a heartbeat: you will have two sharp throwing sticks, your bottle horn, your glass knife, and the limited use of your hind claws and vestigial fangs.

Observing those hind claws and the remains of your ancestors' fangs, I realize that unlikely as you will be to be Henry's descendant, you will be even less likely to be mine. That sort of evolutionary outcome is remarkably unlikely in a big-brained species like mine—in the time needed to evolve those organic weapons, solving a problem in species survival by a slow, random, genetic process, a very few such big brains can easily make the long trip from fire and spear to nuclear fission and rockets, solving the same problem many times more efficiently.

I talked about just such a problem with my father the last time I talked to him on the phone. We saw it as kind of the ground under the mythic figure of original sin—well, I did. Dad called it the "Promethean apple"—I didn't comment on that tangled image, not wanting to offend him. A brainy species can survive only as a brainy species. No beneficent natural process can ever again make you stupid, thus reuniting you with nature. You and your descendants will be cursed with all that excess processing capacity—and thus your potential for malice and ability to act on it, for as long as you walk the planet, just as my species is cursed.

Dad still prefers science to all other topics. Politics, sports, all that's nothing to him. We talked about the irreversibility of the evolution of intelligence for over an hour—an expensive call, but since Mom died it's about the only thing that breaks his loneliness.

Maybe on the next call I'll ask him about Henry. I keep thinking it shouldn't matter to me, and I know it will not be communicated to you, but I'd like to know whether it is at all possible that Henry will have been your ancestor.

You, of course, will be unconcerned with all such things at the point I've narrated you into. You will be standing on that immense heap of fresh carrion, with the aerial scavengers—I call them vulture bats, you will call them something else—circling even lower. On the ground, facing you, will be a pack of what I will call just "big rats"—but by big I mean big as full-grown cocker spaniels, and they will not be rodents, not any more, anyway, but carnivores. What you will call them, and the bats, my palate's shape cannot accommodate.

They will slowly circle, warily, looking but not yet attacking, hoping for your unguarded back.

You will be turning, still up there on the smooth scaly side of the fallen monster, pivoting so that none of them gets a chance. You will be counting on daylight and the cowardice of the scavengers to hold them back. In your right forepaw, you will clutch a throwing stick, raised to stab rather than to throw, and in your left a knife.

They will circle, circle, circle, not quite bright enough to split into two groups and circle opposite ways. Their paws will thud on the thick turf, and now and then their fur will make a little brushing noise against the dry grass, but mostly you will hear only the vulture bats' crying. You will see the big rats' long teeth and staring green eyes, and you will toy with charging through, scattering them, and running away. But you will have blown your horn, and the other hunters will be here soon, and you will want to keep this meat untainted until they arrive.

A thought, perhaps in words, will come to you. You will whirl, careful of your footing on the scales, and fling your sharp, curved stick with a practiced snap of your wrist. It will gash into the leathery wing of a circling vulture bat; you will shout with delight as he struggles some distance from you before crashing to the ground, the stick still in his wing. At once, one of the big rats circling you will give a cry that I might say would sound like that of a bobcat, and charge at your victim. The rest will follow him, ducking and diving around the fallen bat, trying to get in for a death-bite.

The vulture bats will retreat to a prudent altitude. The rats will begin to toy with the shrieking wounded one. Temporarily, you will be master of the bigger prize. If they will not get bored with their game for some time, you will be fine.

You will climb down on the other side of the big dead thing, where some grass will still be smoldering, and find, quickly, as many sticks as you can without getting so far from the carcass as to invite another winged attack. You will hastily build up the fire—you will know how to keep a fire, though not how to make one. You will tie twigs and grass on the end of a long stick, making something that would look to me like a crude broom, and you will set it by the fire, leaned up against the big corpse's back. Then you will leap up again, waving your remaining throwing stick to frighten the aerial enemy back to a respectful height.

By the time you will have done this, the shrieks will have ceased, and your other opponents will be tearing into the flesh of your victim, quarreling over it and pulling it apart between them. You will judge that with luck you may live through this, and you will be vaguely displeased to have enough time to consider the question—like many of my species, you will prefer actions to questions, especially violent busy actions to difficult important questions.

My father is no such person. Not that he tolerates open questions well—he's no better than most people at that. But the problem of his mortality never bothered him much.

In one of those occasional conversations we would have in my room, I remember, the subject came up. His view was that seeing somebody die—he'd been an operating room orderly in the army—was unpleasant, but other than that it was just like having them move away and never write. In my father's scheme, dying would be like having *everyone* move away and never write; sad and lonesome, perhaps, but routine.

I had thought my father held that idea because he was a hero, and I had thought he was a hero because he had been in the army. Actually he had served in peacetime and never left the United States; I knew that then but it somehow did not dim the fact that he had been a soldier, and that helped to fix an image of him in my mind. I don't know what ideas about him I may have derived from that; a lot of my solid certainty about him has slumped back into the fluid mystery of his clumping up the stairs to look in at me, thinking I was asleep, and the brush of his hand on the back of my head as he ran out to the car the next morning. I don't really know how he feels or felt about dying, or much about him from before my own memories of him.

When I talk with him on the phone next week, after we talk about Henry the mouse, we'll talk about death in general. Maybe we won't talk about science or his job or mine at all.

You will not have a job. You will have a role, but you will not have traveled far enough down the road to have jobs as yet, let alone to have individuals who will need them or define themselves in terms of them. There will be only what you will be doing now.

What you will be doing is watching the big rats finish off the vulture bat, also keeping an eye upward against the vulture bats still circling. You will be waiting till the last moment to ignite and use the long torch against the big rats, because when it will be gone you will have to run away, leaving this valuable carcass to the other claimants. But you will be, for the moment, relaxed.

You will have enough attention to spare to enjoy the warm afternoon, but you will snap alert when the rats back away from where they will have been feeding.

A distant relative of the dead thing on which you stand will be coming out of the bushes. This one will have stayed truer to his ancestry—he will want that pile of meat on which you stand, and he will not object to eating you with it. The scavengers will scatter, and you will face the huge thing, ten times your body length, by yourself.

The eyes on the thing will be set close together in front around a short snout—a good arrangement for a solitary carnivore. They will be fixed on the beast under you; when you jump down, they will fix on you. I would call those eyes "catlike," and despite the reptile dullness behind them, there will be something else catlike about all this, because the big thing will move in slowly, as if to play with you, its ridiculous clawed fingers squeezing the ground as if feeling its way.

You will grab your long-handled torch and ignite it. It will blaze up at once. You will have nowhere to run—you will stare into those flat yellow unintelligent eyes endlessly as they draw nearer. In a burst of fury or despair, as the thing weaves sideways, crabbing a little before springing, you will rush toward it, jabbing your torch into that face.

But you will be off center. The hot torch end will destroy an eye instantly, searing the delicate outer surface, grinding black cinders and splinters into the clear jelly.

The creature's head will whip sideways as a thundering whistle of agony rolls from the open mouth. Emboldened or confused, you will thrust again, doing the same to the other eye. The head will snap around again as you jump back.

Bewildered, enraged, blind, it will turn after you, the jaws, big enough to pinch you in two, snapping shut just above your back. You will dodge inside the turn, and the scaly hide will brush against you.

Some notion will form; the thing will not be able to raise its head very high because of the bony ridge at the base of its neck. You will leap, scrambling a moment on its rough side, and seat yourself on the back of the monster.

Sliding forward, drawing your remaining throwing stick from the bag, you will stab under that ridge over and over, looking for a severable artery, an opening to the medulla, the spinal cord, anything you can reach that will kill it.

The throwing stick will draw more blood with each jab, but still the deep hooting howling will go on and on and the head will whip from side to side. Unable to reach you with its short tail or to roll over (the burdens imposed by evolutionary accident and the cube-square law respectively—a point of plausibility), the monster will not throw you off. You will stab and stab again until your arms ache.

At last the thing will collapse under you and you will stagger off it, your breath coming in difficult sobs. Then your head will snap up as a horn sings. The meadow will be filled with one, two, many hunters, and they will all raise their horns, blowing loud and then soft, sending the pitch from a shrill whistle to a deep moan over and over again, wild harmonies filling the meadow. Then you will raise your own horn and make all the sounds you feel, all that you have just felt, and when the horns are finally lowered there will be something new among all of you—the desire for the horns again.

That certainly won't be due to your heredity. I never did get Henry to like music. Lots of other sounds, but not that.

I had come up with the science fair project of doing some behavior mod with Henry—every time I put "Inna Gadda Da Vida" on the turntable, I gave Henry an M&M. The idea was that eventually he would respond only to that sound, ignoring the Beatles, Peter, Paul, & Mary, and the Glenn Miller record I had borrowed from my father's cabinet, but running to the feeding slot at the first sound of Iron Butterfly.

It didn't work because he learned to listen for the switch being flipped. I tried putting a silent membrane switch into the line with an extension cord, and Henry developed an interest in the sound of the tone arm. I set the arm on manually, and he started responding to the electric motor on the turntable. The only thing he never paid any attention to was "Inna Gadda Da Vida." Eventually I took my rock collection to the science fair.

The day Henry got away—I still don't know how; he was just missing from the cage—I kept turning my stereo on and off, hoping he'd pop out looking for an M&M. I even put on "Inna Gadda Da Vida," but of course that didn't work either. Since the next morning I was going to Scout camp for a week, and my mother would be tending Henry, I couldn't very well hide the fact that he wasn't there. If he didn't show up I was going to be in a lot of trouble.

He didn't show up. I had noticed his disappearance at one P.M. At four, I told Mom and Dad. Dad questioned me about it, but then he noticed that I was on the edge of blubbering and stopped in mid-question, blushing and looking cockeyed up at the ceiling as he always did when he was embarrassed. He said Henry would either turn up or he wouldn't while I was gone, and if he did they'd take care of him.

Then he spent about an hour helping me pack up my stuff. The Scout camp was a cabin camp, more for working on merit badges than for real camping. That was fine with me—I had just made Second Class, which meant I could finally work on the Nature, Chemistry, and Astronomy badges. I was worried about Henry, but I was too excited to feel it much.

The week went by in a blur—more fun than anything I had ever done before in my life, because they'd given us a real lab. Certainly it was more fun than wiring up doorbells and putting vinegar on litmus paper like we'd been doing all year in sixth grade science class. When I got home, there was still no Henry.

After a couple of weeks, Dad surprised me with a new mouse. I took good care of him, but I never named him or really talked to him.

Early on in writing this I realized that I knew exactly what my father had done as soon as I had left. He baited a trap, probably with a piece of Hershey bar, and when Henry was killed in the trap he threw the body away, at home (if it was before garbage day) or in some dumpster or trashcan (if it was after). I like to think it was after, because I can easily imagine my father wrapping a dead white mouse in a plastic sandwich bag, tucking it into his briefcase, and scribbling a note in his pocket calendar—something like "Dispose: mouse—2 minutes"—on the Before First Meeting list.

He didn't hate Henry or anything, but it was the simple and easy way to solve the mouse problem. He worked so many hours and spent so little time at home that the random threat a loose mouse posed to his comfort was intolerable.

Knowing him, I know. I know so well that it probably isn't worth bothering him about it on the next phone call. Besides, he'll want to talk about some things in the new issue of *Science News*.

Anyway, that's settled. And I want to get back to what this story is about. You will arrive home heading a triumphal parade of hunters bearing great slabs of the muscles and choicer organs of the dead reptiles. The fires will be stoked up, green sticks sharpened, and flat rocks heated; before sunset the smell of roasting meat will fill the camp. When the whole group, from the toothless old to the just-weaned, has gorged itself, someone will ask you how you came by the meat.

You won't simply tell them that one died by accident and you killed the other by stabbing it in the neck. Instead, you will tell your memories, one at a time, jumping when your story comes to a jump, stabbing at the fire when it comes to a stab. And when you come to the blowing horns, all the horns will blow together again. And again, you will be delighted to hear them.

But you will never hear the story I write now. You would not understand anyway. You could not understand the simplest things in it—microscopes and stereos and merit badges. So I rely on you to tell yours.

MY ADVICE TO THE CIVILIZED

*My most reprinted story, and yet another answer to the question
"Why do you write?"*

The captain says we've got a couple of hours to get letters written.

A year ago I'd have spent the time writing letters for the younger
men. But the literacy class I taught in winter bivouac took care of that.
And I have no one to write to, anymore.

So he comes over to my spot at one of the former picnic tables on the
former high school gym floor, and tries to cheer me up. Why he wants
his company sergeant cheerful, I couldn't say. He's very sincere and sensitive and no help at all, because he can't fix the basic problem—I'm ar-
ticulate and would love to write, but my family died in the St. Joseph
raid, and old friends are all somewhere else, probably dead.

So he gets a dumb idea. "Look, Harry, if I have to I'll order you to do
this. Suppose we don't win—maybe that's it for centuries, right? I mean
we don't know that any other civilized settlement will make it. But
sooner or later people will want to settle down, right, even if all of us are
dead? I mean they are human out there. Or maybe some other settlement will make it all come together. And when civilization gets going
again, they'll do archeology, just like Before."

I agree that all this is plausible because Dave can argue trivia to death.

"Well, then," he goes on, "write a letter to the future. You're a historian—tell the historians of the future what they'll want to know."

"I don't have their ZIP code. Maybe you would know it?"

His eyes widen. His fingers clench. He must be on edge; you don't mention what somebody did Before, like teaching college history. And I must be on edge too, because when someone is rude that way, you don't compound it by being rude back—like by alluding to the fact that Dave used to be a mailman. He sees we're headed for trouble, so he starts back to the big desk in the corner we share—the "Company Office."

He was just trying to help, and I feel bad for him, so I walk after him and say I'll do it. "We'll bury it in a plastic bag someplace before I get on the plane. If we win I can always dig it up and continue it."

I pick up the pen and begin.

I don't know how Before became After. The big cities were smashed and burned first thing, but radio reports from the settlements that can afford expeditions say that there's no detectable radioactivity around Kansas City, Caracas, Honolulu, or Detroit. So it probably wasn't a nuclear war. Things just got violent and ugly one day, or within a week, but communications was the first thing to go, so all we have is the word of some ham and military radio operators that everything went to shit everywhere at about the same time.

Ernwood, a physicist, said he'd been up at the observatory that day and all the instruments went weird, a lot of them burning out. He thought maybe some solar event caused a giant global EMP (I forget what that stands for but it was connected with nuclear winter or something), starting fires wherever conductors ran.

But that didn't explain why some engines and a few radios and so forth still worked, or why nothing in our little huddle of valleys did anything like that—I'd assume my wristwatch would have charred my wrist.

When I asked Ernwood about that, he started talking fast, drawing pictures in the dirt, and his red hair and the flutter of his hands reminded me so much of Cynthia that I got fascinated and couldn't remember what he said afterwards. (This was just after I lost Margie and the kids at St. Joseph, and I couldn't seem to get my mind off Cynthia.)

Anyway, if it will help you, I'm pretty sure Ernwood used words like "shadowing effects," "bounceback," "reradiation," and "induced opaqueness." Science was my dead worst subject, but if that gives you a clue, maybe you'll find a surviving library somewhere to put it all together.

I'd have Ernwood write something for you, but he died in the defense of Providence Falls when we lost it eight weeks ago to Thrasher's Horde.

Because of his red hair, his was about the only head we recognized in the big box they sent to us.

What I can tell you, anyway, is that I got up one Wednesday and there was no electricity, no water, no gas, nothing on the radio, no phone. A few days after, hundreds of refugees came up the highway with wild stories of looting and fighting, cities on fire and towns deserted.

As I re-read what I've written so far, I realize that I'm leaving you the sort of cryptic document that the Dark Ages specialists I knew could spend ages arguing about. My problem is I'm a historian, and no one can write history in these circumstances—history is interpretation, the choice and expression of a view. There's plenty of material for historiographers, establishers of facts and data, in the last decade, but nothing yet for historians.

They announce at least two hours' delay. Fine with me. I feel better about the odds going after dark. So do a lot of the men—they're sacking out all over—but I can't sleep. Might as well keep writing, especially after the promise I was making when I was interrupted.

Anyway, for you historiographers, you grubby fact-grinding establishers of names, dates, and places:

Before
Late XXth century A.D., USA, up until 199-

After
The current period. We are in the ninth year After, which will become the tenth year After five weeks after the next spring solstice. I'm very proud of myself for remembering a word like "solstice" and that that's what starts spring, so you'll have an accurate date to work from.

Civilization
That's what we call ourselves. Politically we're a republic constituted from the old county government of Carson-Bridger County. We used to control about 2500 square miles. We are now down to less than 1000 square miles, which Thrasher penetrated yesterday. He's being slowed by harassment for the moment. The plan is to get him a long way in before we spring what we hope will be a trap.

(Units of measure in above)

Mile = a little over 5000 feet, I think. The number 1760 comes to mind, too, but I can't remember why, and I don't think it's right. Use the land mile—nautical miles are different. One foot (the plural is feet) = 12 inches, I'm sure. One inch = |————————|. (I copied that from an old ruler).

Basic geography

This will be buried at Gallatin High Barracks, which is our main military encampment. One half of a mile west of us is the old UMW Hall, where the Legislature meets, and that's across the street from the old County Courthouse, which is where the President and the Speaker have their offices.

St. Joseph

Nearest town east of here. Clorox's Horde surprise-raided it at the beginning of summer in the year 8. They killed everyone, took all the Before stuff they could carry, and torched the rest. We caught them and killed about fifty, three miles beyond Frederickstein Pass. The next spring they were wiped out by Excess's Horde.

Horde

Gang of raiders. Always named after their leaders. North of us is Wanker's Horde, and then clockwise from them there's Banger's, Excess's, Rover's (due south), Nitrofucker's, Fun Boy's, and Thrasher's. Thrasher seems to be the successful Attila type—Wanker, Banger, and Fun Boy have all been forced to swear some kind of fealty to him in the last couple of years.

The Company

I am in the Northwest Company. In better days we guarded Angel Break Pass. Now the whole Army will try to drive Thrasher's Horde (and its allies) back toward the pass. Northwest Company will try to seal it against them, so the Army—with the help of a couple of other surprises—can corner them for a massacre.

Army

Eleven companies, down from fourteen. They're about the size of US Army companies, Before. We have a colonel, Bob Peterin, and under him there are eleven captains, of whom David Lipowicz is mine. I'm his company sergeant and de facto XO—we've decided civilization can survive without lieutenants, at least for a while. The President is Mrs. Roberta Gibson, and the Speaker of the Legislature is Tiffany Ann Hutchinson, both of the Democratic/No Quarter Party. My party, by the way.

That was off the subject of my annotations, but I couldn't stand the thought that you might know the names of the Hordes' leaders and not ours.

Well, that used up twenty minutes. I stretch and flex my hand, numb from the unaccustomed strain of writing so much in a room that's rapidly getting cold.

The phone beeps. I pick it up. It's Samuelson with confirmation that the plans are go. I still can't believe that our little Cessna was able to get enough parts from other airfields so that we could get all four Dash-8's to fly, after all this time, or even that we managed to make enough methanol, and find enough kerosene, to fuel them.

So strange to think I'll be flying again!

Out the window, the sun has almost set. Dusk has that wonderful October gold color that Margie and I used to walk in for hours. The last fall we had together, Joshua was big enough to walk with us too, not having to be picked up and carried.

I can't believe I'll be flying again, and yet I used to fly into Salt Lake weekly when Harris and I were working on that silly paper about Reconstruction government opposition parties.

Will it all work? Supposedly we'll fly out low, away from Thrasher's Horde, and circle around to land in Angel Break Pass on the old interstate. That will give us most of the night to dig in. But we've had no rehearsals.

I look up from my thoughts. Three men, waiting patiently for me to notice them, want me to witness their wills. I do it, and talk with them for a couple of minutes. They go back to their benches to get some sleep. I should write more if I want to finish before we go, but instead I stand up and stretch.

The October gold fades to indefinite gray, and I look out the window, past the old football stadium, to the airfield. There's an indistinct dark lump out there.

It's a Q-hut, and it contains a collection of scuba tanks, soda machine cylinders, propane tanks, and so forth, all loaded with the nerve gas Bernie Klipfer was finally allowed to make after we won the election. (Well, the party won. I lost to a Democratic Christian by eight votes.) I helped attach the farm-dynamite heads and the bedsheet-strip tails.

So strange to imagine that those crude devices could end the threat within a few days. I wonder what the B-29 crew thought—really thought, not said later to journalists—when they first saw Little Boy? But then they had been winning.

The map of the region swims up in my head, with a red arrow, the kind newspapers used Before, stabbing like a spearhead into the soft, breastlike northwest bulge of civilization. I picture Angel Break Pass at the base of the arrow, and the Army as a dark bar in front of it.

Had we been able to do this last year, we could have dealt with all the Hordes by Dash-8. As it is, we must beat Thrasher or it's all for nothing.

But if we do beat Thrasher—then gas will fall on the other Hordes' winter encampments, some clear night in January when nothing can move far. We'll follow it up with fire bombs that same night, then pneumococcus a week later if Ralph Rogers can get it isolated and into a workable bomb by then. We may have to content ourselves with cholera in their streams in the spring, and with brucellosis in their cattle.

I've never been religious, but I pray now, offering thanks for all three, nerve gas and napalm and germs, my head down on the desk, the wood cool against my forehead.

And then I pray for us as well. The phone beeps again.

There was business to take care of, and we've had one more delay, so it's two hours since I last wrote and we go in about an hour. Now that the annotations are all written, I find myself wanting to tell you things, but I have no order, no scheme, no vision to put them into. As I said before, history isn't yet possible.

The main thing we learn from history is that no one learns anything from history. Somebody said that but I forget who.

Now that I've written all those dusty facts down for the pedants, I'll take what time I've got to say what I think.

Someone is crying, very quietly, in the southeast corner of the gym. It's very dark away from the desk. Maybe I miss electric lights most. It's dusty—no men to spare for cleaning this past month. I don't want to sneeze and draw attention. Besides, I might wake someone.

It's my youngest squad leader, Rodney, who is sixteen. He got his men to go to sleep and then felt bad himself afterward.

We know his age because when we found him seven years ago he had a passport. Back when we still did rescue, and we were still absolutely the good guys.

If it hadn't happened, he'd have been here, or somewhere like it, on a Friday night in October, at a basketball game or a dance.

I ask what's wrong. Just nerves, and a bad dream. He'll be fine—he's been through the whole summer's campaign already. Anyone can get scared. Since he's okay, I go back to the desk.

It's a long way back to the candle. I go slowly, avoiding stepping on people; moments from Before swarm up in me. I remember the cold floors on my way to the bathroom in my pj's, back when all I had to fear was monsters.

Dave doesn't look up from his map. He's asleep with his head in his hands. I sit down in the little pool of red-gold flickering light and pick up the pen again. Beyond our smear of light, it's absolutely dark. I hear only the soft white noise of many people breathing.

Sorry about the time taken from writing to you. I had to comfort a crying kid. I can't help that—I grew up in civilization.

But you understand. Either you're civilized or you're trying—otherwise you would use this to start a fire, not read it.

Unless you've found this *very* late, when you're already dreaming of the lost charms of barbarism. Then no one will read this except some pedant who will grind it up to count how many different verbs I use and the frequency of misspelled words.

That too is civilized.

All I will do now is let myself ramble. I might be decades or centuries older than you are, and you know old people are garrulous.

The moonlight is coming in the window now. Before I begin to write, I go over to look at it. Almost, except for the dead streetlight, this could be the same town, Before.

My Advice to the Civilized

One. *Write down a lot of stuff that doesn't matter.*

Civilization itself isn't much more than accumulated stuff we like that doesn't matter. All that *really* matters is getting enough to eat, sleeping safe and warm, and having somebody to talk to. If you're less strict, there are other things that also matter: politics, GNP, armies moving. Let somebody else write all that down.

Write down stuff that *doesn't* matter.

Like that Margie married me because she liked the University but hated being a grad student. And that I asked her because I knew I wouldn't do any better at my age and salary. And that we had Josh because our birth control stockpile finally ran out.

About the time he was born, we fell in love again. Or maybe just one of us did, and the other was gracious about it. That's how we had Sally.

Graciousness is attention to small details—which you should write down. When Josh learned to hang icicles one at a time and not just hurl them at the tree, he was learning graciousness.

I don't know now why I think of Cynthia so often, but she was gracious, too, and this truly can't matter in the future—it doesn't even matter now—so it's a perfect example.

When she decided the romance was over, she remembered how strongly I associated places with things that happened there, so she made sure she told me in a place I wouldn't ever have to see again.

Even now remembering Larry's Family Dining hurts, but I have no idea whether it was still standing even ten years Before. Just a formica/steel place off the freeway with twenty-four-hour breakfast, a coffee pot on every table, and everything-creme pie.

Cynthia told me as we ate. Uncharacteristically plain in jeans, sweatshirt, and no makeup, she still wore her trademark plastic earrings that looked like a cross between fishing lures and IUDs. Rain thumped against the window next to us and slid down in lumpy sheets.

We had gone in my car: her way of saying she trusted me.

The full moon is higher now. In London in the '40s they called the Harvest Moon (normally the longest full moon in the year) the Bomber's Moon because it made it easy for planes to operate.

I hope it still works. The rhombus of moonlight on the floor is divided by the crosspiece shadows and I think of the end of *Mrs. Miniver.*

I try to concentrate on something serious, but my own advice, scribbled on the candle-shadowed, flickering page before me, disagrees. If I had life to live over, I would think more about whatever popped into my head, and much less about what I was supposed to. The only thing worth doing I did in grade school was daydream.

I look back to the shadowed cross in the dust-yellowed moonlight on the floor and I see the end of *Mrs. Miniver,* again. Greer Garson's face glows, tilted up toward the crossed beams in the bomb hole in the church. Cut to four Spitfires roaring across the sky seen through the upper left corner of the cross—the basic shape of an American flag (= hope?) overlaid on a cross.

I get up to look out the window. There have been some hundreds of days of fighting across the past several years. There will be more if we win. Dave talks about doing what Powell or Pike or Lewis and Clark did, a real exploration of the territory, "once things settle down." He's promised to take me.

As I turn back to the desk, the moonbeam is so bright dust specks shine in it. My shadow blanks them like the Black Thing in *A Wrinkle in Time.*

When I was seven or eight, at Grandma's house, I discovered that if I watched closely enough I could follow a speck out of the sunlight and into the surrounding shadow. As long as I didn't look away I could stay with it. I followed one speck all the way into the hallway and the sunlight of another window. There it was lost in the busy swirl of other specks.

Here's something else that doesn't matter. Margie never learned to love *Mrs. Miniver* the way I did. Probably because it had been Cynthia's and my movie. Some couples have songs (Margie and I had "Scotch and Soda") and foods (one of my roommates and his girlfriend felt that pineapple and green pepper pizza twice a week was mandatory) but Cynthia and I were the only couple I knew who had a movie.

It showed as part of the classic film series, at 7:00 and 9:30 for two nights, every semester. We made it to all eight showings junior year, and six the year before.

Cynthia and I used to fantasize constantly about our living in the "*Mrs. Miniver* Universe." She would be a British Army nurse, because she had always wanted to be British, and I would be a former Okie who had hoboed and worked for the CCC, because I had always wanted a romantic tough background even though (because?) I'd grown up in the suburbs. "Now"—circa 1942 or '43, MMU—I would be a ball turret gunner on a B-17. (I'd rather have flown a Mustang but that was more middle than working class.)

It went on for more than a year. We carried it as far as learning ballroom jitterbug and taking a lot of history courses covering the New Deal period, World War II, and occasionally the early Cold War. Some '40s-style stuff was in fashion so we could sort of dress the part. If there had been Lucky Strikes available then, we'd have started smoking.

You see what I mean. Write down stuff that doesn't matter. If you don't see what I mean, you'll probably just burn this, or wipe your ass with it.

Dave's right. I can't stand the idea.

Two. *Keep the roads open.*

That's what we're trying to do.

Barbarians travel, but *they* only open roads for themselves, just carving holes through human geography and continuing on their lice-ridden way. The Vandals moved a lot by fifth and sixth century standards, but they made it tough and dangerous for anyone else to try. Civilization requires that people who aren't bothering other people have a safe, easy way to go other places. You've got to know the world isn't your village, and you've got to be surrounded by people who know that.

I guess we were losing, Before. In 1910 you could have gone from Shanghai to Capetown, north to Stockholm, and all the way back east to Vladivostok, mostly by land with no problems on the way. Even in 1970 you could still drive from Scotland to India, and from Alaska to Tierra del Fuego, though that was getting dangerous. By the time the big change came, the same trips would have ended in Ankara and in Mexico City.

Anyway, we're going to re-open the roads north and south next spring. There are still a lot of "holds"—ranches with forts—out there, that could feed us if we got the roads safe again.

Gunfire.

I lift the phone to my ear. The connection's always open so I just say "Northwest here. What's the shooting?"

"No problem," Samuelson says. It's his standard answer to everything. "That's our guys. We want them real nervous, so some guys from South Company ambushed a scouting party that was dumb enough to walk up a road. Radio report is six dead, nine to be Plan B'd."

Plan B is what got Mrs. Gibson my vote. Instead of trying to rehabilitate the wounded (they take off as soon as they're well) or exchange prisoners (Hordes don't take any), we hang them, naked, and mutilate the corpses, on the approaches to town. We'd held off on doing that this summer, saving it for shock value.

I voted for Plan B, but I didn't urge anyone else to. Civilization is built on those small ethical distinctions, made repeatedly and recorded.

The rising moon looks smaller now, against stars instead of trees and hills. There are footprints on it. I remember my father shook me awake, made me come downstairs in my T-shirt and pajama bottoms, because there would only be a first time *once.*

Dad was really into the antiwar movement, and the room was full of his students, but unlike any other time I could recall, it was dead silent.

Armstrong bounced around like a kangaroo, sharp-edged with no air to soften the shadows. It was so much like a marionette show under a bright spotlight, like *Thunderbirds* or *Supercar,* that I unconsciously looked for the thin white lines of the strings.

There's no more gunfire. I think of Providence Falls and St. Joseph, and my stomach rolls and my heart pounds to be out there, cutting at their corpses, and to see Thrasher's face when he sees them.

The Hordes would not bother to kill a person before starting to cut— another small, important distinction.

I sit down to write more, but the guns start going again. I pick up the phone.

"No problem. Spiders," Samuelson explains. Those are the young teenagers whose job is to fire a few shots from ambush at the first enemy they see and then get out. It forces the invaders to stop and duck each time, slowing their advance. "Now that they're between Thrasher and his forward scouts, they can slow him down a lot. They can shoot and scoot all night." Samuelson sounds as happy as he ever does.

I thank him, sit down, and pick up the pen.

People who plan roads, bridges, sewers, and so forth are called civil engineers. Civilization happens in cities, where civil society is possible, because of civil engineers. Cities are fed by roads, drained by sewers, watered by pipes that they lay down.

There have been barbarian poets and composers, even painters and some lawyers, but never a barbarian civil engineer. You have to be civilized to care about roads.

I used to take walking tours, from hotel to hotel on foot with just a knapsack. I backpacked too and enjoyed that but it wasn't the same thing. Backpackers walk to see empty useless land; walking tourists walk to see people—where they live and work, what they offer, threaten, sing, or shout to each other along the road. Backpackers say fuck you to people and commune with nature like gibbering savages; walking tourists commune with people.

Backpackers like trails, walking tourists like roads. Roads are civilized. Almost all walking tourists like backpacking but few backpackers like walking tours. Civilized people can enjoy barbaric pleasures, but not vice versa.

Cynthia got me into walking tours, the two summers we were dating. A decade later I got Margie into them.

Cynthia's whole family did walking tours, so there wasn't much choice if I wanted to see her for those two weeks. Besides, I liked her family. We walked in Vermont one year, and Minnesota the next.

I remember Cynthia swinging along on a dirt road through some state park in Vermont. She wore a black, stretchy sleeveless dress and hiking boots. She said it was comfortable; I told her she looked like Olive Oyl, though with her thick red hair hanging down in that French braid, there was no resemblance at all.

Her other dress was blue. Nightly showers, and always being around laundromats in the evening, meant never being more than one day dirty. If you've been backpacking

(will your civilization do such things? I hope so!

Three. *When you no longer* must *walk, walk for fun.*)

As I was saying, if you've been backpacking, you can imagine the pleasures of being clean every day.

One morning, on a deserted back road, when the rest of her family had gotten well ahead, Cynthia and I stopped to fuck. We'd done this often enough to have the technique perfected. For an hour, we'd been talking dirty to each other, quietly, in between some intense kissing—we called it "oral foreplay." We were both ready at the first good spot.

She pulled the black dress off over her head and dropped it on the grass, skinned down her panties, and leaned against a tree in only her bra, hiking boots, and wool socks. I took a rubber from the side pocket in my pack that held the survival kit ("put the stuff that you may need suddenly there," her father had said), and pulled off my shorts and underwear. She put the rubber on me.

As I slipped into her, pressing her against the tree, she gasped, choking down the loud moans she used to make in my frat house room, and pressed her face against my shoulder.

I looked away. Her fifteen-year-old sister Elaine was watching us, standing a few feet away on the trail.

She smiled and gestured for me to go on. As I went harder and faster into Cynthia, her hands clutching my buttocks, Elaine and I stared into each other's eyes. I even moved a little to the side, and Elaine came closer and squatted, so she could get a better look.

As I finished, Elaine stepped into a little side trail and disappeared. I had not thought of Cynthia at all, the whole time.

For the rest of the trip, Elaine would smile at me at odd times. Once she flashed a bare breast at me. I did not know how to respond.

Maybe in penance, or maybe because I didn't want anything else to happen, I didn't fuck Cynthia for the remaining four days of the trip.

When I told Margie about it, years later, she seemed confused and upset. Months later she asked if I wanted to do it outdoors with her, or while someone watched.

I said what she wanted to hear. I would gladly do it with her under any circumstances, but I didn't feel any need to repeat my youthful experiences.

As I said it, I felt disappointment. Margie was affectionate rather than dramatic, and I had always liked drama.

Four. *Enjoy lying, scandal, hypocrisy, and manners.*

Barbarians speak the truth all the time. Thrasher's last message to us was "I am coming. I want loot. I want pussy. Fuck you."

When I was in college the bathroom graffiti used to say hypocrisy was the vaseline of social intercourse. And most manners boil down to hypocrisy—doing a thing the way that pleases others, not the way that comes naturally.

Only barbarians are always honest. Had I been honest with Dave about this busywork, I'd never have enjoyed writing it.

The phone beeps. I pick it up and say "Yeah, Northwest."

"Ready for go in twenty?"

"Sure." Go will mean lining up and crossing the field to board. I hang up. I'll wake the men in ten—they all sleep with boots on and packs loaded, and there's bound to be another delay at the airfield.

I set my watch alarm. In five years at the very most, the last batteries for watches will all be dead.

Gunfire far away—a harassing party shooting up Thrasher's rear?

Has Thrasher found the mutilated corpses? How did he react?

*   *   *

Thrasher's message was all honesty because barbarians rejoice in the rough honesty of discomfort—hair shirts, vision quests, war, gang rape, miserliness, all the ways of injuring yourself to propitiate the Big Booga-Booga in the Sky.

People think honesty is morally correct because all societies are barbarian in their early years, when their moral foundations are laid.

When I learned of Margie's affair with Robertson—an education professor, of all things—I threw the TA who was trying to tell me about it down a flight of stairs, and was disappointed that his arm didn't break. I cried all night after talking with Margie. I spat in Robertson's face when I met him in a bar. (A good move as it turned out—he was not tenured and I was, and the University decided he would be the easier problem to eliminate.)

All that was stupid. There was no style to any of it. I was a stupid jerk instead of the suave, controlled sophisticate I wanted to be.

Five. *Act like who you'd rather be, not who you are.*

I check my watch. Sixteen minutes left. The moon is high; our little town glows. I feel in my bones that this will work.

Six. *Dress well.* Junior year, the night of my frat's May Formal, Cynthia wore a perfectly white strapless dress that clung to her, and elbow-length white gloves. I wore a straight black dinner jacket, ruffled shirt, and black tie.

We moved like perfectly poised dolls or statues through the evening. It was only the next day that I realized I had *been* sophisticated, rather than just feeling it.

I remember that the stench of cigars and the sweet piercing scent of gin plus sweat in the crowded hotel ballroom drove us out onto the terrace.

We kissed, once, lightly, in the moonlight. There were a few other couples out there, along the wall, none near us. The lilacs stung the other smells from my nose, and the alcohol burned in my brain.

A wind came up—it would later become a thunderstorm, and lead to our taking a room in the hotel and spending the night making love in the flashes and thunder, but that came later and didn't matter as much, now that I look back. Right now the wind was still just a warm brushing of spring-soft boughs.

The band played Chad and Jeremy's "Summer Song." I took Cynthia in my arms, very formally, for a foxtrot, and we danced there on the terrace.

Her face was pale and deeply shadowed in the moonlight. When I kissed her at the end of the song, her skin was cool, her breath hot, on my cheek.

I knew then, as surely as I knew anything, that I was going to marry her. I was wrong, but I really knew it.

Ten minutes. I blow the whistle and people start moving. I pull out a plastic bag from the desk, but I won't bury my letter. It should be fine if I just put it in the bag, in the inside pocket of my coat. Raiders will take my watch and wedding ring, but they won't bother with paper, if it comes to that.

This way, if it does come to that, the words might have my body to go with them.

As I fold it I realize I'm not done.

I knew a lot of things. I knew Josh would be a big strong kid and drive me crazy by being a jock. I knew Margie would eventually love me. I knew the power would come back on and the phones start working, by the end of the first week After.

Seven. (Almost forgot!) *Make wine.*

And all good and beautiful things.

And especially make love, in the teeth of the odds.

Time.

I seal the bag, zip it in, and start bellowing at the company now forming up.

RHIP—I'm getting a window seat. I still don't believe, after all these years, an airplane.

THE KIDS ARE ALL RIGHT

First observation:

"Isn't that like saying that your opinion is better than somebody else's? How can you say someone else is wrong?" The question comes at me several times a term, in film class, in theatre history, and most of all in public speaking. It comes at me from cleancut kids who appear to have escaped from the Osmonds, from young women with pierced noses who appear never to have combed their hair or washed their jeans, from young men who wear T-shirts, shorts, sandals, and shades in our Rocky Mountain winters, with the raccoon tan of the dedicated ski bum.

They always sound so startled. Apparently they have not heard it asserted by a teacher before, as starkly as I do, that some ideas are worth more than others, and that some thoughts are worth keeping and some are not. It alarms me considerably that in twelve years of schooling they haven't encountered this thought before, but it doesn't surprise me anymore.

This is, of course, a question which was decently settled 2400 years ago, in Socrates' replies to the sophists. You don't even need to believe in a Platonic capital-T Truth to believe that at the least, the acceptance of an idea necessarily excludes the acceptance of ideas that contradict it, and that ideas derived from observation via a logically correct structure are apt to be more effective as guides to action than ideas derived from vague feelings about vaguely remembered entertainment. So I give Socrates' answers, in informal English, and I walk them through the process of getting there—and something very strange happens in the room.

Everybody relaxes.

It's as if a huge burden is lifted off of them; they don't have to support everybody's right to hold every stupid idea that comes down the pike. I may spend the rest of the term struggling to get them to the point where they understand that there are fair and unfair ways of winning an argument, and that winning is not nearly so important as arriving at whatever a useful picture of reality might be, and so forth, but once they've made that first breakthrough, they wake up, they function, and they do the work—or they get left behind by all the others who do.

Second observation:

I number among my student acquaintances quite a few who are holding full-time jobs and living in apartments of their own. "Wait till you get into the real world," holds no terror for them. They already have a job that stinks, too many bills, and too little time for sleep or friends or family. (Some of them are single mothers, and I ask you to imagine for a moment what it must be like to look after a two-year-old, work thirty or more hours a week, and put in the roughly fifteen hours a week of class time plus thirty hours studying needed to maintain a passing average for a reasonably well-prepared student who hopes to graduate in "only" five years.)

They already live in the real world, probably a realer one than I do.

And yet—at wholly unpredictable times every term—I hit some topic that has nothing to do with waiting tables, or dirty diapers, or the job they hope to pull down someday as a CPA or a second-grade teacher— and the lights go on. They're excited, they can't wait to talk about it, they've got to do an extra project on it. "It" can be anything from my mentioning a couple of ideas out of Lydia Bamber's *Tragic Men Comic Women* while trying to give them a handle on *Twelfth Night,* to the peculiar persistence of figures like Don Juan or Faust in our culture, to Jeremy Whelan's "Instant Acting" method of rehearsal; suddenly there's fire in the room and the best thing you can do is encourage them to bring their individual fuel and pile it higher.

Third observation:

One former student of mine who became a fishing guide after graduation told me that he valued my class because it gave him something to think about when the tourists were sacked out for the night and he was just watching the fire burn down. I wish I recalled what part of the class had interested him so much; I don't think it matters.

What is it I think I'm observing?

Let me start with a blunt confession: I think we of the baby boom have severely dropped the ball. There was never a more promising generation than us, in terms of the education and comforts we received as kids, and there was never one that accomplished less. Don't start about the civil rights movement; that was led by people born around 1920. Forget the moon landing; aside from the fact that only a tiny minority of Americans worked on it, the baby boomers were too young to have had much to do with it (the oldest baby boomers were twenty-four on July 20, 1969). The crusades for racial justice and the ships that reached the moon were dreamt, built, and operated by our parents' generation. As for the collapse of Communism, the people running the show, by and large, were still the Silent Generation that preceded the boomers. The oldest baby boomers were fifteen in 1960; hell, we didn't even invent rock and roll.

So we didn't do much, but we did eventually raise kids—sort of, in between all the piling up of material goods and the rest of that stuff. Those are the kids I'm seeing in college now: close to a majority from what used to be called broken homes, educated in the decayed public schools that everyone decries, latchkey kids, drift-aways, the ones who nobody has quite noticed yet are not really Generation X anymore. (Do the arithmetic if you don't believe me; Gen X are the ones who were teenagers in the eighties. As I write this 1997 is about over; kids entering college this year became teenagers in 1992. They were too young to have direct personal memories of any of the things that were supposedly defining experiences of Generation X; they don't really remember Ronald Reagan, and everything my age cohort called the "New Wave" is "oldies" to them. They are as far from the Gulf War as I, entering college in 1975, was from the Tet Offensive).

So who the hell are they?

They're the people who lived under the boomer thumb for a very long time, because as they grew up the boomers were their parents and were the establishment. And the most notable feature of boomers, I'm afraid, is a passion for fraud—generally phrased nicely as "image" or "how you present yourself" when talking about our relations with others, and as "self-esteem" when talking about our relations to ourselves. (As an atheist I don't know, offhand, what my age cohort calls it when they try to fake out their various gods, but I'm quite sure they have a word for it.) The generation now in college was told to look good and feel positive, but wasn't given much of anything to do.

So they arrive deeply suspicious of everything; anything from the war on drugs to nuclear physics might be an attempt to get them to fall for something. They are at least mildly afraid that no one has ever told them what is going on, or ever will. They are hostile to authority not because it's actually repressing them, but because they suspect it's one more way of putting something over on them.

Every so often, then, I can offer them a deal: Look, guys, the books are open. Here's the evidence for what I'm telling you, here's where you can look up more of it, here are the arguments of the people who disagree with me. Do the work and you'll find out about it.

And every term, some of them do. Not all—after all, college has always had plenty of students who want to have been to college but don't want to do anything while there. Some of them are just not interested in the subjects I teach. Some of them undoubtedly find me so irritating that the thought of doing anything extra in my class is unbearable. But every term, a few of them go off and learn something, just for themselves. Every term I see people, who already work too hard and contemplate too little, make a tiny notch of time to grab onto some little fragment of an idea, a truth, a principle that they can, with enough hard work, make their own.

In those moments, they've gotten past all the nosy poking at their feelings, all the image and glitz, all the endless thumping repetition that life is about success, or feeling successful, or looking like you feel successful. They've lifted their heads above the crappy jobs and the crappier ideology and said, simply, that there is something they would rather know than not know—that they are entitled to some chunk of knowledge and willing to do the work to have it. It's that moment when they get to be human beings, instead of possessors or possessions.

On days when I see that happen, I really look forward to the next century.